More praise for
AMERICAN SHTETL

"Fascinating and original. *American Shtetl* offers a surprising and compelling account of a distinctively American story."
—MARTHA MINOW, author of *When Should Law Forgive?*

"Timely and provocative. From two brilliant scholars and cultural translators of our time comes an honest and compelling window into the secluded, separatist micro-society of Kiryas Joel. Stolzenberg and Myers paint a sensitive and at times searing picture of a Jewish community that is simultaneously a world apart and a quintessentially American invention. *American Shtetl* is riveting."
—RABBI SHARON BROUS, Founder/Senior Rabbi, IKAR

"Anyone interested in the future of Jews in diaspora (not only Hasidic Jews) should be grateful to [Stolzenberg and Myers] for what they've accomplished."
—JONATHAN BOYARIN, *Marginalia*

"[*American Shtetl*] describes in arresting detail the trajectory and triumph of arguably one of the most paradoxical villages in the United States. But the fact-intensive story Myers and Stolzenberg captivatingly tell also permits the astute observer to extract an important insight of constitutional significance: religious minorities do not always lack the political power to protect their interests, as is often assumed. Kiryas Joel may not be rich, but it has clout."
—ZALMAN ROTHSCHILD, *Los Angeles Review of Books*

"*American Shtetl* is a 'must-read' book for anyone interested in the realities of religious pluralism in America."
—SANDY LEVINSON, *Balkinization*

"A tale of religion, race, real estate, identity politics and so much more. An important read for anyone looking to understand American Hasidic Jewishness."
—EMILY BURACK, *Hey Alma*

"Nomi M. Stolzenberg and David N. Myers make a compelling case that the village is far from an unreconstructed throwback to a European shtetl. Rather, it is a thoroughly American phenomenon."
—LEAH LIBRESCO SARGEANT, *First Things*

T0317098

"Fascinating. . . . This is an American story as well as a Jewish one."
—DOMINIC GREEN, *Jewish Chronicle*

"Stolzenberg and Myers have written an engaging and extremely well-researched history of the growth and development of Kiryas Joel."
—BEN ROTHKE, *Jewish Link*

"The Hasidic village of Kiryas Joel is not as anomalous as it looks. It has a history, brilliantly described in this book, that could have happened only in America. And only Stolzenberg and Myers could have turned the extraordinarily complicated legal and political entanglements that make up this history into an accessible and fascinating story."
—MICHAEL WALZER, author of *The Paradox of Liberation: Secular Revolutions and Religious Counterrevolutions*

"A superb, important book. *American Shtetl* is a brilliant work of scholarship that offers a new way of thinking about the complex American Jewish relationship to religious freedom and political liberalism."
—JAMES LOEFFLER, author of *Rooted Cosmopolitans: Jews and Human Rights in the Twentieth Century*

"An excellent book. Stolzenberg and Myers provide a wonderful mix of history and reportage to contextualize and enrich their argument."
—PAUL HORWITZ, author of *First Amendment Institutions*

AMERICAN SHTETL

American Shtetl

THE MAKING OF KIRYAS JOEL, A HASIDIC VILLAGE IN UPSTATE NEW YORK

NOMI M. STOLZENBERG

DAVID N. MYERS

PRINCETON UNIVERSITY PRESS

PRINCETON & OXFORD

Published by Princeton University Press
41 William Street, Princeton, New Jersey 08540
99 Banbury Road, Oxford OX2 6JX

press.princeton.edu

All Rights Reserved
First paperback printing, 2024
Paperback ISBN 978-0-691-25929-1
Cloth ISBN 978-0-691-19977-1
ISBN (e-book) 978-0-691-22643-9

British Library Cataloging-in-Publication Data is available

Editorial: Fred Appel and James Collier
Production Editorial: Jenny Wolkowicki
Text design: Karl Spurzem
Jacket/Cover design: Karl Spurzem
Production: Erin Suydam
Publicity: Maria Whelan and Kathryn Stevens
Copyeditor: Joseph Dahm

Jacket/Cover photograph: Jackson Krule

This book has been composed in Arno Pro

Printed in the United States of America

CONTENTS

ILLUSTRATIONS

ACKNOWLEDGMENTS

Work on this book has been a source of amazement, exhilaration, frustration, patience, and impatience over the past fifteen years. During that time, we incurred debts to a legion of scholars, students, and interviewees. From the very beginning until the end, we were assisted by Chris McKenna, the crack reporter for the *Times Herald-Record* in Middletown. Chris knows more about politics in Orange County and Kiryas Joel than almost anyone in the world. He was boundlessly generous in sharing his knowledge, wisdom, and tips. In a very real sense, this book wouldn't have been possible without him.

At the outset of this project, Barry Trachtenberg provided vital research assistance and ethnographic analysis. Already at that point, as an early-career graduate student, Barry understood the multiple layers of our historical and legal interests and helped to build up an archive of materials that has furnished us to this day. Barry has since gone on to have a productive scholarly career of his own, but his work for us was foundational.

For his unparalleled range of bibliographic knowledge and network of contacts, we thank the inimitable and irrepressible Menachem Butler. Among other gifts, he opened the door to a number of acquaintances in the Satmar world who proved to be invaluable guides.

Among our Satmar sources, regardless of which faction they belonged to, our meetings were almost always productive and pleasant. Even though we appeared as outsiders, we were always treated with courtesy and respect. Frequently, we would be told by an interviewee that he or she did not have much time to talk. And frequently, we would have to excuse ourselves after two or more hours to get to the next meeting. We quickly came to understand that the pathways of curiosity moved in both directions.

Within Kiryas Joel, special appreciation goes to three people: Joel Petlin, the superintendent of the KJ public school, was unstinting in sharing his vast knowledge of education law and the legal affairs of KJ, as well as in providing answers to obscure queries at the drop of a hat. Gedalye Szegedin, the village administrator of KJ (and now town clerk of Palm Tree), is an exceptionally smart and effective public official; despite the fact that he is always busy, he gave hours of time to walk us through his thinking and that of the village and mainstream party leadership. And Shlomo Yankel Gelbman z"l was the preeminent chronicler of the Satmar Rebbe and the empire he created, including in KJ. He had not only encyclopedic knowledge of Satmar history, which he generously shared with us, but also a vast web of informants the world over who helped him retrieve every available reference to the life of Joel Teitelbaum, the founding Grand Rabbi of the Satmar Hasidic group. All three men contributed greatly to the research for this book, even though they may all find (or have found) points in it, perhaps many, with which to disagree.

There are dozens of people in Kiryas Joel and Williamsburg to thank for their openness, kindness, candor, hospitality, and knowledge. For reasons of privacy, many prefer to remain anonymous; we honor this request as we express appreciation to them for opening their homes and offices to us. (In a similar vein, we have anonymized most of the names of those with whom we conducted oral interviews.) Special thanks go to two extraordinary guides, Frieda Vizel and Frimet Goldberger, who agreed to meet with us on multiple occasions to share their deep knowledge of the Satmar community in which they once lived; we also thank Ysoscher Katz for his perceptive firsthand insights into the Satmar community. Debra Fisher generously provided information about her father, Oscar, who was instrumental in buying the land that created KJ. And from the beginning, David Pollock, associate executive director of the New York Jewish Community Relations Council, generously shared his vast knowledge of Hasidic and Satmar life in New York.

In helping to make sense of the often-labyrinthine legal world surrounding KJ, we thank Louis Grumet, the lead plaintiff in the case that brought the village of Kiryas Joel to wide public attention, and Michael Sussman, Jay Worona, and the other lawyers who shared their recollections and legal yarns with us. Veteran reporter Oliver Mackson also provided us with valuable leads and information about various aspects of life in Kiryas Joel.

Over the long period of germination of this book, we had the opportunity to present pieces of it solely and jointly in dozens of institutions including the University at Albany, the University of Pennsylvania, Ben Gurion University, Cardozo Law School, the Graduate Theological Union, Fordham, Haifa University, the Hebrew University, NYU, the Ohio State University, Tel Aviv University, the University of Chicago, the University of Illinois-Champaign/Urbana, UCLA, UC Santa Cruz, the Van Leer Institute in Jerusalem, and the YIVO Institute for Jewish Research. Thanks to those institutions, as well as to these colleagues whose comments improved this book greatly: Orit Avishai, Ayala Fader, Abner Greene, Sam Heilman, Shaul Magid, Naomi Seidman, and Suzanne Stone. We extend a special debt of gratitude to the late lamented William Helmreich z"l, a wonderful character, raconteur, city walker, and scholar of Orthodox life who offered typically perceptive comments on a number of chapters. We, of course, are responsible for any errors in the book.

For their help with research on this project, we thank Stephanie Chasin, Talia Graff, and Lindsay King at UCLA. This book was so long in the making that the number of USC law students who assisted with this project borders on the absurd. That long list includes John Acevedo, Chris Lim, Laura Walluch, David Sheasby, Sarah Truesdell, Donna Chang, David Avraham, Zachary Davidson, Amy Steelman, Christopher Chen, Edrin Shamtob, Aida Bagdasaryan, Ja'Mesha Morgan, Stephanie Rector, Emma Tehrani, Jack Merritt, Will Mavitty, Hannah Waldman, and the late Maren Wright. Mark Smith answered questions about Yiddish throughout the process. Chaim Seidler-Feller, close friend and intellectual partner, addressed queries related to Jewish law with typical perspicacity; on thorny linguistic matters, Shaul Seidler-Feller and Aryeh Cohen offered sage advice. In New York, we had the good fortune to meet Mordechai Friedman, who provided invaluable research assistance with the Yiddish press—and, later, drew on his emerging architectural talents to create a number of maps for this book.

Our respective institutions provided key support to our work. Special thanks are due to the great line of IT experts in the UCLA History Department (Mary Johnson, Hubert Ho, Jonathan Ebueng, and Tam Le) and at USC (Darren Fox, Leonard Wilson, and Rachel Mendoza), as well as the extraordinary law librarians at USC, in particular Cindy Guyer, Karen Skinner, Paul Moorman, Morgan Hagedorn, and Diana Jacque. David Myers expresses gratitude for the resources of the Sady and Ludwig Kahn Chair in Jewish History—and to Jim and Lori Keir who enabled its creation. Nomi Stolzenberg extends appreciation to Katie Waitman, administrative assistant extraordinaire, and to her constant interlocutors at USC, Ariela Gross, Daria Roithmayr, and Hilary Schor. Anne Dailey has been an equally constant source of support and inspiration.

Sally Gordon supplied invaluable commentary at an early stage of this project and ever since. Martha Minow also provided valuable input throughout the long gestation of this project. We'd also like to express gratitude to Uriel Hinberg for his careful reading of this book that allowed for a number of key refinements and corrections in the paperback edition.

The annual meeting of Progressive Property scholars organized by Joseph Singer, Gregory Alexander, Eduardo Peñalver, and Laura Underkuffler graciously provided a venue in which to workshop chapters of this book at both the beginning and the end of our research. We are grateful to all of the attendees, in particular Hanoch Dagan and Bethany Berger.

Toward the end of the project, we were lucky to cross paths with Jackson Krule, who told us of his work as a photographer and chronicler of life in KJ. He shared his remarkable trove of photos of KJ, a small number of which adorn this book. We are deeply grateful to Jackson for his richly evocative work.

It has been a pleasure to work with Princeton University Press. We are deeply grateful to Fred Appel, who passionately and persistently sought out this book, guiding it with his keen editorial eye, finely tuned literary instincts, and seemingly bottomless appetite for scholarship on Haredim in the United States. We thank Fred for connecting us with Thomas Lebien, whose meticulous reading of the manuscript benefitted us enormously. We also appreciate the work of Joseph Dahm and Jenny Wolkowicki in bringing the final version of this manuscript to press after an initial delay. And we thank the three readers of the manuscript for PUP who offered challenging and immensely helpful critique.

This book is dedicated to our three daughters, Tali, Noa, and Sara. They have grown from young girls to women over the long course of researching and writing this book. In tolerating their parents' near-total obsession with finishing a project that never seemed to end, they revealed the very qualities of wisdom, empathy, and understanding with which all three are amply blessed.

PROLOGUE

Approaching Kiryas Joel

Orange County, New York, is a suburban idyll: rolling hills, spacious lots, good schools, and a robust civic spirit. In keeping with the spirit of the modern American suburb, it even has its own high-end outlet mall, Woodbury Common, with more than two hundred stores selling the latest designer fashions. Built to look like an American colonial village, with shingled roofs, a tower shaped like a steeple, and a "market hall" overlooking an ersatz village square, the Common has become a major tourist site since its opening in 1985, attracting millions of visitors every year in search of the archetypal American shopping experience.[1]

Less than four miles away is another notable site in Orange County, also created to resemble a village of yore: Kiryas Joel, often referred to as KJ. The village is a legally recognized municipality whose population of twenty-five thousand consists almost entirely of Hasidic Jews from the Satmar dynasty. Like Woodbury Common, it has been deliberately designed to evoke a traditional past. But the cultural heritage to which KJ lays claim is very different from the one evoked by Woodbury Common. The Common, as its name reflects, is an exercise in nostalgia for a colonial American past; Kiryas Joel, by contrast, expresses nostalgia for a Jewish past. More specifically, it yearns for the past of European Jewry embodied in the shtetl.

Though the pasts to which they seek to return could not be more different, the two "villages" exemplify, each in its own way, what Eric Hobsbawm and Terence Ranger famously called in their 1983 book "the invention of tradition." As Hobsbawm and Ranger contended, many

FIGURE I.1. Overview of Kiryas Joel (4930). Courtesy of Jackson Krule.

"traditions" that "appear or claim to be old are often quite recent in origin and sometimes invented."[2] This is an apt description of the various incarnations of the shtetl that occupy the American mental and physical landscape. The historical shtetl that existed in Europe, as opposed to the mythologized version that entered into the American cultural imagination through *Fiddler on the Roof* in the 1950s and 1960s, was far more diverse than the myth would have it. But it is the mythic, one might say American version, more than the culturally diverse historical shtetl, that Kiryas Joel aspires to replicate. And while the mythic shtetl came to life in the imagination of novelists and storytellers, the shtetl that is Kiryas Joel took rise on the soil of the United States. The village was formed to enable its residents to live a stringently observant religious life, in which all matters—both public and private—are subject to the spiritual guidance and authority of a single religious leader, the Grand Rabbi or Rebbe. The village features a rich network of institutions that cater to the distinctive Satmar way of life, which is consciously patterned on the shtetl of Europe before World War II. The male inhabitants of Kiryas Joel dress in black frock coats, while the females wear modified versions of Jewish women's traditionally modest garb. Their ritual customs, religious piety, and deep reverence for the past all conjure up the well known theme song of *Fiddler*, "Tradition!"

But whereas the lead character in *Fiddler*, Tevya, famously wrestles with the competing pulls of tradition and the secular world, the residents of Kiryas Joel are far less conflicted and far more successful at preserving their traditional way of life. They belong to the strictly observant sector of Jews known as *Haredim*, whose name comes from the Hebrew word for those who tremble—as in the biblical verse "Hear the word of the Lord, you who tremble at his word" (Isaiah 66:5). Haredim trembled at what they saw as the contaminating effects of modern secular culture on their time-honored religious beliefs and practices. In fact, they rejected not only the secularizing trends affecting Jewish life from the latter half of the eighteenth century but also the existing forms of Orthodox Judaism, which they regarded as insufficiently separated from the spiritually polluted secular world. Ironically, their zeal to preserve Jewish tradition led them to invent a new form of Judaism.

Among the fiercest of Haredi leaders was Rabbi Joel Teitelbaum (1887–1979), founder of the Satmar Hasidic dynasty, after whom Kiryas Joel ("Village of Joel") was named and after whom a recent biography was titled *The Zealot*.[3] Rabbi Teitelbaum, also known by the nickname Reb Yoelish or by a Hasidic leader's honorific title Rebbe, came from a region of East-Central Europe that had once belonged to Hungary but after the First World War became part of Romania, before reverting again in 1940 to Hungary and then yet again back to Romania in 1945. It was that region, in the town of Szatmár or Satu Mare (from which the name Satmar comes), where Joel Teitelbaum, the charismatic founding rabbi, settled in 1934. There he presided over the city's Jewish community until the invasion by Nazi Germany in March 1944.

Joel Teitelbaum was saved from the ravages of the Nazi death campaign in a highly controversial organized rescue effort, while most of his followers in northeast Hungary were deported and murdered. He survived the war in the Bergen-Belsen concentration camp in Germany, where he spent four months before being liberated in December 1944. After liberation, he lived briefly in Switzerland and Palestine before arriving in New York Harbor on Rosh Ha-Shanah 1946. With the assistance of trusted lieutenants, he gathered together the tattered fragments of Hungarian Orthodox survivors of the Holocaust. With a small cadre of survivors, he built up a tight-knit Satmar community in Williamsburg, Brooklyn, that has become the largest center of the Satmar world to this day. In addition to Williamsburg, the Satmars established satellite communities in Montreal, London, Antwerp, Montevideo, Melbourne, Jerusalem, and Bnei Brak, and, last but certainly not least, the suburbs of New York. Estimates are that there are 150,000 Satmars today, making the group the largest Hasidic movement in the world.[4] Among all of the Satmar settlements, none has fulfilled the aspiration for spiritual purity and separation from the world more perfectly than Kiryas Joel.

Rabbi Teitelbaum had the intention of creating a shtetl from his first years in America. Shortly after settling in Williamsburg, Teitelbaum set his sights on establishing a community outside of New York City. He instructed his aides to locate land where a shtetl could be established at a sufficient remove from the teeming urban environment and its allures. After several unsuccessful efforts, suitable property was found in Orange County. Shortly after the property was purchased in the early 1970s, Satmars began to settle there, and not long after that, in 1977, Kiryas Joel was formally incorporated as an autonomous village within the town of Monroe.

Unwitting Assimilation in Kiryas Joel

Over the course of the next forty years, the village grew dramatically, doubling in population every decade or so. During that period, KJ became nationally known for both its outsized political influence and its exclusive and seemingly foreign way of life. That foreignness is clearly conveyed to outsiders. While visitors to Woodbury Common are greeted by a welcome booth, visitors to KJ are greeted by a sign at the entrance to the village that conveys in no uncertain terms that it is a world apart. Although it starts with WELCOME TO KIRYAS JOEL and ends, in equally boosterish fashion, with a cheerful exhortation to

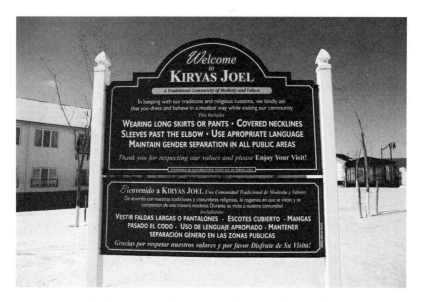

FIGURE 1.2. Sign Warning against Immodesty in Kiryas Joel. Courtesy of Jackson Krule.

ENJOY YOUR VISIT!, most of the sign is filled with admonitions that make it plain that visitors are not welcome unless they respect the community's "traditions and religious customs." Large lettering at the top describes the village as A TRADITIONAL COMMUNITY OF MODESTY AND VALUES. Lest the meaning of "modesty" be lost on outsiders unfamiliar with Hasidic norms, the sign instructs visitors, in English and Spanish, to respect KJ's values by "wearing long skirts or pants," "covered necklines," and "sleeves past the elbow" and by "maintain[ing] gender separation in all public areas."

For all its seeming foreignness, however, KJ is very much a part, indeed a product, of the world from which it purports to have withdrawn. If it is a shtetl, it is a decidedly American one, rooted in the landscape of this country, inescapably subject to its social, economic, and political currents, imprinted with traits that would have been unimaginable in the European shtetl and that clearly reflect its American provenance. In that regard, it results from a process of what we call "unwitting assimilation," an unintended and often undesired process of absorption of norms from broader American society that has been an oft-hidden key to Kiryas Joel's success.

This term does not mean to suggest that Satmars are passive, naïve, or unsuspecting in making their way in the world. On the one hand, they are very mindful of the danger that assimilation—in the form of integration into broader American society—poses to their collective existence. Much of their education is directed to building up discrete spiritual and cultural practices and institutions as a means of insulating themselves from the outside world and preventing assimilation. In this, they are hardly alone. Historian Ibram Kendi contends in his best-selling book *How to Be an Antiracist* that "assimilationist ideas are racist ideas," for they are intended to encourage a putatively inferior group to adopt the culture and values of a "superior" group.[5] Haredim and certain sectors of the African American community are among the many groups that reject the presumption of the superiority of mainstream American white culture and share an aversion to the ethos of assimilation.

This book documents how the growing receptivity to this anti-assimilationist—and anti-integrationist—impulse in many quarters of American society has benefited the Satmars and helped to justify their explicitly separatist aspirations. It shows how conservative forms of religious and economic libertarianism, as well as liberal notions of communitarianism, contributed to the creation of a legal environment that was hospitable to the project of Kiryas Joel as a homogeneous and strictly Orthodox religious community. The story we tell here, which spans the period from the inception of Satmar Hasidism in the early twentieth century up until January 2021, follows the increasing entwinement of Haredi and Christian legal and political interests. Throughout that roughly fifty-year period, the relationship of the Satmars to these trends in American politics was essentially instrumental in nature. Various groups associated with the Christian right took a sympathetic interest in the Satmars' cause and used it as a platform for advancing their own conception of religious liberty. In turn, the Satmars accepted their support and deftly turned their arguments, which were gaining traction in the Supreme Court, to their advantage. In this manner, the Satmars aligned their self-presentation to external authorities with cultural norms drawn from the outside world without deeply internalizing those norms into their own self-understanding.

Indeed, the Satmars and the larger Haredi community held to a far more pragmatic and transactional view of politics—as distinct from an ideological approach—than their Christian courtroom allies. They were equal-opportunity voters, supporting those politicians—Democrat and Republican alike—who could deliver for them. When challenged to defend the legality of their practices in court, they advanced interpretations of the Constitution that often dovetailed with the vision of the Christian right. But they by no means subscribed to the Christian right's political ideology.

This is no longer the case. A seemingly striking change has occurred, which reached a sharp inflection point in the 2020 presidential election and the concurrent COVID-19 pandemic. As witnessed in their participation in protests against mask wearing and other COVID-19 safety regulations, some Haredim have come to resemble conservative white Christians, especially Evangelicals, in both their daily political behavior and their broader political beliefs.[6] What once were overlapping yet distinct outlooks have evolved into a shared ideology premised on a fervent commitment to "religious liberties" as a paramount constitutional guarantee. Not long ago, most Satmars believed that the United States was unique in the annals of the Jewish Diaspora in affording liberties to Jews. Now, many of them subscribe to the Christian right's belief that religious liberty is being threatened by the government and that it may even supersede government authority, granting them the right to defy the state (which many of their neighbors in KJ have accused them of doing for years).

So too they have come to adopt the Christian conservative animus toward liberal elites, who are cast as guardians of an "identity politics" that cares about people of color at the expense of beleaguered white people of faith. For many Haredim who live in Brooklyn and the surrounding areas in the New York metropolitan area, simmering tensions with African American neighbors—punctuated by a surge in violent attacks by African Americans on Jews in 2019—seem to have stirred up a new sense of beleaguered whiteness. Like the Satmar response to the

COVID-19 virus and Trumpism, this reflects a novel development in Satmar culture, albeit one whose seeds began to germinate decades earlier.

In their important new book *A Fortress in Brooklyn: Race, Real Estate, and the Making of Hasidic Williamsburg,* Nathaniel Deutsch and Michael Casper examine the tensions that began to develop between Satmar Hasidim and their African American and Puerto Rican neighbors in Williamsburg in the 1950s. Deutsch and Casper also show that the Satmars were forging a sense of themselves as a racial minority, akin to Hispanic and African Americans. They actively sought units in public housing where minority populations predominated, while other Jewish and white Brooklynites participated in white flight. The result was an extremely complex set of attitudes toward those racial minorities and an equally complex sense of their own racial identity as both other than white and yet, increasingly in the racially coded landscape of America, white.[7]

Like Deutsch and Casper's book, *American Shtetl,* which focuses on those Satmars who left the city, is also a tale of real estate, which, in America, is always a story inflected by race. At the same time, Kiryas Joel is a story about religion—and the politics of religion that was reshaping Americans' sense of identity in the 1970s and 1980s when the village took rise. It is in this period that strategic alliances between conservative Christian advocacy groups and Haredim first began to form. But it is not until very recently that we have seen the hardening of Haredi identity in the mold of Christian conservatism with shades of white Christian nationalism.[8]

Indeed, the shift from an instrumental pragmatism to ideological conservatism in Kiryas Joel accelerated at an astonishing rate in 2020. A telling illustration of this development was the spike in support for Donald Trump; in the 2016 presidential election, Trump received 55 percent of the vote against Hillary Clinton in KJ, while in 2020 he received 99 percent! This change in electoral behavior was accompanied by a growing public demonstration of support for Trump and the political agenda favored by conservative Christians among Haredim, including Satmar Hasidim; a small number of Haredim even participated

in the infamous Capitol insurrection on January 6, 2021. This new political behavior may well reflect the ultimate irony of unwitting assimilation. The Satmars' long-standing fear of assimilation has given way to
assimilation into the present-day culture of right-wing libertarianism
and antigovernment conservatism.[9]

But unwitting assimilation does not mean that Satmars in KJ regularly sit down for coffee with their Christian neighbors in Monroe. They
continue to maintain strict social segregation from the gentile world.
But they still are inescapably products of their environment and, more
than that, active participants in the political life of the "outside" world.
Even in the segregated precincts of their shtetl, they cannot hermetically
seal themselves off from important political, economic, and even social
trends in the surrounding society any more than they can seal themselves off from the coronavirus.

Most notably, the Satmars have learned the rules of American
interest-group politics. Without declaring any intent to join that game,
they simply did so—and in the process they developed tools to be effective participants in local and state elections, to influence politicians,
and even to form and run their own local government. Paradoxically,
these tools are used to promote the community's separatist interests,
which KJ leaders sometimes justify as part of America's tradition of
"cultural pluralism"—the term American Jewish philosopher Horace
Kallen promoted in 1915 to represent an alternative to the "melting pot"
model of assimilation.[10] Using these tools is reflective of a high degree
of integration of American norms that defies yet coexists with the
Satmars' professed separatist aims. In taking stock of the effects of
this barely visible process of assimilation, the late supervisor of the
town of Monroe, Harley Doles, once said of Kiryas Joel that it was "as
American as apple pie."

How can this be? In what way is Kiryas Joel an *American* community,
given all the ways in which it self-consciously rejects the norms and
practices of mainstream American society? In making this claim that
Kiryas Joel is quintessentially American, we are not merely saying that
it fits into the long U.S. tradition of cultural and religious pluralism,
which countenances group self-segregation, nor even that it has (of late)

begun to merge with other, more populous segregationist groups. We are making the more counterintuitive claim that the very features of KJ that appear to be most at odds with American values, most separate from American culture, and thus most indigenously Jewish arose because of, not despite, the American political system. The community's insularity and separation from other groups, its extreme homogeneity and religious uniformity, and its political empowerment are uniquely American characteristics. These characteristics were not present in the Jewish communities of Europe, even in their most strictly Orthodox precincts. They are characteristics that have been actively fostered by America's political, legal, and economic institutions.

This is a claim that defies received wisdom about both the shtetl of yore and present-day American society. The United States, we typically assume, fosters individualism and secularism and forbids segregation and the establishment of religion. The truth is a lot more complicated. While the prohibition against the establishment of religion is enshrined in the Constitution, the wall of separation between religion and government of which Thomas Jefferson famously spoke is far from impermeable. In fact, over the past four decades or so, it has cracked under the combined weight of pressure from religious conservatives and growing sympathy for multiculturalism (and criticism of assimilation) from the left.

And thus, far from being an alien graft, Kiryas Joel was wholly in sync with the political moment in which it arose. By the late 1970s, conservatives were pushing back not only against the countercultural ways of the 1960s, but against the ethos of integration born of the Supreme Court's landmark desegregation decision in *Brown v. Board of Education* (1954) and the decades-long civil rights movement. They heralded the right of Christians to assert their own religious and cultural identity and "civil rights movement," and advanced novel interpretations of the Constitution to support their claims. The founding of the Moral Majority by Reverend Jerry Falwell in 1979 gave a significant push forward to the effort to promote Christian values in the public sphere—and to retool the principle of "religious liberty" to mean freedom from the perceived ravages of liberalism and secular humanism. The election of Ronald

Reagan a year later heralded a new era of receptivity to, and influence by, religious conservatives in halls of political power from town halls to the White House.

But it was not only conservatives who sought to move beyond the liberal integrationist spirit of the 1960s. Already in that turbulent decade, advocates of Black Power sought to lift up African Americans by developing economic self-dependency and cultural autonomy at a remove from white society. This new movement for Black self-empowerment was closely and causally related to a similar movement in the Jewish community, which until the late 1960s had allied itself with the African American struggle for civil rights. While the new language of Black separatism scared some erstwhile Jewish partners, it inspired others to "turn inward" and to seek to fortify traditional Jewish values and institutions rather than integrate and melt into the cultural mainstream, as Marc Dollinger has recently chronicled.[11]

This separatist impulse was manifesting itself in many communities in the 1970s and early 1980s, the moment when KJ took form. Among them were the separatist enclaves known as "womyn's land," established by lesbian activists at various rural sites across the United States. Countercultural communes and religious communes were also popular at the time, and the boundary between the two often blurred. (One notable example that blended the two is People of Praise, the insular charismatic Christian community founded in the 1960s in which the newest Supreme Court justice, Amy Coney Barrett, was raised).[12] These movements, drawing on different sources of inspiration, were not foreign to Americans. They tapped into a long-standing tradition of separatism and intentional communities in U.S. history, of which Kiryas Joel became a constituent part.

In this regard, one immediately calls to mind the Amish, who are often thought of in the same breath as Hasidim, owing to their maintenance of traditional customs and forms of dress, their use of a non-English language in daily life (Pennsylvania Dutch in the case of the Amish, Yiddish in the case of the Haredi Jews), their traditional sexual and gender practices, and their commitment to the theological principle of withdrawal from the world.

But a more apt comparison may be the Mormons, who, unlike the Amish but akin to the Satmars, created their own autonomous government. Joseph Smith, founding Prophet of the Mormon Church, served as city councilor and mayor of the new town of Nauvoo, Illinois, in 1840 as well as lieutenant general of the local militia. After Smith was killed by an anti-Mormon mob in 1844, the group's new leader, Brigham Young, led them across the Great Plains to the Great Salt Lake Valley in Utah in July 1847. The site on which they settled, which they called Salt Lake City, became the spiritual as well as political capital of the Mormon world. A year later, ownership of the territory of Utah passed from Mexico to the United States, and in 1851 President Millard Fillmore appointed Brigham Young its governor as well as commander in chief of the militia. At the same time, Young served as president of the Mormon Church, the effect of which was to join "the civil and religious authority of the territory in one man."[13]

This blending of civil and religious authority continued in this country well after the founding of Salt Lake City. In 1893, the Seventh-day Adventists founded a city named Keene in Texas, about which it was said: "The town doesn't have an Adventist church. The Adventist church has a town."[14] Later, in 1913, breakaways from the mainstream Mormon Church established the town of Colorado City, Arizona, as an enclave in which they could continue the practice of plural marriage, or polygamy. And seventy years later, in 1982, followers of an Indian spiritual guru who established Rajneeshpuram, an intentional community in rural Oregon, briefly attained the status of an officially incorporated city.[15]

These religious communities are commonly perceived as, and criticized for, establishing forms of government—and, in turn, establishing religion—that violate the principle of separation between church and state. But that assertion is complicated by the fact that they all began as private property associations, established by individual property owners or by privately owned collectives that held title to the property on which members are granted the right to live. Ronald Reagan came to office exalting both private property and the image of America as a "city on a hill," a metaphor for American exceptionalism derived from the sermon given in 1630 by John Winthrop, one of the Puritan founders of the

Massachusetts Bay Colony and its first governor. But unlike the Massachusetts Bay Colony, the original shining city on a hill, which was established through a "top-down" method of obtaining a charter from the government (in that case England), most separatist communities that have taken root in America have been created through the "bottom-up" method of purchasing land through the private real estate market.

KJ's Liberal Illiberalism:
A Tale of Religious Communitarianism

This phenomenon of using private property and contract rights to create culturally homogenous enclaves is what we call "communitarianism from the bottom up."[16] "Communitarianism" is a term that was coined in mid-nineteenth-century England to refer to the desire to form strong, self-contained communities, typically animated by utopian and/or religious motives. "Bottom up" refers to the use of private property rights and other market-based mechanisms, as well as individual rights to freedom of religion, freedom of association, and freedom to control the upbringing and education of one's children, to create and sustain subcommunities. These mechanisms stand in contrast to top-down mechanisms, such as land grants and government charters, that bestow legal protection on officially recognized subcommunities as well as various legal privileges including limited powers of self-government. These privileges for subgroups existed in many traditional societies in Europe and the Middle East prior to the modern age. Vestiges of this system of group-based privileges are still found outside of the United States, including in Canada, England, and Western Europe, the other "liberal democracies" to which the United States is often compared. In this regard, America truly does seem to be exceptional. Many critics of modern liberal societies have lamented this, claiming that the replacement of top-down forms of governmental protection with market-based mechanisms and individual rights leads to the atomization of strong forms of community. But, as Carol Weisbrod observed in her seminal study of nineteenth-century utopian societies, private property and contract rights, the building blocks of the free market that Ronald

Reagan exalted, have served equally well as the building blocks of communitarian societies, belying the oft-repeated claim that liberalism will destroy them.[17]

In the 1980s, an era marked by the Reagan presidency and the growing power of religious conservatives, the ideal of communitarianism was undergoing a revival among academics. One key symptom was the popular belief that liberal individualism had become, as the book *Habits of the Heart* proclaimed in 1985, potentially "cancerous" and a threat to "the survival of freedom itself." For thinkers who subscribed to this view, communitarianism was an alternative to, if not outright rejection of, the values on which liberal societies are based. They saw the openness of liberal societies, with their strong emphasis on individual liberty, rights, and freedom of choice, as a challenge to the preservation of cultures with distinct identities, particularly those that deviated from the values of a liberal society. Communitarianism and liberalism were thus presented as antithetical philosophies and forms of social organization.[18]

But in practice American communitarianism has always been intertwined with liberalism. Indeed, at the very same time that communitarian philosophers were lamenting liberalism's baleful influence on groups with nonconforming cultural values, many such groups were using economic and legal tools provided by America's liberal legal regime to build their own separate communities. It is no accident that when KJ was first gaining its footing at the start of the Reagan era, communitarianism came into public prominence alongside libertarianism, a variant of liberalism with deep roots in American culture that espouses maximal personal liberty, a free market, and a minimal state. The individual rights that communitarian critics of liberalism inveigh against and libertarians hold dear have long served as the building blocks out of which thick self-governing communities in America are built.

Literally hundreds of utopian and separatist micro-societies have sprouted up on American soil, thanks in no small measure to the foundational liberal principle of the right to private property.[19] By exercising this right, their members were able to acquire land and cement the social bonds on which enclave societies depend. Following the model laid down by past sectarian groups, the Satmars of Kiryas Joel purchased and developed land and then invited their coreligionists to settle on it. Only after following these steps did they create a public entity by incorporating as a separate municipality, an outcome that was neither intended nor desired by the Satmars at the outset. It was this pathway, from private enclave to elected local government, that turned Joel Teitelbaum's dream of a place of refuge into an official subdivision of the state of New York.

The result of following this private pathway to political empowerment has been a degree of insularity, homogeneity, and religious uniformity never before seen in the Jewish world, not even in the dense Jewish communities of Eastern Europe. In only a small fraction of cities, towns, and villages in Europe did the Jewish community constitute a majority of the population. In none of them did Hasidic Jews constitute the sole group or hold the reins of government. Yet that is exactly what we see in Kiryas Joel, where the Satmars constitute over 99 percent of the population. That homogeneity is a result of both Joel Teitelbaum's vision and the bottom-up, market-driven process by which the village was formed. That process has led the Satmar population of Kiryas Joel to amass far more governmental power than any Jewish community in Europe ever did. The village's unique demography—its dense concentration of Satmar Hasidim and the huge birthrate (the highest in New York State, with families of ten to fifteen children a common occurrence)—has produced a formidable voting bloc. The community has been able to use that electoral power to gain influence with higher levels of government. Millions of dollars of government support have streamed into the village, leveraged by the Satmars' political clout—a fact that is bewailed by critics of the village who regard it as a theocracy breaching the constitutional wall of separation between religion and state.

Interestingly, some of the loudest critics come from within the community itself. They lament the day that the Satmar settlement became a bastion of local sovereignty, possessed of the same powers of government as any other municipality in the state of New York. That formal act, they maintain, effectively empowered the community's acknowledged leaders, its leading rabbis and their aides, to exercise control over every domain of life in the village. When the founding leader, Joel

Teitelbaum, was alive, there was no such controversy over rabbinic control over all matters, as his authority was universally recognized among Satmar Hasidim. However, he died only two years after KJ was formally recognized, leaving behind no heirs and a huge crisis of legitimacy for his successor.

As this book traces, deep rifts developed within Kiryas Joel (and the wider Satmar world) soon after Reb Yoelish's death. Dissidents emerged within the community who felt strong-armed and even oppressed by the new rabbinic establishment led by Rabbi Moshe Teitelbaum, Joel's nephew, who was closely allied to the official village leadership. What had been unquestioned in Joel's time—the absolute nature of his authority in all matters—now became the source of great dispute, enmity, and litigation.

Meanwhile, external critics pointed to an array of unsettling features within the community—the pronounced difference in gender roles, the limited exposure to secular studies (especially for boys), the intolerance for any form of religious or cultural dissent—to prove the undemocratic, and potentially illegal or unconstitutional, nature of Kiryas Joel. Even the village's most robust supporters would maintain that KJ does not adhere to the principle of liberal democracy that values the rights of the individual above all. In this regard, Kiryas Joel is not only an example of religious communitarianism but a site of the confounding phenomenon of liberal illiberalism, the counterpart of "illiberal liberalism," which is the term political theorists have adopted to refer to the ways in which liberalism is intolerant of cultures that reject liberal values, as it uses the authority of the state to promote the spread of liberal values.[20] The flipside of that phenomenon is what we call liberal illiberalism, a particular variety of communitarianism from the bottom up. This means that while KJ rose as a result of the exercise of the most basic liberal right to private property, it came to assume the powers of (local) government. Village leaders use both public and private powers to promote a decidedly illiberal and hierarchical form of authority that prioritizes total obedience to the strict norms of the community over individual freedom. This form of social control, at once rooted in American soil and seemingly alien to it, is a second key feature that helps us explain KJ's success in preserving a strong form of community and the very American nature of that success.

Productive Tension: A Way of Life

As we have noted, the rise of Kiryas Joel coincided with a golden age of conservative political and legal activism that began in the late 1970s. Since that time, American politics has been marked by a continuous erosion of the "high and impregnable wall" of separation between religion and state, as Justice Hugo Black described it in 1947. That erosion was largely the result of a concerted political campaign to overturn the principle of "strict separation" between church and state led by religious conservatives and the broader conservative legal movement of which they formed a key part. Reflecting the conservative restiveness with then-prevailing doctrines of "strict separation," Chief Justice William Rehnquist declared in *Wallace v. Jaffree* (1985) that "the 'wall of separation between church and state' is a metaphor based on bad history, a metaphor which has proved useless as a guide to judging. It should be frankly and explicitly abandoned."[21] Rehnquist would soon be succeeded by even more conservative justices, but his leadership of the Court was at the time widely regarded as an emblem of the retreat from the liberal Warren Court era and the rise of judicial conservatism. Emboldened by expressions such as Rehnquist's in *Wallace v. Jaffree*, the religious conservative movement made steady gains from that time onward in reinterpreting the Constitution to reflect its belief that public support for religion is permissible.

Kiryas Joel might seem to be an unlikely beneficiary of a movement devoted to America's status as a "Christian nation." But the Satmar village not only profited from that movement; it also played a role in propelling the return of religion to the public square by mounting a remarkably effective defense against numerous legal challenges to its practices and its very existence. Starting in the mid-1980s and accelerating over the course of the 1990s, KJ became a battleground for disputes about the interpretation of the First Amendment. The village found itself facing growing public criticism for its perceived fusion of religious and political forms of authority, which led to lawsuits calling into question its legality on various grounds.

Here too the story of KJ resembles that of other American religious communities that succeeded in creating their own cities on a hill. Utah itself became a state only after a prolonged period of conflict between Mormon residents and the federal government that included the enactment of laws prohibiting polygamy and limiting the amount of property the LDS Church could own. Mormons were vigorously prosecuted under these statutes, and the Supreme Court refused to overturn these statutes or recognize the Mormons' right to a religious exemption from the anti-bigamy law. The price of the Mormons' political success—recognition as a state—was a significant theological concession: the surrender of plural marriage.[22]

Closer in time and circumstances to Kiryas Joel is the case of Rajneeshpuram, the Oregon community founded by followers of Bhagwan Shri Rajneesh that was incorporated as a city in 1982. After bitter hostility between the new city and its neighbors, the state of Oregon sued the city of Rajneeshpuram in 1982, alleging that "recognition of the municipal status of the city of Rajneeshpuram constitutes the establishment of a theocracy." Accepting the argument that the city's existence violated the Establishment Clause, a federal district court issued a judicial order in 1984 requiring that the city be dissolved.[23]

KJ has also been repeatedly hauled into court. Indeed, since 1985 the village has been embroiled in more than a dozen lawsuits challenging its municipal institutions and practices. But none of the legal challenges brought against the village's public institutions has stuck. That is not to say that the courts have delivered a definitive pronouncement that the village and its actions are constitutional and fully in compliance with American law. In many of the cases, the village has prevailed either on a technicality or as a result of the parties settling the case.

In other cases, especially in the key realms of education and zoning, the village has been the initiator, demonstrating tremendous skill in picking lawyers and legal forums that serve its ends. Even when it has suffered legal defeats, KJ has found ways to adapt to the law and to adapt the law to its purposes. Indeed, over an exceptionally intense four decades of continuous litigation, the village has not just survived but thrived. Ironically enough, the constancy of strife and tension has been—along with unwitting assimilation and illiberal liberalism—a third key to KJ's success, steeling village leaders for battle in the rough-and-tumble world of American politics and law.

A Jewish American Story

From the vantage point of Jewish history, Kiryas Joel appears to represent a novel phenomenon: a self-standing, homogeneous, Yiddish-speaking shtetl that became a legal municipality recognized by the state—a vision long fantasized by utopians and novelists, but without precedent in European Jewish history.[24] By contrast, through the lens of American history and law, it is the rather *unexceptional* nature of KJ that stands out. The goal that we set out to accomplish together, a scholar of American law and a scholar of modern Jewish history, was to bring these perspectives together, to expose the seams that both hold the community together and connect it to the surrounding culture.

In addition to being a Jewish story and an American story, the tale of Kiryas Joel is also a *Jewish American* tale, reflecting the internal divisions within America's Jewish community as well as the bonds that hold it together. KJ's history features many—and many different kinds of—American Jews, often bitterly arrayed against one other. Drawn into KJ's orbit, they face off as neighbors, school administrators, rabbis, lawyers, and judges, transforming the political and legal battles over the village into a larger proxy battle over what it means to be an American and what it means to be a Jew in America.

Waged in the hallowed space of the American suburb, these battles call to mind "Eli the Fanatic," the short story published in 1959 by a young Philip Roth in his breakout collection *Goodbye, Columbus.* Roth's searing story depicts the vast social chasm between newly arrived Haredim and their more Americanized brethren. The central character is an assimilated Jewish lawyer, Eli Peck, who has moved out to suburban paradise in mythic Woodenton, New York. Peck is egged on by his close friends, all Jews, to confront an unseemly site in their midst: a yeshivah on the hill (echoing the mythic city on the hill) populated by Jewish orphan-survivors of the Holocaust and presided over by an enigmatic immigrant headmaster named Leo Tzuref. Pondering the spectacle with incredulity, a friend spits out, "A Yeshivah! Eli, a Yeshivah in Woodenton! If I want to live in Brownsville, Eli, I'll live in Brownsville."[25] (Brownsville is the poor Brooklyn neighborhood, lyrically memorialized by Alfred Kazin, that was once populated by Jewish immigrants from Eastern Europe.)[26]

Mr. Tzuref, the foil to the "typical" American Jews portrayed in Roth's story, who came to the suburbs precisely in order to escape the insularity of immigrant Jewish communities and gain entry to the world of the gentiles, has come to the suburbs in order to escape interference from the outside world. He can't imagine why Peck would be so opposed to the enclave he has created. And in fact Peck ultimately disappoints his friends by failing to remove the enclave from Woodenton. Instead, in one of the story's final tragicomic scenes, Peck suffers a nervous breakdown and dons the garb of a traditional Orthodox Jew.

This kind of "Jew versus Jew" struggle, as Samuel Freedman titled a book devoted to the subject, played out repeatedly over the decades following the publication of Roth's incendiary story.[27] More and less observant Jews took up opposing sides in suburban battles over taxes, resource allocation, and zoning in suburbs all across America, from Airmont, New York, and Beachwood, Ohio, to the Hancock Park neighborhood of Los Angeles. Could the basement of a private home in a residential area serve as a synagogue on Saturday? With such a *shtibl* (small prayer space) as an anchor, would the neighborhood turn Orthodox? If so, what then would happen to the "integrity" of the neighborhood as well as to property values? More often than not, non-Orthodox Jews were at the forefront of the neighborhood organizations that objected to the Haredi "intrusion" into American neighborhoods and suburban communities.

This was precisely the situation that confronted the Satmar Hasidim when they first made their way to Monroe in 1974. Jewish residents of

Monroe report that they initially welcomed Satmars as fellow Jews but quickly came to understand that the new arrivals were not interested in participating in local Jewish life, which revolved around Reform and Conservative synagogues. In fact, the Satmars were not much interested in interacting with any of the residents of Monroe, Jews or otherwise. Like Roth's Tzuref, they came to Monroe with the intention of creating an enclave, at a remove from New York City and from their immediate neighbors, where they could live their distinctive religious lives without interference. They would discharge basic civic obligations of paying taxes and voting in elections, the latter to ensure their interests were met. But they had no desire to integrate since assimilation would spell the end of their sacred way of life.

This realization was a bitter pill for the veteran Jewish residents of Monroe, who came to regard the Satmars as not only unfriendly but ungrateful exploiters of the services of the town. The Satmars, for their part, regarded the local Jewish population as no more friendly to them than the non-Jewish population. The confrontation between American and traditional Jewish values triggered by the Satmars' arrival in Monroe thus also became a confrontation between two radically different types of American Jews.

These differences are reflected in the fact that the leadership in KJ often found itself at odds with national Jewish organizations for which the village was a manifest violation of their vision of Americanness. Groups such as the American Jewish Committee, the American Jewish Congress, and the Anti-Defamation League had been steadfast in their support of the principle of separation between religion and state from their inception. When the village administration decided to address the problem of how best to educate children with special needs by creating a public school in KJ, these national Jewish groups, joined by dissenters in the village, lined up in opposition, writing amicus briefs in the various rounds of litigation that ended up in the U.S. Supreme Court in 1994. Arrayed against these liberal Jewish groups, especially in their approach to church-state issues, were more observant Jewish groups such as the Orthodox Union and the Agudath Israel, whose outlook was much more aligned with conservative Christian organizations.

Hostility between Jews has also been a prominent feature of life inside KJ since the death of Rabbi Joel Teitelbaum in 1979. The Rebbe's
passing inaugurated a new era in Satmar history marked by fierce battles
over the legitimacy of his successors. The appointment of his nephew,
Moshe Teitelbaum, inspired a first wave of opposition gathered around
Reb Yoelish's widow, Alta Faiga. This opposition continued throughout
the 1980s, consolidating into a group known as Bnai Yoel (the Sons of
Joel), who see themselves as the true followers of the founding rabbi. In
addition to Bnai Yoel, a pair of larger groups of opponents arrayed
around two of Moshe's sons: Aaron, who has been the chief rabbi of
Kiryas Joel since 1984, and Zalman Leib, who has served as the chief
rabbi of the large Satmar community of Williamsburg since 1999. Over
time, their rivalry has given rise to outbreaks of violence and to two
competing sets of institutions—religious schools, synagogues, rabbinical courts, aid societies, and wedding halls—one run by Aaron, the
other by Zalman. Making matters even more complicated is the fact that
the Bnai Yoel have their own set of institutions in Kiryas Joel. In this
regard, KJ is itself an arena of "Jew versus Jew" battle.

The radically divergent perspectives and visions at play—within and
outside of the village—make the story of Kiryas Joel a highly complicated one. Many inside the village regard it not only as a great American
success story but also as an organic and beautiful way of life. But many
others, Jews and non-Jews alike, believe that KJ altogether fails to uphold the American—and American Jewish—ethos of civic engagement. What joins these divergent views together is the shared perception that KJ has succeeded in its goal of achieving physical and cultural
separation. Indeed, despite the fact that critics castigate the Satmars for
their exclusionary and self-segregating ways, it often seems like they
desire separation as much as the Satmars do. The most recent chapter
in the legal and political saga surrounding Kiryas Joel reinforces this
point: in their attempt to achieve greater autonomy and segregation, the
village entered yet again into conflict with the town of Monroe, which
was ultimately resolved by mutual agreement; the two sides supported
the creation of a new self-standing town called Palm Tree (the English

translation of Teitelbaum), which has replaced Monroe as the town of which the village of KJ is a part.

Yet, as we have suggested above, and as we will elaborate in the following pages, KJ is less separated from the outside world than either its boosters or its critics recognize. It is precisely because the Satmar village—and now town—cannot avoid affecting its neighbors any more than it can avoid being affected by them that it has become an object of controversy. Indeed, Kiryas Joel elicits intense emotions—and judgments. The drama of the story makes it into a sort of passion play from which observers draw deep, often conflicting, moral lessons. Most people with whom we have spoken expect us to endorse their version of the story and condemn the others. But our motivation is neither to condemn nor to condone. We, the two authors of this book, don't share the exact same opinion of the community. But we hope, by combining our perspectives and sifting through the many different outlooks portrayed here, to be able to present it in a fair-minded and multifaceted way.

We also hope that readers inclined to judge Kiryas Joel will extend the ambit of their judgment beyond the perimeters of the village to include the larger society that produced it. For the ultimate conclusion we draw is that KJ is not an isolated island but an integral part of American society, a product of the country's political, social, legal, and economic institutions. As such, it illuminates the deep tensions between competing visions of law, politics, and religion that so roil public life in this country today. In the midst of these deep-seated tensions, it has transformed adversity into a position of power and solidity that its founding fathers and mothers never could have imagined. Herein lies the fascination of the American shtetl.

PART I

THE PAST AND PRESENT OF
THE SHTETL

CHAPTER 1

Life in the Shtetl

Every Friday in the late afternoon, as the sun gives way to dusk, a series of loud sirens pierce the air of a densely packed village located in a suburban town in the Catskill Mountains fifty miles north and slightly west of New York City. As in American company towns of yore, the blare marks an end to the busy work week. But instead of releasing thousands of laborers from the factory to their homes or the nearby bar, the sirens clear the streets of Kiryas Joel. The frantic pace of the hours leading up to the sirens, with women and men scurrying about to complete their chores, gives way to calm as the twenty-five-hour-long Jewish Sabbath enters, during which most forms of labor permitted during the week—the Talmud records thirty-nine varieties—are forbidden. The sirens thereby delineate the border between labor and rest, profane and sacred, weekday and *Shabbes*.

Rather than being controlled by a single business corporation, KJ is dominated by a religious corporation, the Congregation Yetev Lev D'Satmar, to which all of the residents, at least originally, belonged. It is the all-encompassing religious character of KJ life that leads members of the community to declare that their mode of living is the most organic way of life around.[1] When the main Yiddish newspaper of the Satmar community published a long article in 1978 declaring that Kiryas Joel was "a dream that became a reality," the sentiment was no exaggeration. The first residents who made their way from Brooklyn to Orange County four years earlier knew well the difficulties they faced on the path to their suburban community.[2] They retained their deep faith that it was God's will, along with the leadership of their spiritual shepherd, Rabbi Teitelbaum, that allowed the community to rise. And they were proud that their small settlement had become what they had originally hoped—a place of purity, an enclave at a remove from the rest of a society that, for all its willingness to countenance the creation of a Hasidic village, was still irredeemably *golus*, exile.

At the same time, they were proud of the community's success, as measured by its stunning growth; Kiryas Joel quickly became the fastest growing municipality in the state of New York, with an annual rate that sometimes reached 13 percent in a given year. Indeed, the village has grown from 2,000 people in 1980 to 7,500 in 1990, 13,000 in 2000, 20,000 in 2010, and 25,000 in 2019. According to one estimate, it may well reach 96,000 residents in 2040, thereby making it the first all-Hasidic city in the world.[3]

The chief official responsible for planning growth in Kiryas Joel is village administrator Gedalye Szegedin, an exceptionally capable Satmar Hasid, now in his early fifties, who speaks English with a Yiddish inflection, although he was born and raised in New York. Bespectacled and bearded, Szegedin wears the familiar workday outfit of most men in the community: a white shirt buttoned to the top, black pants, a black vest, and, when the occasion arises, a long black caftan (outer coat), and big round black hat. But he is unlike his Satmar peers in many other regards. He mixes the tasks of city manager, town planner, savvy politician, and decisive CEO to guide virtually every aspect of municipal life in Kiryas Joel, from residential development to traffic patterns and garbage collection. Admired by friends and resented by foes, who accuse him of working only on behalf of the establishment faction, Szegedin exudes an air of confidence born of more than twenty-five years of service as administrator as well as by his extensive web of local and statewide political ties. He is related to some of the leading figures in the village. His uncle is Mayer Hirsch, a wealthy and well-connected developer who is one of the most powerful people in KJ, serving as the moving force behind the semiofficial Vaad hakirya (which oversees land acquisition and sale in the village); and his stepfather, Rabbi Wolf Gluck, was head of the largest private school system in

Aerial Photos of KJ Over Time

Photos From www.historicaerials.com

FIGURE 1.1. Aerial Photo of Kiryas Joel over Time. Courtesy of Mordechai Friedman.

town, the United Talmudic Academy. During his time in office, KJ has grown dramatically in terms of both population and village services. Szegedin observes with a mix of pride and amusement that some have called him the Robert Moses of KJ, referring to the legendary and controversial New York city planner.[4]

This picture of a blessedly insular but rapidly growing rural community is a key part of the story of Kiryas Joel. But this is only one strand of the story. In many regards, the village is not a model of tranquility and orderly growth but is rather rife with tensions, both within and beyond.[5] Satmar Hasidim may look to the uninitiated eye as identical to one another in appearance and worldview, but there are sharp divisions separating factions in the village, each of which follows its own leaders and maintains its own set of religious and educational institutions. The faction associated with the chief rabbi of the village, R. Aaron Teitelbaum, dominates the major institutions in town and has presided over the dramatic growth of the community; the main opposition party is associated with his younger brother and rival, R. Zalman of Williamsburg. And there is the smaller dissident group, Bnai Yoel, which follows neither rabbi.

In a curious reenactment of history, the Bnai Yoel are known as *misnagdim* (opponents), while the mainstream party goes by the name "Hasidim," which literally means "pious ones." This is the very set of terms—Hasidim and misnagdim—used to distinguish groups of Jews in the late eighteenth and early nineteenth centuries in Eastern Europe, although the "Hasidic" camp was then the renegade upstart, whereas now it is the establishment. The misnagdim, in that earlier context, were precisely the opponents of Hasidim—in fact, the anti-Hasidim.

In the context of Kiryas Joel, the so-called misnagdim not only claim to be more pious and to maintain greater fidelity to the first Satmar Rebbe's path but also assert that the establishment party of R. Aaron denies them religious and civil services and, in doing so, reveals KJ's true colors as an authoritarian theocracy. They report being intimidated, pressured, excluded, and even attacked.[6] By contrast, those associated with the ruling faction maintain that there is a "live and let live" policy that allows each group to provide for its members within the framework of a Satmar way of life. For the outside observer, it is difficult to reconcile the two sharply divergent accounts, both of which seem to contain more than a grain of truth.

Both the establishment and the dissidents are steadfast in their commitment to *halakhah* (Jewish law). They do, however, have different outlooks regarding how to approach neighbors beyond KJ's borders, which stretch just to 1.5 square miles. The dissidents are keen on forging harmonious relations with the gentile world and believe that the mainstream *k'hul* (from the Hebrew word *kahal* for congregation) has been needlessly aggressive in throwing its weight around. Since the early 2000s, an organization called the Kiryas Joel Alliance, associated with the Bnai Yoel, has sought to create a more favorable image of the community in the broader public eye by distinguishing between the residents and leaders of KJ.[7] These good neighbor policies coexist, paradoxically, with the dissidents' commitment to religious separatism, which they believe has been breached by the establishment party's assumption of the powers of secular local government.

The leadership of KJ, for its part, maintains that the problem is neither politics nor an absence of neighborly relations. It is demographic, plain and simple. As Gedalye Szegedin formulated it in 2016, Kiryas Joel must continue to expand in order "to accommodate the needs of the community and secure the necessary infrastructure." Szegedin noted that there have been 2,500 babies born in the community since late 2013, during which time he himself issued 750 marriage licenses.[8] It is that explosive growth that impels him to seek out more land, sewage capacity, and water at every turn.

It is also that rate of growth that makes Kiryas Joel an outlier in Orange County, New York. Neither its physical appearance nor its population density conforms to the classic American suburban ideal that one encounters in the rest of the town of Monroe, where the village of Kiryas Joel is located.[9] There one finds, over twenty square miles, a mix of American creature comforts (restaurants, a movie theater, and small businesses), a diverse range of architectural styles, and generously spaced lots on which ranch-style homes sit. By contrast, KJ has had to cram more than 30,000 people into its 1.5 square miles, which, given its birth rate, has necessitated constant efforts to annex new territory. These have been met with vocal opposition by neighbors, who have felt the threat of encroachment by Kiryas Joel for decades. In fact, in 2013 a group of citizens in the town of Monroe, of which KJ was a part and constituted a majority until 2019, established an organization called United Monroe in order to check the expansion of KJ beyond its then present borders. In particular, United Monroe strenuously objected to the village's desire to gain control over an additional 507 acres of land. It took aim at what it called, in somewhat ominous terms, the KJPE— the Kiryas Joel Political Elite—which it described as "masters of manipulation" intent on securing gain for themselves and their community at the expense of neighboring groups and individuals.[10]

The fact of the matter is that, over the course of its history, Kiryas Joel has punched well above its weight in the political arena, using its ability to deliver a bloc vote to elect candidates sympathetic to the community who, in turn, deliver economic and other benefits to it. Although KJ is a town of 25,000 residents, its leaders can pick up the phone and quickly reach top state and federal officials. A key question is whether the presence of increasingly assertive and independent dissenting factions within the community will mean the end of KJ's extraordinary political clout through the bloc vote. It is worth noting that in the town of Palm Tree, available voter registration records from 2019 revealed that 35 percent of the community identified as Democrats, 38 percent as Republicans, and 9 percent as Independents.[11]

Past voting results yield conflicting signals. In the November 2016 election, the competing camps in KJ joined forces to support the reelection of Republican state senator Bill Larkin by a vote of 5,852 to 140. KJ voters were more divided on the race for state assembly in which a Haredi candidate from neighboring Spring Valley, Aron Wieder, garnered 4,598 votes in the village to his opponent's 1,491, though Wieder eventually lost. Meanwhile, the presidential contest was even more divided, with Donald Trump receiving 55 percent (1,592) and Hillary Clinton 45 percent (1,291). What was noteworthy in the 2016 election was that 3,000 fewer voters cast ballots in the presidential election than in the local races.[12] This suggests that, until the dramatic shift to Donald Trump in 2020, the Satmars of KJ had much more at stake, in terms of the welfare of their community, in local elections in which candidates are expected to bring direct, tangible benefits to their constituents.

The recent trend toward a more assertive national political presence requires much careful analysis in coming years. It reveals a new sensibility among Satmars—a conservative, libertarian, ideological Americanness. In the past, it was not at all uncommon to hear Satmar Hasidim express appreciation and loyalty to the United States, which offered safe haven to the surviving remnant of their community after the Holocaust. But the 2020 presidential campaign featured a more forceful form of political identity, exemplified by the sight of flag-waving Haredim at pro-Trump rallies. In many ways, Satmar Hasidim operate with a good deal of cognitive dissonance, recognizing that America has been uniquely hospitable to Jews while still expressing the daily hope that the Messiah will come and liberate Jews from the state of exile in which they dwell. One of the sharpest formulations of this belief came from Zalman Teitelbaum, who declared in the midst of the 2020 campaign—and on the day marking the liberation of Joel Teitelbaum from Bergen-Belsen— that "we need to understand that we are in exile, we live here but we are not Americans."[13] In many regards, Satmar Hasidim today live in two zones of time: in the realm of messianic hope and in the everyday reality of their own legally recognized municipality, which, as we shall see, transformed a relatively small collection of private property owners into a sovereign shtetl.

An Uncommon Suburb

Out-of-towners are offered an eye-opening introduction to KJ's unusual nature when they drive down Forest Road into the village; there they can see the sign that, since 2010, has urged those entering the village to respect THE TRADITIONS AND RELIGIOUS CUSTOMS of the Satmar community. As one proceeds further into town on Forest Road, one sees color-coded signs posted on either side advising men and women to walk on different sides of the street during the Sabbath and holidays.

Sidewalk segregation is actually not practiced in Kiryas Joel. Men and women cohabit public spaces in the heart of the village, where just to the left of Forest Road is a large lot of land containing the village's first shopping center, to which is appended a suite of village government offices. Directly adjacent to the village offices is the Ezras Cholim, Kiryas Joel's own health center.

Heading in the opposite direction, straight down Van Buren Road and then a right onto Quickway Drive, one arrives at a small body of water known as Forest Road Lake, around which the first eighty garden apartments of the community were built between 1972 and 1974 in the subdivision known as Section I. The original residents had the benefit of proximity to water, but they eschewed the typical American suburban dream of single-family ranch homes with a lawn in an isolated wooded area. Rather, they moved into two-story rectangular red brick apartment buildings.

Apartment living became the norm in Kiryas Joel, where the density of housing units is seven times that of the regional norm.[14] It had to be in order to accommodate large numbers of Satmar families interested in moving out of the city and finding affordable housing. Today, over 90 percent of the community live in rows of tightly packed multifamily dwellings, many of which are three, four, or even five stories high, with anywhere from twenty to forty apartments.[15] If you drive around the village, you will see construction crews everywhere building new and larger buildings far beyond Section I. And yet there is no evident master plan at work.[16] A small handful of private Satmar developers have put up edifices of differing style and scale, with far less attention paid to aesthetics than to functionality, which is the name of the game in a market that requires hundreds of new units each year to meet the housing demands of newly married couples.

The extraordinary density of Kiryas Joel, so unlike the suburban villages and towns that neighbor it, is reflected not only in the waves of multistory buildings but also within the apartments themselves. Given that procreation is a sacred ideal in the community, it is quite common for Satmar families to have between eight and fifteen children. Parents must become master interior designers to apportion space wisely. Suffice it to say that children rarely have their own bedrooms. (Parents, however, each have their own beds.) The sharing of space is, in the first instance, the product of necessity. As of 2018, nearly 50 percent of the community lived below the poverty line, making KJ, in statistical terms, one of the poorest communities in America.[17] As a result, for many residents, there is little disposable income to make major home improvements.

But the sharing of space serves another purpose. It reinforces the importance of assuming one's place within the collective. While Kiryas

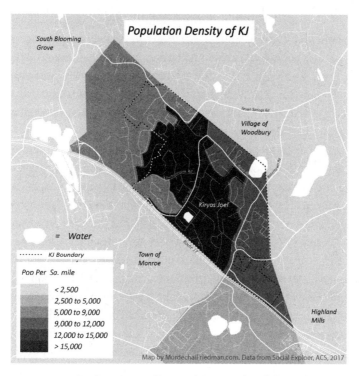

FIGURE 1.2. Population Density of Kiryas Joel. Courtesy of Mordechai Friedman.

FIGURE 1.3. Man Walking in Front of Typical Multiunit Apartment Buildings in Kiryas Joel. Courtesy of Jackson Krule.

Joel manifests its Americanness in various ways, one way in which it does *not* is by opting out of the celebration of individualism in American society. The Satmar Hasidim of Kiryas Joel place the collective above the individual, and children from an early age are taught to appreciate that principle. Conformity, not difference, is desired. Deviation is dealt with harshly.

Here is a subculture of America in which personal choice does not reign supreme. For a small number of people who grew up in Kiryas Joel and other communities like it, the absence of freedom to express themselves as individuals becomes unbearable. Testimonies from people in this group describe how the restrictions, whether they be on clothes, reading material, or open questioning of beliefs or practices, led them to transgress the norms of the community as teenagers. The vigorous reprimands they received from their parents might well have been bolstered by the suspicions of neighbors, which were then passed on to the village's Vaad hatsnius, or Modesty Committee. The resulting threats of the committee—or even an audience with Rabbi Aaron—deepened their sense of alienation and in some instances paved the way for exit.[18] Struggles such as these have inspired a flurry of memoirs from those who fled communities such as Kiryas Joel. For example, Shulem Deen, who grew up in New Square, a nearby Hasidic village, writes eloquently in his memoir, *All Who Go Do Not Return*, of his inability to stifle his doubts about faith and thus the entire system of regulation in the community in which he grew up.[19] He and others who have left attest to the primacy of community in a place such as Kiryas Joel, where the needs of the group heavily outweigh those of the individual member.

Following in "the Path of Ancient Israel"

A recurrent phrase in insider accounts of Satmar Hasidism and Kiryas Joel is that the community follows in "the path of ancient Israel" (*derekh Yisroel sava*), that is, in the way of one's forebears.[20] Fealty to the ideal of an unchanging tradition is considered a supreme obligation. Satmar leaders hold to the famous injunction of one of the nineteenth-century forebears of modern Haredi culture, the Hatam Sofer (Moses Sofer), who declared that "innovation is forbidden as a matter of Torah."[21]

FIGURE 1.4. Audience of Satmar Men and Boys Gathered to Hear R. Aaron Teitelbaum.
Courtesy of Jackson Krule.

This commitment begins with physical appearance. At large gatherings in Kiryas Joel, one sees a sea of uniformity—men dressed in black pants, with *tzitzis* (fringes) hanging outside of their pants from their prayer shawl undergarment. On the Sabbath and holidays, men dress in their more formal garb of a long silk black coat called a *bekishe* and a large circular fur hat called a *streimel* (both of which differ in style from those worn by men of other Hasidic groups). Almost all men in the community have long beards and carefully twisted sidelocks known as *peyes*, the latter of which are left uncut in fulfillment of the injunction from Leviticus 19:26 that "ye shall not round the corners of your heads, neither shalt thou mar the corners of thy beard."

The penchant for sartorial uniformity is also reflected in dressing children in identical clothes. Women are permitted somewhat more variety in their dress. But if conformity is the expectation for men in their dress habits, then its corollary, modesty or *tsnius*, is the paramount expectation for women in Kiryas Joel. Women are instructed, as the sign at the entrance to the village indicates, to wear long skirts as well as tops that cover their necklines with sleeves that extend to the beginning of the wrist. When clothing deviates from established norms, the wrath of the community, in the form of the Modesty Committee, may fall upon the violator. This is the fate that befell a woman named Toby Greenberg in 2007. She was given to wearing jean skirts and colorful shirts, both of which were deemed inappropriate by the Modesty Committee. When she refused to modify her dress, self-appointed extremists disseminated flyers that accused her of contaminating the village. A group of them also slashed the tires of her car and delivered a letter to her home demanding that she and her family leave the village, which they eventually did.[22]

In addition to modesty in outer clothing, Joel Teitelbaum insisted that girls and women should wear thick, not sheer, stockings, lest "a terrible breakdown of *tsnius*" (modesty) occur.[23] To guarantee this, he had one of his followers create a distinctive brand of tights for Satmar women known as "Palm" (the English translation of the Yiddish "Teitel") of at least 90 denier (a measurement of thickness). He also insisted that married women should not merely cover their hair but also shave their heads every month. This was not an innovation of Satmar Hasidism but had become a major tenet of Teitelbaum's stringent approach already in Europe. In Kiryas Joel today, there is a mix of head covering styles among women, with some favoring a *shaitel* (wig) over a *shpitzel* (a head covering with only a partial wig in the front). Some also wear a *tichel*, a scarf worn over the wig that covers the shaved head.[24] Most women accept these hair-related strictures as consistent with the values of modesty that they hope to uphold as virtuous "daughters of Israel." Violating the standards—for example, by not fully shaving one's hair or wearing insufficiently modest attire—carries a powerful threat. It was thuggish intimidation in the case of Toby Greenberg. For others, it is the real prospect of censure from the community and perhaps expulsion of one's children from the community's private religious schools.

Another expected, supervised, and mostly desired communal norm is the practice of regular visits to the ritual bathhouse (*mikveh*). Men are expected to go on Friday before the onset of the Sabbath, but many go on a daily basis before morning prayers. Married women, meanwhile, are required to make regular use of the mikveh. They must adhere strictly to family purity laws that require a menstruating woman in a state of *niddah* (the Hebrew term for menstruation, which also carries the connotations of impurity and separation) to remain beyond the touch of her husband for two weeks every month; he is not even supposed to hand her a plate of food. After a week in which no menstrual blood is identified, a woman must go to the mikveh to be purified, after which she can return to sexual relations with her husband. Some formerly observant women regard this process of purification as intrusive and demeaning—and an attempt by male rabbis to control their bodies.[25] Many others regard it as a natural and integral part of the rhythm of Jewish life, which brings them not only a sense of order but a higher state of purity. It is also the case that some women and men in the Haredi world, in general, and in KJ, in particular, believe that abstaining from sex for two weeks enhances their mutual desire and the overall quality of their sex life during the other two weeks. To facilitate that practice, Satmar wives and husbands sleep in separate beds in their bedrooms.

Men and women in the Satmar world pair up at an early age, almost always through arranged marriages. Young women get married shortly after graduating high school. Prior to that time, they have virtually no contact with boys or young men other than family members. They live in an insular culture in which sexual attraction and flirtation are not only discouraged but, according to various accounts, often absent—at a time of peak interest and development among adolescents in mainstream American society.[26] This dissonance reveals but one of the ways in which Kiryas Joel is very different from the surrounding world.

But Kiryas Joel is also part of that world. Satmar Hasidim are people—flesh and blood like others. While there are strict rules about dress, Satmar girls and women devote a good deal of attention to style. Teenage girls in the community follow their American contemporaries in seeking thin bodies.[27] While they are strongly encouraged to resist sexual impulses throughout high school, abstinence is not a lifetime commitment. Sex in the community is circumscribed but not proscribed—freely practiced for two weeks a month within the confines of marriage.

Marriage in Kiryas Joel is a socially regulated part of the Satmar life cycle at age eighteen for girls and twenty for boys. The first step toward a possible union is taken not by the young prospects themselves but usually by a woman matchmaker or *shadkhente*, who assesses the compatibility of the two families. Among the key criteria considered by the matchmaker are whether the families place a great deal of value on learning Torah, how committed they are to high ethical standards (*midos*), and whether they tend to the more conservative or open-minded side of the spectrum in terms of exposure to the wider world. After preliminary vetting by the parents, the prospective couple meets for a first encounter known as a *besho*, often at the home of one set of parents, spends a short amount of time together, often in awkward conversation, and reports back to the matchmaker who shares information with both sides and then tells their parents whether to move forward or not. If the couple gives a green light, it is usually a matter of months up to a year before the wedding takes place.

Immediately thereafter, the new husband and wife settle into a new home and begin to attempt to have children, which is seen as the ultimate *mitzvah*—a combined religious commandment and moral imperative. From the perspective of village officials in KJ, this oft-repeated pattern poses a significant, but quantifiable, problem. Given that the tradition in Satmar is for married daughters to remain close to their mothers, village officials can gauge the minimum number of apartments needed every year by the number of girls graduating from high school in a given year, usually around 250. In the past five years, there have been substantially more families seeking apartments in Kiryas Joel than available domiciles. In 2015–2016, for example, village planners estimated that 325 new families needed housing, although there were only 138 apartments available. They also projected that between 275 and 415 new apartments would be needed every year to satisfy demand.[28]

How to make room in the already densely packed village? At various points in KJ's history, the village has sought to grow by annexing land

from the village of Monroe. These efforts have invariably elicited concern
and opposition that have grown in intensity. For example, six years after
the village was incorporated, in 1983, developers associated with the
village leaders sought and eventually succeeded in annexing 370 acres
from the town of Monroe.[29] Again, in 2003–2004, controversy arose
when Kiryas Joel sought to build a thirteen-mile pipeline to tap into the
New York State aqueduct, a move that prompted a new round of protests, including a spate of unpleasant antisemitic outbursts against the
Satmar community. By 2004, when the pipeline plan had stalled, the
Vaad hakirya proposed to transform more than 300 acres that it owned
outside of the community's boundaries into a second village.[30] A decade later, village officials set in motion the proposal to annex 507 acres
from the town of Monroe to deal with the demands of growth. That plan
was whittled down to a more modest 164 acres, which were added to KJ
to make the new town of Palm Tree.[31]

Village leaders have justified the various annexation plans as not only
logical and necessary but as intended to avoid imposing direct Satmar
political control beyond Kiryas Joel. This would happen, they say, if
Satmar Hasidim settled in large numbers in locations beyond the current boundaries of the village.[32] That scenario would deviate from the
KJ model of a self-standing Hasidic polity and make KJ more like
nearby Ramapo, New York, and Lakewood, New Jersey, places where
Orthodox Jews represent a substantial percentage of the town's population and have gained control over political institutions in the towns,
including the school districts. This despite the fact that virtually none
of the Orthodox children attend the district schools, leading to widespread public ire in both locales.[33]

KJ, on one hand, and East Ramapo and Lakewood, on the other,
represent two distinct models of political organization; the former
favors complete separation between Haredim and the rest of the world,
while the latter places Haredi Jews of various stripes in a religiously,
economically, and racially diverse population. Even though the three KJ
factions had different strategies for engaging the outside world, all came
to accept the idea that the best—or least bad—solution was to sever KJ
from Monroe and create the new Hasidic town of Palm Tree.

The Internet and Its Discontents

Even that step could not seal off the Satmars from the outside completely. In the internet age, residents of Kiryas Joel are exposed to more of the broader world than ever before. As a matter of policy, the internet is seen as a dangerous threat, and community officials seek to limit its use. According to census data, 32 percent of KJ residents have computers and 17 percent have internet subscriptions—in contrast to the national averages of 92 and 80 percent respectively.[34] Many in KJ stay off the internet out of the sincere conviction that it poses grave peril; but others abide by the norms because private religious schools require that parents sign a document affirming that they do not use the internet at home.

And yet a good number of KJ residents, especially those who work outside of the village, *do* have smartphones, with regular access to the internet, albeit with a "kosher" filter that limits exposure to pornographic or other potentially transgressive material. In fact, possession of cellphones is so widespread that the Modesty Committee cannot win the battle to eliminate them.

This reveals one way in which Kiryas Joel has been swept up in the tide of unwitting assimilation, even as it declares steadfast adherence to the "path of ancient Israel." To give texture to the point, one encounters in the community a subset of young people who, while fully intending to remain there, are, in a sense, freethinkers: first, in letting their intellectual and cultural curiosity roam beyond the bounds of communal inhibitions, principally through the internet, though also via literature and travel; and second, in straining against what they perceive as the overly stringent authority structure of the community through subtle forms of resistance such as a man trimming his beard, a woman letting her hair grow, or a parent playing video content for children.[35]

This kind of resistance was slowly revealed during a lengthy discussion among a group of a dozen proudly open-minded men in the community in an hours-long *melaveh malkah*, the meal that escorts the Sabbath queen out on Saturday night. As the eating and drinking extended into the wee hours of Sunday morning, the assembled guests became more candid about the restrictions in the community. One person cast residents of KJ as "ignorant people" who blindly follow rules without any idea of why. Following on that comment, another participant took note of the fact that after making a brief appearance in the community, sushi was no longer available, having been deemed by some religious leaders too blatant a symbol of assimilation into American society to be acceptable. A third person, familiar with the widespread availability of sushi at many Orthodox Jewish restaurants and celebrations outside of KJ, jumped in to say that the ousting of sushi from KJ was a case of "manipulation for no reason."

The topic of the freewheeling conversation then shifted, in somewhat random fashion, to the subject of marijuana. One participant averred, quite remarkably, that "it was the only thing that keeps us going." It turned out that many of the guests at the table were personally familiar with marijuana and regarded its use as completely unproblematic. And clearly, they let on, they were not the only users of marijuana in the village. For them, it was a necessary escape valve from the strictures of the rabbis and their lay allies, many of which they found senseless. They even rolled their eyes.[36]

In this conversation and several others, KJ residents made mention of another interesting deviation, seemingly of a less transgressive nature: the growing popularity of the Breslov brand of Hasidism within Kiryas Joel.[37] Given the expectation of lockstep adherence to Satmar ways, it is surprising, on first blush, to hear of the entry of Breslov Hasidism into the community. The two forms of religious expression are at the opposite ends of a wide spectrum of Hasidic cultures. Satmar, some say, is not really Hasidic, in that it does not subscribe to the same principle of ecstatic devotion on which the original movement—and many of its offshoots—rest.[38] Its bookishness is the opposite of the Breslov way, which is proudly ecstatic and whose followers revel in joyful singing and dancing, sometimes even at busy intersections (in Israel). The fact that hundreds in KJ are increasingly drawn to Breslov reflects a deep spiritual thirst that is not being met by Satmar Hasidism.

So why do these spiritual seekers not stray "off the *derech*" (OTD) in a more conclusive sense—that is, off the path of Orthodoxy? Why do they choose to live as "double lifers," as Ayala Fader calls them—holding to a critical perspective on life in the community and yet continuing to go through the motions of an observant life, complete with thrice-daily prayers and continuous Talmudic study? The assembled guests made clear that, for all of their criticism of the ruling regime in KJ, they loved their Jewish lives in the village. The regulated nature of life in the community, while excessive in their eyes, still lent structure and meaning to them. And they choose to remain because they feel that Kiryas Joel is a safe and healthy environment for their children, especially in guaranteeing that they will remain committed Jews. The importance of this point cannot be overstated. Kiryas Joel is a children's society. The median age of its population is 12.4, and more than 60 percent of the community is under the age of eighteen.[39] During school hours, they are nowhere to be seen. But before and after and on the Sabbath, the streets and sidewalks of KJ abound with children racing after one another, jumping rope, or riding their Big Wheels.

To be sure, life is not idyllic for all. Former Satmar residents of KJ recall facing the wrath of their parents as adolescents when they transgressed the rules.[40] Their decision to leave the community was profoundly difficult, given the intensity of family ties and the insularity of their world. Their biggest fear, and an oft-voiced threat, is that by leaving they will lose custody of and contact with their children, which can lead to excruciating legal battles, exacerbated by the perception that courts frequently side with the parent who remains and even go so far as to award that parent "spiritual custody." Another source of concern is that, coming from the sheltered world they do, Satmars have little understanding of how the outside world works; in the case of men, they may even lack functional levels of English required to make their way into a competitive labor market. In order to meet the needs of this cohort of exiters from KJ and other Haredi communities, a network of organizations and online resources has arisen to provide support, advice, training, legal and material resources, and community for those navigating this difficult journey—the most prominent of which is called Footsteps.[41]

FIGURE 1.5. Young Boy on Big Wheel. Courtesy of Jackson Krule.

Because of the risks and difficulties involved, the rate of exit is very low. Although there are no hard data, the total number of those who leave is likely no more than a few handfuls of people every year, including those who transition to a less stringent Orthodox life in neighboring Monsey, New York. Yet because the Satmar population itself has grown so large, there is a solid contingent of ex-Satmars in the community of former Haredim that groups such as Footsteps seek to assist after exit.

Gender and the Rhythms of Ritual and Work in KJ

The laws and customs of Satmar Hasidism provide a well-defined framework for the conduct of daily life. Men wake up between five and seven each morning, often going to the mikveh for ritual immersion before *shil* (as Satmar Hasidim pronounce the Yiddish word *shul* for synagogue). Kiryas Joel offers many options in this regard. Each of the three factions has its main synagogue on or near Forest Road, although there are scores of other synagogues or prayer spaces, as many as one hundred, closer to where many residents live. Most are small *shtiblekh* (often a room or couple of rooms in the basement of a house) in which members of one faction will join together in prayer. Not all synagogues begin services at the same time, which means that there are *minyanim* or prayer quorums running throughout the morning, afternoon, and evening. Men may study with a partner before morning prayers and then remain after for a short Talmudic *shi'ur*, or lesson. Joel Teitelbaum insisted that male followers not only pray the prescribed three times a day but also devote themselves to Talmud study in the morning and evening.

That said, he neither insisted nor desired that men in the community dedicate their entire lives to study. Whereas other Haredi rabbis encouraged men to continue full-time study throughout their adult lives—a phenomenon especially noticeable in Israel—the Satmar Rebbe expected men to go to work after getting married. In fact, one of the criteria in choosing a site in Orange County was that it had to be close enough for men to commute to New York for work every day. Over time, the premium placed in the community on excellence in Talmud Torah, the study of sacred texts, has prompted more and more young

FIGURE 1.6. Men in Study Hall in Main Aroni Synagogue. Courtesy of Jackson Krule.

men to lengthen the time they study in *kollel*, the religious institution in which married men study on a full-time basis. The trend represents a curious kind of religious innovation, one that pushes toward a more traditionalist or stringent form of religious life and inverts the original Hasidic impulse to reject the overly intellectual study-based approach of rabbinic Judaism.

One of the consequences of this new trend is that the burden of economic responsibility for young couples shifts to women. In general, women perform a mix of diverse and somewhat contradictory functions in Kiryas Joel. They do not have the same obligation as men to pray three times a day. Nor do they typically make their way to synagogue on the Sabbath. But they are the custodians of the domestic realm with responsibility to provide for the physical and emotional well-being of many children. As schoolgirls, they learn the intricacies of maintaining a strictly kosher kitchen and do most, if not all, of the cooking. They also learn through observation how to raise and organize a large number of children, whom they must pack up and send off to school every weekday morning, which includes Sunday.

In going about these tasks in Kiryas Joel, women are limited in their mobility because they are not permitted to drive, as a matter of long-standing Satmar custom.[42] It is common to see mothers pushing strollers on the sidewalks of the community. To accommodate their transportation needs, there are bus lines within KJ and to New York City as well as a number of car services staffed by Satmar men to ferry them around. This is a rare setting in which women interact with men other than their husbands in unsupervised fashion. In many other public social settings, women and men are separated, often by a wall or divider known as a *mehitsah*.

For the most part, Satmar Hasidim seem to hold to a traditional "separate spheres" ideology according to which men and women inhabit different social and spiritual realms: men dominate in public, women in the domestic sphere. This division, as Rosalind Rosenberg noted in 1982, necessarily entails a significant difference in power between men and women.[43] But in at least one regard, women have a considerable advantage in dealing with the outside world. Girls receive far more exposure in school to secular subjects, especially the English language, than boys, who get a heavy dose of Jewish studies at the expense of secular subjects. Yiddish remains the language of the community, with more than 96 percent of residents declaring that a language other than English is spoken in their home. In some households, women use English in communicating with other women and their children, while retaining Yiddish in interactions with their husbands. Women's fluency with English also makes them valuable assets in the workplace where, as office managers, clerks, and secretaries, they can effortlessly engage the outside world.[44] In this way, the division of gender roles associated with the ideology of separate spheres is inverted in ways that bestow significant privileges on women, even if they are expected to use those privileges on behalf of their families in fulfillment of traditional roles, and without subverting the man's traditional role as head of the household.

Already in 1972, sociologist Israel Rubin, whose field study in Williamsburg yielded the book *Satmar: An Island in the City*, observed that "expectations concerning division of labor between husband and wife are undergoing radical change." Increasingly, he noted, Satmar "women share with their husbands the responsibility of providing for the family."[45] This trend has only increased over the past forty years, as feminism has led to greater opportunities for women in virtually every domain of American society. In today's world, Satmar women go to work after graduating high school, often as teachers in the KJ private schools, and, increasingly, continue working after giving birth to their first children. Work is, in the first instance, a matter of a large family's economic sustenance. Even if a man is working and not studying in *kollel*, making ends meet is challenging for the average Satmar family. The population density of the village makes real estate extremely expensive, for both renters and buyers.[46] Private school tuition, even though heavily subsidized, quickly adds up with families of more than five kids. And the most basic expenses—feeding and clothing a large family as well as a cleaning woman to help tend to the house—are substantial.

Women's work outside of the home is important both for economic reasons and for imparting a sense of purpose. Here is another instance in which Kiryas Joel, the insular Satmar Hasidic community, betrays traces of assimilation. Notwithstanding the widespread acceptance of traditional gender roles, many women, and some men, have absorbed, often unwittingly, elements of a most secular modern ideology, feminism. A conversation involving three women in Kiryas Joel, each of whom came from a family belonging to a different faction in town, revealed a range of attitudes in this regard. One of the women professed to having a limited understanding of what feminism was; she said she was content with the role that she had as a wife and mother who did not need to work outside of the house. Two of the other women chafed against the community's constraints on women. Of those two, one explicitly embraced the cause of feminism, especially in her desire to pursue her professional aspiration. Once, as a younger married woman, she had given thought to leaving KJ for a somewhat less confining Orthodox community. But she has stayed and raised her family in the village. Despite the limitations she experiences—on her attire, her desire to drive, and her passion for physical fitness, among others—she continues to believe in the virtue of the way of life in Kiryas Joel, particularly in ensuring the ongoing Jewish identity of her children.[47]

The conversation among these women also pushed to the surface the question of the status of women relative to men in KJ. Echoing various versions of separate spheres ideology, the women all declared that their husbands treated them as equal partners in the raising of their families but recognized that this was not universally the case in the community. One woman reported that she had heard, and was drawn to, the claim that women did not have to perform all of the commandments that men did because they were born in a more perfect state. The women very much resonated with the view that men, including their husbands, were in an imperfect state and required constant efforts at self-improvement.

They also clearly felt a tension in living their lives in Kiryas Joel. Of course many Jews, though surely not Jews alone, experience a tension between their religious or ethnic identity and the inexorable pull of American society. The case of Kiryas Joel is an intriguing laboratory for observing how, in a society that professes to reject the values of modern society, that balance is struck. Seen from the outside as entirely cut off from the surrounding culture, KJ in fact draws from and is continually being reshaped by that culture—even as leaders within sternly warn against any surrender to it.

One of the last havens from the surrounding world and the tensions that emanate from it is Shabbes, the Jewish Sabbath. Shabbes is the culmination of the week, marking a twenty-five-hour period of abstinence from work, driving, and all forms of electric or electronic devices. Automotive traffic on the streets comes to a halt, save for the drive-bys of the village's non-Jewish Public Safety officers and the occasional forays of the Satmar-manned Hatzolah ambulance corps.

Adults and children alike look forward to the arrival of Shabbes (with the exception of the mostly silent minority for whom its many restrictions are suffocating). It is regarded as a temporal site of holiness, as distinct from the more mundane work or school week. All of the restrictions against work on Shabbes make preparing for it extremely labor-intensive, especially on Friday. Residents in KJ race around furiously to purchase the necessary items, clean the house, set automatic timers for lights, rip up toilet paper to avoid violating the rule against tearing on the day of rest, study the weekly Torah portion, place phone calls to family members elsewhere, and smoke a final cigarette before the sounding of the siren. Well before that, the mother of the house (often aided by her older daughters) has prepared vast quantities of food for the main family meals on Friday night and Saturday lunch, since cooking is not permitted on the Sabbath. In home after home, including in the residences of the small number of Sephardic and Yemenite Jews in the community, the same menu is repeated in lockstep Satmar fashion. It is classic Ashkenazic fare: for dinner, chicken soup, gefilte fish, chicken, and then meat, with an assortment of side dishes; for lunch, gefilte fish, egg salad, and then the pièce de résistance, "chulent," the traditional meat and bean stew that Jews have been eating for centuries because it can be kept warm without violating the laws of Shabbes (or losing its tastiness).[48]

The Sabbath brings its own form of "separate spheres" between men and women. Men and boys shuttle back and forth for prayers in synagogue three or four times from the onset of Sabbath to its exit on Saturday night.[49] Women remain at home, chatting with other women friends or tending to their children. When meals come, the male head of the house will make the blessings over wine and bread, as will other men and boys above bar mitzvah age. Hewing to traditional gender roles, the women and girls first serve food to the men and then take their seats on the other side of the table. In some homes, the conversation is divided along gender lines, with men and women clustering in separate groups, whereas in other homes, the conversation is more integrated. In both cases, the pace of the meal is much slower than on a normal workday, allowing for more extended and intimate conversation among family members.

Shabbes in Kiryas Joel is illustrative of the multiple faces of the community. Its observance rates as one of the highest priorities of residents, as evidenced not only by their punctilious attention to detail but also by the amount of money they expend to mark it. Shabbes also contains the most traditional and, in some sense, restrictive elements of Jewish observance, while at the same time embodying the quintessence of joy in Judaism—as embodied in the phrase *oyneg Shabbes* (the pleasure of the Sabbath). It requires a tremendous amount of work and advanced preparation but also symbolizes freedom from the rigors and strains of the week.[50]

Just like Shabbes, the major holidays of the Jewish calendar are an intense mix of restriction and pleasure: Rosh Ha-Shanah, Yom Kippur, and the three major festivals of Sukkot, Passover, and Shavuot. Each of these holidays is governed by many of the same constraints as Shabbes as well as by its own distinctive customs.

In addition to these holidays, which are widely celebrated throughout the Jewish world, there are a number of days on the ritual calendar that reflect the particular customs of Rabbi Joel Teitelbaum and his followers. The first is the twenty-first day of the Hebrew month of Kislev (Kaf Alef Kislev), the day that commemorates Joel Teitelbaum's liberation from the Nazi concentration camp, Bergen-Belsen, and his passage across the border to Switzerland on December 7, 1944. Rabbi Teitelbaum's release from the clutches of Nazi captivity is marked every year by his followers with a celebratory banquet in Brooklyn. Initially staged in very modest fashion, eventually the annual dinner grew in size to include thousands of attendees, all male, who listened to hours of speeches extolling Joel Teitelbaum and warning against any deviation from his path (including regular admonitions against the internet and smartphones). It was also an opportunity for New York City politicians and public officials to pay tribute to and receive a blessing from the Rebbe. Following the split in the community between R. Aaron and R. Zalman Leib, two lavish dinners have been held at massive armories in Brooklyn, each of which attracts close to ten thousand participants. Busloads of men make their way down from Kiryas Joel to participate in these events, which are the social highlight of the Satmar year as well as the most important fundraisers for Satmar educational institutions or *moysdes*. True to form, the Bnai Yoel hold their own celebratory dinner in Kiryas Joel. Meanwhile, schoolchildren put on their Shabbes best and are inculcated with a sense of the grandeur of the occasion, which one KJ resident referred to as "Satmar Independence Day."[51]

If Kaf Alef Kislev captures the community's joy over the survival of their towering leader, Hay Iyar captures his wrath. The fifth day of the Hebrew month of Iyar is Israeli Independence Day; it was on this day, on May 14, 1948, that David Ben-Gurion formally proclaimed the state of Israel. While much of the Jewish world rejoiced at this occasion, Joel Teitelbaum considered it one of the darkest moments in Jewish history. For him, it represented a monstrous usurpation of God's prerogative to bring the Messiah by those whom he identified as Zionist "transgressors."[52] Unlike some Haredi rabbis whose intense opposition gave way to tacit acceptance of the state of Israel, Teitelbaum's anti-Zionism never abated. He wrote fiercely against it and enjoined his community to remain vigilant against Zionism's dangers. Satmar boys study his major anti-Zionist treatise, *Va-yo'el Mosheh*, on this day.[53] A particularly extreme anti-Zionist group that draws inspiration from Joel Teitelbaum, the Neturei Karta, even arrives from nearby Monsey to Kiryas Joel to burn the Israeli flag.[54]

A third day that reflects the distinctive outlook of the Satmar world is the twenty-sixth day of Av, which is Joel Teitelbaum's *yahrtseit*, or anniversary of his death. Veteran residents of KJ still remember with painful exactitude the last hours of their revered Rebbe, who fell ill on Shabbes, August 18, and expired at seven thirty in the morning of August 19, 1979.[55] Notwithstanding his advanced age of ninety-two, residents of Kiryas Joel greeted his passing with disbelief. It was hard to imagine life without the charismatic founder. Later that day, in keeping with the Jewish tradition of rapid burial, some hundred thousand mourners converged on Kiryas Joel for the funeral. Any Satmar Hasid who could get to Upstate New York in time came, overflowing all routes of transportation from New York. The *New York Post* reported: "Roads into the Catskill mountain town were clogged by the caravans and traffic was brought to a standstill for 15 miles."[56] Ever since that dark day in Satmar history, thousands of his followers have made their way to Kiryas Joel annually to commemorate the day of Teitelbaum's death, which reveals the enduring depth of his impact on the community. Moreover, every day men and women make their way from Kiryas Joel and around the world to his *ohel*, or burial place, where he lies alongside his wife and next to his successor, Moshe Teitelbaum, and his wife. They come to the main cemetery in KJ to engage in prayer and quiet meditation and to place *kvitlekh*, notes of supplication, at his grave.

Unquestionably, the memory of Joel Teitelbaum continues to play a huge role in the Satmar world, particularly through the three major days

FIGURE 1.7. Graves of Alta Faiga (1912–2001), R. Joel Teitelbaum (1887–1979), and R. Moshe Teitelbaum (1914–2006) at Main Kiryas Joel Cemetery. Courtesy of Jackson Krule.

of ritual observance just mentioned. At the same time, his grand-nephew, Aaron, the chief rabbi of Kiryas Joel, has introduced his own annual variation of a ritual commemoration that draws thousands of participants. On Lag Ba-Omer (the thirty-third day of the Omer period that stretches from Passover to Shavuot), Aaron presides over a large sea of black-clad men in front of the main synagogue in KJ, with women off to the side. He transfixes the rhythmically chanting and swaying crowd by lighting a huge bonfire to mark the death of the second-century sage R. Shimon bar Yochai. Neither his father nor great-uncle marked Lag Ba-Omer in such a visible way. Since 2000, he has turned the commemoration into a major event that draws tens of thousands of participants and wide coverage on social media.[57] This event is one of the ways in which Reb Aaron seeks to escape the shadow of his predecessors and promote Kiryas Joel as capital of the Satmar kingdom, competing with his brother Zalman Leib's base of operation in Williamsburg.[58]

FIGURE 1.8. R. Aaron Lighting Lag Ba-Omer Fire, 2019. Courtesy of Jackson Krule.

FIGURE 1.9. Women at Lag Ba-Omer Celebration under a Sign for Water, 2019.
Courtesy of Jackson Krule.

FIGURE 1.10. Crowd of Men and Boys Gathered for Lag Ba-Omer Celebration.
Courtesy of Jackson Krule.

The Primacy of Torah: Education in Kiryas Joel

Education is the essential complement to ritual observance in the Satmar community. It is an activity of the highest value in Kiryas Joel and attracts a great deal of attention and resources. Indeed, there is no more cherished or prestigious designation for a young man than to be a *talmid chukhem* (a Torah scholar). The KJ private school network educates well over ten thousand students, employs the largest number of people in the community, and boasts a range of institutions designed for students ranging in age from toddlers to adults. Each of the three factions in KJ has its own school system with its own presiding Education Committee (*Vaad ha-chinech*) to raise funds and ensure curricular conformity; the mainstream faction's United Talmudic Academy (known also by its Hebrew name Torah V'Yira) has its institutions in Kiryas Joel itself, while the other two, the factions associated with R. Zalman Leib and the Bnai Yoel, have their schools just across the village lines.[59] Meanwhile, there is also a public school in the village that exclusively serves special needs children, most of whom come from KJ. As we shall see,

·FIGURE 1.11. Kiryas Joel Public School. Courtesy of Joel Petlin.

the public school district has been the source of very intense controversy within and beyond the community. Nevertheless, it has also been
the beneficiary of substantial local and state support and occupies a
state-of-the-art facility in the village.

Education was deeply rooted in the worldview of Rabbi Joel Teitelbaum, who believed in the unquestioned primacy of Jewish studies over
secular studies. As he first developed this vision in pre–World War II
Europe, his focus was on the intensive religious training that boys and
young men should receive in yeshivahs. By the time he arrived in America, he had come around to support an idea that he vigorously opposed
in the old country: girls' schools.[60] Indeed, one of his first steps to lay
an institutional foundation for his community in America came in 1950,
when he instructed followers to build schools for boys and girls. Out of
this effort came the United Talmudic Academy (UTA), the umbrella
organization for Satmar education, including the Bais Ruchel girls'
schools, based in Williamsburg. A quarter century later, in 1974, UTA
established satellite boys' and girls' schools for the first Satmar residents
of Kiryas Joel.

Propelling his investment in education in the United States was the
omnipresent sense of threat. In his view, America was a wild and dangerous environment, full of seductions that could lure deeply committed
Jews into full assimilation. As a result, it was necessary to "establish

educational institutions like those founded by our fathers, without any compromises or changes, Heaven forbid."[61]

This general principle of resisting any change—curious in light of Joel Teitelbaum's own concession on girls' education—was translated into strict communal supervision over education and related behavioral areas. In a directive from early 1978, KJ school officials advised parents on the following matters:

- The length of girls' skirts (below the knees)
- The danger for boys of *bitul Torah*—neglect of Torah study—by making frequent visits to New York City for celebrations
- The importance of parents monitoring their children's learning through weekly quizzes
- The necessity of inculcating reverence for prayer, the study hall, and, above all, the Satmar Rebbe
- The prohibition on bringing candy or extra money to school, since it might induce envy or even stealing[62]

Along with edicts of this sort, both gender separation and curricular content in the three private school systems are closely regulated. Boys begin school at three or four years old, usually after the ceremony known as the *upsherin*, marking their first haircut when their heads are shaved except for their earlocks. The language of instruction is Yiddish, though a primary task over the next few years is to gain familiarity with written Hebrew since it is the language of the most foundational of Jewish texts, the Five Books of Moses and the *siddur* or prayer book.[63] Only later, at six or seven, do boys take up the study of English, math, and writing, which they study until the age of bar mitzvah, thirteen. As distinct from their "sacred studies" of rabbinic texts, they will also study Jewish history in Yiddish (and in a highly reverential traditional format).[64] From that point forward—that is, by the time they make it to *yeshivah ketana*, or high school—religious studies will occupy all of their time. Here is what a typical day looks like at a KJ boys' high school:

5:30–6:30 Immersion in mikveh (ritual bath)
6:30 First Talmud class

7:30 Study of Hasidic works and preparation for prayers
8:15 Morning prayers
9:15 Breakfast
10:00 Talmud lesson
11:00 Chavrusa learning (with a study partner in study hall)
1:00 Lunch (depending on the season, the afternoon mincha prayer is either in early or late afternoon)
2:00 Lesson on the major code of Jewish law, *Shulhan ʾArukh*
3:00 Chavrusa study
5:00 15-minute break
5:15 Chavrusa study
7:00 Dinner
8:30 Chavrusa study
9:30 Evening prayer[65]

The nearly exclusive attention on Jewish studies in KJ high schools reflects an extreme version of the claim to the free exercise of religion endorsed by many KJ residents who want their sons to be educated in this fashion. In point of fact, private schools do not have total discretion to decide on their own curriculum under American law. In a series of cases extending back to 1923, the U.S. Supreme Court determined that states have the authority to impose "reasonable regulations on all schools."[66]

In New York, the Department of Education seeks, at least in theory, to ensure that "nonpublic" schools, as both parochial and secular private schools are called, adhere to minimal standards regarding educational content and the safety and maintenance of the physical plant. To enforce these standards, it sends inspectors to nonpublic schools to supervise compliance, though their main task is often overseeing whether state funding is being properly spent. It is important to note that nonpublic schools in New York, as elsewhere, are entitled to receive state funds for a variety of purposes, especially transportation of students and professional support for special needs pupils. In Kiryas Joel, the services provided by the state, through the KJ public school district, are indispensable to the functioning of the private school system.

In recent years, however, there has been new public scrutiny on Kiryas Joel and other Haredi communities in New York City and its surrounding counties regarding the degree to which boys' schools comply with state standards. One important source of information has been former members of these communities who decry, often from painful personal experience, the lack of preparation for making one's way into the wider non-Jewish world. An organization called Young Advocates for Education (Yaffed), which was founded by a former student of a Hasidic yeshivah, aims to "encourage compliance with relevant state guidelines for education while maintaining respect for the primacy of Judaic studies and the unique cultural and religious values of the ultra-Orthodox community." Yaffed maintains that in many Haredi schools, no more than ninety minutes a day is devoted to boys' education—and only until the age of thirteen.[67] It further asserts that state inspections and enforcement of minimum education standards are inadequate, if not nonexistent.

In 2015, Yaffed threatened both the state and city with legal action.[68] Three years later, in July 2018, Yaffed filed suit against New York State officials, including Governor Andrew Cuomo, alleging that they had wrongfully agreed to exempt Haredi yeshivahs from the requirement to provide "substantially equivalent instruction" in secular subjects.[69] This newly instituted requirement represented a relaxation of the former rule. Instead of following the prescribed curriculum, the new law said, religious schools could substitute "substantially equivalent" educational materials. In November of that year, in the face of widespread resistance to complying with even this relaxed rule, New York State education commissioner Mary Ellen Elia issued an order requiring that nonpublic schools, including hundreds of yeshivahs and other religious schools, meet the "substantial equivalency" bar. In response, a coalition of like-minded religious actors—Haredi organizations and Catholic diocesan officials—appealed to state court for exemption from the state's regulations, which they saw as a violation of their religious freedom. In April 2019, a state court struck down the guidelines, prompting Commissioner Elia to issue a new set of regulations intended to ensure that private religious schools meet the public school standards in subjects such as English, math, history, and science.[70]

The fact that state regulators have been lax in enforcing standards in KJ and other Haredi schools is not merely a function of respect for religious freedom in these communities. It is also a product of the groups' considerable political power and their ability to elect political candidates who can protect them. This political heft has granted Haredi communities, and Kiryas Joel in particular, substantial latitude in a variety of domains of life, including control over the nonpublic educational system. At the same time, it also generated resentment from neighbors about their outsized influence and seeming disregard for American rules and norms.

To date, the focus of Yaffed has been on boys' education, perhaps because it was formed by young men and reflects their perspective and because there is more focus on secular education in the girls' schools. The underlying assumption within the Satmar world is that girls *should* receive more English training and less text study than boys. This has made state regulation of the girls' schools less fraught than is the case in boys' yeshivahs. That said, Joel Teitelbaum made clear from the early days of girls' instruction, as he conveyed to the long-standing English principal Hertz Frankel in Williamsburg, that the Bais Ruchel system should "be a Yiddish school with an English department."[71] In Kiryas Joel, a heavy emphasis is still placed on Jewish studies. In the morning, after prayers and breakfast, girls in high school study the following subjects in Yiddish: *halukhe* (Jewish law), *parshe* (the weekly Torah portion), *Yahadus* or Judaism (customs and ritual calendar), *tefile* (prayer), *muser* (ethics from *Ethics of the Fathers*), Jewish history, and Yiddish language.[72]

Following lunch, they study in English. One woman who was born and raised in KJ but left the community has vividly described the excitement that attended these studies: "We all had crushes on the English teachers, who were incredibly worldly by our measurement, as some of them came from Monsey and all of them spoke in better accents than us, so we liked to watch them arrive in their vans and straight skirts and pointy heels and fur rimmed coats. Everyone dreamed of being picked out by those goddesses for attention. How popular you'd become overnight!"[73] In half-hour segments, girls study language and literature, math, history, and some science (though nothing that smacks of evolution, which hardly fits with the Satmars' view of creation). While the school produces its own colorful and attractive materials for Jewish studies classes, the options for English materials are far more limited. In order to maintain control over content, a dedicated team of Bais Ruchel teachers sits in a room and crosses out sentences in English-language text materials that might offend.

This kind of censorship points to the ideological boundaries that shape and limit education in KJ for both girls and boys. The girls in English class are naturally curious; the woman above mentions that often "a robust conversation" would ensue in history class over the relative virtues of, say, the British versus the colonists in revolutionary America.[74] But the classes in secular subjects are short. And there is no opportunity to do additional reading since there is no public library in town. The notion that there be a library with unfettered access to a wide range of books, especially "secular" books, is anathema to much of the community.

Likewise, there is a powerful communal taboo on university education. In this respect, KJ differs sharply from the general population of Jews in America. Whereas 58 percent of American Jews had graduated from college according to the 2013 Pew Research Center study, only 5.8 percent of KJ's residents had a bachelor's degree.[75] In September 2016, the *New York Times* reported that the UTA in Williamsburg had issued a new ruling that women "shouldn't God forbid take a (college) degree which is according to our sages, dangerous and damaging," for it would invariably expose them to secular students, Jews or non-Jews, as well as increased use of the internet.[76] The UTA did so not out of the blue but because there has been an increase in women seeking education beyond the eleven years that is standard in the Satmar world, either through online courses or by enrolling at local colleges.

The community's main educational message for girls is that they should aspire to be pious Satmar women who are modest and competent and who understand their life mission as mothers and custodians of the domestic sphere. This was how the longtime principal of the Bais Ruchel high school in KJ, Malka Silberstein, articulated her objectives.

Silberstein is herself a formidable and dynamic woman who oversaw the high school for nearly thirty-five years beginning in 1982. She brought to her work a steely determination and a sense of worldliness, having grown up as the main contact between her immigrant parents and the outside world in postwar Brooklyn. Mrs. Silberstein was also primarily responsible for introducing special needs education into the community. She reported to Eliezer Shlomo Kohn, a high-energy, gregarious rabbi who was summoned by Joel Teitelbaum in 1978 to run the Bais Ruchel system, which numbers some thirty-five hundred pupils in kindergarten through high school.[77]

There is a tension built into girls' education in KJ. While communal norms determine that English studies are secondary in importance to Jewish studies, girls often ascribe to them more prestige and interest. They recognize that English education affords them functional skills in the workforce. Some also feel a real and unsatisfied hunger for learning and books. The study of history and literature can open the door to a vast outside world of which they yearn to know more.

The small handful who take the bold step of entering that door often find that, even with their fluent English, they are unprepared for its rigors. They don't know everyday language and slang. They are inexperienced in dealing with non-Jews. And they are forbidden to drive. Of course, the overwhelming majority of young women stay in the community and are, by external appearances, content within the framework of a Satmar life. For a small minority, the strictures of life, punctuated by the glaring eye of the Modesty Committee, are unbearable. In between are various degrees of freethinkers, highly critical of everything from the frequency of garbage pickup to internet restrictions in the village, but who ultimately choose to stay and raise their children in the ways of their parents.

Part of what keeps them in Kiryas Joel is the sense of connection to one another. Most residents in KJ would say that it is important to be respectful to, and solicitous of, the gentile world; many would say that every human life, Jewish or non-Jewish, is precious. But almost all feel a special sense of commitment to *Klal Yisroel*, concern for the well-being of fellow Jews, particularly fellow Haredim. Included in this sphere of compassion are those with special needs, especially children. As one parent of a special needs child, a prominent community leader, averred, once upon a time special needs children were kept out of sight. But they have since come out of the closet, in part as the result of broader attitudinal shifts toward disabilities and disability rights in American society, and in part due to the activism of special needs advocates within the community, foremost among them girls' school principal Malka Silberstein.

A Public School in the Shtetl:
Essential Service or Trojan Horse?

A key question arose with this shift in consciousness in the mid-1980s. What was the best way of educating special needs children in the village? The Satmar parents, who began to ask the question with new urgency, realized that the community lacked the expertise and resources to do the job themselves. They also became increasingly aware that they were legally entitled, indeed obligated, to obtain publicly funded services for their children. As will be explored at greater length in chapter 4, they began to explore their options, including sending children to regional public school programs and arranging for public school teachers to provide instruction in Kiryas Joel at "neutral sites," that is, sites that were neither in the public schools nor in the community's private schools. When the latter option was blocked, due to a combination of legal and administrative actions, Assemblyman George Pataki from Peekskill put forth a bold idea: the creation of a new public school district within the bounds of KJ intended for special needs kids from the village.[78] The idea ignited a huge storm of controversy within the community: some said that such an institution would introduce foreign values to the students; outside of the community, critics claimed that such a district would be a clear violation of the separation of church and state.

Faced with a difficult choice, the village leadership decided to proceed with the creation of a public school and then mobilized its formidable political power. Assemblyman Pataki, who would go on to be elected governor of the state three times, was a key point person.

Although not a Jew, Pataki shared Hungarian roots with many Satmars and was known as a good friend of the community; he also understood the potency of the Satmar voting bloc. Chapter 748, the Assembly bill authorizing the creation of an independent school district in KJ approved in 1989, was Pataki's brainchild. Another friend of the community, Governor Mario Cuomo, surprised many observers by setting aside constitutional concerns and signing the bill.

At that point, the legal battles began to heat up. Leading the charge against the school district was Louis Grumet, who served as director of the New York State School Boards Association—and whose name adorns the case that made its way to the U.S. Supreme Court in 1994: *Grumet v. Board of Education of Kiryas Joel School District*. In 2016, Grumet published a book describing his experience litigating the case. Co-authored with John Caher, *The Curious Case of Kiryas Joel* details the tortuous path of the multiple lawsuits that were brought against the KJ School District, three by Grumet, who challenged its constitutionality, and one final one by KJ dissidents, who challenged the district's legality on nonconstitutional grounds. Although much of the book focuses on the victories Grumet's legal team scored, ultimately his side did not win the day. The KJ leadership persisted in its efforts and put an end to legal challenges to the Kiryas Joel Union Free School District after more than a decade of litigation.

Like many outside critics, Grumet and Caher see this success as a reflection of the Satmars' separatist vision of how to live in the world. As they put it, Satmar Hasidim do not support the idea of an American melting pot, choosing instead to dwell in "isolation in a self-designed ghetto."[79] This is true in the most evident ways; Satmars self-segregate by language, dress, housing, modesty norms, and limits on interaction with the wider world. But at another level, this description does not capture the extent to which the community unconsciously absorbs political and social trends in the larger American society. Nor does it reflect the extent to which changes that were occurring in American attitudes toward cultural diversity enabled the Satmars' success. There was, of course, no explicit decision made in KJ to "assimilate" these external norms. Rather, geographic contiguity and the intentional use

of tools of the outside world—in this instance, special education profes-
sionals, highly sophisticated lawyers, and the secular legal system—
introduced into the community new standards, aspirations, and operating assumptions.

The Kiryas Joel Free Union School District is the product of this kind
of unintentional and largely unacknowledged assimilation. The district
is the governmental body responsible for running the public school in
KJ as well as for providing educational, therapeutic, and transportation
services to the nonpublic schools willing to receive them. The district's
founding superintendent, Dr. Steven Benardo, was a secular Jew who
had served for decades as a New York City school administrator. Haredi
opponents both inside and outside of the village railed against the new
district, fearing that, as a public institution, it couldn't be a Jewish
school; there would be no mezuzahs on the walls nor instruction in
Jewish studies, and non-Jewish holidays such as President's Day and
Martin Luther King Day would be celebrated.[80] They were correct in
their apprehensions. In order to meet state and federal requirements,
the public school must operate as a secular public school, and it does.
At the same time, the school has the discretion to determine its own
schedule provided that it meets 180 days a year; thus, it could arrange
the calendar to allow students time off for Jewish holidays. Moreover, it
was within its rights to use Yiddish as a working language alongside
English in the school; this was especially important in communicating
with children who had not yet been exposed to English in their homes.
In promoting his vision of the school, Benardo consistently spoke of KJ
as a bastion of distinctive cultural values in a country that has always
been tolerant of and fortified by cultural diversity.[81]

This line of argument has been continued by his second-in-command,
Joel Petlin, who replaced Benardo as superintendent of the KJ public
school in 2007. Like Benardo, Petlin is not a Satmar Hasid. He is a Modern Orthodox attorney from Los Angeles who was involved in the legal
defense of the school district and knows the intricacies of education law
as well as anyone in New York State. Similar to his predecessor, Petlin
serves a variety of roles in KJ. Along with Ari Felberman, the Bobover
Hasid who since 2003 has served as the government affairs liaison in KJ,

he is one of the most prominent public spokesmen for the community. He explains the seemingly alien ways of Kiryas Joel to an often mystified outside world; he is also the interface between the school district and the New York State education system. And he works closely with the village leadership to promote the school district, including overseeing the construction of a new forty-four-thousand-square-foot building in 2008. It is a telling indication of how porous the boundary can be between public and private realms in KJ that the school district does not own its own building but leases it on a long-term basis from the Vaad hakirya, which is affiliated with the Rabbi Aaron–allied mainstream.

The public school district receives most of its funding from federal and state sources. Its total budget is approximately $38 million, of which about $23 million goes to the public school and another $2–3 million to the pre-K program. The remaining amount of $12 million, which comes from the federal Title 1 program designated for low-income districts, is intended to provide remedial instruction in math and English to non-public schoolchildren. Of the total public school budget, $9–10 million comes from local taxes, and the remainder comes from state and federal sources.[82]

By way of comparison, in the neighboring Monroe-Woodbury School District, nearly 70 percent of the budget comes from the local tax base. Moreover, the cost to educate a child in the KJ district is many times more than the state average; the school superintendent places the figure at between $70,000 and $80,000, in comparison to the average state expenditure per child of $24,712. Of course, a key difference is that every student in the KJ public school is a special needs child. The statewide average for providing special education is $32,794 per child (excluding added expenses such as transportation and district administration costs).[83]

Nonetheless, the disparity between the KJ district's cost per pupil and that of other school districts (in which students requiring special educational services are a relatively small portion of the overall student population) creates the perception that Kiryas Joel unfairly benefits from public support relative to other locales.[84] Complicating the image problem is the fact that government institutions in the village tend not to share information in the public domain as do other municipalities, which is partly the result of a lower level of interest among KJ residents and partly the function of a deep-seated Satmar suspicion of revealing too much to the outside world. Thus, there is no readily accessible on-line information about budgetary outlays, village services, or election results.[85] Nor are there accessible records of village board meetings, as required by law.[86] The public school district, by dint of its public mission and media-accessible superintendents, is much more connected to the wider world than most of KJ's institutions are, but it still does not have its own website.

Within the community, the school district plays two important roles. First, it provides, through a staff of 150, remedial instruction and therapy to children in the nonpublic schools. These services are in addition to the transportation of thousands of nonpublic schoolchildren that is overseen and paid for by the public school district. This is both a massive logistical challenge (given the different starting times and age groups, the village traffic patterns, and the large number of transported students—8,000 in total) and a significant budgetary consideration (about 20 percent of the budget).[87]

The school district's second and main task is to educate kids who require full-time attention. The public school had, as of 2017–2018, 162 full-time K–12 students (of whom 81 percent came from economically disadvantaged homes) and 472 prekindergarten children.[88] Approximately three-quarters come from Kiryas Joel, with the remainder being Haredi children from surrounding towns. There is an in-school staff of 250, 100 of whom are therapists. It has long been speculated by some outside of KJ that, because of endogamy in the community, there is a higher rate of birth defects and hence learning disabilities. In addressing this claim, Joel Petlin clarifies: "There are 10,000 kids living in Kiryas Joel. We serve about 400 of the kids, so our referral rate is about 4 percent, which is much lower that the statewide average (15 percent). It's concentrated here because we have one building."[89]

What is clear is that Kiryas Joel has fully embraced the idea that special needs children deserve careful and expert attention—in ways that depart from previous communal norms. The public school building is a technologically sophisticated and pleasing environment; physical space is divided by age, with primary and high school kids inhabiting different color-coded rooms and floors. There is a small gym, a room for students to practice yoga, and a large playground outside. Although almost no time is devoted to physical education in the private school system, the public school principal, Jehuda Halperin, a Swiss-born Orthodox Jew with advanced degrees in special education administration, insists on it, believing it to be essential to the health of students.

Unlike the private schools in KJ, the public school uses computers and other forms of technology to aid in educating its students. Curiously, all of this is known, tolerated, and supported, including through tax dollars, by the community. In this sense, the school evidences a certain degree of cognitive dissonance between what is expressly forbidden in one setting and permitted in another. It also affirms that Kiryas Joel is, in important but largely unarticulated ways, a part of the American landscape, particularly to the extent that it has absorbed best practices regarding the educational well-being of children with special needs.

Making Ends Meet: Economics in Kiryas Joel

One of the most widespread images of Kiryas Joel in the wider American imagination relates to its poverty. Writing in a front-page article in the *New York Times* in 2011, reporter Sam Roberts cast it this way: "The poorest place in the United States is not a dusty Texas border town, a hollow in Appalachia, a remote Indian reservation or a blighted urban neighborhood. It has no slums or homeless people. No one who lives there is shabbily dressed or has to go hungry. Crime is virtually nonexistent."[90] That place, of course, was Kiryas Joel, where the median household income of $26,000 was half of the national average and 57.3 percent of the population lived below the poverty line, according to the 2010 national census. By 2019, the percentage had fallen to 45.1 percent, reflecting a gradual process of upward mobility as more residents of KJ make their way into the middle and even upper-middle classes through stable wages, new internet-related pursuits, and successful investments—all part of the American suburban dream.

That said, the rate of poverty in KJ is still four times higher than the national average of 10.5 percent.[91] There are many extremely large families, with ten to fifteen children, whose annual earnings fall well below the adjustable poverty line (dependent on number of persons in the household). They live in reasonably well-kempt, if overcrowded, apartments—and in a small number of cases, single-family homes (though a growing number of those who can afford houses are moving outside of the village bounds). Even under strained physical and financial conditions, parents usually manage to feed their large broods, with the added demand of celebrating the Sabbath and holidays with copious amounts of food and drink. One way in which this is possible is because there are private food kitchens in KJ that provide supplies to families in need, with regular deliveries on the eve of the Sabbath.

In fact, the existence of a large network of individuals and organizations devoted to social services is one of the reasons that Kiryas Joel is able to maintain a basic level of sustenance as a community. The work of groups such as Hamaspik (catering to the developmentally disabled), Ezer Nesuin (assistance to young married couples), and the Kiryas Joel Social Services rests, in part, on a profound communal commitment, even obligation, to charity. Indeed, it is a nearly universal expectation in KJ that anyone with even the most minimal capacity should assist others in need, especially other Jews. For most residents, this may mean setting aside a few dollars each week from an already strained budget. One KJ resident explained the matter in simple terms: Satmar Hasidim do not go out to dinner or to the movies. They don't have widescreen televisions or cable bills. Nor do they have to pay five-figure college tuitions for their children. Thus, they have more disposable income to give to charity within the community and to meet their basic needs for food, clothing, and shelter.[92]

Of late, there has emerged a noticeable and growing class of affluent residents in Kiryas Joel who offer support for a range of communal tasks. In fact, from its inception in the United States, the Satmar community benefited from the generosity of legendary patrons such as Israel Zupnik and Getzel Berger (from London), who heeded the call of Joel

Teitelbaum and gave wherever and whenever the Rebbe designated. Even after his death, some supporters, such as Nachman (Nathan) Brach, remained loyal to the Rebbe's legacy and aligned themselves with the Rebbetsin rather than with Moshe. Meanwhile, in KJ today, figures such as Mayer Hirsch and David Eckstein provide major financial support and advice for the ruling faction of R. Aaron, overseeing some of the most central institutions in the community. In parallel, the Zali and Bnai Yoel factions have major financial sponsors of their own. Across the spectrum, people of means in KJ routinely give money to pay for the construction or upkeep of schools, synagogues, ritual baths, and cemeteries. They also regularly contribute to less fortunate individuals and families in the community who require extra funds to cover school tuition or weddings for their children or to put enough food on the table. In recent years, a new group of charity seekers has surfaced in KJ (and other Haredi communities such as Lakewood, New Jersey): professional money raisers from Israel, *shnorrers* (Yiddish for beggars), who go door to door at night in support of the sick or Torah institutions in the holy land.[93] So routinized is this practice by now that KJ residents can purchase communally generated vouchers to hand out to the supplicants.

In a more general sense, this private charitable network is one of the ways residents of KJ escape the debilitating effects of poverty. A second and more controversial means is through government support. Given the low incomes in the village, it is not surprising that the rate of federal subsidies granted to individuals and families runs high. In 2009, 41 percent of KJ residents received food stamps, while a 2014 report declared that twenty thousand residents—a whopping 93 percent of the village—were enrolled in Medicaid programs intended for low-income individuals and families.[94] This rate is disturbing to many outsiders, including United Monroe leader Emily Convers, who stated, "The disproportionate number of citizens using these services is cause for alarm."[95] Convers vehemently disputes the charge by some in KJ that she and her organization are motivated by hostility toward Jews.[96]

That said, the high degree of dependence by Kiryas Joel residents on government support plays into the image of the village as replete with welfare cheats, crooked politicians, and "parasites" intent on exploiting the system.[97] The fact that there have been periodic criminal charges filed against individuals arrested for massive welfare fraud fortifies the impression. In November 2014, members of two Orthodox families with branches in KJ were arrested on charges of defrauding the government and banks to the tune of twenty million dollars by alternating underreporting and overstating their income. Less than a year later, in July 2015, two KJ men and their corporations were swept up in Operation Million Dollar Mark, a federal operation aimed at welfare and Medicaid fraud.[98]

The perception of corruption extends to the governing regime in KJ. As far back as 1990, an uncompleted medical center that was funded through federal grants was burned down in what investigators assumed to be a case of arson committed by someone in the community. Subsequently, the local *Times Herald-Record* newspaper wrote a series of stories in the 1990s alleging that the community "filed sham documents and misled the government," most egregiously by diverting money intended for the medical center to a swimming pool at a girls' school in the community.[99]

These perceptions lead critics to suggest that Kiryas Joel upends the established rules of the game in order to achieve an unfair advantage. This is not an invention out of whole cloth. The federal inspector inquiring into the 1990 arson/fraud case noted the difficulty he faced in piercing the veil of silence in KJ. "The presence of special agents and their interests," he observed, "are immediately communicated to officials within the community." In related fashion, a state investigator assumed, correctly as it would turn out, that the county district attorney would not file charges against KJ officials in this episode for it would be politically dangerous to do so.[100] It is understandable that those outside of KJ—and some within it—fear its political power. No one can deny that the village has benefitted from a huge amount of state and federal support enabled by the active efforts of a long line of prominent politicians including George Pataki, Mario Cuomo, Benjamin Gilman, Sheldon Silver, Hillary Clinton, and Chuck Schumer.[101]

Reconciling the diametrically opposed images of KJ—as pure embodiment of religious communitarianism versus abyss of corruption—is a daunting task. We should bear in mind four factors. First, the insularity and perceived foreignness of Satmar Hasidim, especially given their place in suburban New York, invite suspicion on the part of their neighbors. KJ's own proclivity for secrecy and lack of transparency only heightens the distrust.

Second, KJ residents undeniably draw a huge amount of government support. But many families in Kiryas Joel not only meet the federal standards of poverty; they require and are entitled to that support in order to feed and clothe a large number of children.

Third, the success of the village and residents in gaining government support, which is extraordinary, can easily be seen as exploiting the system. But alternatively, it can be seen as playing the game better than anyone else. American politics is an unwieldy contest involving not merely individual voters but interest groups vying for power. The Satmars of Kiryas Joel are hardly the first group to try to marshal their electoral assets into political and economic advantage. Many other religious groups, political parties, lobbyists, corporations, and nonprofits have sought and continue to seek to do so. KJ has been particularly effective at it.

Fourth, KJ is a village that bustles with energy and industry where most adults work hard to scrape by. To be sure, it is a most unusual setting in which women bear and raise a very large number of children over the course of their adult lives. As a result, 39 percent of KJ women over sixteen reported working in the labor force, according to the 2020 census, as against a national average of 58 percent. This is a notable figure, reflecting either the decidedly un-twenty-first-century gender norms in the community or a serious degree of underreporting of actual employment, or both. But the constancy of giving birth and raising kids is, for many women, an all-consuming job. Moreover, the percentage of working women leapt nearly 60 percent from 2000 to 2010 and another 20 percent from 2010 to 2020. In contrast to women, the percentage of men who are in the labor force is around 64 percent, comparable to the national average of 68 percent.[102] Here, we see yet another notable confluence between Satmar practices and mainstream cultural norms. Contrary to common misperceptions, the rate of (male) participation in the workforce is not dramatically low. And, as another sign of the indirect permeation of feminist norms, the rate of female participation is rising.

Where do people work in KJ? The largest number of employees can be found, not surprisingly, in the community's educational institutions; one-quarter of adult workers in KJ are employed in the extensive network of private schools, along with the much smaller public school. Over eight hundred people are employed as teachers in KJ. Women populate the ranks of teachers and administrators in the girls' schools, just as do men in the boys' system. The next largest areas of employment, according to census data from 2003–2014, are retail trade (18.4 percent), health care and social assistance (13.3 percent), and manufacturing (10.7 percent).[103] A glance at the local Yiddish phone book reveals that among the most prominent services and businesses in town are accounting, advertising, children's clothing, gift stores, insurance, plumbing, printing, vitamins, and car services, as well as a wide range of religious services and products not typically found in other suburban communities.

One of the most prominent local businesses in the village is the Kiryas Joel Poultry Processing Plant. It is a five-minute walk from the KJ public school and the multistory building on Bakertown Road that houses a number of stores, one of the few restaurants in town, village offices, and the office of school superintendent Joel Petlin. The poultry plant, which was established in 2003, employs some three hundred workers, most of whom are Latinos from outside of the village. It is described on its website as the largest kosher poultry plant in New York State, with thirty to forty thousand chickens slaughtered per day.[104] Over the course of its history, the plant has encountered legal difficulties. In October 2014, the U.S. Attorney in the New York area filed civil charges against the plant alleging violations of the Clean Water Act, as evidenced by the "slaughtered chicken parts, salts, fat, oils, and grease" found in the Ramapo River. The plant quickly agreed to settle for a $330,000 fine, acknowledging that past violations occurred but were "inadvertent" and "sporadic."[105] This development relates to a broader concern of KJ's neighbors that the community is largely inattentive to environmental issues, all the while consuming everything in its path in order to foster growth. Here again, there is more than a grain of truth in the claim—and a fair bit of exaggeration. Environmental consciousness is not nearly as heightened as one might find in most suburbs of Orange County, whose populations tend to be highly educated and middle to upper-middle class. But it has grown somewhat and is an oft-invoked priority of village administrator Szegedin.[106]

An ever-expanding form of economic activity in KJ is, ironically enough, internet commerce. Young entrepreneurs have created a KJ version of "start-ups" that engage in third-party retail sales, purchasing products at wholesale prices and then reselling on Amazon.com or other sites. The items they sell range from clothing to scratched or dented household appliances, many of which generate a considerable profit margin. This activity obviously requires a good deal of familiarity with the internet and provides access to a wider consumer world beyond KJ. In that respect, it is unusual in terms of sanctioned or desired activities in the highly regulated world of KJ. But it is a good example of how KJ residents, especially the younger generation, can satisfy their curiosity about the outside world, principally through constant internet use, without abandoning the Satmar way of life. It is also an instance of change being driven from the bottom up in the face of official disfavor.

In addition, many adult residents work in small-scale retail activities such as food markets, toy stores, book shops, clothing, and garages, either in KJ or in nearby communities. Defying the usual suburban rules against mixed-use zoning, many of these small-scale businesses operate in residential areas. The average commute to work for a KJ resident is twenty-five minutes, though that figure rests on the fact that a majority of adults work in or near the village, with little commute required, while 17 percent of KJ residents have commute times of sixty minutes or more.[107] The latter are the workers, ranging from clerks to company executives, who make their way on a daily basis to jobs in New Jersey, Brooklyn, and Manhattan. One of the most popular places of employment is B&H Photo, the large Satmar-owned camera emporium on Thirty-Fourth Street and Ninth Avenue in Manhattan, to which a dedicated bus line runs from KJ every day. Buses also run, at peak times on an hourly basis, between KJ and Williamsburg and Borough Park in Brooklyn. (Incidentally, the buses often become miniature synagogues in morning and evening, as men stand in quorums of ten to say their prayers, curtained off from women who sit in a different section.) Those who commute to New York serve not only as a conduit of much-needed income for KJ but also as a cultural bridge to the more cosmopolitan ambience of New York City. Even those Satmars who live in KJ and don't work in the city frequently visit to see family, attend celebrations, and shop. This constant traffic fosters competition between the Satmar capitals in Williamsburg and Kiryas Joel. One communal leader in Williamsburg gave voice to a common perception that KJ was a *gashmiesdike shtetl*—that is, a materialist community where people go to live the life of upper-middle-class suburbanites.[108] That reputation stands in tension with two other images of the Orange County shtetl: first, its high rate of poverty and, second, the view of its own residents that theirs is the more spiritually pure and less materialistic setting. KJ's self-image is that of a holistic community imbued through and through with sacred spiritual values.

Theocracy or Two-Party System?
The Webs of Political Power in KJ

Internal opponents of the KJPE (Kiryas Joel Political Elite), as the internal and external opponents have dubbed the establishment, often describe the village as a theocracy in which there is no separation of political and religious authority. Once marginal in numbers and influence, the dissidents have gained ground in the community over the years; estimates are that they have gone from a small handful after the death of Joel Teitelbaum to anywhere between 40 and 55 percent of the population of Kiryas Joel. In 2001, they mounted for the first time a candidate, Mendel Schwimmer, to challenge the incumbent mayor, Abraham Wieder. Confounding most expectations, Schwimmer pushed Wieder to a recount, eventually losing by 650 votes out of 5,000 cast. Allegations of voter fraud committed by allies of Wieder abounded at the time, including claims of intimidation and double voting. Indeed, the assertion that some voted in both Brooklyn and KJ surfaced in a 1997 investigation by the *Times Herald-Record* and has dogged elections in KJ since the contested 2001 vote.[109] Many in the dissident ranks have a fatalist attitude, assuming that the establishment party will find a way to declare victory regardless of the votes cast. For his part, Gedalye Szegedin has long defended politics inside KJ as "a two-party system," a characterization that captures the extent to which this insular shtetl has assimilated to a basic norm of American political culture.[110]

As in most matters involving the village, the truth lies somewhere in the middle, between the poles of a repressive theocracy, on one hand, and a fully functioning two-party democracy, on the other. One key layer of complexity owes to the fact that while the Rebbe and leadership of the main religious congregation are private, nongovernmental actors from the standpoint of American law, they are, in the eyes of their followers, public authorities who *govern* the community and enforce its (religious) laws. Indeed, the Rebbe, especially Joel Teitelbaum, has been deemed to be the ultimate religious authority, whose edicts regulate every aspect of Satmar life and carry greater authority than the edicts of any secular political institution. The whole point of creating a separate enclave was to have a jurisdiction governed by Jewish law, which is to say, governed by the Rebbe and his religious aides.

But the porousness of the line between public and private in KJ is also attributable to American law and to the practices of local sovereignty that are designed to subject government to the will of private citizens. These are the laws, norms, and practices that allowed a group of private property holders to become a legally recognized village in a matter of months in 1976–1977. The laws of the state of New York mandated that the newly established village of KJ hold elections for mayor and village board. Venerable community leader, patron, and close aide of the first Satmar Rebbe, Leibish Lefkowitz, was elected mayor in 1977, a position in which he served without opposition until just before his death in 1998.[111]

At that point, his deputy mayor, another successful businessman, Abraham Wieder, assumed the office, which he has continued to occupy up to the present. Wieder, who was born in Paris in 1948 to Hungarian

Jewish survivors, was raised in Montreal and went to a Satmar yeshivah in New York. An affable and avuncular man, he has served as the titular head of the village for the past two decades, combining the functions of spokesman, lobbyist, and cheerleader-in-chief for Kiryas Joel. He oversees the four-member village board and appoints the village administrator to a ten-year term. That kind of security of employment has been instrumental in granting the administrator, Gedalye Szegedin, wide latitude to run the village. Szegedin oversees the village's various departments including planning, public safety, sanitation, water, and fire. (Although the village contracts out for its law enforcement services, it has hosted its own volunteer fire department since 2000.)[112] For his services, Szegedin is well compensated, earning a salary of over $200,000.[113]

Wieder and Szegedin are the elected and appointed leaders of the village and wield a tremendous amount of power. Both are key supporters of Rabbi Aaron Teitelbaum—and before him, of his father, Moshe Teitelbaum (the nephew of Joel). As such, they are frontline partisans in a major battle in the Satmar world extending back to the transition from the first to the second Rebbe in 1979–1980. The elevation of Moshe to that position prompted the rise of the first group of dissidents who rallied around the first Rebbe's widow, the core of which would become the Bnai Yoel faction. A few years later, the ranks of dissidents expanded further when Moshe appointed Aaron as chief rabbi of KJ in 1984, a clear signal that he saw his eldest son as heir apparent. But fifteen years later, Moshe shocked the Satmar world by leaving Aaron in control of Kiryas Joel, while elevating his third son, Zalman Leib, to the position of chief rabbi of the main Satmar congregation in Williamsburg. This act created a deep breach between the two brothers that manifested itself in a torrent of public denunciations, rabbinic prohibitions, lawsuits in secular courts, and even outbreaks of violence—as in 2005, when followers of R. Aaron allegedly broke into and destroyed a Williamsburg school associated with R. Zalman Leib.[114]

Violence was certainly known in the Satmar community well before this point; it is a recognizable feature of the history of the Teitelbaum family. What followed after the death of Moshe in 2006 was a period of intense acrimony between the two brothers. And yet, by 2009, the seeds of an interesting shift in Satmar self-understanding were visible. In that year, Moshe Friedman, a key community leader and aide to the second Satmar Rebbe (known as Moshe Gabbai to distinguish him from another leader of that name), gave an interview in which he maintained that the Satmar world had become too big for one head and that this was the underlying logic of Moshe Teitelbaum's division of the empire a decade before. That claim has since morphed into a decidedly American—and capitalist—truism: competition is healthy.[115] To be sure, tensions did not disappear immediately after Friedman's interview. But by the latter half of the 2010s, observers reported that the once inviolable taboo on social interaction among members of the different camps in KJ had significantly weakened.

And so today Kiryas Joel has three sets of moysdes, or religious institutions, belonging to the three congregations: the mainstream Yetev Lev D'Satmar associated with R. Aaron, the V'yoel Moshe congregation of R. Zalman Leib, and the Bnai Yoel group, whose main shul is the Khal Charidim. Each has its own lay leaders who conduct the entwined business, religious, and educational affairs of the congregation—for example, building, maintaining, and overseeing the institutions.

In many ways, Kiryas Joel resembles the medieval corporate Jewish body, the kehillah. The difference is that the premodern kehillah was not sovereign over its domain in all the ways that KJ is. It had the formal protection of the local ruler. And it exercised certain governmental powers that were delegated to it by the ruler—for example, the power to establish courts of law that adjudicated internal disputes according to Jewish law.[116] But the premodern kehillah did not exercise control over nearly such a wide range of affairs as is the case in KJ. This control is manifested not only in the village's mayor and administrator but also in the Vaad hakirya, whose power over many aspects of life in the village ranges widely. Despite its quasi-official status, the Vaad's leaders are not elected nor are its activities subject to public oversight; from the point of view of American law, it is a private entity.

Alongside this powerful village-wide body, each faction has its own quasi-public bodies. These include the beis din, or rabbinical court, which is the jurisdiction of first resort in a wide range of civil matters,

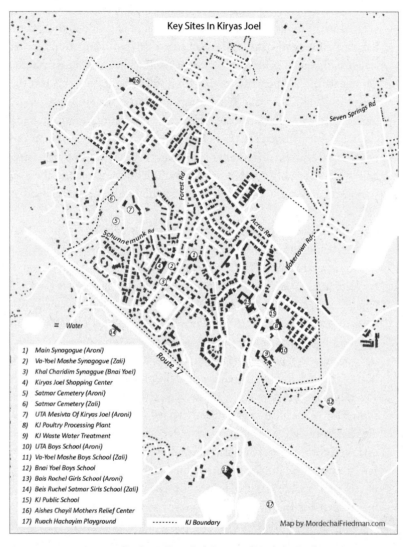

Key Sites In Kiryas Joel

Seven Springs Rd

Forest Rd

Acres Rd

Bakertown Rd

Schunnemunk Rd

= Water

Route 17

1) Main Synagogue (Aroni)
2) Va-Yoel Moshe Synagogue (Zali)
3) Khal Charidim Synaggue (Bnai Yoel)
4) Kiryas Joel Shopping Center
5) Satmar Cemetery (Aroni)
6) Satmar Cemetery (Zali)
7) UTA Mesivta Of Kiryas Joel (Aroni)
8) KJ Poultry Processing Plant
9) KJ Waste Water Treatment
10) UTA Boys School (Aroni)
11) Va-Yoel Moshe Boys School (Zali)
12) Bnai Yoel Boys School
13) Bais Rochel Girls School (Aroni)
14) Beis Ruchel Satmar Sirls School (Zali)
15) KJ Public School
16) Aishes Chayil Mothers Relief Center
17) Ruach Hachayim Playground

-------- KJ Boundary

Map by MordechaiFriedman.com

FIGURE 1.12. Key Sites in Kiryas Joel. Courtesy of Mordechai Friedman.

and particularly in the areas of divorce and child custody; indeed, no Satmar man would marry a woman who had not received a kosher *get*, or writ of divorce. In addition to the beis din, each faction maintains its own Vaad ha-chinech (education committee) to oversee the schools under its control.

In a village run by and for Satmar Hasidim, the authority of each of the factions within KJ achieves a higher degree of compliance than one might find in more heterogeneous municipalities with a large Haredi presence. Many consider Jewish law to have the same standing as—or even more standing than—state law. Each camp thus acts as an island of sovereignty within the village. From the standpoint of American law, these are private forms of authority. By contrast, the village administration, run by and for the Satmars of Kiryas Joel, is officially recognized as a public authority. It exercises a degree of control over life inside the boundaries of the village that few other localities do. It draws strength from the porous boundary between public and private, state and religious law. The entwining of the two legal systems lends special potency to this rare form of local sovereignty.[117]

This is what makes KJ the stuff of legend—and the source of such divergent opinions. Some of its reputation is deserved, and some of it is exaggerated. Some of its activity skirts the bounds of legality, and some of it is interest-group politics at its finest. The next two chapters delve deeper into how this extraordinary cultural, political, and religious phenomenon—at once so foreign and yet so quintessentially American—came into being.

CHAPTER 2

Satmar in Europe

The birth of Kiryas Joel would have been unimaginable without the commanding presence of the man after whom the village was named, Joel Teitelbaum. Although the Satmar Rebbe was not initially intent on a legally recognized municipality, he did aspire to create a shtetl, as we hear from the account of the leading Satmar court historian, Shlomo Yankel Gelbman: "The idea of a 'shtetl' was a subject that never left the agenda during all of our years growing up; at every turn, one spoke of the Rebbe's desire to build a settlement outside of the city that would be four pure cubits devoid of any defect or flaw in which the Satmarer could devote themselves to Torah and awe of G-d, in the pure path and way of the holy Rebbe who taught us."[1] The Rebbe's goal of a shtetl was to consecrate a pure space at a remove from the allures and seductions of the city—in this case, from multiethnic and multiracial Brooklyn where the remnant of the Satmar community that survived the Holocaust made its home from the late 1940s. This ideal of a shtetl as a self-contained paradise of Jewish observance resonates with the romanticized popular image mentioned in the introduction.

That said, it required more than a bit of imagination to invent a mythic past that could serve as the model for Kiryas Joel. For the Satmars' point of origin, the Romanian city of Satu Mare was not a homogeneous Eastern European village but rather a multiethnic East-Central European city. In 1941, it numbered slightly more than 50,000 residents, of whom a quarter—12,960—were Jews.[2] Today Satmar Hasidim live alone among themselves in KJ. But as in Satu Mare, they do not dwell in a total state of insularity. They are contiguous to their American neighbors with whom they do business on a daily basis and from whom they absorb cultural, social, and political values.

This reflects a simple but important point about Satmar Hasidim. They do not live beyond time or place. They are products of their context, living next to or among people quite unlike them (including other Jews). This is true now, but it was also true when the Satmar brand of Judaism was first founded. To wit, Joel Teitelbaum served as the chief rabbi of Satu Mare, but it was hardly the case that the entire Jewish community heeded his every edict. There was a diverse array of non-Orthodox groups in the city, including the Zionists whom Rabbi Teitelbaum loathed and who loathed him. There were also strictly Orthodox groups who neither accepted his authority nor followed the customs of the Satmar Hasidim. As a result, there was vigorous opposition to Teitelbaum's election as rabbi of the community in 1928, prompting him to wait six years until the controversies had subsided to take up his position.

This reminds us of another important point: Satmars were relative latecomers in the Hasidic Jewish world, coming into existence only with the appointment of Rabbi Teitelbaum as chief rabbi. Given its youth, how did Satmar Hasidism become as large and well established as it did, especially after nearly being extinguished in the Holocaust? We might also ask: what was it in the Rebbe's personality—and in the Satmar culture he created—that explains the group's desire to create a shtetl sheltered from the outside world, the likes of which they had never seen or lived in previously?

The answers lead us back to an area of East-Central Europe whose boundary shifted several times over the course of the twentieth century between Hungary and Romania. Prior to the redrawing of borders in the Treaty of Trianon of 1920, this area belonged to the Hungarian Kingdom of the Austro-Hungarian Empire. (This is a significant fact to bear in mind since Satmar Hasidim tend to conceive of their geographic and cultural roots as Hungarian, and decidedly not Romanian. They feel a particular sense of identification with the Hungarian Unterland, the northeast quadrant of pre–World War I Hungary that was often cast as the cultural foil to the western Oberland.)[3]

Over the course of the nineteenth and early twentieth centuries, the Unterland region developed a distinctive brand of Orthodox Judaism, marked by intense ritual stringency, fierce resistance to "modernizers," and a combative public culture. Although the call to battle against Jewish modernizers was joined by Hasidim throughout Eastern Europe in the nineteenth and twentieth centuries, the Unterland became a main center of the modern, though self-consciously antimodern, Haredim. Munkacz, Sighet, Puppa (Pápa), Vishnitz, and, of course, Satmar—these were some of the place names attached to Hasidic groups from the Unterland known for both their extreme piety and their intolerance of ritual laxity.

Groups such as these helped to create—and help us understand—what may be called the "Hungarian exception" in modern European Jewish history. Hungary was poised not only between East and West but also between the large and dense concentrations of Yiddish-speaking Jews in Eastern Europe and the smaller but still sizable centers of acculturating Jews in Western Europe.

It was in this environment that the Teitelbaums established themselves as a leading Haredi family, beginning with R. Yoelish's great-great-grandfather, Rabbi Moshe Teitelbaum (1759–1841). Known as the Yismah Moshe (following the habit of notable rabbis assuming the names of their most renowned books), Rabbi Moshe was the progenitor of the Teitelbaum family—and its tradition of pugnacious defense against the threat of impure innovation of any sort. He bequeathed to his descendants a belief that they were soldiers in a battle against the very modern world of which they were inescapably part. Joel Teitelbaum was a devoted admirer of the Yismah Moshe and was once described by a biographer in terms that would have made the family patriarch proud: "From his youth, Rabbi Joel Teitelbaum revealed himself to be a man of stormy ferocity; particularly in religious matters, he proved himself to be a *man of war* without surrender or compromise."[4]

Joel Teitelbaum was not merely one among the soldiers. He was the unquestioned religious and political leader of his community, cast in regal terms as a sort of Hasidic king. Some would even call the realm over which he presided, particularly in America, the "Kingdom of Satmar."[5] This kingly language was not unique to Satmar. The various centers of Hasidism that began to take rise from the late eighteenth century—all of which were sites of the teaching of the movement's founder, the Baal Shem Tov (1800–1865)—were referred to as "courts."[6] At the heart of the court stood the *tsadik*, or Rebbe, a new kind of Jewish leader distinguished not chiefly by his erudition but rather by his piety, charisma, and above all perceived gift of communication that permitted him to mediate on behalf of his followers with God. The tsadik, in this regard, was a "ladder" between the human and divine realms—a claim that, not surprisingly, brought down torrents of scorn and opprobrium from Hasidism's Jewish opponents.[7]

As a youngster, Joel Teitelbaum was inclined to the ascetic side of the personality spectrum; he exhibited an obsessive attention to personal hygiene and purity as a child, frequently availing himself of the mikveh (ritual bath).[8] When he reached adulthood, his personal norms of purity carried over to a broader communal vision. Along with fellow Haredi rabbis, he grasped the modern age as the very embodiment of contamination, no more dangerously represented than by Jews themselves—in the form of deviants such as the Maskilim (Enlighteners), Reformers, Zionists, and their unwitting Orthodox collaborators.[9] For Teitelbaum it was the Zionists who posed the gravest danger. As he wrote in his most renowned book *Va-yo'el Mosheh* (1959), the chief source of impurity in the world was the state of Israel. It was this alien political form that blinded and deceived Jews, prompting them to place the value of the idolatrous state above that of the holy Torah.[10]

Teitelbaum's fierce critique of Zionism in *Va-yo'el Mosheh* rested on a distinctive reading of the well-known "Three Oaths" found in the Babylonian Talmud. Whereas modern Zionists regarded the Oaths as a metaphor without any legal validity in the present, Teitelbaum disagreed. The first of the Oaths was a demand by God that Jews refrain from "ascend[ing] as a wall (i.e., en masse)" to the Holy Land through their own human action.[11] It was Zionism's willful violation of this oath that so unsettled Teitelbaum, prompting him to describe Zionism repeatedly in *Va-yo'el Mosheh* as "that impure idea."[12] The present state of disorder and pollution could not be overcome by human efforts; only God could restore the proper moral balance.

The contrast between Teitelbaum's quietism here and his own forceful vision of Satmar politics is striking. It was not just his unrelenting commitment to do battle against the forces of impurity in the modern world that stood in contrast to his avowed quietism. It was also the affirmative side of this commitment, the vision of creating a society in which Jewish law (halakhah) and the distinctive Satmar path—*derekh Yisra'el sava*, the "way of ancient Israel"—would dominate all spheres of life.

This vision was first hatched in the Hungarian Unterland, but it came much closer to realization in the United States. It was in America that Satmar Hasidim realized a theological-political vision predicated on opposition to Zionism—which became, paradoxically, a sort of mini- or counter-Zion—whose success stands in contrast to other modern attempts at achieving a large degree of communal autonomy in the Diaspora, perhaps most notably the secular Yiddish experiment in the Soviet region of Birobidzhan.[13]

Joel Teitelbaum did not consciously derive inspiration from secular Diaspora nationalists—nor even from his Orthodox rivals in the Agudat Yisrael. But he did live next to and do battle with them. As a result of this proximity, he and his Satmar followers absorbed, internalized, and recrafted the values and beliefs of the very modern world they rejected. It is this kind of oppositional assimilation that leads us to understand Hasidism as both estranged from and immersed in the world—in ways that challenge the familiar division between the categories of traditionalist and modern, religious and secular.[14]

Satmar and the Hungarian Unterland

The birthplace of Satmar Hasidism, Satu Mare, is located on both sides of the Someş River in the northwest region of present-day Romania. It sits on an alluvial plain about a hundred fifty kilometers from the Carpathians, one of Europe's longest mountain ranges. Satu Mare's current proximity to the borders of Hungary (thirteen kilometers) and Ukraine (twenty-seven kilometers) recalls not only its former existence as a Hungarian city known as Szatmár but also the multinational and multiethnic ambience of a region whose boundaries changed frequently. Alternating over the past century between two regional rivals, Hungary and Romania, the area was under the control of various empires in previous centuries, including the Ottoman, Austrian, and Austro-Hungarian.

Szatmár is commonly said to be in Transylvania, the region between Hungary and Romania from which the fictional legend Dracula took rise (named after a bloodthirsty medieval prince named Vlad III Dracula). Historical works on the Jews of Transylvania frequently include Szatmár in their discussions. But the term "Transylvania" is used in various ways, referring to a more limited geographic region in which Szatmár did not fall as well as to a wider geocultural region in which it did. Thus, the city was not within the boundaries of the semi-independent Principality of Transylvania in the sixteenth to eighteenth centuries, but it was subject to the principality's strong influence. During this period, Szatmár belonged to a narrow strip of land known as Partium to the immediate west of Transylvania and to the east of the Kingdom of Hungary. Following the end of Ottoman rule in Hungary in the early eighteenth century, Transylvania and Partium became part of the Habsburg and the successor Austro-Hungarian empires. By the nineteenth century, the county of Szatmár and its Jewish community began to grow substantially in size.

Szatmár was next to Máramaros county, which included Sighet, the town with which the Teitelbaum family was long associated and in which Joel Teitelbaum was born in 1887. The two counties—Szatmár and Máramaros—became sites of Haredi life in the late nineteenth century and, as such, sites of conflict with other Jewish groups. They were also the two most populous counties in this part of northeastern Hungary and underwent rapid growth over the course of the late eighteenth and nineteenth centuries. Szatmár's Jewish population grew more than sixfold, from 2,569 in 1787 to 16,588 in 1869. Meanwhile, the number of Jews in Máramaros country rose almost thirteen times, from 2,254 in 1787 to 26,296 in 1869.[15]

This dramatic growth took place under the Habsburgs, whose overall policy toward the Jews was marked by a mix of intolerance (Empress Maria Theresa) and tolerance (as in the case of Emperor Joseph II). The Habsburgs also held control over the northern territory of Galicia, from which Jewish immigrants began to flow southward in the nineteenth century. The central authorities in Vienna were keenly interested in promoting the integration of Galician Jews and adopted a particularly heavy-handed approach in the first decades of the nineteenth century toward Hasidim, whom they regarded as clannish, fanatical, and fettered by "chains of superstition."[16]

It was in this period that the patriarch of the Teitelbaum family, Moshe Teitelbaum, moved from Galicia to the Hungarian town of Sátoraljaújhely (also known as Ujhely), which is located some hundred fifty kilometers northwest of Szatmár. Born in 1759 in the Galician city of Przemyśl, Teitelbaum was raised in a traditionally observant family. It was his encounter with the early Hasidic rabbi Ya`akov Yitshak, the Seer of Lublin, that transformed him from an opponent of Hasidism into a Hasid himself. Subsequently, Rabbi Moshe served as rabbi for twenty-four years in the Galician town of Sieniawa before being called to the post of rabbi of Sátoraljaújhely in 1808. There he disseminated his unique blend of Hasidic teachings throughout the region, drawing around him devoted disciples and students.[17]

Moshe Teitelbaum was a mix of erudite scholar, messianic mystic, and folk healer. Regarding the first vocation, Teitelbaum defied the popular image of the Hasidic leader who eschewed serious Talmud Torah (Torah study); he was renowned for his learning and authored a number of important works of halakhah and commentary, including the multivolume biblical commentary published after his death bearing his name, Yismah Moshe. Regarding the second vocation, Teitelbaum was so anxious for the coming of the Messiah that, later in life, he took to wearing his Sabbath finery all week long in anticipation of his arrival; at the same time, he anticipated the stance of his descendent, the Satmar Rebbe, by insisting that Jews should not emigrate to Palestine unless and until led there by the Messiah. And with respect to his vocation as a healer, Moshe Teitelbaum was both renowned and reviled by fellow

Jews for distributing amulets for health and success. Legends of his healing powers included claims that he bestowed his gift on non-Jews, the most famous case of which was a young Lajos Kossuth, destined to become a leading Hungarian political figure.[18]

After moving to Sátoraljaújhely, Moshe Teitelbaum encountered the most prominent rabbinic figure on Hungarian soil, the famous Hatam Sofer (Rabbi Moshe Sofer, 1762–1839). Similar to Teitelbaum, the Hatam Sofer was not native to Hungary but rather a transplant. He moved from his birthplace, Frankfurt am Main, in 1806 to assume a rabbinical post in the northwestern Hungarian city of Pressburg, home to the Hungarian legislature (and known today as Bratislava, capital of Slovakia). The two religious leaders could not have been more different in their spiritual background and disposition; the German-born Hatam Sofer was heir to the tradition of early modern Ashkenazic Judaism, while the Galician Teitelbaum was an adept of the upstart Hasidic movement that took aim at the former.

In spite of their varied origins, the two rabbis shared an agenda. Although German in origin and resettled in the western Oberland region of Hungary, the Hatam Sofer strongly advocated for Yiddish rather than German as the language of rabbinic sermon. Like Moshe Teitelbaum, he saw the replacement of Yiddish by German as emblematic of a dangerous tendency to modernize and reform Judaism.[19] In fact, the two rabbis were allies in a campaign against perceived transgressors who sought to reform or move away from traditional Jewish religious culture.

In waging this battle, the Hatam Sofer was most renowned for his principle that innovation is forbidden as a matter of Torah.[20] This credo made him a founding father of the traditionalist battle against modernizers. Moshe Teitelbaum, for his part, was a fellow soldier on the Hungarian front. Operating from his base in the Unterland, Rabbi Teitelbaum brooked no deviation from strict observance—notwithstanding his own "conversion" to Hasidism, which was often deemed by its opponents as a dangerous deviation itself. He urged observant Jews to segregate themselves from those who violated the Torah. As he once wrote, there is, in the natural course of affairs, hatred between the righteous and the transgressors—and it is not a bad thing. Hatred serves to wall off the good from the evil.[21] This belief in the necessity, even virtue, of hatred was an article of faith for the Yismah Moshe's notable descendent, Joel Teitelbaum. As he wrote in his own Torah commentary, *Divre Yo'el*, hatred of *resha'im* (evil ones or transgressors) "was good and beneficial."[22]

The century that separated the activity of the two Teitelbaums was one of intense conflict for Jews in Hungary. The early nineteenth-century efforts to introduce reforms into Hungarian Jewish synagogue and ritual behavior, associated with Rabbi Aaron Chorin of Arad (1766–1844), prompted a ferocious reaction by the traditionalist camp, led by the Hatam Sofer and Moshe Teitelbaum in their respective spheres. As is often the case, this contentiousness began to creep into Hungarian Orthodoxy itself, with some leaders, typically in the western Oberland, favoring a degree of engagement with modern secular culture, whereas others, especially in the Unterland, countenanced no such concession. The latter faction asserted itself in aggressive fashion in late November 1865, when twenty-five rabbis—later joined by fifty-six colleagues—signed a declaration in the northeastern Hungarian town of Michalovce (Michalowitz). The signatories produced a nine-point resolution that began with a ban on sermons in synagogue in a language other than Yiddish and concluded with a sweeping prohibition on change to "any Jewish custom or any traditional synagogue practice."[23] The Michalovce Decree was a foundational text of the separatist branch of Orthodoxy that took rise in Hungary during the last third of the nineteenth century. Among the signatories to this text was Rabbi Yekutiel Yehuda Teitelbaum (1808–1883), who briefly succeeded his grandfather, the Yismah Moshe, as rabbi of Sátoraljaújhely.

The career journey of Rabbi Yekutiel Yehuda, known as the Yetev Lev after his most famous book, points to the denouement of the earlier partnership between Hasidic and non-Hasidic Jews in Hungary symbolized by his grandfather and the Hatam Sofer. It also points to the fragility of the Yismah Moshe's legacy after thirty-three years. His own son, Eliezer Nisan (1788–1855), did not wish to succeed his father and made his way to Sighet, where he became rabbi—but not without facing opposition from both Hasidic and non-Hasidic Jews.[24] Eliezer

Nisan's son, Yekutiel Yehuda, assumed the Yismah Moshe's post, but he was forced to leave Sátoraljaújhely six years later—on the eve of the Sabbath, we are told—because the Jewish community had had its fill of the ways of the Hasidim. In particular, the Yetev Lev refused to adhere to his contract, which stipulated that he was to refrain from the Hasidic practices of dispensing amulets and receiving notes containing penitential prayers (kvitlekh) as well as from delivering sermons of longer than an hour and a half.[25] Throughout his career, he was forced to leave communities when his practices and personality raised opposition among local Jews.

Charismatic authority does not always pass on in neat dynastic succession. It surely did not in the generations that followed the Yismah Moshe, whose own success in establishing an enduring Hasidic presence in Sátoraljaújhely was rather limited. His grandson's position as rabbi was forever being challenged, there and elsewhere, by Orthodox and non-Orthodox Jews alike. In one especially striking case in Sighet, the Yetev Lev became involved in a campaign to impose new stringencies in the laws of *kashrut*. He saw to the creation of a new butcher shop whose ritual slaughtering met his exacting standards, but whose existence threatened the livelihood of the town's butchers—to the point that one night a large rock was thrown through the window of his home, presumably by those affected by the new shop.[26] Meanwhile, in the last months of his life, in 1883, the Yetev Lev had to struggle to overcome the opposition of communal leaders to his favored son, Chananiah Yom Tov Lipa Teitelbaum (1836–1904), known as the Kedushas Yom Tov, whom he wanted to inherit the position of rabbi of Sighet.[27]

And yet, if the Yetev Lev did not possess his grandfather's charisma, he did inherit another quality: an extremely combative attitude toward adversaries. Both the Yetev Lev and the Kedushas Yom Tov were warriors, waging battle against Hasidim, non-Hasidic Orthodox, non-Orthodox, and later Zionists. As a reflection of that martial impulse, it is no surprise that the collection of rabbinic opinions that the Yetev Lev had a major hand in compiling over the kashrut struggles in Sighet was *Milhemet mitsvah* (Commanded War). It was a title that recurred within Hungarian rabbinical culture over the course of generations.[28] War was, indeed, an appropriate metaphor to describe the posture of the Hungarian Jewish community in the latter half of the nineteenth century.

In 1867, Jews gained formal emancipation in Hungary. In the following year, the liberal minister of education and religion, Joseph Eötvös, set out to create a central national body akin to the French consistory that would represent the Jews vis-à-vis the state. He convened 220 delegates in December. But rather than achieve unity and forge an effective national voice, the Hungarian Jewish Congress instead laid bare the deep fault lines among Hungarian Jews. These differences were reflected in the very choreography of the meeting hall, with "Progressives" on one side and "Orthodox" on the other. Disagreement arose at virtually every turn, whether in attempting to elect a Congress president or accepting the rabbinic code *Shulhan ʿArukh* as authoritative.[29] After protracted disagreements, the Congress delegates passed a series of statutes intended to regulate local communities and the central organization.

In response, the Orthodox, who were a minority of the delegates at the Congress, turned to the Hungarian parliament to request the right to be exempted from the Congress's regulations. In 1870, parliament granted this request, and shortly thereafter an independent organization of Orthodox communities was established. Subsequently, the new centrist Status Quo community was established, so called because of its members' commitment to retain their Jewish way of life as existed before the Congress. This series of developments bespoke a new and sharper key in Jewish denominational politics in Hungary and prompted a virtual civil war between Jews in that country. It was in the midst of this war—one fought with words not arms, but a vicious fight nonetheless—that Joel Teitelbaum, the son of the Kedushas Yom Tov, the grandson of the Yetev Lev, and the great-great-grandson of the Yismah Moshe, was born.

Confronting the Enemy: The Birth of a Life Mission

To gain a sense of the worldview that Joel Teitelbaum developed over the course of his life, it might be helpful to think of four circles of enmity in which he was embedded from his early years. The outer circle represented the tension between the world of the Jews and the world of the gentiles. The Teitelbaum family's professed reverence for "the way of the ancient Israel" meant separation from the gentile world, to the greatest extent possible. For that world was the ultimate source of attraction for wayward Jews and, as such, a grave threat that the Teitelbaums felt compelled to fight.

The second circle of enmity signified the chasm between Torah observant Jews and those who sought to reform or modernize Judaism by moving away from strict observance of Jewish law. As had his ancestor R. Moshe in Sátoraljaújhely, so too Joel Teitelbaum in Szatmár regarded as grave transgressors those Jews who no longer heeded the sixteenth-century *Shulhan 'Arukh* as the authoritative code of Jewish conduct. Included in that group were the Status Quo and Neolog communities as well as most Zionists. Just as one should separate oneself from the gentiles and their ways, so too one should avoid contact with these modernizers.

The third circle of enmity represented traditionalists and modernizers within the Orthodox camp. Although united by a shared commitment to strict observance of halakhah, the two groups differed over the extent to which a Jew should absorb the culture, language, and norms of the land. In Hungary, the modernizers, perhaps most prominently Esriel Hildesheimer, the German-born rabbi who served the community of Eisenstadt (Kismarton) in the Oberland, were willing to speak German (or Hungarian) and to deliver sermons in the vernacular. They were also prepared to establish a modern rabbinical seminary in which new subjects such as history and homiletics would be taught alongside the traditional subjects of Talmud and Jewish law. For Joel Teitelbaum and his forebears, such concessions marked precisely the kind of innovation that the Hatam Sofer sought to avoid.

The fourth circle of enmity, and perhaps the most difficult to comprehend, was defined by the tensions between Hasidic and non-Hasidic traditionalists, both of whom sought to maintain the boundary against the encroachment of modernity—and who were known respectively in Hungarian Jewish parlance as Sephardim and Ashkenazim (based on their preferred prayer rite). The rift between the two was based on mutual suspicion: in one case, that the Sephardim were introducing ritual innovations into Torah-true Judaism (e.g., times of prayer, the nature of ritual slaughtering); and in the other, that the Ashkenazim were bent on the suppression of a new pietistic movement devoted to upholding the law without diminishing the spiritual experience of Judaism. The tension between these two groups of traditionalists in the Hungarian Unterland in the late nineteenth century signaled the parting of ways of followers of the early allies, the Hatam Sofer and the Yismah Moshe.

At the center of these four circles of enmity stood Joel Teitelbaum, who was born in Sighet, Hungary, on the eighteenth day of the Hebrew month Tevet 5647, corresponding to January 13, 1887. He was the youngest of five children born to Hannah and Chananiah Yom Tov Lipman Teitelbaum, the Kedushas Yom Tov. Joel's father succeeded his own father, the Yetev Lev, as rabbi of Sighet in 1883 and served there for twenty-one years until his death in 1904—a crucial year in Joel's life, as we shall soon see.

The Kedushas Yom Tov is said to have remarked once about his fifth child: "Mayn Yoylish iz keyn mol keyn kind nisht geven" (My Joel was never a child).[30] The young boy not only was very studious but possessed a razor-sharp analytical mind and a seemingly limitless memory. He was not sent to school—neither to a traditional Jewish *heder* nor under any circumstance to a state school in which he might be exposed to secular subjects (such as history, mathematics, and literature). These were completely off-limits to him, as indeed were the vernacular languages spoken where Teitelbaum lived. It was left to his mother to teach him how to sign his name in Latin characters. In his own adult life, Joel Teitelbaum enjoined his followers to abstain from studying anything more than the bare minimum of secular subjects necessary to achieve economic sustenance.

As a child, Joel's education was entrusted to two *melamdim* (instructors), Nachman Kahana and Joseph Hoffman. Later, as an adolescent, he spent time studying with prominent rabbis in the Unterland, including in Szatmár. He was so devoted to his studies that, according to his biographer, he spent nine hours consecutively throughout the day, and even more at night, poring over his books.[31] This rigorous regimen did little to enhance the young prodigy's health. Like his elder brother, he was a sickly young man, so much so that his father forbade him from fasting on fast days. As a general matter, Joel Teitelbaum's version of piety tended to the abstemious. Accordingly, he ate little as a matter of principle and sought to avoid developing an appetite for any particular food or drink.[32] It is said that he even minimized drinking plain water, for, according to the early modern kabbalist Hayim Vital, this most basic human need only increased one's appetite.[33] In similar fashion, he consciously limited his hours of sleep, both to allow for more study and to prevent impure (that is, sexual) thoughts from entering his subconscious state. He even avoided sleeping in a bed, it was said, except on the Sabbath.[34]

From his earliest years, Joel Teitelbaum was fastidiously concerned with purity. He spent a long time every morning cleansing himself—washing his mouth and using the bathroom repeatedly—so as to enter prayer in a pure state. Contemporaries reported that in the dire conditions of a Nazi concentration camp, where he spent a number of months in 1944, Joel Teitelbaum was so concerned about personal hygiene that he traded food for toilet paper.[35] But the concern carried over to other parts of his life, with obsessive regularity.[36] Purity and impurity were organizing principles of his worldview. Joel Teitelbaum conceived of the world as filled with hostile forces, both at the deepest cosmic level and at the level of mundane human behavior. He lived his life in daily battle against the "evil inclination" (*yetser ha-ra*) lest he stray over to the dark "other side" (*sitra ahra*) of which the Kabbalah frequently warns.

This gloomy vision of the world, and especially of a modern world wracked by impurity, accompanied Teitelbaum throughout his life. The year 1904 was a significant date in commencing that journey; it was in that year that he was married, his father died, and he left his birthplace of Sighet. Although the marriage had been arranged ten years earlier, Joel Teitelbaum was wed to his first wife Hava, daughter of the Plontcher Rebbe, Avraham Chaim Horowitz, in February 1904. Because of his father's illness, the wedding was held not in the bride's hometown but in Sighet, where the ailing Kedushas Yom Tov officiated from his sick bed. Immediately after the wedding, the Kedushas Yom Tov designated Joel's elder brother Hayim Tsvi as his successor as rabbi of Sighet. The father was said to have spoken these words to his younger son: "Your elder brother will take my place; he will become the rabbi of Sighet. I don't want two kings serving one crown, and you would make two rabbis in Sighet. I don't have a rabbinic position to bestow upon you, and so I will bequeath to you the spiritual powers that I received from the holy one, our teacher and master, the Yetev Lev, who received them from our distinguished forebear, the Yismah Moshe."[37] The Kedushas Yom Tov's words about not having two kings serve one crown are an ominous anticipation of what would transpire a century later when the later Moshe Teitelbaum divided the Satmar kingdom in 1999, producing two warring factions. But back in the time of Joel Teitelbaum, it was customary in Hasidic circles for the younger sons of a recently deceased rabbi to take leave of their hometown to allow their elder brother to establish his authority. By the time of his wedding, the eighteen-year-old Joel Teitelbaum was a recognized prodigy who was granted ordination by eight prominent rabbis. But after his brother became rabbi of Sighet, he had no discernible means of livelihood.

In the summer of 1904, the young rabbi's mother consulted with the Belzer Rebbe Yissachar Dov Rokeach about her underemployed son. The Belzer Rebbe suggested that Joel Teitelbaum make his way to Szatmár, which was beginning to attract a large number of Hasidim, including students of his father, and was a rapidly growing Jewish town.[38] Shortly thereafter, Joel Teitelbaum followed the rabbi's advice and moved to Szatmár. More than five thousand Jews lived within the city limits, constituting a fifth of the population (and a quarter of the Jewish population of the larger county). Joel Teitelbaum's precocity, erudition, intense devotion, and ascetic ways attracted a growing following, including within the established non-Hasidic community as well as from Hasidim from the wider Unterland region.

Not long after his arrival in Szatmár, Joel Teitelbaum displayed signs of his family's characteristic zeal. He expressed concern over the close proximity of a women's ritual bath (mikveh) to a men's bathhouse. When communal leaders refused to move the women's facility, he gathered a group of supporters in the middle of the night and proceeded to raze it.[39] This fervor earned Teitelbaum both enemies and admirers. Potential opponents in the Orthodox community were impressed, and perhaps a bit intimidated, by his uncompromising stance toward those Jews whom he deemed transgressors. As is often the case in matters of religious observance, the more punctilious or, at least, visible the performance of obligations, the greater the degree of authenticity and authority ascribed. Joel Teitelbaum benefited from this dynamic, but he also gained respect among fellow Orthodox Jews for his intense commitment to Torah study. Over time, he became a highly regarded religious figure in the Unterland, ripe for a plum rabbinical assignment. In 1910, at the age of twenty-three, he was elected to the post of rabbi and presiding judge of the rabbinical court in the small Jewish community of Ilosva (known in Yiddish sources as Orshava), a Hungarian town some ninety-five kilometers northeast of Szatmár.[40] Devoted followers of Teitelbaum's from Szatmár, including Chief Rabbi Judah Grünwald, accompanied him on his way in the spring of 1911 for part of the journey. Meanwhile, the local governor of the Ilosva district came to receive the new dignitary but was surprised to find a man so young that he barely had a beard. This prompted him to ask, it is said, if the new arrival came with an accompanying wet nurse.[41]

Teitelbaum had an immediate impact on Ilosva, attracting a cadre of devoted disciples whose Hasidic dress and habits changed the complexion of the local Jewish community. He set about transforming Jewish life in the town by focusing attention on the realms of education, dietary regulations, and sartorial modesty. At every turn, he opposed whatever he deemed a grave transgression. In one written admonition to the Jews of Ilosva and its environs in 1919, especially directed against those who promoted mixed dancing, he declared: "It is necessary to employ very strong tactics to prevent this, and to pursue in every manner possible these youth—and also the fathers of these young men and women who do not protest to their children sufficiently. It is necessary to separate them from the community of Israel and from all its sectors, and not to allow them to participate in any holy matter and not to call them to the Torah, because they are rebels in the eyes of God and the Holy Torah."[42]

Reflected in this statement are two interrelated traits of Teitelbaum's public persona: the insistence on preserving a pristine state of purity in the face of calls for innovation and the willingness to segregate transgressors from the steadfast core. The resulting regime of ritual stringency became the model for his leadership, both in Ilosva and beyond. It was a mode of existence predicated on intimate familiarity with Jewish law, especially for men (upon whom the burden of the performance of the obligations of Jewish law fell heavily). Consequently, Joel Teitelbaum placed a great deal of emphasis on institutionalizing the study of Torah. Upon arrival in Ilosva, he established a yeshivah, or advanced academy for Talmud study, to which more than fifty students from across the region, and not just Hungary, came to learn. As Sh. Y. Gelbman, Teitelbaum's biographer, wrote with pride, there was not "any trace of progress according to the spirit of the time" in the yeshivah.[43]

Teitelbaum had many potential allies in the Hungarian Unterland. The region, as we have seen, was known for its rabbinic opponents to modernizing trends. The followers of one of Joel Teitelbaum's heroes (and his father's teacher), the Sanzer Rebbe, Rabbi Chaim Halberstam, were amply represented in Szatmár and other neighboring towns and villages. Teitelbaum made his way back to Szatmár just as chief rabbi Grünwald was preparing to take leave.[44] Teitelbaum persuaded him to stay and remained there himself for eight years. There he met not only Sanzer Hasidim, but Hasidim of other courts as well (for example, Belz, Spinka, Vishnitz, and Munkacz). These Hasidim shared his concern over the cultural threats lurking in their midst: modernizers, reformers, assimilationists, and Zionists.

The arch-traditionalists of the Unterland were not given to compromise. Just as they sought to ensure the primacy of Yiddish in Jewish life (as at the Michalovce conference), so too were they prepared to defy government regulations about language by discouraging the acquisition of Hungarian. Rather than send their children to public schools or Jewish schools with a modern curriculum, they established their own schools with traditional sources at the heart and instruction in Yiddish.

In a similar vein, Joel Teitelbaum regularly encouraged and assisted fellow Jews in the midst of the First World War to avoid service in the Austro-Hungarian army, for fear of the physical and spiritual dangers that enlistment might entail (e.g., exposure to foreign habits and norms).[45] A similar concern was raised regarding Kiryas Joel more than fifty years later; some Satmar Hasidim, including one of Joel Teitelbaum's most trusted lieutenants, Lipa Friedman, feared that young men would be much more publicly identifiable in a self-standing rural village than in a dense urban neighborhood like Williamsburg and, as such, susceptible to the draft for the Vietnam War.[46]

Joel Teitelbaum actively promoted the principle of segregation—not only from gentiles, but, as we've seen, from most other Jews. In this regard, the language used in Satmar sources is telling: gentiles, men in particular, were referred to by a traditionally derogatory term, "uncircumcised" (`arelim`), while deviant Jews were called "transgressors" or "heretics" (*kofrim, apikorsim,* or *minim*). From the perspective of Satmar Hasidim, a large majority of Jews fell into this category, including Zionists, the reform-minded Neolog, Status Quo, modern Orthodox, and even strictly observant "Ashkenazim." In fact, it often seemed that the greatest venom was reserved for the most proximate.

For example, the young Joel Teitelbaum took aim not only at the Zionists but also at the religious Zionist Mizrachi party, which was founded as an alternative to the secular factions within the Zionist movement in its early years. The Balfour Declaration issued by the British government in November 1917 added considerable legitimacy to the Zionist cause and thus raised alarm bells for Teitelbaum and likeminded rabbis.[47] In 1920, he and a number of colleagues issued a stern warning at a rabbinical conference in Großwardein, Hungary, that called for "an absolute prohibition on associating in any way with the band of Zionists or Mizrachi members, or assisting them in any way . . . or studying, God forbid, in their schools."[48]

Taking matters a step further, Teitelbaum expressed unbridled disdain for the Agudat Yisrael (known as the Aguda). The Aguda was founded in 1912 by traditionalist Orthodox Jews from Germany and

Poland with the intention of blunting the thrust of secular Zionist settlement of Palestine. Among its chief supporters were renowned Hasidic rabbis, who lent the group a Haredi character. But the fact that the Aguda supported its own project of settlement in Palestine, as well as a somewhat less restrictive attitude toward secular studies, made it an enemy of Unterland Haredim. In the summer of 1922, a prominent neighboring Haredi leader, the Munkaczer Rebbe, convened a meeting of rabbis in Csap, Czechoslovakia (Chop in Ukraine today) in order to condemn the Aguda's errant ways. The gathering signaled a sort of *Kulturkampf*, a cultural war, between Hungarian (and neighboring) Orthodox rabbis, on one hand, and German and Polish rabbis, on the other.[49] The delegates at Csap approved a unanimous decision that "it is forbidden to us, according to the view of the Holy Torah, to associate with the 'Aguda.'"[50] The first signatory was the Munkaczer Rebbe; the second was Joel Teitelbaum, who shared his older colleague's contempt for the insufficient vigilance of the Aguda toward Zionism.

True to form, Joel Teitelbaum and the Munkaczer Rebbe found themselves at loggerheads with one another on more than a few occasions. Not only did each follow his own particular customs, but each imagined himself as the leader of the Haredi camp. Both rabbis sought to establish and maintain order in a time of upheaval, as refugees from Galicia entered Hungary and placed new strains on existing communal resources during and after the First World War.

Indeed, the balance of power in Europe was altogether recalculated after the war. The map of East-Central Europe was redrawn, with dramatic consequences for the Unterland. According to the terms of the Treaty of Saint-Germain-en-Laye in September 1919, the Austro-Hungarian Empire was dissolved, yielding an independent Hungary and Czechoslovakia, along with Austria, Poland, and the state of Serbs, Croats, and Slovenes that later came to be known as Yugoslavia. A little less than a year later, in August 1920, the Treaty of Trianon was signed in which Hungary was required to cede more than 70 percent of its terrain—including Transylvania and adjoining areas to Romania, and other nearby regions to Czechoslovakia.

Trianon remains a painful memory seared in Hungarian national consciousness. The country's sense of territorial integrity was deeply compromised, and boundaries shifted in what seemed to be arbitrary fashion. Overnight, Szatmár became Romanian (Satu Mare), and Ilosva became Czechoslovakian (Iršava). The redrawing of the borders prompted economic, cultural, and psychic dislocation for Hungarian Jews. Before the war, the vast majority of Szatmár's Jews—90 percent of them—declared their mother tongue as Hungarian, with the remainder clinging to Yiddish.[51] Now Romanian was the language of the land. Those previously employed in public functions, Jews and non-Jews alike, were unable to compete with those who spoke the new language of the land. Merchants too were required to reorient themselves toward Romanian. Some Jews were unwilling to make the transition and moved back to areas under Hungarian control. Other Jews, displaced from neighboring regions by the war, now came to live in Satu Mare, but without any means of livelihood.

One effect of the demographic and economic turmoil, as we notice elsewhere in interwar Eastern and Central Europe, was a burst of cultural innovation that disrupted established norms and patterns of leadership. In encountering a new language and culture, Jews were prompted to create new schools, organizations, and vehicles of literary expressions, including novels and plays on Jewish themes. It was not only secular Jews who strained to break free of the shackles of the past. The post–World War I period also witnessed new energy in the traditionalist camp, with scores of rabbinic treatises and journals rolling off the city's Hebrew presses.[52]

Joel Teitelbaum was both the beneficiary of this stimulating new ambience and a sharp critic of it. Consistent with the battle cry of his forebears, he reiterated his opposition to innovations of any sort in Judaism, even as he belonged to a generation of leaders creating a new brand of Haredi Judaism. His Satu Mare was a particularly interesting site of activity. Its Jewish community of now over ten thousand was far bigger and more diverse than Ilosva's, with substantial non-Orthodox and Orthodox populations dwelling in different quarters of the city and interacting warily with each other. A new opportunity presented itself to Teitelbaum in March 1920, when Judah Grünwald died, creating a vacancy for city rabbi that he considered filling. The prospect of Teitelbaum's candidacy won enthusiastic support among his closest supporters but generated opposition among non-Hasidic "Ashkenazim" as well as various Hasidic groups in town. In fact, two Hasidic members of the town council reconsidered their erstwhile promise to support Teitelbaum, resulting in his failure to win the unanimous approval of the council required for selection as chief rabbi. In his stead, Eliezer David Grünwald (1867–1928), no relation to Judah, was invited from a neighboring town to become the chief rabbi of Satu Mare.[53]

A few years later, in 1922, Joel Teitelbaum took leave of Satu Mare and returned to the much smaller community of Iršava (previously Ilosva), which had fewer than eight hundred Jews.[54] He was joined by a solid core of disciples, who helped him breathe new life into the town's yeshivah, which grew in number to more than one hundred students. Rabbi Teitelbaum's reputation as a charismatic and stringent leader made him a source of both attraction and fear in the region, where his influence spread beyond the confines of Iršava. He served there for four years until he was chosen to succeed Rabbi Shaul Brach as the rabbi of the Jewish community in the larger Romanian city of Carei (known previously by its Hungarian name, Nagykároly, and in Yiddish as Krule). Carei had substantial numbers of both "Ashkenazim" and Hasidim, not all of whom cohabitated peacefully. After initial disagreement, the two groups managed to reach consensus on Joel Teitelbaum as town rabbi, a post to which he was elected in March 1925.

Slightly less than a year later, on a rainy day in late February 1926, Teitelbaum arrived in Carei to a celebratory reception. He left little doubt that he would act there as he had elsewhere. Shortly after his arrival, Rabbi Teitelbaum went off early in the morning to a butcher shop to ensure that his exacting standards of kashrut were being met. He also made clear that he would do all within his power to change the physical appearance of Jews in line with his norms—more modest clothing for women, and long beards and *shtreimels* (wide fur hats) for men. Gelbman reports that there were only two Jewish men who wore shtreimels when Teitelbaum arrived in Carei, but, after several years, nearly a third of the Jewish male population did.[55] In parallel, Joel Teitelbaum followed the path of his father, the Kedushas Yom Tov, by urging Jews not to send their children to the local gymnasium (high school) lest they be exposed to secular subjects.[56]

This series of steps, which was designed to guard the boundaries of his community, engendered fear and hostility among opponents. But it also reinforced Teitelbaum's reputation as a forceful and desired leader known throughout the Unterland. Meanwhile, back in Satu Mare, supporters raised his name again as a candidate for chief rabbi in 1928 following the death of Eliezer David Grünwald, who had served in the office for eight years. Moving quickly to fill the position, the town council voted on June 11 to nominate Joel Teitelbaum to succeed Grünwald. Teitelbaum responded several days later by thanking the council but turning down the proposal, pleading his own inadequacies in assuming such a large job as well as his commitment to the Jewish community of Carei.[57] His supporters in Satu Mare persisted, arguing that the threat posed by the modernizers, and especially the Zionists in town, was increasing. The opponents of Teitelbaum, for their part, appealed to officials at the Romanian Ministry of Religion to remove the entire Jewish council of Satu Mare—and further, to invalidate the candidacy of Joel Teitelbaum on the grounds that he was too fanatical and did not speak the language of the land.

These divisions necessitated two additional elections involving Teitelbaum on August 14 and September 27.[58] In the last one, the results were clear: Teitelbaum won 779 of 780 eligible voters. Nevertheless, he understood that even with a landslide victory in the third election, the time was not right to come to Satu Mare. Tensions between the competing sides remained too high. It was only in 1934, six years after the elections, that Teitelbaum decided to make his way to his new rabbinic position. He stole away from Carei just after dawn on February 27 for the two-hour car ride to Satu Mare. A sense of shock, and even bitterness, hovered over the community, as we hear in this account by an admirer from Carei the day after: "The Jews of Carei awoke to a most unpleasant surprise: our beloved and revered rebbe, Rabbi Joel Teitelbaum, left us in the early hours of the morning without giving us any advance notice or an opportunity to part from him; ever since it became known that he plans to leave us, his followers have walked around in a state of mourning and perplexity. It pains us that we must part from our beloved leader."[59] On the other hand, the prospect of Teitelbaum's arrival in Satu Mare was cause for celebration among his supporters there. To accommodate all who wanted to greet him in his new city, Romanian officials decided to open the borders with Hungary and Czechoslovakia to allow for easy passage. The Hungarian Jewish newspaper *Hoemesz* reported that Teitelbaum was accompanied on his walk to the main Satu Mare synagogue by a military band; he delivered his first sermon there to an audience estimated at between five and six thousand. Stores were closed for the day, work came to a halt, and city officials received Teitelbaum as a distinguished dignitary.[60]

As in his earlier rabbinic postings, he moved quickly to transform the Jewish community over the next few years. By the fall of 1937, Teitelbaum felt confident enough to set in place a series of new communal regulations that included the following strictures:

- Women were admonished not to let their hair protrude onto their foreheads
- Women should not be seen in the market or on the street with a wig made of gentile hair that resembles real hair
- Women should not go outside in transparent stockings
- Jews should avoid going to the theater or museums, and they should warn members of their household against doing so
- Jews should send their children to high school only for the period required by law and no more
- Jews should not indulge in leisurely reading lest it lead to the commission of more dangerous acts[61]

Along with this new ritual stringency came new waves of Hasidim, who regularly visited Satu Mare on the Sabbath and Jewish holidays. Some studied at the yeshivah over which Joel Teitelbaum presided, the largest of four in town with close to four hundred students. While the enhanced

Haredi presence in town was unnerving to the less observant Jews of Satu Mare, it also was something of a boon to the local Jewish economy, especially for poor Jews who rented out rooms and provided meals to the visitors. This new demographic factor, according to the Satu Mare memorial book, altered the "physiognomy of Jewish life" in the city.[62]

Satu Mare was, by far, the largest of the Unterland communities in which Joel Teitelbaum served as rabbi, numbering nearly thirteen thousand Jews in 1930 (and nearly twenty-five thousand in the surrounding county). Although two-thirds of the county's Jewish population declared themselves to be Yiddish speakers, Satu Mare did not conform, as we noted earlier, to the model of the mythic Eastern European shtetl. It was far more ethnically and religiously diverse, with Jews constituting between 20 and 25 percent of the urban population (and about 8 percent of the total rural and urban population).[63] Even within the Jewish world, heterogeneity was the norm. Religiously, there were substrata of Status Quo, Neolog, Ashkenazic, and Hasidic communities. And notwithstanding Joel Teitelbaum's fierce objections, there were some eight hundred self-identified Zionists in town, ranging from Ha-Shomer Ha-Tsair on the left to Betar on the right.[64]

For all its lack of homogeneity, the size of Satu Mare actually made it a good laboratory for Teitelbaum. He could experiment with his distinctive brand of religious politics, balancing tightened supervision over the community with a willingness to work with gentile authorities. Indeed, while he discouraged interaction between his followers and less observant Jews, he was always willing to meet public officials and display loyalty to them in order to advance his community's interests. Perhaps the most striking visual evidence of this willingness was Rabbi Teitelbaum's famous encounter with Romanian king Carol II in November 1936. Carol was passing through Transylvania after a state visit in Czechoslovakia with President Edvard Beneš. His twelve-wagon train stopped in Satu Mare, where he was received by local politicians and religious figures. A widely disseminated, blurry photograph captures Teitelbaum in a large fur coat bending forward to shake hands with the king.

FIGURE 2.1. R. Joel Teitelbaum Greeting Romanian King Carol II in
1936. Public domain, Wikimedia Commons.

The event is well known and celebrated in Satmar lore. Reverential
biographies of Teitelbaum spare no detail in recounting it. They report
that he was asked by the organizers to stand in the row of dignitaries
that included the head of the Status Quo community as well as representatives of the Greek Orthodox and Catholic churches. When the
king approached, we hear, the two men's eyes locked, and Teitelbaum
uttered the Hebrew benediction upon seeing a gentile head of state. The
king then proceeded past the two Christian clergymen and, according
to a contemporaneous account, "shook his hand warmly and for a

prolonged time." The account continues that "the honored guests and the assembled masses were astonished and looked on with bated breath at the shaking of hands of the king and the holy Rabbi. They saw it as an expression of kingly grace, on one hand, and civic loyalty, on the other."[65]

This hagiographic account exemplified a key feature of the Satmars' emerging political culture: their accommodation to gentile power. Throughout their history, Satmar Hasidim laid claim to a time-honored Jewish tradition extending back to third-century Babylonia, the principle of *dina di-malkhuta dina*, which held that Jews should accept the law of gentile kingdoms while living in Exile. Joel Teitelbaum's bow to King Carol II offered graphic evidence of his acceptance of the ancient doctrine. It also undergirded his belief in the benefit of allying with government power in order to promote the community. It was this belief that Teitelbaum carried with him as Europe entered into the darkest of historical epochs.

The "Return" to Hungary and the Collapse of the Satmar World

In 1936, the same year that he met the king, Teitelbaum suffered a painful loss. His wife of thirty-two years, Hava, died after a long illness, made all the more bitter by the fact that two of the couple's daughters predeceased her (Esther in 1921 and Rachel in 1931). Teitelbaum remarried quickly—in August 1937.[66] His second wife, Faiga, was half Teitelbaum's age, a twenty-five-year-old who came from a renowned Hasidic family in Poland, where the wedding was held. She was a formidable, worldly, and self-assured person, who jealously guarded the authority of her husband and voiced her opinion on a wide variety of personal and institutional matters. After her wedding, she took over management of the household from Joel Teitelbaum's surviving daughter, Roysele, who had stepped in after her mother's death, resulting in tensions between stepmother and stepdaughter that would last for decades and even figure in the succession controversy after Joel Teitelbaum's death in 1979.

The first years after her marriage to Joel Teitelbaum proved to be profoundly trying ones for their community. The outbreak of the

Second World War on September 1, 1939, sent shock waves through every Jewish community in Europe. The sense of imminent danger to Unterland Jews was felt less than a year later. In late August 1940, the region in which Satu Mare was located, known then as Northern Transylvania, was returned to Hungary as part of the Vienna Award that Germany and Italy imposed on smaller East-Central European states. The fact that Jews from this region continued to identify with Hungary and Hungarian culture twenty years after the Treaty of Trianon did not guarantee a happy reunion. Since the late 1930s, the Hungarian government led by Admiral Miklós Horthy had grown closer to Germany, in which it saw the greatest prospect for advancing its own goals of territorial restoration. Consistent with the terms of that relationship, and riding a wave of antisemitic nationalism, the government introduced a series of discriminatory laws in 1938 and 1939 designed to minimize Jewish involvement in Hungarian economic, cultural, and public life.

As of 1940, the Jewish community of Satu Mare, along with those of Carei, Sighet, Cluj (Klausenberg), and Oradea (Großwardein), was again formally part of Hungary, but under far more hostile circumstances than previously. Facing intense discrimination themselves, Jews of Hungarian origin still fared better than foreign-born Jews, especially those who found refuge in Hungary after the Germans commenced their territorial conquests in 1938. In 1941, with the announcement of a third racial law, Hungary began deporting tens of thousands of foreign Jews. Some eighteen thousand Jews were deported in August to Ukraine, where they and thousands of local Jews—nearly twenty-four thousand in total—were massacred in a matter of days in what became a terrifying adumbration of the Final Solution.[67]

The rapidly altered circumstances of Jewish life in this period posed a major dilemma for Joel Teitelbaum. Would he dare join forces with those whom he considered less than scrupulous in their observance in order to ameliorate the dire condition of Jews at large? The events of the day exposed a deep tension between his belief in acquiescence, both to God and to the sovereign government, and his combative, activist impulse to struggle against evil and impurity in the world.[68]

That tension between quietism and activism assumed outsized significance during the Holocaust, which was one of the most controversial chapters in Joel Teitelbaum's controversial life. Among his followers, his survival was regarded as nothing short of a miracle. To this day, the day of his liberation from Bergen-Belsen, the twenty-first day of the Hebrew month of Kislev, is occasion for huge celebration within the Satmar world.

And yet the story is complicated, on both theological and historical levels. In theological terms, the Holocaust—the great rupture in the fabric of European Jewish life—was cast as a continuation, albeit at a dramatically escalating pace, of the demonic forces that had run amok in the modern age. As Teitelbaum expounded in his theological treatise, *Va-yo'el Mosheh*, God instructed the angel Samael to put before the Jews a test of their faith in the form of Zionism. Should they succumb to its allures, they would be surrendering their adherence to the sacred oaths that they had pledged to God, particularly the one forbidding a return to the Holy Land in advance of the Messiah. By violating this oath, Teitelbaum argued, Jews incurred the full force not only of Hitler's wrath, but far more ominously, of divine judgment; the result was the explosion of evil forces that generated the Holocaust.[69]

The stunning causal link posited by Teitelbaum between Zionism and the Holocaust was anchored in his quietistic view that only God could commence the return of Jews to their homeland.[70] At the same time, it was rooted in a decidedly aggressive attack on Zionism. These two elements together forged a distinctive theological politics, borne of the perpetual state of crisis that Teitelbaum regarded as the condition of modern Jewish life. And in between these seemingly irreconcilable poles was a certain pragmatism that allowed Teitelbaum to join forces with longtime enemies. One example was Teitelbaum's letter in the early 1940s to Rabbi Chaim Yisrael Eis of Switzerland, a member of Agudat Yisrael, who was actively involved in efforts to rescue Jews in danger. Notwithstanding his long-held disdain for the Aguda, Teitelbaum turned to Eis with the request to mobilize Jews "in every place where they sit in peace" to act on behalf of their brethren. Teitelbaum himself made secretive overnight trips to Budapest in this period to participate in efforts to save Polish Jews.[71]

These missions came to an end on March 19, 1944, when the Germans decided to retract the limited autonomy afforded Hungary since 1940 and occupied the country. The strange netherworld in which Hungarian Jews had dwelt up to this point—managing to eke out a semblance of normality while the rest of Europe was aflame—collapsed. The arrival of the Nazis in 1944 signaled a rapid shift to mass murder. Jews outside of Budapest were rounded up into ghettos and in April began to be deported to Auschwitz. In a mere two months, Hungarian gendarmerie and German SS officers dispatched more than 425,000 Jews to the death camp.

On May 3, 1944, a ghetto was established in Szatmár. Joel Teitelbaum and his wife were spirited out of the city the night before, under the cover of darkness in a Red Cross vehicle driven by some willing Hungarian soldiers. They made their way to the Romanian city of Klausenberg (Cluj) when the driver lost his way and asked the passengers for directions. In a state of panic-stricken bewilderment, they were unable to offer any guidance, and as the sun began to rise the driver ordered them out of the vehicle. Joel Teitelbaum, his wife, and a few remaining passengers were left to their own devices, walking from home to home in search of a sympathetic presence to take them in. Within a matter of hours, they were arrested and jailed. A few days later, on the eve of the Sabbath, Teitelbaum and his wife were sent to the Klausenberg ghetto just outside the city.[72] There they remained for five weeks under difficult conditions. One of Teitelbaum's close advisors and biographers wrote of this period in almost Christological terms: "The travails and sufferings of our Rabbi were much greater than the pain and travails of the rest of the inhabitants of the camp, for our Rabbi suffered not only in body, but also, indeed mainly, in spirit."[73]

What followed thereafter has become the source of considerable controversy at many different levels. During this dire period of deportations, a Hungarian Zionist official by the name of Rudolf Kasztner entered into negotiations with Adolf Eichmann, the notorious SS official responsible for the "Jewish Question," with the aim of winning the freedom of as many European Jews as possible in exchange for cash, gold, and other precious items. Initially, the plan was to exchange ten thousand trucks for a cessation of the deportation of Jews, but that deal never came to pass. The key question that has been raised and debated—in print and film for decades—is whether Kasztner was a noble and courageous defender of his people or an opportunist who befriended a Nazi enemy for his own gain.[74] So inflamed were those who believed the latter that Kasztner was assassinated by a fellow Jew in Israel, his transplanted home, in 1957.

Joel Teitelbaum was, on the face of it, a sworn enemy of Kasztner, the committed Zionist. And yet he was included among the four hundred Jews who were brought from the Klausenberg ghetto to Budapest in June 1944 as part of a larger group designated for passage to freedom on a special rescue train Kasztner arranged with Eichmann. Legend has it that Teitelbaum, the arch-anti-Zionist, was included because Kasztner's father-in-law, a lawyer and community official named József Fischer, had a dream in which his late mother instructed him to ensure the safety of the rabbi.[75] In fact, it was a fellow member of the Jewish council (*Judenrat*) of Klausenberg-Cluj, Dr. Theodor Fischer, who persuaded József Fischer, who headed the council, to insist that Kasztner include Joel Teitelbaum in the transport.[76] As a general matter, Kasztner tended to include relatives, fellow townsmen, Zionists, and wealthy Jews, though not typically prominent anti-Zionists. Teitelbaum and his immediate entourage were exceptions to the rule. They were included not only or principally due to his prominence, but rather owing to the financial incentives offered to Kasztner by a wealthy Budapest Jew, Chaim Gross.[77] One can hardly avoid the irony that it was the intervention of a Zionist official that saved his life. Teitelbaum, for his part, insisted, in the midst of the legal entanglements in which Kasztner found himself in Israel in the 1950s, that it was not Kasztner but rather God who rescued him.

The "Kasztner transport," as it was known, left Budapest on June 30, 1944, with 1,675 passengers, including Joel Teitelbaum. Although Eichmann originally claimed that the train would head to a neutral country, he decided to divert it to the Bergen-Belsen concentration camp on

July 8. Upon arrival, the passengers were cast in a state of deep fear and uncertainty, not knowing whether they would be liberated, left to die in Bergen-Belsen, or deported eastward to a death camp. While there, Joel Teitelbaum held firm to his regimen of ritual stringency. He adhered to the rules of kashrut (fasting several days a week per his custom), prayed regularly, and refused to shave his beard and earlocks, in violation of Nazi directives. This unyielding commitment to tradition left an impression on his fellow camp mates, one of whom recalled that "in the filthy barracks the Rebbe remained as pure as crystal. The terrible filth had no hold over the Rebbe."[78]

Liberation from captivity came in two parts for the fortunate members of the Kasztner transport. A smaller group of 318 was freed on August 21, after which an additional round of negotiations was conducted up to the end of November involving Kasztner, SS officer Kurt Becher, and a representative of the Joint Distribution Committee from Switzerland, Saly Mayer. Three and a half months later, in early December, a second group of more than 1,350 Jews, including Joel Teitelbaum, was released, making its way from Bergen-Belsen to the Swiss border. Before transferring to Swiss trains, the passengers had to wait out another several hours of harrowing negotiations before finally crossing the border and gaining freedom. The day on which the second group arrived at the Swiss border, December 7—the twenty-first day of the Hebrew month of Kislev—is, as noted, one of the most celebrated days on the Satmar ritual calendar.

Joel Teitelbaum's devoted biographers go to great lengths to herald his efforts to rescue Jews in Hungary.[79] The resulting portrayal stands in sharp contrast to the image of a charismatic religious leader who was saved by virtue of his own renown, but left behind his followers in a time of grave crisis. Indeed, there are those who still recall being told by Rabbi Teitelbaum to remain in Europe into the 1940s rather than seek refuge in Palestine.[80] So great was the sin of abetting the Zionist enemy, they recall being instructed, that it was better to remain in Europe in the hope of divine salvation.

Teitelbaum did indeed hold on to his view of the demonic nature of Zionism even after the full weight of destruction of the Holocaust was known. He declared in *Va-yo'el Mosheh* that if one were to measure all the transgressions of the world on one side of the scale against the Zionist state on the other, the latter would tip the balance. At the outset of the book, he wrote that "one need not search and seek out in hidden places the evil that brought upon us the great travail [i.e., the Holocaust]. . . . The [Zionist] heretics and transgressors made all sorts of efforts to violate the Oaths—to ascend the wall and take for themselves a government and liberation before their time, which is to say, to hasten the end."[81] As a result of this sin, the gentile nations were released from their obligation (in the third Oath) not to subjugate the Jews excessively, thereby enabling the genocidal assault of Nazism.

In considering this position, two ironies should be noted. First, Teitelbaum's major writings, including his anti-Zionist works, were authored in Hebrew, the language of the Zionist movement. For most observers, it is virtually impossible to dissociate Hebrew from the Zionist project of national cultural revival. Of course, it is also the case that Hebrew was the language of rabbinic discourse over the centuries—indeed, the primary medium through which Jewish legal discussions were conducted. Teitelbaum's attitude toward Hebrew is quite striking. Whereas rabbinic Hebrew was perfectly acceptable to write in, the modern form spoken and taught by Zionists was, according to him, "an impure language."[82]

And in a second irony, Teitelbaum warned repeatedly against "ascending the wall" of the Holy Land through Jewish immigration. But he himself, upon gaining freedom in Switzerland, sought to move to Palestine. While colleagues and admirers were trying to arrange a visa for him to come to the United States, Teitelbaum was attempting to secure a highly valued British certificate of immigration to Palestine. Zionist officials were not enthralled with the idea of granting one of the precious certificates given them by the British to an avowed anti-Zionist. British authorities overcame the obstacle, however, by granting seven hundred certificates directly to Jewish refugees in Switzerland, including Joel Teitelbaum. On August 19, 1945, after nine months in Switzerland, he boarded a ship for Palestine.

These ironies remind us that for all of his unyielding principle, there was in Joel Teitelbaum a willingness not only to confront but also to accommodate. This willingness was a trait forged in the fractious culture of Hungarian Unterland Jewry, but which Joel Teitelbaum brought with him to America, where he arrived on the second day of Rosh Ha-Shanah 1946. It was a quality that he and his followers in America would develop to rather striking effect, using it to revive their decimated community into what would become the largest Hasidic group in the world.

CHAPTER 3

Satmar in America

FROM SHTETL TO VILLAGE

The path to the creation of a Satmar shtetl in America was not a direct one. It took almost thirty years for Rabbi Joel Teitelbaum and his followers to break ground on the community that would become Kiryas Joel.

The Satmar village was a decidedly new entity. In Europe, Jews had never formed their own legally recognized entities populated exclusively (or even predominantly) by Jews, let alone one populated exclusively by followers of one Hasidic rebbe.[1] Nor had they agitated so audaciously for land and other public benefits and utilities—water, electricity, housing, education, and welfare relief. But in the United States, the Satmars, along with other Haredi groups, developed a higher degree of political sophistication, effectiveness, and boldness in promoting their interests than Jews demonstrated in Europe—in large part because the United States afforded them that opportunity. The culture to which they adapted in America presented them with unprecedented opportunities and a new set of tools for advancing their interests. Through the use of skilled intercessors, bloc voting, well-crafted political alliances, economic capital, and mastery of the American legal system, they were able to achieve many of their communal goals, including a degree of group insularity unimaginable in Europe.

This is a central theme in the story of this book: the success of Satmar Hasidim in securing a separatist enclave was paradoxically accomplished through accommodation to the outside world. More specifically, it entailed becoming American and absorbing American values and practices into their own political culture.

This chapter describes the paradoxical process of assimilation through separation (and vice versa), which commenced with the arrival of Rabbi Joel Teitelbaum in New York just after the Second World War. At the very moment when American Jews whose forebears had landed in America in an earlier generation were heading to the suburbs in large numbers, Rabbi Teitelbaum chose to settle with his followers in New York City. It was there that the Satmar community gathered itself anew.

And yet the suburbs beckoned to Rabbi Teitelbaum, who sought many of the same benefits for his community that other Americans did: affordable and ample housing, clean air, and less traffic and congestion than in the city. The impulse to move from a crowded urban center to more spacious suburban surroundings was a classic American white middle-class step.

But in this regard, the Satmar Hasidim appear to be outliers. Unlike other American Jews, they didn't aspire to enter the American middle-class mainstream. Nor did they share the quest of other American Jews to pass as white gentiles in the fashion of Philip Roth's eponymous antihero in "Eli the Fanatic."[2] Rather, what they aimed to do was to hold on to their distinctive garb and customs within a homogeneous enclave in which everyone would be a strict adherent of Orthodox Judaism.[3]

And yet, the typical American suburb, populated by upwardly mobile descendants of immigrants, and the Satmar suburb whose raison d'être was to resist assimilation and economic mobility are less different than they appear. For the establishment of culturally—and racially—monolithic residential concentrations in the suburbs is more the rule than the exception in the United States. It is not only religious groups such as the Amish or the Mormons that have been intent on realizing a strong form of communitarianism. The creation of private enclaves embedded in local governments that are responsive to their interests (and are largely indifferent, if not hostile, to outsiders) is a much broader American phenomenon. As has been well documented, the post–World War II American move to the suburbs has generally been characterized by socioeconomic, cultural, and racial conformity. Scholars have called attention to the role of federal policies and local government law in promoting segregation.[4] The role of local government, in particular, has long been understood. For example, in their 1993 book *American Apartheid*, Douglas Massey and Nancy Denton offered convincing evidence that typical patterns of racial segregation found in cities were replicated in suburbs in the seventies and eighties. Whites moved to the suburbs to live among other whites, whereas "black entry into suburbs did not bring integration."[5]

The Satmars occupied an intermediate space on the racial spectrum between white and Black with regard to exclusionary zoning and other local government practices that fostered residential segregation. By virtue of their perceived whiteness and, equally importantly, their access to capital, they had more latitude and mobility to move than did African Americans. Nonetheless, the prospect of their arrival in suburbs evoked trepidation on the part of largely white and proto-NIMBY communities which repeatedly sought to thwart the Satmars' efforts to buy property in their backyard. Undeterred, the Satmars kept searching for a suitable site in the suburbs where they could live and grow, while preserving the homogeneity of the community they first built in the United States in the Brooklyn neighborhood of Williamsburg. This was a process of years, decades even, in the making.

From Satu Mare to Williamsburg

When Joel Teitelbaum arrived at the Port of New York on September 27, 1946, he could not have imagined the extraordinary success he would have in this country.[6] After all, he was still recovering from the collapse of his world. The Jewish community of Satu Mare and its environs was largely wiped out; eighteen thousand of its members were deported to Auschwitz with terrifying speed in the last twelve days of May 1944. Teitelbaum made his way from Bergen-Belsen to Switzerland at the end of 1944 and then on to Palestine, together with his wife and a number of followers.[7] As he had in Switzerland, Teitelbaum spent long hours in prayer and study. At the same time, he began to get involved in the political intrigues of the 'Edah Haredit, Jerusalem's staunchly anti-Zionist religious community. Along with his wife Faiga, he also devoted a good deal of attention to the cause of war orphans, whose physical and spiritual well-being he sought to ensure. He established the Yetev Lev yeshivah, named in memory of his grandfather, which provided poor and orphaned Jewish boys with basic material needs as well as a place to study Torah.[8]

One of the declared reasons that Rabbi Teitelbaum came to the United States in 1946 was to find supporters for the school, which faced constant financial difficulties.[9] His followers in America had other plans. Various groups of Orthodox Jews, with Hungarians prominent among them, had been raising money with an eye toward luring Teitelbaum to settle in America, even before his liberation from Bergen-Belsen. His arrival was cause for great joy among his admirers, even though his reception was somewhat delayed. His ship docked in New York on the second day of Rosh Ha-Shanah, and he did not alight until the end of the holiday that evening.[10]

After a few weeks in Manhattan, Teitelbaum moved to the Williamsburg section of Brooklyn, where he stayed at the home of a follower, Mordechai Fleischman, until Passover 1947. Fleischman lived on Rodney Avenue, which, along with Lee Avenue, became the main thoroughfare of Satmar Williamsburg. In this first year, Joel Teitelbaum still spoke of his stay in America as temporary; he declared his intention to return to Palestine to continue his work there.

Especially instrumental in convincing him to stay in the United States was Rabbi Michael Ber Weissmandl (1903–1957), a Slovakian-born rabbi who gained renown for his attempts to rescue Jews during the Nazi assault even as he himself was at great risk. Weissmandl, who survived the war and resettled in the United States, founded his own yeshivah known as Nitra (after the Slovakian town where he studied). Joel Teitelbaum spent a number of months with Rabbi Weissmandl in the summer of 1947 at the yeshivah's first home in Somerville, New Jersey; there, according to the legend, Weissmandl took Teitelbaum's passport and ripped it up to prevent his return to Palestine.[11]

Weissmandl's decision to establish a yeshivah in the suburbs may have set Joel Teitelbaum's mind in motion because shortly thereafter Teitelbaum began his pursuit of a suitable venue outside of the city for his own community. But in deciding to stay in the United States, he also made a serious commitment to building a major Satmar presence in Williamsburg.

Located just off the bridge that bears its name, Williamsburg is a bustling neighborhood in Brooklyn that has undergone a number of transformations in its history. Williamsburg assumed its name in the early nineteenth century after the district's surveyor, Jonathan Williams. It became an incorporated city in 1851 before merging with Brooklyn four years later. At that point, Williamsburg was home to wealthy New Yorkers, including German Jews, who lived on tree-lined streets in the neighborhood, especially on Bedford Avenue. In the wake of the First World War, by which time Brooklyn was integrated into New York City as a borough, Williamsburg attracted a new group of residents: Eastern European Jewish immigrants who established traditional synagogues, clubs, and schools. One of the new additions was the Torah Vodaath yeshivah founded in 1922 by Rabbi Zev Gold. At that point, "Williamsburg became really Jewish," as one longtime resident observed, noting the increasing presence of men with beards and earlocks on the streets.[12]

This is to say that Williamsburg had a Jewish, and specifically Orthodox, population already by the time of its next major transformation—the period marked by the arrival of refugees from Europe during and after the Second World War. Curiously, on the eve of this new demographic wave, experts on New York predicted the decline of Williamsburg as a desired place of settlement for white ethnic groups. The long-established Jewish community, in particular, was moving away and assimilating into the American cultural mainstream. But Williamsburg, Jewish Williamsburg in particular, was altogether remade by new immigrants—first hundreds of German, Austrian, and Czech Jews from 1939 to 1942 and then thousands of Hungarians from 1944 on. It was the latter group that left the deepest imprint on Williamsburg, prompting one older Eastern European immigrant to label the neighborhood

"Hunksville," after a common derogatory term used in America for Hungarians ("Hunkies").[13]

As part of this Hungarian emigration, Joel Teitelbaum came to Williamsburg and did what he had done in every community in Europe that he served; he introduced new norms of stringency in education, dietary regulations, dress habits, ritual purity, and interaction between Jews and non-Jews. If the terrain of early twentieth-century Europe posed serious challenges to the purity of Torah observance, America appeared at first to present an even bigger challenge. The reputation of the United States as a *treyfe medine*—an unkosher and impure country—was deeply rooted in the minds of the postwar immigrants, who recalled the unsuccessful efforts of the European-born Rabbi Jacob Joseph to establish a unified Orthodox presence in New York at the turn of the century. The fact that synagogue affiliation was still high and new houses of worship were being built at a rapid clip in suburban America in this period was of no moment to Rabbi Teitelbaum. His main concern, as he made clear to his followers in his early years in Williamsburg, was not the majority of American Jews scattered across different denominations but rather the small circles of Haredim in the country, many of whom had barely survived the war. In characteristically grave language, Rabbi Teitelbaum described the new crisis he encountered in the United States: "If a house is on fire, you try to salvage as much as possible, even if partially damaged. But if the flames are threatening to engulf the neighboring houses, it is foolish to spend time saving charred items. . . . In our generation, the fire of assimilation has taken hold of many Jewish homes. We must devote our energies to saving those homes that have not yet been damaged."[14]

In early June 1948, Teitelbaum convened a group of men at the Satmar study hall on 500 Bedford Avenue with the goal of creating a formal congregation to be known as Yetev Lev, named after his grandfather. Consistent with his traditionalist view of modesty, he insisted on gender segregation, inviting only men to be members of the congregation. In this first phase of Satmar in America, some seventy men agreed to join as founding members by paying an annual fee of ten dollars.[15] In the bylaws that were adopted four years later, it was stated that "the most revered teacher, Rabbi Yoel Teitelbaum, may he live long and be well, is our local rabbi, may it be for many years to come. Nobody can perform his functions without his consent. *He is the only authority in all spiritual matters.*" This formulation would become the source of considerable controversy a half century later in the litigation between the two competing sides in the Satmar world.[16]

During his lifetime, the Rebbe's authority was absolute in the Satmar world. He was the shepherd to a tattered flock whom he was trying to lead to safety. His close associate, Sender Deutsch, wrote an insider biography that described Teitelbaum's message to his followers: "It is forbidden to learn the ways of the land. We should be separate and segregated from the transgressors. And he also taught us the laws of impurity and purity. The Rebbe taught us to guard against the impurity of Zionism, to separate ourselves from these transgressors, from the fathers of impurity and all of their offspring."[17] Indeed, the principle of segregation from others—Jews and non-Jews, but most especially from Zionists—was an oft-declared ideal of the newly constituted community in Williamsburg. It was planted in the minds of young Satmar children through the educational system that Teitelbaum devoted much energy to building. In fact, the Satmars' most urgent institutional task in the early years was to create a school system to inculcate the group's values. In the spring of 1949, the Torah V'Yirah yeshivah, also known by the English name United Talmudic Academy, was founded with seven students. A year later, the decision was taken to proceed with building a primary and secondary school system, according to Rabbi Teitelbaum's animating vision: "We must establish schools and yeshivahs like those bequeathed to us by our forefathers according to their distinctive path, when they created yeshivahs to uphold and observe the commandments without any compromises or changes G-d forbid."[18]

With the United Talmudic Academy as the anchor of the nascent Satmar community in Brooklyn, Teitelbaum turned his attention to other aspects of Jewish life in Williamsburg. He encouraged his followers to build a school for girls so that they would be instructed in the practices of the Satmar community. In 1951, the Bais Ruchel school, named after his late daughter, took rise, developing over time into a network of schools for thousands of girls in Williamsburg, Kiryas Joel, and other Satmar communities around the world.[19]

At least as important to him as girls' education was the "purity" of women after menstruation, which explains why the creation of a mikveh, or ritual bath, was part of the early planning of Satmar leaders in Williamsburg. Indeed, women's purity, regulated by the Talmudic tractate Niddah, has been an important concern of rabbinic Judaism for centuries and was a matter of fastidious attention for Rabbi Teitelbaum and the male-dominated Satmar world. The creation of a Satmar mikveh in Williamsburg in the early 1950s was perhaps the most concrete expression of his search for an island in a sea of impurity.

The same do-it-yourself instinct guided his concerns about kosher food. He placed a great deal of importance on the establishment of a Satmar bakery to produce *matsah*, the unleavened bread consumed by Jews on the holiday of Passover. He also called for the establishment of a Satmar-owned store to sell kosher meat. As he had in Europe, he insisted on the strictest supervision over food production. But his role in the United States was different from the role of a rabbi in the old country. He was not the officially recognized chief rabbi of the Jewish community but rather one among many rabbis operating in a private, unofficial capacity.

Teitelbaum called upon two of his most trusted lay advisors, Joel Klein and Lipa Friedman, to oversee the bakery and butchery, respectively.[20] The two European-born men served, in succession, as president of the Yetev Lev community. One of the keys to the success of Satmar in expanding its empire was its lay leadership, which drew on the tradition of political engagement from prewar Hungary. Friedman was tasked with developing bylaws for the congregation, which was officially incorporated under New York's nonprofit religious corporation law.

Satmar's lay leadership consisted of men, typically ones with rabbinic ordination, who engaged in the outside world as businessmen and who maintained channels of communication with local political officials and fellow businessmen. It was these leaders who invested their own funds, cajoled others, and sought public support for the growth of the Satmar community. Many were quite successful in their business endeavors, which tended to focus on import-export, factory production, and real estate. It was they who raised money for the fledgling institutions in the early 1950s and forged relations with politicians in New York City, Albany, and Washington who could provide assistance in matters deemed essential to the community such as housing. And it was they who helped transform Williamsburg into a dense center of Satmar Hasidim.[21]

This was not an overnight process. One can trace the transformation of Jewish Williamsburg through the pages of the Yiddish newspaper *Der Yid* (The Jew). In describing the early history of the newspaper, its editor, Sender Deutsch (the Rebbe's advisor and biographer), maintained that the chief reason for the lowly spiritual state of the Jewish community in Brooklyn in the postwar era was the presence of four "unkosher" Yiddish newspapers (the *Morgan Zhurnal*, *Der Tog*, the *Forverts*, and the *Frayheyt*).[22] These papers had been the chief outlet for secular forms of expression, from modernist poetry to left-wing politics and the famous advice columns that guided generations of Jewish immigrants bent on assimilating into American society. By the early 1950s, the audience for these Yiddish papers had shrunk precipitously. It was in these years that an observant writer for the *Morgan Zhurnal*, Dr. Aaron Rosmarin, decided to establish his own weekly newspaper for the Orthodox population of the New York area called *Der Yid*. It included articles of a varied nature: Torah commentaries, reverential accounts of past sages, and news about prominent rabbis and leading developments in the present. It also contained frequent advertisements for trips to Israel, including from the Israeli national shipping company Zim.

The tenor changed in February 1956, when Aaron Rosmarin stepped down as editor of *Der Yid*. The paper was purchased by a group of Satmar Hasidim under the guidance of Joel Teitelbaum. Uriel Zimmer was initially appointed editor to replace Dr. Rosmarin, who was soon succeeded by Sender Deutsch. The paper now began to promote a more uniformly Haredi editorial line. Striking a combative tone, the lead article of the new regime took aim at "those who destroy religion."[23] From that point forward, the paper abounded with articles focusing on the dangers posed by the state of Israel, such as one on March 2 under the headline "Zionist Propaganda Places Education in Europe in Danger."

The anti-Zionist line revealed the influence of Joel Teitelbaum, who declared that he wanted a newspaper "because I have no other outlet to spread the Torah view on the Zionist state."[24]

As the combative Satmar style began to assert itself in the Yiddish newspaper, the complexion of Williamsburg became more Hasidic, particularly Satmar.[25] One important factor that reshaped the neighborhood in the 1950s was the highly disruptive and unpopular construction of the Brooklyn-Queens Expressway (BQE) that began in the late 1930s. For more than two decades and culminating in 1957, pieces of the BQE were added under the watchful eye of New York City's omnipotent master planner Robert Moses. In his definitive biography of Moses, historian Robert Caro remarks that "in a city such construction requires the eviction of people from their homes," and the BQE project was no different. Whole streets were taken over for the project, and high rents drove out previous tenants of Williamsburg, including Irish, Italian, Slavic, and some Orthodox Jewish residents. Moses himself averred, in his brusque and commanding style, that "when you operate in an overbuilt metropolis, you have to hack your way with a meat ax."[26] The major project that he imagined as a connector between Brooklyn and Queens engendered deep resentment among the Satmars of Williamsburg since it cut through the heart of their neighborhood. But rather than leaving, they stayed by the side of their rabbi. And they stayed by the side of their rabbi when large numbers of Puerto Ricans and African Americans moved into Williamsburg, including close to the Rodney-Lee intersection, the center of Satmar Hasidic life. From that point until the present, Satmar Hasidim, Puerto Ricans, and African Americans have competed for precious affordable housing stock, especially in the large public projects such as Bedford Gardens and Roberto Clemente.

Religious Communities in Search of Autonomy

Even as the Satmar community in Williamsburg grew by leaps and bounds in the 1950s, Joel Teitelbaum determined that it would be necessary to seek a space outside of New York City to create a safe enclave where the Satmars could pursue their way of life, free from the intrusions of outsiders. He had several models on which to draw. The Lithuanian sage Rabbi Aharon Kotler (1891–1962), founder of the renowned Lakewood, New Jersey, yeshivah, came as a refugee from war-torn Europe to the United States in 1941 and almost immediately set out to re-create the religious world he left behind. He emanated from a different religious tradition from Joel Teitelbaum's—the non-Hasidic rabbinic culture of Lithuania. And yet he and Teitelbaum were friendly and held each other in high esteem.

The Lakewood community formed by Rabbi Kotler marked out the approach of settling in an existing locale and carving out an oasis of Torah within it. Kotler established the Beth Medrash Govoha in Lakewood in 1943 with an original cohort of fourteen students. It grew dramatically over the decades and is today one of the world's largest and most prestigious yeshivahs, with more than six thousand students. Its faculty and students, along with the many religious institutions and commercial establishments that serve them, have fundamentally altered the character of Lakewood, transforming the onetime winter resort town into a city of nearly a hundred thousand, half or more of whose population is Orthodox.

A second model for Joel Teitelbaum was that of a fellow Hasidic rebbe who led a small group of followers to a rural area in Rockland County, about thirty miles from New York City, in 1954. The rebbe who led this expedition of Hasidic Jews to the suburbs was Yaakov Yosef Twersky, known as the Skverer Rebbe after the town of Skvira in Ukraine. Rabbi Twersky was a descendant of the Chernobyl Hasidic dynasty who had survived the war in Romania before making his way to Brooklyn. Once in America, he was confronted by the same challenges that Rabbi Teitelbaum faced, especially the challenge of living in the midst of strangers. Consumed by the fear that corrupting cultural forces would encircle his followers, Rabbi Twersky sought out a rural area where he could lead and guard over his flock.

Like Leo Tzuref in "Eli the Fanatic," Rabbi Twersky and his followers expected simply to be left alone in their new rural environs. That did not happen. Having settled within the bounds of the town of Ramapo in

Rockland County, they were subject to its laws, and especially its zoning regulations. The new Haredi residents of Ramapo unnerved their neighbors by making use of edifices in ways that violated local zoning ordinances. They built dwellings in which more than one family lived, defying the suburban predilection for low-density housing. And in direct contravention of the classic suburban blueprint that segregated residential from commercial uses, they placed synagogues, bakeries, and other commercial establishments in the basements of private homes. Town officials in Ramapo did not hesitate to cite the Skverer Hasidim for these violations, prompting Rabbi Twersky and his followers eventually to seek authority from New York State courts to incorporate as an independent village. In July 1961, the courts approved the plan, and New Square, New York, a clever anglicization of Skvira, was born as an autonomous municipality comprising 530 Hasidic Jews.[27]

New Square was the prototype of a self-conscious, homogenous, and legally incorporated shtetl on American soil. It bears many of the features of Kiryas Joel, but on a significantly smaller scale, with one-third the number of residents (8,500 vs. 25,000).[28] As in KJ, the population of New Square is extremely young (60 percent below the age of eighteen), speaks a language at home other than English (i.e., Yiddish) in overwhelming numbers (95.5 percent), has low rates of college attendance (4.0 percent have completed a bachelor's degree), and is very poor (with a median household income of $23,000, and more than 63 percent of the community below the poverty line).[29]

Over time, more and more traditionalist Orthodox communities followed this example and chose to settle within an hour's radius of New York City, principally in three nearby counties: Rockland, Westchester, and Orange. The hamlet of Monsey within the town of Ramapo in Rockland County was a particularly popular destination. With the arrival of large numbers of Orthodox and Haredi Jews beginning in the 1970s, Monsey was transformed from a community with a small Jewish presence to a major concentration of Orthodox families. A report in the *New York Times* from 1997 estimated that there were at the time 112 synagogues and 45 yeshivahs in Monsey's 2.2 square miles. As in New Square, tensions between new arrivals to the area and local officials frequently arose over zoning disputes, prompting one group of Hasidim to carve out the new village of Kaser within the town of Ramapo in 1990. As a local Jewish leader wryly observed, reflecting on the boomeranging dynamics of exclusion that have led to more and more incorporation and secession: "There are two reasons villages get formed in Rockland. One is to keep the Hasidim out and the other is to keep the Hasidim in."[30]

Most of the satellite Haredi communities that formed in the suburbs did not end up forming their own separate villages. But they did dwell as more or less isolated pockets within the established boundaries of their towns. In this way, they were an indicator of the postwar pattern of suburbanization that fostered a high degree of residential segregation.

The postwar homogenous suburb as we know it had roots in an earlier federal initiative, originating in the Harding administration (1921–1923), which developed model laws that became the basis of suburban zoning ordinances adopted throughout the country.[31] These zoning laws deliberately sought to exclude the lower classes, especially Black Americans, first through explicit racial restrictions and then, after the Supreme Court ruled racially restrictive zoning to be unconstitutional in 1917, via economically costly building restrictions intended to produce the same effect.[32]

The resulting racial and economic segregation, as we have noted, became one of the defining characteristics of the American suburb.[33] Orthodox Jews who moved into the suburbs may have been largely unaware of the segregationist governmental policies that led to their creation. But they quickly found themselves confronting exclusionary zoning laws, first as victims, when town residents tried to exclude or limit them—and then as beneficiaries, when they learned to control the laws of local government themselves.

Orthodox Jews left the city in search of the same things other suburbanites were looking for—respite from the noise, grime, and congestion. And even though they deviated from the conventional suburbanite profile in terms of income level, educational choices, and residential preferences, they have exhibited a growing comfort with suburban habits and behavior. Not only do Hasidim go to their local malls to shop and socialize, they also have felt enough at home to throw their weight around in local politics, including in the domain of public education. In a number of suburban locales outside of New York, most notably in Ramapo, Orthodox Jews have voted members of their own community onto public education boards that preside over schools in which their children are not students. This has aroused complaints that the Orthodox school board members are interested not in the well-being of the public school district but rather in reducing their own taxes and diverting funds to support their own children's educational needs in private religious schools. In response, Orthodox school board members have argued that they are aiming to ensure that the public school was run efficiently and that private school kids receive all the support from the school district that they deserve.[34]

The recent "takeovers" of suburban school boards are a striking example of the increasing assertiveness that Orthodox suburbanites have demonstrated in the political sphere. In the old country, traditionally observant Jews often aligned themselves with the government, especially with conservative authorities with whom they shared the desire to preserve the status quo. That did not reflect political naïveté on their part. They were savvy guardians of their communal self-interest, who understood the political environment in which they were required to maneuver. They were aided by the *shtadlan*, the community's designated representative for interacting with gentile authorities. The role of the *shtadlan* in Europe was to ingratiate himself *with* the authorities, not to challenge or confront the political authorities to make policy changes, as interest groups in America do.

This points to a key difference between Europe and the United States. The political behavior of American Haredim reveals a far greater degree of independent-mindedness than their prewar ancestors exhibited. If the latter aspired to "a loyal attitude of peace and goodwill to the state," American Haredim have been far more willing to play and manipulate the political game, even if that means challenging established power.[35] They have felt justly entitled to the benefits of citizenship that the American democratic system provides. They have also felt an added, largely unspoken sense of entitlement owing to the enormous losses that they and their relatives suffered in Nazi Europe. There is an unarticulated belief in the Haredi community that, as a measure of earthly and divine compensation, they are entitled to live their religious lives without external hindrance or prejudice.

This sense of entitlement has often been nurtured by the American political system. It is not just that American politicians actively covet the votes of Haredi communities. It is also that the American political game both encourages the pursuit of individual self-interest through the exercise of individual rights *and* facilitates the creation of private associations, which enjoy what are in effect collective rights, exercised in the pursuit of a group's collective self-interest. These rights endow groups with the ability to maintain their separate cultures, live according to their own rules, and exclude people who are not members of their communities.

In this sense, the United States has been more accommodating of the communal aspirations of traditionalist Jews than the European countries from which they came. The system not only has allowed Jews at large to exert a significant role in the political process through the usual mechanisms of interest-group politics but also has granted traditionalist Jews in particular the opportunity to create communities that surpass in homogeneity and size what existed in Europe. For this reason, Haredim often regard the United States in reverential terms, as a *malkhus shel hesed* (a kingdom of grace), even while continuing to see themselves in a state of exile (*goles*).

Satmar Takes to the Suburbs

The vision of creating an enclave that was a sufficient distance from New York City yet close enough to permit a daily commute was born early in Joel Teitelbaum's American career. A rural site could provide refuge from the city, Satmar chronicler Sh. Y. Gelbman noted, "for it would not be touched by the influence of the gentile world and could differentiate and segregate itself from gentile ways." Teitelbaum famously declared that the creation of such an enclave would be the most important measure of his leadership; if he did not succeed in that task, then he would conclude that "I have done nothing [in my life]."[36]

The Rebbe's associates began to inquire into the possibility of building a settlement on Staten Island in 1952. A Satmar representative met with Staten Island borough president Cornelius Hall, who saw the potential of identifying a rich new trove of Democratic voters and offered the Satmars 190 acres of land at a cheap price. It was in that period that the construction of the BQE was beginning to wreak havoc on Williamsburg, and some Satmars thought it advisable to move the community to Borough Park. The Rebbe was more interested in Staten Island, where a higher degree of isolation could be achieved; in fact, at that time, there was no Verrazzano-Narrows Bridge connecting it to Brooklyn.[37] It was precisely that feature—and the fear of being noticed and singled out—that prompted Joel Teitelbaum's aide-de-camp, Lipa Friedman, to oppose the creation of a Satmar enclave on Staten Island. Rabbi Teitelbaum was always surrounded by close advisors—both gabbaim who attended to his religious and personal needs and latter-day shtadlanim, political advisers and intercessors, such as Friedman, who served as head of the Satmar school system and president of the Satmar community from 1948 to 1972. Ever the loyal follower, Friedman dropped his opposition to the creation of a self-standing shtetl when R. Teitelbaum made clear his strong support; Friedman subsequently devoted himself to fulfilling the Rebbe's desire.[38]

For a variety of reasons, Staten Island did not work out as the site of the Satmar enclave, so the search continued. A number of locales in neighboring New Jersey, where the Lakewood yeshivah was established nearly two decades earlier, were investigated in the early 1960s. A break came in 1962, when a group called Satmar Associates, Inc. purchased five hundred acres in Mount Olive Township for $850,000. The funds had been collected at the request of Joel Teitelbaum, but they represented just the beginning of the proposed community. Mount Olive was to be the site of a $20 million investment by the Satmars that would eventually include eight hundred houses, a yeshivah, a shopping center, and an industrial park.[39] This ambitious plan, whose public face was Lipa Friedman, was to be three times the size of the village of Skverer Hasidim in New Square, New York, that had been incorporated in 1961.

But the plans ran into fierce opposition, and in ways that would establish a pattern in the history of Satmar settlement. Facing opposition from local residents, Satmar officials filed a complaint against the township committee of Mount Olive a little over a year after purchasing the land, accusing it of "arbitrary, unreasonable and discriminatory" acts. The complaint alleged that the township refused to allow the Satmar group to file a municipal improvement bond that was required to begin building the infrastructure (sewers, streets, water supply) necessary for the new community. According to the complaint, the motivation behind the denial of the bond was simple: it was "the nature and ancestral characteristics of the persons who were to inhabit the residences" that prompted the township committee to block their path. Simply put, the complaint alleged a case of antisemitism.[40]

This kind of tension would become a defining feature of Satmar—and more broadly, Orthodox Jewish—efforts to move to the suburbs. At times, opposition to their attempts to establish enclaves with homogenous neighborhoods and new zoning norms came from uncomprehending non-Jews. At other times, it was the result of the "Jew vs. Jew" phenomenon.[41] This is what happened in Beachwood, Ohio, in the late 1990s when a group of Orthodox Jews tried to build a number of institutions—synagogues, schools, and ritual baths—and were opposed by the largely Jewish residents and officials of the city. And it happened in Ramapo, which included, we recall, the village of New Square. In response to a new influx of Orthodox residents in the 1980s, local inhabitants, Jews among them, borrowed a page from the Haredi playbook and used state law to create their own self-standing and exclusionary villages. This "village movement" was intended to carve out boundaries in which Haredim would not dwell; the villages of Wesley Hills (1982) and New Hempstead (1983) took rise in this way in the early 1980s.

The process of carving out exclusive enclaves from the town of Ramapo continued in the early 1990s. It was then that a group of Vizhnitz Hasidim founded the village of Kaser in 1990, which prompted a group of non-Orthodox Jews to join with non-Jews to agitate for the establishment of the village of Airmont a year later. Both sets of Ramapo residents followed the same script—one seeking to safeguard its particularistic way of life, and the other to prevent the alteration of their more conventional suburban way of life. In commenting on the latter impulse, Herbert Reisman, a town supervisor in Ramapo who was himself Jewish, stated unmistakably: "The motivation of some people is that they do not want the ultra-Orthodox or the Hasidim to move in."[42] Toward that end, the new village of Airmont quickly passed zoning regulations forbidding the creation of boarding schools in its midst.

This, in turn, led to a suit by the federal government and a number of individual plaintiffs against Airmont alleging that the village discriminated against prospective residents on the basis of their religion. The jury in the trial held that the village had in fact violated the plaintiffs' free exercise of religion, as well as the Fair Housing Act. But their judgment was thrown out in 1993 by U.S. district judge Gerhard Goettel, who declared, with astonishing candor, that if there was hostility against Orthodox Jews in the village, "it is largely the result of the lawsuits brought against it by the various plaintiffs and the extensive publicity plaintiffs have intentionally generated." Judge Goettel's decision was itself struck down by the U.S. Court of Appeals for the Second Circuit, which reinstated the original jury verdict and maintained that the village was created illegally in order to exclude those whom it deemed undesirable.[43]

What was at stake in Airmont was not only a clash between two competing groups of Jews, Orthodox and non-Orthodox. It was also a clash between two different conceptions of Jewish Americanness, as painfully portrayed in Roth's "Eli the Fanatic": on one hand, the ideal of cultural integration into the mainstream and, on the other, the ideal of preserving discrete cultural strands as part of a pluralistic American mosaic. From the standpoint of the integrationists, the Haredim were exclusionary. But from the perspective of the Haredim, it was the integrationists themselves who were exclusionary, seeking to prevent the entry of outsiders into their enclaves and insisting that they conform their land-use practices to the exclusionary zoning norms of the American suburb. Like other religious and spiritual communities that had the temerity to upset the peace of "typical" American suburban communities and challenge their cultural norms, Haredim were at once the excluded other and the excluding other.

This paradox of exclusion, born of the tension between the competing ideals of cultural assimilation and integration, on the one hand, and cultural preservation and separation, on the other, would express itself in Kiryas Joel in waves of litigation that surfaced in the village starting in the mid-1980s. Before those waves of litigation hit KJ, however, familiar tensions arose in the first attempts to create the village.

Purity + Property = Shtetl

Following the collapse of the effort to move to Mount Olive in the early 1960s, Joel Teitelbaum's aides continued to search out new venues in the New York metropolitan area. By the late sixties, their focus had turned to Orange County, New York, where they noticed an uptick in the sale of land in and around the town of Monroe. This increase in activity in the real estate market was motivated by a significant rise in the town's population over the decade, growing from 5,900 inhabitants in 1960 to over 9,100 in 1970.[44] At the same time, private investors seized on the opportunity to purchase land in a bucolic area that was still undeveloped, cheap, and, significantly, an hour or less from New York City. More than twenty development projects regularly appeared on the docket of the Monroe town planning board.

Meanwhile, in early May 1967, a group of New York doctors, who incorporated themselves as Monwood Realty, bought a parcel of land from Monroe resident John DeVos at the juncture of Forest and Schunemunk roads.[45] Monwood had in mind to develop the land into a residential area to be known as Rosewood Village and immediately began to seek approval for water and sewage use with the town board and planning board of Monroe. After five years of vetting, scrutiny, and authorization by Monroe officials, the parcel of land was sold, in 1972, by the doctors' group to another party, Monfield Homes Inc., which was a real estate purchasing organization acting on behalf of Satmar Hasidim.[46] The Satmars were familiar with this area; they, along with other Orthodox Jews, frequented a number of summer bungalow colonies located a short distance from the property in question. Previous attempts to buy land had failed, most recently at Congers Lake near New City in Rockland County. As one Satmar intimately involved in the plan to purchase a 175-acre lot at Congers Lake observed of the locals: "They were afraid for Jewish people like they were afraid from Negroes. . . . Jewish people shouldn't come in. . . . They didn't want to have us especially in their neighborhood; they didn't want to have another New Square."[47]

This analogy drawn between religiously observant Jews and African Americans is worth pondering. It recalls the ambiguous racial status of the Satmar Hasidim, who were, in a sense, neither Black nor white. Although they undeniably enjoyed the privileges that whiteness accorded in American society, they were nonetheless marked by the white (and white Jewish) mainstream as foreign in appearance and demeanor, sometimes fetishized as an emblem of the nostalgic past, and often stigmatized as an undesirable element best kept out of one's own community. Either way, they were regarded as separate and other, tolerated when they kept to the margins, but unwelcome when they sought to enter into the physical precincts of suburbia. The experience of New Square had made the residents of Rockland and Orange counties wary, leading gentile and Jew alike to take active steps to prevent an ultra-Orthodox influx.

But the Satmars were not to be deterred. It was not just the allure of the undeveloped landscape of Orange County that attracted them. There was also a push out of Williamsburg, which in the 1960s was becoming more ethnically and racially diverse. Hasidim soon found themselves locked in battle with their Puerto Rican and African American neighbors for government resources, especially government-built, low-income high-rise apartments. In addition to this economic competition over public housing units, there was a culture clash between the minority communities that lived side by side. The linguistic, religious, and political culture of the new Puerto Rican arrivals was at odds with the conservative and insular Satmar way. Cultural tensions with the African American community in Williamsburg also were growing, especially when the Black Power movement arose in the 1960s.

As a general matter, the countercultural Zeitgeist of the sixties, marked by youthful rebellion in politics, music, dress, and sex norms, heightened the sense of alienation that Satmar Hasidim felt toward and in the city. These factors intensified the push to leave the city—just as the Satmar community experienced a great shock. In 1968, the same year that a housing discrimination suit was launched in which the city of New York was accused of favoring the Satmars over their Black and Puerto Rican neighbors in Williamsburg, the Rebbe suffered a major debilitating stroke. This prompted his close advisors to redouble their efforts to find a site of refuge outside of the city.[48]

Most prominent among them was Leopold (Leibish) Lefkowitz (1920–1998), who succeeded Lipa Friedman as president of the Satmar community. Lefkowitz was a Hungarian-born Jew and successful businessman who was widely admired within and outside the Satmar community for his intelligence and integrity. In stark contrast to the Rebbe, Lefkowitz was worldly and at ease in a non-Jewish setting; in fact, he survived the Second World War by disguising himself for a time as a gentile. The Rebbe relied heavily on the counsel of Lefkowitz, who served as his liaison with the outside world, both in Williamsburg and in Orange County. Lefkowitz operated a business, Crystal Clear Industries, in Ridgefield, New Jersey, that employed scores of Satmar Hasidim. From 1969, he was entrusted by the Rebbe to find a suitable venue for the community. In that role, he was intimately involved in the overall strategy and financing for the land purchases in Monroe and came to be regarded as one of the founding fathers of the Satmar community there. In fact, because of his extensive contacts and importance within the community, Lefkowitz was elected the first mayor of the village of Kiryas Joel in 1977.[49]

Two other personalities figured centrally in the story at this stage. The first was Oscar Fisher (1928–1993), another Hungarian-born Jew who survived the Holocaust and moved to America, where he, too, became a successful businessman. Fisher was Leibish Lefkowitz's brother-in-law. His sister Dina was married to Lefkowitz, and the three were partners in Crystal Clear Industries, which produced imitation crystal. Oscar Fisher was not a Satmar Hasid, but he played a crucial role in the history of Kiryas Joel as president of Monfield Homes. It was he who made the initial purchase of land in Monroe from Monwood Realty on September 27, 1972. Additional real estate transactions followed, in which Fisher presented himself to the sellers as an enterprising businessman intent on investing in property in Monroe with an eye toward developing it.

Fisher was recruited to the task of aiding the Satmar community by his brother-in-law, Leibish Lefkowitz. It was not principally his business acumen that made him a good candidate for the job. It was rather the fact that he wore no head covering and did not have a beard. Thus, he would not arouse the usual suspicion that a Haredi man with a long beard, earlocks, and *yarmulke* would. Fisher was somewhat conflicted over his Jewish identity, torn between the strict religious norms of his sister and brother-in-law, familiar to him from youth, and his own instincts as a fun-loving bon vivant.[50] That said, he was willing to assist the Satmar community in realizing its goal, in no small part motivated by his desire to be accepted by his sister and brother-in-law and their exclusive world. And so he came to play an essential role as the clean-shaven face of the Satmar purchasing effort. Fisher worked closely with his brother-in-law, as well as with local Orange County attorney Herbert Fabricant, to buy land for a proposed Satmar settlement.

Another important figure in the early years of settling Monroe was Herman or Haim Hirsch Leimzeider (b. 1932), who was the president of a real estate company, 57 Acres Realty Corp., that served as a front for the Satmar real estate acquisition effort. Known beyond the Hasidic world as "Herman the Hammer" for his hard-nosed business practices, Leimzider was, like Fisher and Lefkowitz, a Hungarian-born survivor. He arrived in the United States in 1951 and settled in Williamsburg, where he began to work renovating old boarding houses. Several years later, he entered the jewelry import business with a friend, but eventually split with his partner and returned full-time to construction. Leimzider's experience in business, and particularly real estate, made him a point person in the Satmar acquisition of land and subsequent erection of housing units in Kiryas Joel. As his nickname indicated, Leimzider could be tough-minded and protective of Satmar interests. He worked alongside and, more commonly, in the shadow of Oscar Fisher, who publicly represented Monfield Homes—and the Satmar community—in its efforts to buy property. Leimzider later asserted that his intention from the outset was to achieve the minimal threshold of five hundred residents in order to create a self-standing village according to the laws of New York State.[51] Others in the Satmar community maintain that the decision to create a village did not come until later, in 1976, in the midst of sharp disagreements with the town of Monroe over alleged zoning violations. Leimzider, for his part, claimed merely to be following in the path of the Rebbe whose "main purpose was that he wants to have a legal village." "Why? Because if he's going to have a legal village, we're going to have our own zoning and we'd be able . . . to build two-family houses so that the people should be able to get to it."[52]

It is far from clear that the Satmar Rebbe wanted a legally recognized village from the outset. In 1972, those entrusted with implementing Rabbi Teitelbaum's vision did not pursue formal recognition. Rather, they focused on building an isolated neighborhood of eighty garden apartments and twenty-five single-family homes that would come to be known as Section I on the land that Fisher purchased. Fisher hired lawyer Herbert Fabricant to secure the necessary water, sewage, and zoning permissions from the Monroe town board and planning board. A number of the key players in that authorization process—Fabricant and fellow lawyers Alan Lipman and Morton Marshak, Monroe town attorney James Sweeney, and town engineer Andrew Barone—were involved in many real estate transactions discussed by the two boards in this period, not all of which were approved. For example, it was Marshak who attempted to persuade the town board, unsuccessfully at first, to grant permission to the Jehovah's Witnesses to establish an assembly hall in 1971 that would seat 2,300 people.[53] Several years later, at its June 12, 1973, meeting, the planning board rejected the request of the Sigand Construction Corp. to build 204 garden apartments in Monroe. At the same meeting, the planning board provided preliminary approval for a project of garden apartments named Arden Forest, which was being built by Monfield Homes. At the next meeting on July 10, the board reviewed the plans of Arden Forest more carefully and determined that eight features of them were unacceptable. By the following meeting on August 14, "all changes that were requested" had been made, and the plans were authorized to move on to the next stage of development.[54]

Up to this point, the true purpose of the Monfield company remained hidden to the outside world. And yet within the Satmar community, the march toward the Rebbe's dream was proceeding apace. As Leopold Lefkowitz recruited new investors for the neighborhood, Herman Leimzider assumed responsibility as the on-site construction supervisor in Monroe. He made his way every day from Williamsburg to the Monfield development in Monroe, where he quickly disappeared into the trailer next to the building site so as to avoid detection. From his concealed command center, Leimzider oversaw construction, together with the non-Jewish contractor Anthony Franzese, of the garden apartments, single-family homes, a water supply system, and a sewage treatment plant. On one occasion, in the summer of 1973, as the construction of the apartments and homes neared completion, Rabbi Teitelbaum came to see and bless the work being done.[55]

Secrecy lasted until the spring of 1974, when the first traces of public visibility appeared. In late March, the Monroe town board became aware that dwellings in the Monfield development were being advertised in synagogues in Brooklyn and elsewhere as two-family homes. Prior to that point in the approval process, Monfield had insisted that the homes were single-family dwellings. The town and planning boards had frequently inquired into the layout of the Monfield units, and their concerns had been largely assuaged. Now a local resident by the name of Abraham Genen informed the town board that Hasidic Jews had visited him in Monroe and referred to the availability of two-family dwellings in Section I. In reporting on this exchange, the local newspaper, the *Times Herald-Record* from neighboring Middletown, announced on April 2: "Development accused of fraudulent advertising."[56]

Shortly thereafter, Oscar Fisher and Monfield Homes were summoned by the town board to answer the charge of false advertising, which, if confirmed, would have brought a halt to the work on the units. Town attorney James Sweeney reported at the May 6 board meeting that he had received written confirmation from Monfield that "they are only building 1 family residences in this subdivision." By contrast, town engineer Andrew Barone reported on his site visit of May 3 that he discovered that "houses are being built with piping for two kitchens," as well as for washing machines on each of the units' two floors. Despite this finding, Barone claimed shortly thereafter that he had misread the drawings and that nothing untoward was contained in them, perhaps a reflection of the high regard in which Oscar Fisher was held.[57]

Still, the town board was now alert to the specter of deception and moved quickly to spell out exactly what the term "family" meant so as to ensure that homes intended for single-family use not be sold for use by two families. Nine years earlier, in 1965, the town of Monroe had passed a comprehensive zoning law that superseded the earlier 1942 ordinance. The 1965 law divided the town into distinct districts (residential and nonresidential) and indicated which of the former were restricted to single-family dwellings and what lot sizes were permitted. The task of zoning residential districts for single-family homes had long been considered essential for maintaining a desirably low level of population density and thus the *rural* nature of life in the region (at a time when Orange County was 50 percent rural).[58] In 1974, this law was tightened by inserting an addendum that defined "family" in deliberately restrictive terms as: "One or more individuals related in blood to the third degree of collateral consanguinity, descending from a common ancestor, or by marriage or adoption, also including foster parents and foster children, as defined in Sec. 271 of the Social Service Law of New York State, or two individuals not so related, living as a single housekeeping unit and using cooking facilities and certain rooms in common."[59] In other words, extended families including great-grandparents were acceptable. But distant relations were not permitted in the same house. Boarding houses, clubs, and households made of any more than two unrelated individuals also were explicitly forbidden by the new law.

The passage of this amendment to the town's zoning ordinance was part of a wave of new single-family ordinances enacted in the late 1960s and early 1970s. Single-family ordinances, as such, had been in place since the early twentieth century, a standard feature of the zoning laws first promoted by Secretary of Commerce Herbert Hoover in the administration of Warren G. Harding. These zoning laws deliberately sought to exclude Blacks, first through explicit racial restrictions and then, after the Supreme Court ruled racially restrictive zoning to be unconstitutional in 1926, via economic measures that were intended to produce the same effect.[60] By the 1960s, the fear of "unconventional" people moving in prompted many suburban communities to adopt new measures aimed at strengthening the existing mechanisms of exclusion. The newly sharpened single-family ordinances became a favored tool for keeping out undesirables such as college students and "hippies," whose communes were regarded as a threat to the rural and suburban way of life.

There were several concerns that led towns such as Monroe to adopt new ordinances tightening the definition of the family. In addition to the specter of commune dwelling, there was growing alarm about over-population in the area. More and more New Yorkers were seeking to leave the city in the 1970s, especially during the turbulent reign of Mayor Abe Beame (1974–1978) when New York was on the verge of bankruptcy and infrastructural breakdown.[61] Hasidic Jews were part of a much larger stream of city dwellers decamping to Long Island, Rockland and Orange counties, and parts farther north. In response, suburban municipalities imposed zoning and planning restrictions to regulate the flow of the new residents and the edifices that would house them. For example, the town of Ramapo introduced an ordinance in 1972 that scholars have called the birth of "the modern growth management movement in the United States."[62] According to this ordinance, which was upheld by New York's highest court in *Golden v. Town of Ramapo*, residential development permits would be granted only if essential public services were available for the proposed development.

In addition to placing constraints on the influx of undesirable urbanites, these new single-family zoning laws reinforced the racially and economically exclusionary tendencies of the old single-family zoning laws, a matter that was addressed by a case that reached the Supreme Court in 1977, though the litigation commenced in 1973, around the time that the Satmars began construction in Monroe. In that case, the Supreme Court declared that a zoning ordinance that prevented an African American grandmother from living in a house with her two grandsons, because they were cousins not brothers, was unconstitutional because it "sliced deeply into the family." A concurring opinion by the liberal justice William Brennan expressed particular concern about "the imposition upon the rest of us of white suburbia's preference in patterns of family living."[63]

Just four years earlier, however, a Supreme Court decision, which arose out of a challenge to a single-family zoning ordinance in Belle Terre, a village in Suffolk County, New York, upheld a single-family zoning ordinance that defined the family to exclude more than two unrelated people. The ordinance in that case, which arose out of East Cleveland, had limited the definition of a single family to "one or more persons related by blood, adoption, or marriage, living and cooking together as a single housekeeping unit, exclusive of servants" or no more than two persons "not related by blood, adoption, or marriage, living and cooking together as a single housekeeping unit." Rejecting the claims put forth by a group of college students who said that "social homogeneity is not a legitimate interest of government" and that "the ordinance is antithetical to the Nation's experience, ideology, and self-perception as an open, egalitarian, and integrated society," the Supreme Court affirmed the basic constitutionality of single-family zoning ordinances, holding that "a quiet place where yards are wide, people few, and motor vehicles restricted" is a permissible goal for local governments to pursue.[64]

On the other hand, one year prior to the *Belle Terre* decision, in the 1973 case of *United States Department of Agriculture v. Moreno*, the Court had telegraphed the more liberal message that anticipated the holding in *East Cleveland*. The *Moreno* decision held that the government could not require a household to conform to a definition of the family that excluded "unrelated" members in order to be eligible to receive food stamps.[65] This pattern of confusing decisions illustrated the intense national debate over exclusionary zoning and, more specifically, the constitutionality of restrictive single-family zoning ordinances. It was in the midst of this debate—indeed, between the *Belle Terre* decision affirming a local government's definition of a "single family" as no more than two unrelated household members and the *East Cleveland* decision curtailing the authority of local governments to impose exclusionary definitions of a family—that Kiryas Joel moved from nascent settlement to official village.

The Hasidim were just a trickle in a much larger stream of urban dwellers exiting the city for the suburbs. This outflow placed new strains on suburban municipalities, which struggled to absorb the erstwhile city dwellers. The focus on managing growth that developed in response to this outflow served to make housing more expensive, with predictable consequences for the poor and lower middle class. Racial minorities had long been effectively shut out of the suburbs by the absence of affordable housing, as had working-class and lower-middle-class white people. Some suburbs imposed architectural and lot size requirements that ensured they would be populated exclusively by the wealthy. Others, like Monroe, were populated by middle-class people of more modest means. But all such municipalities, by virtue of their low-density housing requirements, restricted and excluded the lower rungs of the socioeconomic ladder, producing a degree of class- and race-based homogeneity that became the stereotype of the modern American suburb.

But while many Americans had flocked to the suburbs in search of this model, others were coming to question it. The pejorative term "exclusionary zoning" was virtually unheard of prior to 1969. But in that year, the National Committee Against Discrimination in Housing held a training seminar to assist lawyers in bringing lawsuits challenging the constitutionality of zoning ordinances that effectively excluded the poor and racial minorities. In 1971, an article taking stock of the flurry of anti–exclusionary zoning activity of the preceding two years was published with the optimistic title "Racial and Economic Zoning: The Beginning of the End?" It was not the beginning of the end. The Supreme Court, as we just saw, subsequently rebuffed the efforts of affordable housing advocates in *Belle Terre*. Even the decision in *Moore v. City of E. Cleveland* three years later, denying the right to exclude an extended family, did not alter the broad grant of authority given to local governments as a matter of federal constitutional law.

In contrast to the confusing and mixed record of the Supreme Court regarding exclusionary zoning laws, some state courts were leading in a different direction. Animated by the newly energized federal campaign to combat racial residential segregation (the Fair Housing Act, prohibiting discrimination in the housing market, had been passed in 1968), some state judges were open to interpreting their state constitutions in a more liberal fashion than that offered by the U.S. Supreme Court. New Jersey proved to be particularly receptive to claims that were being made by advocates who maintained that excluding affordable housing violated the state constitution because of its racially and economically discriminatory impact. The New York courts, by contrast, resisted the argument that the racial and economic effects of exclusionary zoning violated New York State's constitution.[66]

Smack in the midst of this controversy over exclusionary zoning, the Satmars arrived in Monroe. By the time they first faced off against town officials and residents in 1974, the battle between the opponents of exclusionary zoning and the defenders of "reasonable measures of growth control" was pitched. The Satmars, however, occupied an ambiguous place in that controversy. In many ways they fit the profile of the typical excluded minority; they were viewed as different, poor, and in need of high-density housing. But they also differed from the typical excluded minority, especially people of color, and shared key characteristics with the typical suburban excluders: they were white, politically favored, able to purchase property, and desirous of living apart from people who were different from them. As a community whose difference was not racial but rather cultural in character, they represented an early instance of a conundrum that would bedevil the American courts and American politics for years to come: whether "lifestyle" differences should be treated as akin to racial groups or religious beliefs, which governments are legally forbidden to exclude—or rather as cultural or economic choices that governments are presumed to be free to promote. The legal flux that existed at the time the Satmars first moved to Monroe and the ambiguous position they themselves occupied made it difficult to predict what the outcome of their struggle with the town's zoning authorities would be. But it meant that they had a variety of legal and political tools available to them to conduct their version of the fight over zoning then being waged nationwide.

Meanwhile, on the ground in Monroe, the Satmars' perceived difference made them a frequent target of criticism. But so too did their apparent dissimulation. By the spring of that year, it was known that Monfield's agents and Satmar leaders had concealed the nature of their plans, a practice that they felt was justified in order to overcome the exclusionary antisemitism to which they would likely be subjected. Prior to this point, Monfield's own lawyer, Herb Fabricant, believed that he was working only for Oscar Fisher.[67] But by the spring, the Yiddish press was openly reporting that "over one hundred Satmar families are moving out of Williamsburg to settle in a town 100 miles from New York."[68] Despite the inaccurate distance reported from Monroe to New York— only fifty miles—the cat was out of the bag. Back in the city, rumors of a mass exodus prompted widespread anxiety among Satmar Hasidim in Williamsburg over the prospect that the center of gravity in their world was decisively shifting. They not only feared that the Rebbe would be leaving his home of nearly thirty years, since a home had been purchased for him on Bakertown Road in Monroe, but also worried about declining real estate values if there were a flight to the suburbs. Mayor Beame, for his part, directly appealed to Leibush Lefkowitz not to take the Satmars—a valuable political asset—out of Brooklyn.[69]

Lefkowitz was busy on various fronts: updating and receiving advice from the Rebbe, working with Oscar Fisher and Herman Leimzider on permits and construction, and raising money for the new settlement. The project of building a shtetl required millions of dollars, and this from a community with an exceptionally high rate of poverty. Lefkowitz had the benefit of the Rebbe's unqualified endorsement, which meant that rich and poor alike were inclined to give. At the same time, he worked in tandem with fellow Satmar leaders Sender Deutsch, Shlomo Mikhel Rosner, and Moshe (Monroe) Friedman to tap into the wealthy elite of the global Satmar community, which provided generous support to the branches in Europe, Australia, South America, Canada, Israel, and the United States. Two key figures in laying the financial foundation for KJ were Getzel Berger, the well-known Haredi real estate tycoon in London, and Israel Zupnik, the renowned industrialist and donor in Israel and the United States. Closer to home, Herman Leimzider was working with local New York banks to arrange for mortgages for the property.[70]

With construction well under way, funding rolling in, and increasing public attention, Satmars from Brooklyn began to visit Monroe in April and May 1974 to explore housing prospects. Community leaders were concerned that the desirability of life in Monroe would lead to a dangerous spike in housing prices. The fear of a price war induced them to impose tight regulation on costs. Lots for new houses would be sold for $18,000, while rent in apartments would range between $280 and $325 a month depending on size.[71]

All property purchased in Monroe by Monfield Homes and other Satmar-related companies was concentrated under the control of a Satmar development agency—precursor to the Vaad hakirya—that sold individual lots and sold or rented apartments to individuals according to a fixed price schedule. This activity took place well in advance of the formal recognition of the village of Kiryas Joel by the state. Because of its private character, this activity was not subject to the strictures that would apply to state action, even though, from the point of view of the followers of the Satmar Rebbe, his directives were even more authoritative than the orders of a government official. American legal and economic practices thus enabled the Satmars to regulate the market for housing units in Monroe, a clear example of communitarianism from the bottom up.

Unelected community leaders, who were appointed to run the development agency by the Rebbe, regulated the market for housing units. They also regulated the pace of migration from Williamsburg. They remained deeply concerned that the arrival of Satmar Hasidim in Monroe might induce panic in local residents. After initially welcoming prospective buyers from Brooklyn, the leaders stopped encouraging them by the late spring of 1974. By temporarily suppressing the demand for housing, it was hoped that resistance from Monroe residents would lessen.

Satmar leaders also engaged in a public relations campaign to explain the community's distinctive values and practices to the broader Monroe community. It was in this period that Leibish Lefkowitz emerged from behind the scenes to replace Oscar Fisher as the public face of the Satmar effort, impressing those he encountered with his formidable diplomatic skills.

But the challenges he faced were serious and not easily overcome by personal charm. By August 1974, the mood in Monroe was palpably tense, as the first Satmars from Brooklyn began to move into the Monfield development.[72] A month earlier, the local *Times Herald-Record* had started to raise public awareness—and concern—by publishing daily stories on the Satmar community. A headline on July 17 read: "How Many People? Monroe Officials Jittery." The story noted the odd configuration of the Monfield homes, which did not seem intended for small nuclear families. For example, the TV rooms in the original plans curiously did not have space for televisions, which Satmar Hasidim were forbidden to watch; instead, there were sinks, which suggested the possibility of occupancy by more than one family, or at any rate a denser form of occupancy than the typical nuclear family. Reflecting a growing sense of apprehension, the article observed that Monroe officials "have gotten a little nervous at the prospect of 600 to 2000 (or more) 'new' people moving into their town in the next five years." One estimate suggested, with prophetic accuracy, that eventually some 20,000 "new" people—that is, Hasidim—could dwell in Monroe.[73]

The next day, the *Times Herald-Record* ran a story under the headline "Hasidic Settlers Face Uphill Fight." It detailed the Satmar plans to move beyond the initial 170 acres and 500 residents in Section I to encompass a total of 270 acres that could be home to as many as 2,000 people. Residents were fearful that they would be prevented from driving through Satmar neighborhoods on the Sabbath or denied the use of a small lake now contained within Section I. It was not altogether surprising, as the *Times Herald-Record* article averred, that "the harshest reaction to the Hasidim came from non-Hasidic Jews in the neighborhood." One Jewish resident, who lived on Forest Road near the Monfield subdivision, proclaimed that the Hasidic arrivals "are the most

horrible people that God put breath in."[74] A few days later, another Jewish resident opined that the arrival of the Satmars "is not complimentary
to me as a Jewish person. I find it very undignified that they live
4,000 years behind everyone else. It is an embarrassment to me."[75] The
fear of guilt by association was also voiced by an active member of the
local Conservative synagogue in Monroe who, after an initial period of
enthusiasm over the arrival of a new group of Jews, found herself having
second thoughts. As she recalled her thinking years later: "I was concerned that the non-Jewish population would lump us all together and
say, 'Well, look at the Jews, they're so aggressive, they don't care what they
do and not know the difference.'"[76]

Such private reservations soon mounted into a public furor that
prompted the *Times Herald-Record* to run a series of eight lengthy letters
to the editor on July 27 in defense of the Satmars. The gist of these letters
was, as one was titled, that Hasidim are "people, too." Another letter
writer opined that while the dress of the Satmars was different, "it is no
more shocking than that of the Amish," a comparison that was often
made, perhaps because of a recent Supreme Court decision that recognized the right of the Amish to maintain their way of life.[77] That decision, in *Yoder v. Wisconsin*, had been handed down in 1972, as the Satmars were engineering their first purchase of land in Monroe. Notably,
the one justice who (partially) dissented from that decision, William O.
Douglas, expressed concern that exempting the Amish from compulsory education laws would violate the rights of their children by de-
priving them of a secular education—a concern that foreshadowed
complaints, many decades later, from people who grew up in Haredi
communities.

In the summer of 1974, as the Satmars began to arrive, the local newspaper sought to strike a balance between informing its readers about the
history, habits, and leaders of the Satmar Hasidim and reporting on
tensions with town bodies over zoning rules. Thus, there was a flattering
profile of Leibish Lefkowitz in early August and later that month an
interview (conducted in Yiddish by a *Times Herald-Record* reporter)
with Rabbi Joel Teitelbaum, newly resettled in Monroe.[78] On the other
hand, there were reports of growing tensions between Satmars and

Monroe residents over access to the local lake as well as over plans to build an additional forty-four single-family homes next to the Monfield development. In mid-August, the Monroe planning board rejected the proposal for new homes when a representative of Herman Leimzider's 57 Acres development company refused to answer questions about links to the Monfield property. One of the audience members, local real estate lawyer Alan Lipman, pushed the point, seeking more comprehensive information on the links between the original Monfield site, the proposed forty-four-unit land, and a rumored third parcel adjoining the first. Prodding the board to adopt a more aggressive attitude, Lipman asserted: "I don't think it should be kept a deep, dark secret what they plan to do with the land."[79]

The piecemeal fashion in which the Satmars unfolded their plans exacerbated tensions. Chastened by unsuccessful attempts to purchase property in the suburban New York area in the past, they shared as little of their intentions as possible, a defensive maneuver that frustrated town residents and officials alike.[80] Further escalating the conflict, both sides held to the self-fulfilling belief that the cultural differences between them were "colossal," as one journalist asserted in the *Times Herald-Record*. He used Satmar dress norms to illustrate this point in a column he wrote in 1976: "The father clung tightly to the elbow of his look-alike son. Both wore bottle-like glasses, baggy black pants and dusty black jackets. To them the look is beautiful. To others it is sloppy and monotonous." Such widely held views led Satmars to believe, as Leibish Lefkowitz claimed in response, that their Monroe neighbors "just don't like us."[81] The pervasive assumption that their neighbors were antisemitic reinforced the Satmars' desire to have as little contact with the surrounding world as possible. They believed that this aspiration was their prerogative as part of the American experiment in cultural pluralism. And they grasped that group segregation was the effect—and, for many, the intent—of the great American move to the suburbs.

Without a doubt, segregation *was* the ideal of the Satmar shtetl in Monroe: to create a closed and insular society that operated according to its own rules and without interference from the surrounding world. Tales from the early years of the community recalled the case of a non-Satmar man from the Adas Jeshurun congregation of Washington Heights named Birnbaum, who wanted to live in the new community. It was said of Birnbaum that although he wore a modern hat and kept a neatly trimmed beard, he was a strictly observant Jew who was drawn to the personality and views of Rabbi Teitelbaum, especially on Zionism. And thus he was permitted to settle in Kiryas Joel, where he lived for ten years, during which time he developed a number of Satmar ritual habits.[82]

The fact that Birnbaum merited special mention in the history of Kiryas Joel attests to his uniqueness. The community would not let him dwell in its midst unless he conformed to its norms. No one would have dared sell or rent property to him otherwise. He was an outlier in physical appearance—and thus the exception that proved the rule. All residents of the community were expected to adhere to a strict code of conduct that included fastidious observance of Jewish law, dress norms, and gender separation. In addition, Rabbi Teitelbaum conveyed to his aides that he insisted on the following rules for prospective residents in the new community: (1) married women must not have any of their own hair and must shave it regularly; (2) "impure" recreational books or magazines are not permitted in private homes; and (3) the "impure" language of modern Hebrew should never be spoken.[83]

For many Satmars, the opportunity to live in a community bound by such rules, in a suburban setting proximate to New York, was the fulfillment of a dream. "A wonder of the world," *Der Yid,* the Satmar weekly, euphorically proclaimed of the new settlement that took its name—the village of Joel—from its guiding inspiration, Joel Teitelbaum.[84] To be sure, KJ in its early days lacked some of the core features of Satmar life in Williamsburg—markets, shuls, schools. In fact, some of the first settlers in Monroe wanted to return to Brooklyn for the high holidays in September 1974, but the Rebbe instructed them to stay put. Over time, the desire moved in the opposite direction, particularly as Joel Teitelbaum spent more and more time at his home on Bakertown Road in Monroe, and Satmar Hasidim wanted to come to KJ to be in his presence.

Ironically, the price of preserving the requisite degree of communal purity was a descent into a messier, less pure world: the world of

American law. From the very beginning, Satmar lawyers made their way to state courts to ward off attempts to impinge on the group's plans—for example, by delaying approval of development beyond Section I or by restricting Satmar control over the lake in that area.

Satmar leaders were prepared to use all available legal and political instruments at their disposal to ensure the group's well-being. They were ready to withhold information or even dupe town officials about their true intentions.[85] When asked by the *New York Times* in September 1974 about plans to develop a village of three thousand people, Leibish Lefkowitz responded: "Such nonsense. We—Monfield Homes—will be happy to build 50 more homes in the next few years."[86]

But construction at the Monfield site was proceeding apace. The supervisors, Leimzider and Franzese, now had to contend with frequent visits by Monroe town engineer Andrew Barone, who came to ensure compliance with zoning regulations. Leimzider was actively engaged in converting traditional single-family homes into domiciles that could be used by larger Satmar families; this entailed adding walls, sinks, and kitchens, among other features. Frequently, he was slapped with stop orders for alleged zoning violations. But a string of skilled local lawyers—first Herbert Fabricant, followed by Jerry Markovits and later Bernie Davis—were successful in persuading the town planning board and local courts to approve the construction in 1974 and beyond.[87]

For a short while, even as the zoning tug-of-war continued with the town, tensions between Monroe residents and the Satmars seemed to subside. The Satmars, for their part, attempted to demonstrate a growing sense of civic belonging. In November 1974, a delegation led by Leibish Lefkowitz paid a visit to the Monroe Ambulance Corps and left a donation of a thousand dollars. The next month the *Times Herald-Record* invited sociologist Israel Rubin, who two years earlier had published his sympathetic ethnographic study *Satmar: An Island in the City*, to author a pair of articles about the community. The two pieces, "Satmar's Arrival in Monroe No Cause for Alarm" and "Satmarer Can Live in Peace with Neighbors," were an attempt to explain the beliefs and practices of the Satmars and assuage fears that they sought to impose their religion on others.[88]

Rubin's articles contributed to the new sense of peace and goodwill. Monroe residents who lived close to the settlement reported that they had overcome their initial concerns and now regarded the Satmar as "good neighbors." One Monroe man declared enthusiastically in July 1975: "They're dolls." His children regularly played together with the grandchildren of Leibish Lefkowitz. Even Lillian Roberts, a Jewish woman who frequently complained to town officials about Satmar violations, especially around the lake, regularly engaged her Satmar neighbors in friendly conversation. Meanwhile, local merchants attested to the fact that Satmars were good for business. They bought in large quantities and, according to a Shop-Rite supermarket manager, "never complain. They're very courteous; probably our best customers."[89]

By this time, the Satmars had begun to lay the foundation for their communal lives. They had established synagogues, mikvehs, markets, and schools, often in the basements of apartment buildings, which made them violations of Monroe zoning law. They also had rented buses to drive men in the community to their jobs in Brooklyn and Manhattan so a regular source of livelihood could be assured. With this basic infrastructure in place, Kiryas Joel became a desirable destination for the Satmars of New York. Having land and open space made it especially desirable around the holiday of Sukkot when families, unlike in Brooklyn, could build their own booths to eat and sleep in, as mandated by religious law. The ability to live a strictly Orthodox lifestyle in the country marked, for a key Satmar observer, the "opening of a new chapter in the annals of Haredi Jewry in America." Joel Teitelbaum communicated a sense of the importance of the new venue by insisting that Kiryas Joel be known not as a "shtetl" but as a *shtot*—not just a little village, but a Jewish town.[90]

Renewed Tensions and KJ's Formal Recognition as a Village

The Satmars' growing sense of confidence lent itself to an even greater willingness to enter the political fray. While community officials were prepared from the outset to utilize legal means to advance their interests, they were aware that they did not yet have a critical mass to exercise a significant hand in electoral affairs, as they were able to do in Williamsburg. But in Monroe, local politicians knew what the future might hold. One official observed already in the fall of 1975 that the Satmars "could control elections when there are enough of them here."[91]

At that point, residents from the Monfield development, then numbering 105 families, began to register to vote: 122 new voters enrolled in the Ninth District, newly created to account for the Satmar presence.[92] They were a small fraction of the 3,700 or so registered voters in town. But the Satmars were a rapidly growing population, due to both a steady stream of arrivals from Brooklyn and a high number of children per family. By this time, they had already started to cultivate relationships with local politicians in Orange County such as U.S. congressman Benjamin Gilman. This engagement belonged to the long-standing tradition of Satmar political behavior, evident in the close ties that the group's leaders had forged with political officials in Europe and especially in Brooklyn, where the Rebbe met regularly with a steady stream of New York officials including congressmen, senators, and mayors from Robert Wagner and John Lindsay to Abe Beame and Ed Koch.

The combination of the Satmars' growing political heft and Monroe residents' ongoing fears about their neighbors upset the short-lived honeymoon between the two groups. The town's patience with new groups seeking to settle in its midst, particularly religious groups, was waning. As noted earlier, the town board was asked in 1971 to approve plans for a Jehovah's Witnesses convention center.[93] The man who would become the Satmars' attorney, Herbert Fabricant, argued strenuously against the new center, which was quite close to what was then the Monfield development, though the plans were eventually approved. And in 1976, the town of Monroe got in a legal dustup with the Yoga Society of New York that had set up an ashram twelve years earlier. The Yoga Society had done some building on its property without the required permits, prompting the town to issue zoning citations. The society then went to court to invalidate the town's zoning law of 1965, arguing that the law was illegal because it had not been published in the local newspaper in the proper fashion. Initially, the Yoga Society won its case in New York State court, before losing on appeal in 1977. It is no coincidence that the society's lawyer, Bernie Davis, would become the Satmars' hard-hitting attorney. Satmar community leaders had noticed his success in beating back the Monroe zoning law on behalf of the Monroe ashram. One day in July 1976, three of those leaders—Moshe (Monroe) Friedman, Shlomo Mikhel Rosner, and Herman Leimzider—came into his office and asked Davis to "do the same thing that I did for the people in the white and orange robes."[94]

Davis's services were urgently needed in the summer of 1976, when the town of Monroe began to up the ante in enforcing its zoning laws. Until this point, town officials had been rather inconsistent in issuing violation notices. Some said that this was due to the lack of rigor of town inspector Andrew Barone.[95] But the town board and town planning board approved additions to the Monfield development at almost every one of their meetings. Records from those meetings betray no antipathy on the part of board members toward the Satmars, who were repre-sented by friends, colleagues, and not infrequently law partners of town officials—all of whom constituted a small and tight circle of intimates.

Town attorney Jim Sweeney insisted that the new scrutiny in 1976 was not the result of antisemitism. Rather, it was purely a function of the desire to uphold the letter and spirit of the 1965 zoning law to main-tain the rural character of residential homes in the area located north-east of Route 17 (also known as the Quickway) where the Monfield development took rise.[96]

The same could not be said for residents of Monroe, whose ire at perceived violations by the Satmars and the relative indifference of town officials was escalating and unveiled. A group of about a hundred resi-dents came to a town board meeting on July 12 and angrily "demanded the town enforce its zoning laws and force the religious community to tear out house renovations."[97] Local lawyer Alan Lipman, who was ac-tively involved in efforts to control Satmar growth, feared that violence could break out.[98]

By this point, the town had begun to take more forceful steps. In early June 1976, a member of the Satmar community, Nuchem Friedman, was arrested for refusing to close a grocery store he ran. Originally, the store was in his house, but he moved it to a pair of tractor-trailers outside of his house, after receiving a stop order from inspector Barone. That arrangement was deemed illegal, but Friedman did not close it down, and he was arrested. In his defense, members of the community argued that since Satmar women did not drive, it was important to have a strictly kosher grocery store in walking distance of their homes. But this argument did not hold sway.[99]

On the contrary, Friedman's arrest was a clear intensification in the battle between the town and the Satmars. Subsequently, the town stopped work on five new homes in an adjacent development known as Section II in late June; and then in early July, it charged eighteen homeowners (out of twenty-five) in Section I with violating the building code by converting one-family homes into two- or three-family residences.[100] This new enforcement policy was the outcome of a poorly worded regulation adopted by the town in June and announced in the official *Monroe Gazette* on July 1, 1976:

> *Single Family Dwelling*: A dwelling designed for and used by one family. The existence in design or otherwise of more than one room in a dwelling designed or used for cooking and food preparation and designed to or containing cooking facilities and food storage and preparation facilities, commonly known as a kitchen shall be a prima facia [sic] evidence that the dwelling is not designed for or used by one family. *This evidenciary [sic] rule, however, shall not apply to a kitchen designed for use solely in observance of religious holy days or feast days.* The existence in design of a floor and room layout for a second story substantially similar to design to the floor layout of the ground floor of the same dwelling which second story can be isolated from the ground floor by a single door or partition shall likewise be prima facia [sic] evidence that the dwelling is not designed for used by one family.

The new definition went well beyond previous ordinances intended to limit residence in homes to single families. Moreover, it was unmistakably drafted with the Satmar community in mind. That raised the strong possibility that it could be deemed to be illegal, even though it evinced a measure of cultural sensitivity toward the Satmars. The provision underlined above suggests that the town of Monroe had come to learn that some Satmar Hasidim maintained a separate kitchen for the Passover holiday in their homes; moreover, the town was willing to accept such kitchens as an exception to their zoning laws. What they were not prepared to countenance, however, was the existence of two or more apartments—or family units—in a home zoned for single-family residence.

The Satmars were growing more and more upset by the intrusions of inspectors and the threats of violations. They saw them as blatant discrimination against a group of people based on their cultural and religious values. They were particularly opposed to the single-family residence definition, which did not conform to their understanding of what a large, multigenerational Jewish family was. One woman, Lea Wertzberger, who was among the eighteen homeowners accused of a violation, said: "They're just after us up here. We pay our taxes. We have our own school up here, but we pay school taxes anyway. I don't know what they want from us."[101]

Just who were "they," in the Satmars' view? Town officials and local newspapers were deemed chiefly responsible for the growing scrutiny.[102] But there was also a bit of the "Jew vs. Jew" dynamic at work. At town board meetings, Jewish residents, by now over their honeymoon, were especially vocal in opposing the growth of the Satmar community.[103]

But the Satmars had no intention of reversing course. Their investment in Monroe was substantial, as they bought up more property to support a growing portfolio of religious institutions, or moysdes. Community members had made the transition to suburban life rather easily, and they weren't going to be discouraged easily.

In the midst of the rising storm, Leibish Lefkowitz tried to calm passions, issuing a statement in the official *Monroe Gazette* on July 29. He admitted that the size of Satmar families creates "understandable doubt by those who do not know us and our customs." But he hastened to add that his community was tax-paying, crime-free, self-sufficient, and an economic boon to the area. He continued by appealing to the American tradition of tolerance for difference: "We intend only good. Though our customs are different, the American system of protection of all people with all beliefs is profoundly important to us. The law, applied evenly and equally, must protect all of us." Lefkowitz concluded by calling for "a cooling-off period, where full discussions can take place." In the meantime, a court of law would decide whether the Satmars were in violation of valid zoning laws.[104]

While awaiting the court's decision, Lefkowitz brought up an idea that he had raised earlier in the year in January. He proposed at the beginning of August that the Satmar neighborhood establish a PUD, planned unit development. The PUD was a regulatory tool introduced in the post–World War II period that allowed designated neighborhoods considerable latitude in determining their own zoning patterns and rules—for instance, it permitted mixed residential and commercial uses or the coexistence of single-family and multiple-family homes in the same area. This indeed could have been a suitable path to an accommodation, but it was not pursued. Two other prospective solutions were raised in this period: The first was to convert private Satmar property holdings to tax-exempt status by aggregating them under the umbrella of the religious congregation. Given the quasi-public nature of Satmar institutions, the shift away from individual private ownership to formalized communal possession was not far-fetched. Such a strategy would allow Satmars to have greater control over their tax dollars as well as over the use to which their property was put.

Ultimately, it was another, more dramatic idea that gained traction with the Hasidim: the creation of an incorporated, legally recognized village.[105] The precedent of New Square was on the minds of Satmar and town leaders. But this option was hardly a foregone conclusion. Notwithstanding Herman Leimzider's claim that incorporation was desired from the outset, Gelbman and others maintain that the original idea was not to create a legal village for which Satmar Hasidim would be entirely responsible.[106] But the goalposts had clearly moved by the late summer of 1976 as the conflict with Monroe reached new depths.

One Friday night, Lefkowitz's associates, Moshe Friedman and Shlomo Rosner, went to seek guidance from Joel Teitelbaum, who was in an infirm and debilitated state at ninety. They believed that an impasse had been reached, but the Rebbe told them that "since the entire village is the result of a miraculous act, you can rely on a miracle" to salvage the situation.[107] All will resolve itself, the Rebbe assured them.

There is little doubt that Friedman and Rosner—and for that matter the entire Satmar community—believed in the capacity of the Rebbe to work miracles. And yet Satmar leaders did not leave it to Rabbi Teitelbaum's powers alone; they engaged in their own mundane actions to tip the balance of power to their side, some of which reveal a striking degree of worldliness. For example, they hired the veteran New York City public relations expert Howard Rubinstein in the summer to help craft a message of firmness and goodwill that Leibish Lefkowitz delivered in a variety of forums to the wider community.[108] Shortly thereafter, they made another stunning move. According to Gelbman, they engaged a local lawyer to spy on town officials at local restaurants and bars and report back to Satmar officials on their intentions. In the course of his undercover work, the lawyer was said to have caught a town official expressing his desire to "go to war against the Hasidim."[109]

This fortified the impression among the Satmars that the town operated with ill will toward them. What was required in response, they felt, was steadfastness. Accordingly, the Satmars decided, in late August, to fight the zoning violation notices against the eighteen homeowners in Section I. Their lawyer, Bernie Davis, a proud iconoclast who favored cutoff jeans in court, introduced an aggressive strategy designed to show that the town failed to provide equal protection to Satmar residents by selectively enforcing zoning laws.[110] Continuing the line of argument he had used on behalf of the Yoga Society, Davis maintained that the town's zoning law, including the recent addendum defining a single-family home, was invalid. What he and his clients particularly objected to were intrusive daily inspections by Andrew Barone, backed by search warrants when Barone was denied entry to houses. The matter made its way to the court of local supreme court judge Edward O'Gorman, a friend of town officials whom the Satmars regarded as singularly unfriendly to their cause. (In the state of New York, the term "supreme court" applies to the highest level of trial courts that exists in each county; the highest level of appellate court, the state equivalent of the

Supreme Court of the federal judiciary, is known as the Court of Appeals.)[111]

Meanwhile, tensions were rising on the ground. Over one hundred irate residents came to a town board meeting on September 13. Eight residents spoke at the meeting, all of whom called for more severe action to be taken against the Satmars, including criminal charges.[112] Wasting no time, the Satmars filed a petition the very next day with Monroe's chief executive, Supervisor William Rogers, calling for the creation of their own village to be known as Kiryas Joel. In an accompanying statement, Leibish Lefkowitz declared that town officials treated Satmars as "criminals." He also pointed to the hysteria of Monroe residents who "want us thrown out of town."[113]

As Satmar leaders and their lawyers already knew from the case of New Square, the path to creating a village in the state of New York was not overly complicated. According to the state's Village Law, "a territory of 500 or more inhabitants may incorporate as a village in New York State, provided that the territory is not already part of a city or village" and contains "no more than five square miles at the time of incorporation."[114] Since the territory in question was part of a *town* and measured 450 acres, it could petition for incorporation if 20 percent of the eligible voters or those holding more than 50 percent of the assessed property value signed a petition. The Satmar petition was signed by landowners who held five million dollars of the seven million of assessed property in the community.

At a special meeting of the town board on September 29, Supervisor Rogers set November 3 as the date of the hearing to address the petition to create the new Satmar village. Meanwhile, a majority of the town board passed a resolution declaring opposition to its formation. In explaining the board's logic, Supervisor Rogers declared that the Satmars' move was a simple ploy to avoid adherence to the town's zoning laws. It also set a dangerous precedent that "any development" or group could choose to follow, thereby risking a further depletion of Monroe's resources.[115]

The next move in the rapidly shifting legal chess game was made neither by the Satmars nor by the town of Monroe but by local lawyer

Alan Lipman, who was a frequent critic of the Satmar development. In a daring gambit, motivated in no small part by his own qualms as a Jew about the insularity and methods of the Satmars, Lipman filed a petition proposing that a chunk of Monroe's territory, 556 acres that included the Monfield settlement, be annexed to the existing village of Monroe, which was an administrative unit under the town of Monroe.[116] If the annexation plan succeeded, the Satmars would not be able to create their own village, since their property would come under the authority of the village of Monroe. According to state law, a village cannot be created out of an existing village.

The town now had two competing petitions to address: Lipman's for annexation and the Satmars' for a village. In what would be a fateful decision, it scheduled a hearing on the Lipman annexation proposal for October 28, whereas the meeting on the Satmar petition was scheduled for November 3. The Satmars feared that their plans for a village were being intentionally thwarted by this sequence, which had the potential to render moot their petition to create a village on November 3. That decision may have tipped the balance. In a bold response, the Satmars filed suit in federal court alleging religious discrimination by town officials and the seventy-five Monroe residents who had signed the Lipman petition, all of whom would be financially liable if the suit succeeded. Since they were moving beyond the jurisdiction of the state courts, the Satmars did not use their regular local lawyers, Bernie Davis and Jerry Markovits, for this case. Rather, they hired a highly regarded Albany firm, Nolan and Heller, with expertise in annexation cases.

A key to the Satmars' strategy was their sophistication about the American legal system, as reflected not only in their discernment in choosing lawyers but also in prospecting which judges might be most sympathetic to their concerns. Their legal team engaged in the practice of forum shopping by searching out the most sympathetic jurisdiction; after careful study, they decided to file suit in the court of the Southern District of New York.[117] On October 21, Albany attorney Richard Weiner laid out the case to Judge Lee Gagliardi in a preliminary hearing in New York, asserting that the Lipman annexation plan amounted to a violation of the civil rights of the Satmars.[118]

With the clock ticking toward the next hearing in Judge Gagliardi's court on October 26, town officials began to sense—and hear from their constituents—that village incorporation for the Satmars would be a far more preferable path to a long and costly religious discrimination lawsuit. As a result, intensive negotiations were jump-started between town and Satmar leaders, facilitated by an unlikely mediator: none other than Alan Lipman, author of the competing annexation petition. Mindful of the urgency of the situation, Lipman invited Moshe Friedman and Shlomo Mikhel Rosner to his house to commence discussions on Friday evening, October 22—the Sabbath eve! Friedman and Rosner walked with their wives to Lipman's house on the edge of the Satmar development. After they arrived, Lipman asked the Satmars to "put your [religious discrimination] petition on the shelf," at which point a mutually agreeable plan could be forged. Friedman and Rosner were unmoved: "We need our own village. . . . We want to govern ourselves." The conversation ended inconclusively, but it was decided to continue the next day.[119]

The decisive meeting occurred at Lipman's house on Saturday night. Throughout the night and into the early hours of the morning, Lipman shuttled between two rooms in his house, in one of which sat town leaders and in another the leaders of the Satmar community. The town wanted the Satmars to put an end to its suit as a precondition to an agreement; the Satmars insisted that the town permit it to proceed with its plans to create a village. At the end of one long and tense exchange, Friedman exploded in anger and accused the Monroe officials of antisemitism. At that point, after hours of negotiation and two years of growing tensions, Lipman conceded in the name of the town of Monroe: "Relax gentleman, you have your village." With that utterance, the meeting concluded at six o'clock on Sunday morning, October 24. Agreement was reached to create a legal municipality to be known officially as the village of Kiryas Joel. The Satmars hurried over to the home of Joel Teitelbaum to inform him and receive his blessing.[120]

All that remained were technicalities, albeit important ones. The following day, Satmar lawyer Jerry Markovits conducted a lengthy negotiation with Monroe officials over the precise borders of the new municipality, arriving at a map that was smaller than the original petition (320 vs. 450 acres) but included the main areas of Satmar settlement in Monroe that were north of the Quickway. The day after—Tuesday, October 26—was the scheduled date of the hearing in Judge Gagliardi's court to discuss the discrimination suit. Instead of presenting their arguments, the two sides met briefly with Judge Gagliardi to finalize the details of their agreement. The Monroe residents withdrew their petition for annexation, and the Satmars withdrew their discrimination suit.

Two final steps remained. The first was the formal authorization by the town of Monroe of the Satmar petition to create a village of Kiryas Joel. Notwithstanding ongoing objections by some neighbors of the Satmars, the town board approved the petition after a hearing on December 2. In a remarkably candid statement that reflected the stress of months of high-stakes legal machinations, Supervisor Rogers opined: "To me, and I believe to the town board, the compromise is almost as distasteful as the dispute it settled." The Satmars, he continued, were exploiting the state's Village Law to evade enforcement of Monroe's zoning laws. Moreover, the creation of a self-standing village reflected their "disdained isolation from the rest of the community." He concluded with a warning that if the Satmars "believe that they are above or separate from the rules and regulations" of Monroe, they should prepare for "more confrontations as bitter as the one this decision purports to resolve." With that ominous warning, Rogers did what he believed the law required him to do: he approved the petition.[121]

The next and final step was for the residents of the area seeking incorporation to hold a vote, which was scheduled for February 15. In the intervening months, town officials explored a variety of steps intended to limit the future expansion of Kiryas Joel, including merging with the village of Monroe. They also sent on, in the form of a letter from town attorney James Sweeney, a proposal to the New York State Legislature to emend the Village Law. With more than a trace of exaggeration, Sweeney made the case by claiming: "In the summer of 1976, the Town of Monroe had on its hands perhaps the most flagrant, brazen and widespread zoning violation ever visited upon a town anywhere in the

United States." He then expressed concern at the granting of "unfettered and absolute power" to the petitioners, employing language that would later be used by Satmar dissidents within Kiryas Joel.[122]

Notwithstanding this rancor, the Satmars had the legal wind at their backs. They proceeded to an election, which resulted in a vote of 148 to 1 in favor of village incorporation.[123] The results of the election were sent on to New York State Secretary of State Mario Cuomo, who quickly affirmed the petition. On March 2, 1977, the village of Kiryas Joel was formally established.

PART II

LAW AND RELIGION IN THE
VILLAGE AND BEYOND

CHAPTER 4

Not in America?

Seeds of Conflict

Kiryas Joel was established just as American society was retreating from the high point of liberal integrationism. Notwithstanding the successes the civil rights movement had achieved in the preceding decades, integration had been met with continuous popular resistance. The landmark Supreme Court decision of 1954 mandating school desegregation, *Brown v. Board of Education,* sparked particularly intense, often violent protests. White resistance to desegregation continued throughout the sixties and seventies. Black Nationalists also criticized *Brown,* asserting equality was better achieved through Black empowerment and racial separatism than through desegregation. By the late 1970s and early 1980s, when the village of Kiryas Joel was being formed, Americans of many different racial, religious, and political stripes were questioning the integrationist mantra of the civil rights movement and championing a variety of nationalist, separatist, and communitarian causes.

At the same time, the political mobilization of (mostly Christian) religious conservatives was altering the complexion of American politics. The emergence of the Moral Majority, a coalition of evangelical Christians with conservative Catholics that was actively involved in the effort to elect Ronald Reagan, took place against the backdrop of a broader "return to tradition" that was revitalizing faiths across denominational and political lines. The village of Kiryas Joel was unmistakably a part of these larger trends. Its creation in 1977, just three years before

Reagan's election, reflected the unwitting process of assimilation the Satmars were undergoing into a culture that itself was undergoing radical transformations.

As the liberal 1960s gave way to various illiberal movements in the 1970s, liberalism itself was evolving in the direction of multiculturalism, which challenged the model of equality as the elimination of racial, cultural and other kinds of differences. In place of a sameness model of equality, a different model was gaining ground that embraced cultural differences and their perpetuation as an ideal.

One early manifestation of this shift, foreshadowing struggles to come in KJ, was the New York City teachers' strike of 1968, which pitted the United Federation of Teachers (UFT), the predominantly Jewish teachers union, against the African American Teachers Association and the Ocean Hill and Brownsville neighborhoods of Brooklyn. Black and Puerto Rican communities in both of these neighborhoods banded together to withdraw from the citywide school district and establish their own school district that would be committed to hiring minority teachers and administrators and to implementing a curriculum that emphasized Black and African culture and history. The new community-controlled school district sought to hire its own teachers and administrators by firing the existing corps of teachers, almost all of whom were Jews. This prompted a strike by the UFT, which favored color-blind hiring policies and objected to abandoning New York State's long-standing policy of consolidating local school districts into a single, centralized unit. The union couched its objections in terms of the value of transcending differences by maintaining a citywide school district whose overall population was racially diverse—although schools within the district were de facto segregated.

The episode pushed to the fore tensions between Blacks and Jews in Brooklyn. Accusations and real expressions of antisemitism surfaced in the tense period from April through November 1968; so too the UFT and its powerful president, Alfred Shanker, were accused of racial insensitivity and ignoring the needs of the poor, underserved community of Ocean Hill–Brownsville. Some have seen this episode as a pivotal moment in the passage of Jews into the white American mainstream.

Author James Baldwin reflected on the tensions of the day by declaring, "It is cowardly and a betrayal of whatever it means to be a Jew, to act as a white man."[1]

Complicating matters even further was another version of the "Jew vs. Jew" friction. Many Jews in New York City, including a sizeable number in the teaching profession or with family members in it, supported the union, mobilized against antisemitism, and saw themselves on the other side of the Black community. This included the growing population of Hasidim, who lived in close proximity to Black and Hispanic communities in Brooklyn. And yet there were other Jews, including in the UFT, who supported school decentralization and the vision of empowering minority groups and celebrating their cultural differences that animated it. This "difference model of equality," most prominently associated with the Black Power movement, was enthusiastically embraced by many on the left. Still others found themselves torn between the two competing visions of equality.

This tension manifested itself not only in the politics of race and religion that were roiling American society but also in the disability rights movement that was emerging in this era and would come to play a surprisingly large role in Kiryas Joel. Federal and state laws mandating special education were passed just as the Satmars began to settle in the town of Monroe. By the time the village was established, the nationwide process of implementing these laws was well under way. This created a serious problem for the Satmars, who had to figure out a way of complying with these laws that did not breach the village's boundaries. This was a daunting challenge that quickly turned into a point of conflict with the authorities responsible for administering special education. Soon enough, political battles with the regional school district devolved into litigation, during the course of which KJ's separatist practices were exposed and denounced before the entire country as being un-American.

It may seem strange that such a seemingly marginal issue as disability rights would assume such an outsized role in shaping the village's history. But in 1994, precisely forty years after the landmark decision in *Brown v. Board of Education*, the Supreme Court would hand down a decision addressing the special education controversy in KJ, which not only affected the Satmars in profound ways but also affected how American courts interpreted constitutional law. *Grumet v. Kiryas Joel,* as the case was known, dealt not with the Equal Protection Clause, which *Brown* was based upon, but rather with the Establishment Clause of the First Amendment, which prohibits the "establishment of religion" and embodies the basic principle of separation between church and state. But it, too, addressed the relationship between equality and segregation. More specifically, it addressed KJ's practices of political and religious separatism—and America's tolerance for such practices.

Dragging on from 1985 until 1999, the litigation over special education in KJ had paradoxical effects on the village. It simultaneously challenged and fortified the Satmars' separatism and thrust them into prolonged contact with the very outside culture they sought to escape. It was a perfect example of the unwitting absorption of American cultural values that took place in KJ, reflecting the growing convergence between the Satmars' separatist values and various trends in American political culture that were pulling away from integration and toward the difference model of equality.

It also demonstrated the Satmars' continuing propensity to thrive in conflict. The creation of the village was meant to calm tensions with the surrounding world. But from the outset, Kiryas Joel was beset by challenges from outside authorities and civil rights advocates who questioned the constitutionality of its insularity and its peculiar mixture of religious with political authority. This was the basic paradox of municipal incorporation: while it promised—and indeed delivered—an unparalleled degree of political autonomy and insularity, it also brought increased visibility and notoriety. What from one point of view was a more perfect form of separation was, from another point of view, a maneuver that shined a spotlight on the village and its perceived deviations from American norms.

Yet, far from undermining the fledgling village, the conflicts that proliferated after its incorporation seemed only to strengthen it. Its leaders' powers continuously expanded, and their commitment to separation never wavered, even as it became increasingly enmeshed with American political and legal institutions. KJ's leaders withstood the challenges visited upon them by outside parties. And they also faced down opposition from within, which began to surface less than a year and a half after the village's formation. Like the village's external adversaries, its internal opponents made education the focal point of their criticism. They made common cause with the outside critics of the village's way of handling special education. And they also voiced objections to the village's private system of religious education.

But the first seed of internal dissent was planted before any of the education controversies arose. It emanated from a source even more fundamental than the schooling issue—the question of leadership succession—a matter that had long been avoided. And yet on August 19, 1979, it could no longer be forestalled. That was the day on which Rabbi Joel Teitelbaum suffered a heart attack and took his last breath at the age of ninety-two.

The Dawn of a New Era

The immediate response to the Rebbe's death in the global Satmar community was crushing grief, followed by shock. Despite his advanced age and years of infirmity, R. Yoelish had remained up until his passing not only the unquestioned spiritual leader of the Satmar community but also the guiding compass in all aspects of his followers' lives. Life without him left his followers in a state of profound disorientation.

That sense of being adrift was accentuated by the fact that the Rebbe left no male heirs. Feelings of loss shaded imperceptibly into a widespread sense of anxiety about who his successor would be. Typically, the position of Grand Rebbe in a Hasidic court would pass on in dynastic fashion to the Rebbe's son, usually the first born—as was the case when R. Yoelish's older brother, Hayim Tzvi, known as the Atsei Hayim, was appointed to succeed his father, the Kedushas Yom Tov, in Sighet. But the challenge of transmitting dynastic authority in a system based on charismatic leadership is always great—and all the greater in cases where there is no obvious successor.[2]

Not only did R. Yoel leave no sons, but he also had given no clear indication as to who should succeed him. Nor did the community have any established procedures for appointing a successor. After all, R. Yoelish was the first Satmar Rebbe, and his followers had found it so difficult to countenance the world without him that talk of succession had been virtually taboo prior to his death.

And yet, once he died, Satmar Hasidim accepted his death without question—in marked contrast to other some other Hasidic groups, such as the Bratslaver Hasidim who refused to accept a new leader after their rebbe, R. Nahman, died in 1810, or the Lubavitcher Hasidim, some of whom continue to believe to this day that Menachem Mendel Schneerson, who died in 1994, will come back as the Messiah.[3] Unlike these two groups, the Satmars immediately faced up to the need for a new leader. The only question was who that leader should be.

In the fog of uncertainty that followed R. Yoelish's death, the names of a small number of candidates were aired.[4] The leading contender was the Rebbe's nephew, Moshe Teitelbaum, son of the Atsei Hayim, who had spent time in his uncle's house as a young boy of eleven after being orphaned in 1926. Moshe lost his wife and children in Auschwitz, came to the United States after the war, married again, and had five children. He settled in Borough Park in Brooklyn, where he established a synagogue and became known as the Sigheter Rov after his hometown. In the last decade of R. Yoelish's life, he spent more time in his uncle's court, though he had a tense relationship with the Rebbetsin, Alta Faiga, who held tight control over the household.[5]

The perception that Moshe was the Rebbe's logical heir was cemented by his noble lineage (he descended from illustrious rabbis on both his mother's and his father's sides) and by the absence of any obvious alternative. As one member of the Satmar congregation board noted, "there was really no second choice."[6] Bowing to this logic, the Satmar community governing board began to hold discussions with Moshe about assuming leadership in the days after the Rebbe's death. At a meeting on Monday evening, September 10, 1979, a mere three weeks after the passing of Joel Teitelbaum, the board affirmed Moshe's selection as Rov and Av Beis Din (head of the rabbinical court). Immediately thereafter, seven members of the board went to Moshe's home in Borough Park to convey the decision. According to the account in *Der Yid*, he responded with great emotion to the honor bestowed on him and pledged to assume a leading role in "all matters pertaining to the administration of the holy community."[7]

The position of Rov in the late twentieth-century Satmar world was akin to that of an executive who stood at the top of an organization with many institutional units and holdings. Moshe and the governing board agreed that the job of Rov should be separated, at least for the first year of mourning, from the "seat of rabbinic authority" (*kise ha-robones*) that Joel Teitelbaum possessed as Rebbe. In Hasidic culture, the exalted status of the rebbe demanded total devotion and veneration. All agreed that Moshe Teitelbaum neither merited the unquestioned adulation his predecessor enjoyed nor wanted it, at least not right away. Instead, it was decided that he wait out the eleven-month mourning period following his uncle's death, during which time he would be able to consolidate power as Rov, and after which he could assume the prestigious second job from a position of greater strength.[8]

In accord with this plan, Moshe Teitelbaum ascended to the position of Rebbe during the week of the first anniversary of R. Joel's death. A lavish series of events was held that culminated in a coronation ceremony known as the *hakhtore*, literally, a crowning.[9] The event took place in the main synagogue/study hall in Kiryas Joel on Saturday night, August 9, 1980. Just two days earlier, presidential candidate Ronald Reagan had delivered his infamous states' rights speech in Mississippi. The fact that a presidential election was being waged in the outside world barely registered in KJ, where attention was riveted by the transfer of power taking place in their own world. *Der Yid* captured the drama of the event: "A crowd of over twenty thousand Satmar Hasidim from all over the world, featuring hundreds of rabbinic luminaries and Hasidic rebbes, assembled last motsa'e Shabbes when our teacher and rabbi, the righteous sage Rabbi Moshe Teitelbaum was chosen as the Satmar Rebbe, as successor to his illustrious uncle, the rabbi of all of the Diaspora, the holy of holies, our teacher and master, whose first yahrzeit fell on the 26th of Av (August 8)."[10]

The crowning ceremony marked not only Moshe's ascension as Rebbe, but also Kiryas Joel's newfound status as a rising center of the

Satmar world alongside Williamsburg.[11] As host of the coronation, KJ simultaneously embodied the legacy of the old Rebbe and signaled that the Satmar community had regained its equilibrium and was moving forward. To all outward appearances, it had weathered the period of uncertainty following Reb Yoelish's death, and all was well in Satmar Land. But not for long.

The Appearance of Internal Opposition

Almost immediately following the crowning ceremony, a small but vocal group of critics emerged, casting doubt upon Moshe's fitness to assume the mantle of the Rebbe. Indeed, these grumblings had preceded the coronation, commencing from the moment when Moshe was appointed Rov. It was perhaps inevitable that many Satmars would doubt Moshe's ability to approach the high bar of leadership set by R. Yoelish. The contrast between his personality and that of his revered uncle did not help. Skeptics described Moshe as "a very plain man" who did not come close to the holiness of his uncle.[12] Some of them adopted a wait-and-see attitude, hoping he would grow into the role. But a small number were vehemently opposed to his leadership from the get-go, believing Moshe to be a faint echo of the founding rebbe and an unworthy successor.

Dubbed *misnagdim* (opponents) by the new Rebbe's supporters, Moshe's foes were, for the most part, loyalists of the Rebbetsin, Alta Faiga (Old Faiga), the widow of Reb Yoelish. Faiga was now living full-time in KJ, having moved into the newly constructed apartment behind the main synagogue. Originally intended to serve as a parsonage where both she and her husband would live, Faiga's new home became a hub for Moshe's opponents, who formed an entourage around her, attending to her personal needs, helping her to implement her charitable endeavors, and using her house as an alternative prayer space, while hatching plans for keeping control of as many *moysdes* as possible in the Rebbetsin's hands.

The fact that the opposition camp had coalesced around a woman was, in and of itself, a striking departure from the traditional power dynamics of Hasidic life. While Faiga shied away from the title of "leader," her role in spearheading the resistance to Moshe's leadership was undeniable and shattered the model of the quiescent and subordinate rebbe's wife. That she managed to become "a power among the Satmar Hasidim" (as she was described in her obituary in the *New York Times* twenty-one years later) was testimony to her own forceful personality.[13] Like her late husband, she was a charismatic figure. She also had a gift for seizing opportunities and turning apparent disadvantages into advantages. Most notably, she was childless in a culture that celebrated and expected very large families. Not unexpectedly, this was initially held against her. But over time, she overcame the stigma of not producing progeny and an heir. By lavishing her attention—and charitable largesse—on children and schools, Faiga became known as the mother of the entire Satmar community. She thus took the traditional gender role assigned to women in her community and turned it on its head.

In keeping with this strategy, she parlayed her proximity to Reb Yoelish to gain clout in a man's world. Feisty and combative, she did not suffer rivals gladly. She already had a long-running feud with her husband's surviving daughter from his first marriage, Roysele, that had begun in Europe and continued after the war. Even more significantly, she deeply disliked Moshe Teitelbaum, who, it is said, had counseled his uncle for decades to pursue the halakhic option (and, in the view of some, obligation) to divorce Faiga because she bore him no children.[14] The lingering animus between Faiga and Moshe, along with her own formidable public persona, made her a focal point of opposition to the new rebbe. Within a short time after her husband's death, a small circle of misnagdim developed around her who refused to accept the legitimacy of Moshe's appointment as the new Satmar leader.[15]

Among the prominent figures in her circle was a real estate wheeler and dealer by the name of Nathan (also known as Nachman) Brach. As a man of means with diverse business interests in both Satmar centers, Brach played a role in helping to finance construction in Kiryas Joel in its earliest years and would go on to play a prominent role in the gentrification of Williamsburg by those known in Satmar parlance as the *artistn* (artists).[16] Following the Rebbe's death, he held himself up as a standard bearer for uncompromising devotion to Reb Yoelish's legacy. Unable to reconcile himself to Moshe as successor, Brach emerged early on as a ringleader in the camp formed around Faiga, aiding and abetting byzantine financial dealings through which the Rebbetsin and her followers sought to thwart Moshe.[17] Brach's and Faiga's claims to ownership of various properties would become an extremely valuable weapon in the ensuing fights between their camp and Moshe's and the ever-growing schisms that soon followed. Over time, Brach became a flashpoint and one of the first catalysts of litigation emanating out of the internal disputes in KJ. This litigation, which Moshe's supporters initially resorted to as a means to suppress the internal challenge to his authority, was separate from the special education litigation initiated by KJ's external opponents. But the two legal battles commenced at roughly the same time, and together they stamped the village with the strong imprint of American law.

Conflict and even violence were hardly unknown in the Hasidic world, and particularly in the Teitelbaum family, extending back to nineteenth-century Hungary. What was distinctive about the post-Yoelish era was that conflict and violence turned inward, pitting one Satmar Hasid against another. The timing of the Rebbe's illness and death cast a shadow over the village's earliest years. Without the unifying force of his charismatic personality, the community very quickly began to splinter. It took time, however, for the conflicts to reach a point of deep fracture. In the immediate aftermath of the Rebbe's death, the full implications of the developing feud between Faiga and Moshe were not yet clear. Most Satmars managed to stay out of the simmering controversy, concentrating instead on the daily business of raising children, making a living, and observing religious law. The main focus of the community was neither the succession dispute nor the special education controversy, but rather building up the institutions of the shtetl that the Rebbe had envisaged: the synagogue, the *beis midrash* (study hall), the wedding hall, and the all-important schools where boys and girls were taught—separately—to fulfill their respective ritual duties. All of these institutions were still in nascent form when the village was established in 1977. But thanks to the community's concerted effort, they developed at a rapid clip.

As did the village population. From a few dozen families in 1974, the number of village residents at the time of its incorporation in 1977 had shot up to around five hundred—a fourfold increase in a mere three years.[18] By 1980, the population of the village again jumped four times to two thousand. This meteoric growth was partly attributable to the arrival of new families, each bringing with them the Satmars' typically high birthrate. This "natural" population growth was augmented by the influx of yeshivah *bokhers*, boys sent to study in the KJ central yeshivah, which quickly acquired a strong reputation in the broader Satmar community. Attending the KJ yeshivah became a source of prestige for Satmar boys—and a prized feature in a prospective bridegroom. Nothing could serve as a better demonstration that the village was thriving, even with the first stirrings of internal dissent. Day by day, birth by birth, bokher by bokher, bridegroom by bridegroom, KJ was fulfilling the late Rebbe's dream of a shtetl in the suburbs, separated from the outside world.

External Opposition

But the very things that reflected the Satmars' success in creating their own autonomous enclave reignited the conflict that incorporation was expected to extinguish. The exponential population growth, in particular, threatened to disturb the relatively placid conditions that prevailed in the village's first few years. The first sign of open tension between KJ and its neighbors was a direct consequence of the village's need to accommodate the burgeoning population that resulted from its stunning rate of growth. In the first of many efforts to respond to this challenge, Kiryas Joel annexed another 370 acres of land in 1983.

The annexation was one of the first major exercises of municipal power undertaken by the village. As such, it required village leaders to follow state regulations. All local government units in America are regarded as subdivisions of the state and are required to act in conformity with state municipal law. Among the requirements that have to be met for a municipality's actions to be considered legal are rules designed to harmonize the activities of smaller units with the interests of the larger regions of which they are a part. The first of these rules to confront the Satmars was a New York municipal law that requires annexations to be approved by a majority of voters in both units affected by the proposed act: the municipality engaging in annexation and the municipality from which land would be annexed. When applied to the proposed land annexation in Kiryas Joel, that meant gaining the approval of the town of Monroe.

That proved to be extremely contentious.[19] Seven years earlier both parties to the "divorce" settlement that established Kiryas Joel had hoped that the creation of a separate village would lead to the Satmars' effective withdrawal from the town of Monroe. Indeed, Monroe's residents wished for that no less ardently than the Satmars did. But the land annexation of 1983 was perceived by many of them to be an ominous sign that this expectation was misplaced.

The realization may have been dawning on Monroe's residents that conflicts over scarce resources, such as land, would not come to an end just because a legal boundary had been set up around the Satmar community. This was exactly why state law required localities to act in ways that took neighboring communities' interests into consideration. An official boundary would not prevent the area now designated a village from drawing upon the same water table nor from laying claim to the same contiguous landmass to which the rest of the town lay claim. In recognition of this unsettling prospect, over a thousand residents in Monroe signed a petition submitted to the town board before the vote to approve the annexation took place, expressing their concern that the land grab, as they perceived it to be, would lead to overdevelopment.

The board, however, summarily rejected the petition. Reflecting the diversity of opinion within the town of Monroe, it did not merely disappoint KJ's opponents; it denounced them. Raising the specter of invidious motives that had haunted the earlier conflict with the Satmars, the board sharply rebuked the petitioners: "We reject summarily the . . . concern relating to the erosion of the current sociological base within the Monroe community. The comments . . . border on base sociological and religious bigotry."[20] With this public statement, the board announced its decision to approve KJ's acquisition of the undeveloped land.

Monroe's divided response reflected divisions emerging in American society more broadly. Thus, while KJ's land annexation provoked conflict with the outside world, it also reflected congruences with nationwide trends. Indeed, at the same time that KJ was seeking to enlarge its land base beyond its original 340 acres, another religious enclave, on the opposite side of the United States, was seeking to do the same. This was the community of Rajneeshpuram, Oregon, founded by spiritual guru Bhagwan Shri Rajneesh and settled by legions of his followers. Rajneeshpuram was like Kiryas Joel in a number of regards. Both were sectarian spiritual communities that sought to remove themselves from mainstream society, and both sought to do so by carving out a large degree of territorial autonomy and incorporating themselves as municipalities. The confluence of their respective incorporation and annexation strategies signified a bold new form of communitarianism that was then sweeping the country. But not all communitarian experiments were equally successful. Indeed, there were many attempts to secede and incorporate made by different communities with different identities at this time, some of which worked and others did not. Paralleling KJ's success was the neighborhood of West Hollywood, which became the "first gay city" in America in 1984, having formerly been an unincorporated part of Los Angeles County. By contrast, a few years later, the predominantly African American population of West Roxbury, Massachusetts, tried and failed to establish a separate city named in honor of Nelson and Winnie Mandela after being branded and denounced as a movement of "Black separatists." Even the Rajneeshees' initially successful effort to establish their own city ended in failure. Their attempted land annexation was disallowed by the regional Land Use Board of Appeals (a decision upheld by the Oregon Court of Appeals), and the City of Rajneeshpuram itself was found to be an unconstitutional "establishment" of religion in violation of the First Amendment.[21]

By contrast, the Satmars' municipal project was a marked success. But it did not escape intense, ongoing controversy. Indeed, the reaction to its first land annexation in 1983 was a harbinger of external challenges it would face for years to come. The fear of Monroe residents that the Satmars would constantly try to procure more land continued for decades. Meanwhile, another conflict emerged, this one between KJ and the Monroe-Woodbury School District, the regional school district that encompassed the town of the Monroe, the neighboring town of Woodbury, and all of the villages within them.

It was in this arena that the controversy over special education arose. But special education was not the only, or even the first, source of disagreement between the Monroe-Woodbury School District and the village of Kiryas Joel. Special ed, as it was coming to be known, was just one of several services regional school districts were obliged to provide to all children within their territory. By state law, the Monroe-Woodbury School District had to provide bus transportation, remedial education, and special education services to children in its jurisdiction, regardless of whether they were enrolled in public schools. This was not a special arrangement for KJ. In New York State (as in other states), all school districts were legally obligated to deliver these services to children in their jurisdiction even if they attended parochial or secular private schools.

These legal obligations drew KJ into the district's regulatory orbit, despite the fact that, to a one, Satmar parents eschewed public education. All Satmar children attended KJ's private religious schools at the time the school district controversies arose, except for a very few who, because of severe disabilities, did not attend school at all. But the village of Kiryas Joel lay within the physical boundaries of the Monroe-Woodbury School District. And KJ properties were subject to taxation. Those taxes were used to support the district. In return, the school district provided a variety of services to children in KJ, even though they did not attend public school.

Meeting the needs of KJ children for these services while respecting the community's religious and cultural norms proved to be an exceptionally difficult balancing act that would lead to years of tension between KJ and the Monroe-Woodbury School District. Even as seemingly innocuous a service as bus transportation became a point of controversy. Remedial education was another flashpoint. And special education became nothing short of explosive. Eventually, in much the same way that the earlier standoff over zoning had led to the creation of the village of Kiryas Joel, the tension over access to special educational services culminated in the creation of a public school in KJ devoted exclusively to serving children with special needs. This was the development that sparked the case of *Grumet v. Kiryas Joel*, the lawsuit that challenged the creation of a separate school district and ended up placing KJ on display in front of the entire nation.

By the time this litigation reached the Supreme Court, a large cast of characters had been assembled, each of whom played a key role in the developing legal drama. In addition to already familiar figures such as Reb Moshe, Reb Aaron, and KJ's titular mayor, Leibish Lefkowitz, new leaders emerged inside KJ whose rise was linked in various ways with the special education controversy. It was at this time that Abe Wieder rose to political prominence. By his side was his wife, Schayndel, who herself played an important, albeit accidental, role in bringing awareness to the village of the rights of children with special needs. Another woman, who played an even larger role in raising consciousness in the community, was Malka Silberstein, the first Satmar advocate for children with special needs. Joining Mrs. Silberstein in her fight for children with disabilities was Wolf Lefkowitz, a wealthy businessman who became the benefactor of the first program established for children with disabilities in KJ, which was set up inside the girls' religious school.

It was also at this time that the internal dissent in KJ blossomed into a full-blown dissident movement. The leaders of this growing dissident movement enthusiastically supported the litigation challenging the constitutionality of KJ's school district. One in particular, Joseph Waldman, whose brother Zalman was Faiga's personal assistant, did everything in his power to aid and abet the plaintiff, Louis Grumet. Waldman was in regular, unsolicited contact with Grumet's litigation team.

The dissidents themselves were aided by their own personal lawyer, civil rights attorney Michael Sussman. Sussman was but one of a number of outsiders, including lawyers, judges, elected officials, and educators, who came to loom large in KJ. Many outsiders were drawn into the

life of the village through the special education controversy, some as
adversaries of the Satmars, some as representatives and allies. On the
adversarial side were Daniel Alexander, the Monroe-Woodbury School
District superintendent, and his assistant superintendent, Terry Olivo.
Yet another thorn in the side of KJ was the union that represented
school bus drivers in the Monroe-Woodbury School District, which
brought a grievance on behalf of Patricia Dugan, a woman bus driver
who became the subject of an early protest in KJ, which proved to be
the opening shot in the protracted legal battle. But by far the most indefatigable outside opponent was Grumet, the self-appointed civil
rights crusader who spent ten years, aided by his lawyers, Jay Worona
and Pilar Sokol, suing New York State for authorizing the creation of a
public school district inside KJ.

On the allies' side were numerous politicians, including the two gov-
ernors who presided over New York during the time of the special education controversy, Mario Cuomo and George Pataki, both of whom
were huge champions of the Satmars. So too were several influential
members of the state legislature, most notably Joseph Lentol. Outside
the governmental arena, KJ's interests were represented by George Shebitz, the village's chief lawyer, alongside legions of other lawyers employed by the village over the years. After the KJ School District was
established, its superintendent, Steven Benardo, became one of the most
vocal and effective spokespersons for the village. And once the school
district became the subject of Grumet's lawsuit, KJ also was represented
by one of the country's foremost litigators, Nathan Lewin, whose client
roster included the likes of Richard Nixon, Edwin Meese, John Lennon,
and Jodie Foster in addition to Orthodox Jewish groups.

Beyond this circle of outsiders who directly engaged with KJ on a
regular basis were legal and political actors who stood at a further remove from the village but whose actions nevertheless had a significant
impact on the litigation and, by extension, KJ itself. These included the
numerous judges who participated in the special education dispute as
it wound its way up and down the different tiers of the federal and state
courts, most notably, Judith Kaye (the first woman to serve as New

York's chief judge), Lawrence Kahn (the federal district court judge who first addressed the constitutionality of KJ's school district), and all members of the Rehnquist Court, no fewer than six of whom—Justices Souter, Blackmun, Stevens, O'Connor, Kennedy, and Scalia—wrote separate opinions weighing in on the KJ dispute. Appearing in a cameo role in the *Grumet* litigation was John Roberts, the current chief justice of the Supreme Court, but back then a young and relatively unknown lawyer, though already a well-respected member of the nascent conservative legal movement. Another conservative lawyer yet to become a household name whose actions affected the course of the litigation was Jay Sekulow, today best known as a radio and TV host and as a member of former president Trump's legal team. He entered the KJ story as the newly appointed chief counsel for the American Center for Law and Justice, a self-described "politically conservative, Christian-based" legal advocacy organization established in 1990, just as the *Grumet* case was getting started.

It was a high-profile crowd that surrounded KJ by the time the *Grumet* case reached the Supreme Court in 1994. But in 1980, the year of Moshe's anointment, the village existed in relative obscurity, and most of these figures had yet to be drawn into KJ's orbit. Although the events that would bring about the conflict with Monroe-Woodbury were already under way, nobody then could have anticipated its eruption. To the contrary, the matter of special needs seemed, at the time, to be a very small concern, a family matter that few were focused on, other than the mothers of a handful of children with disabilities. As with the Rebbetsin's rise to influence, the work of these women remained under the radar for quite a while, only to explode into public consciousness at the end of the decade.

1974–1984: The Road to Special Education

In 1974, the same year when the first Satmar families moved to the town of Monroe, Malka Silberstein, a twenty-four-year-old woman living in Williamsburg, gave birth to her fourth child. Named Shayndel (Yiddish for "beauty"), the baby was born with Down syndrome. The way Mrs. Silberstein tells the story, "At the moment of her birth, I decided I'm going to accept it and this is going to be my mission."[22] That moment marked the birth not only of her daughter but also of an advocacy movement for children with disabilities inside the Satmar community.

Prior to the emergence of this advocacy movement, people with disabilities were heavily stigmatized in the Satmar and the wider Hasidic community. Family members with disabilities were a source of shame, who were excluded from many community activities and often kept hidden away in their homes. Well aware of these negative attitudes toward children with special needs, Malka Silberstein became an advocate for change soon after her daughter Shayndel's birth. In 1976, she turned for support to Leibish Lefkowitz, the leading Satmar official, and one of the first to make his home in KJ.[23] At that time, KJ was not yet a legally recognized village, though its incorporation was less than a year away. Mrs. Silberstein would eventually move to Kiryas Joel herself, carrying her activism with her. But when she first approached Lefkowitz, that prospect was not on her mind.

What occupied the attention of Mrs. Silberstein and Lefkowitz at their first meeting in Brooklyn was a matter seemingly far removed from issues of local government or national politics. In Mrs. Silberstein's recollection, what she had to say to Lefkowitz came down to a simple moral principle: "It's not fair," she told him.[24] It was not right to deny children with disabilities and their families the essential services they needed. And it was not right, in her view, to isolate people with disabilities and exclude them from community life.

Mrs. Silberstein's most fundamental goal was to overcome that isolation. As she saw it, "the community did not have the right attitude."[25] The entire community revolved around the performance of *mitzvos*, or ritual commandments. Schools were key agents in imparting the required skills and knowledge to boys and girls to perform their respective obligations.[26] For boys, this meant being prepared for a life of Torah study and stringent ritual observance. For girls, the focus was on preparing them for their future roles as guardians of the home, as wives, mothers, and housekeepers—roles that were also viewed as a fulfillment of religious duties but that did not involve mandated Torah study. Because the focus of boys' education was on religious studies, those who lacked the mental faculties to be able to study the Torah and perform the prescribed rituals of daily worship were, by common practice, excused. A similar logic was applied to "defective" girls. Since one of the chief goals of education was to learn how to perform obligations one would assume as an adult, those who were viewed as incapable of performing adult religious obligations were seen as not being in need of education.

This was the logic that Mrs. Silberstein set out to challenge. Her vision was integrationist to the core—though a vision of integration that would take place only within a segregated Satmar society. The goal, as she saw it, was not just to provide support for children with special needs. More fundamentally, it was to integrate them into the life of the community. That meant, first and foremost, developing an educational program that would permit children with special needs to participate fully, or as fully as possible, in school and in the ritual life of their families and the wider Satmar community.

Mrs. Silberstein was unwittingly replicating the logic of integration that was then being promoted by the nascent disability rights movement. At the same time that she was beginning to organize support for families in the Satmar community, a nationwide movement to raise consciousness and change practices in the treatment of people with disabilities was gaining steam.[27] The mantra of the American disability rights movement was "mainstreaming." Its goal was to overcome widespread practices like labeling people as defective and "warehousing" them in institutions. In combating the isolation and stigmatization of people with disabilities, the disability rights movement took its cues from the civil rights movement, which had fought against Jim Crow segregation by linking the cause of racial equality with the objective of desegregation. Thanks to the civil rights crusades of the 1950s and 1960s, the segregationist logic of "separate but equal" had been roundly repudiated in America. The landmark 1954 case *Brown v. Board of Education* that demanded an end to racial segregation in the nation's public schools held that separate is "inherently unequal."[28] Ten years later, that same integrationist logic was incorporated into the Civil Rights Act of 1964.[29] Another ten years later, in 1974 (the year that Shayndel Silberstein was born), a similar logic was incorporated into a special education bill that disability rights activists were proposing and lobbying for in Congress. That bill, the Education for All Handicapped Children Act (later renamed the Individuals with Disabilities Education Act and known now as IDEA), was passed in 1975. It was one of the first pieces of disability rights legislation to be enacted in the United States and the first to recognize special education as a legal right.[30]

The Education for All Handicapped Children Act echoed the integrationist credo of the Civil Rights Act. But in addition to calling for mainstreaming, the new statute required school districts to accommodate the needs of each qualifying child with an individualized education program (IEP). Thus, both integrationist and accommodationist principles were embodied in the new special education regime, notwithstanding the fact that the principle of accommodating differences and that of overcoming them often pulled in opposite directions.

The dominant belief enshrined in the new disability rights laws was that the path to equality for people with disabilities was through mainstreaming, that is, integration.[31] But integration into *what*? Mrs. Silberstein's vision of integrating the disabled more fully into Satmar society would come to be seen by outsiders as a segregationist practice that prevented the integration of Satmar children into the outside world. This was a paradox that beset many groups other than the Satmars. Advocates for the Deaf, for example, were deeply divided at this time over the question of whether integration was best achieved by raising children with hearing impairments *within* the separate world of the Deaf community or by mixing them into mainstream environments. Proponents of the former position argued that forcing Deaf children to learn to speak orally and lip-read in order to join the hearing world impaired their linguistic and mental development and denied them the opportunity to become fully fluent in their own culture and language (Sign).[32] The other side of the debate claimed that Deaf separatism denied children the ability to become more fully integrated into society at large.[33]

A similar tension surfaced in Camphill, a residential boarding school in Pennsylvania to which New York had been sending children with developmental disabilities for decades. Camphill was among the first targets of Louis Grumet, who took the reins of the newly established Office of Children with Handicapping Conditions, which was formed by New York State's Education Department in response to the new federal legislation. Grumet himself was a specialist neither in special needs nor in education. He was a veteran behind-the-scenes player in New York State politics with a particular expertise in the field of state and local government. At the time IDEA was passed, he was working for Mario Cuomo, who was then New York's secretary of state. In 1975, Grumet, a protégé of the future governor, had served at Cuomo's suggestion as New York State's delegate to the White House Conference on Individuals with Handicapped Conditions. Subsequently, he represented Cuomo in the negotiations that led to the passage of legislation establishing the new program on handicapped children's education in the state's Department of Education. He was tapped to run that new special ed program by Gordon Ambach, New York State's commissioner of education, in 1977—the year that the village of KJ was created.[34]

From the very beginning of his tenure as assistant commissioner, Grumet adopted an aggressive approach. Trained as a lawyer (though he never practiced law), he saw it as his mission to enforce the new mandate, using the threat of litigation to spur reforms and, if necessary, close institutions that were not in compliance. Together with his chief aide, Dr. Hannah Fleigenheimer, he set about identifying schools that operated in violation of the new special education laws. His first targets were examples of the notorious facilities branded as "warehouses." One, the Harlan School, was an institution to which poor Black children in New York City were routinely sent. The other was the sole program for Hispanic children with disabilities in the city.[35] Then he took on Camphill.

Camphill was a curious and illuminating choice for the man who would spend the 1990s waging a legal campaign against the creation of a school district in Kiryas Joel. A favored placement of New York's elite families, Camphill was more than a boarding school; it was a "children's village," a residential community based on the utopian philosophy of Austrian educator and philosopher Rudolf Steiner (1861–1925). Founded in a Pennsylvania farmhouse in the late 1950s, the Camphill School was part of a network of youth and adult villages where people with developmental disabilities lived and worked side by side with people without such disabilities in an environment intended to nurture each individual's "inner healthy self."[36] Its bucolic setting, its progressive educational philosophy, and its predominantly white middle- and upper-class student body placed Camphill in a world apart from the prototypical warehouses that Grumet had taken on in New York City. At Camphill, students played musical instruments, gardened and farmed, and frolicked in nature. The educational curriculum included the classics (Milton, Dante's *Divine Comedy*) and the arts.[37]

Yet Grumet determined that Camphill, despite all of its attractive features, was in violation of the new special education law. Staff members sent in to monitor the situation at Camphill observed numerous deficiencies. By their account, students spent their time in the vaunted Milton class masturbating, tuning out, and generally failing to be engaged by a program that catered more to the hopes and dreams of their parents than to their actual abilities.[38]

Armed with this report, Grumet confronted the New York Board of Regents, which initially resisted his demand to cease paying for placements at the Camphill school. One of the regents had two of his own children at Camphill. Another, the sole African American on the Board of Regents, was Kenneth Clark, the psychologist whose studies of children's reactions to Black and white dolls (conducted with his wife, Mamie Phipps Clark) famously supplied the Supreme Court with its support for the proposition that "separate is inherently unequal" in *Brown v. Board*.[39] Because of his role in *Brown* and his ongoing efforts to promote desegregation, Clark was a personal hero to Grumet, whose own lifelong dedication to integration began when he was a teenager in West Virginia in 1955 experiencing the implementation of *Brown* first-hand. Clark, who had not previously taken an interest in the issue of segregating children with special needs, told Grumet after his presentation, "You really put me in my place," and invited him to what turned out to be a four-hour dinner with him and his wife Mamie. The encounter led to a personal friendship with the Clarks and fortified Grumet's vision of special education as a civil rights issue. Indeed, he viewed his job "from the beginning to the end as to have each child educated in the least restrictive environment," which, to his mind, meant integration.[40]

In the eyes of its many supporters, Camphill was a visionary community where children with serious disabilities could learn and thrive far better than they could anywhere else. But to Louis Grumet, it was just another example of an institution that segregated disabled children and failed to meet their educational needs. In response to one regent's assertion that the children were loved and well treated there, his provocative retort was that "we're not paying for love and well treatment, sir. We call that prostitution. We're paying for education, and they're not getting it."[41]

Reflecting back on that time, Camphill's longtime director Bernard Wolf (then a young house parent, "coworker," and teacher at the school) acknowledged that, from one point of view, the school was failing to fulfill the goal of mainstreaming children.[42] But he insisted that what looks like segregation to outsiders was, from Camphill's internal point of view, the most successful form of integration: into a small and nurturing community.

Much the same could be said of the programs for special needs children in the Satmar community. In calling for children's integration into the life of the Satmar community, Mrs. Silberstein could be seen as embracing a separatist vision—in keeping with the religious separatism that defined the community as a whole. But from the perspective of the Satmar community, what she was calling for was a form of mainstreaming that would reverse the practices of isolating people with disabilities that had long existed in the Haredi community.

From this point of view, Mrs. Silberstein's vision of integration was perfectly in sync with the new mantra of mainstreaming that was being written into American law. It was only in 1970 that the first piece of disability rights legislation in the United States was passed, guaranteeing "handicapped access" to public buildings. In 1973, disability rights activists scored their second legislative victory with a law guaranteeing equal employment opportunities and forbidding discrimination by employers on the basis of either physical or mental handicaps. The first federal law to recognize the right to special educational services for children with special needs, the Education for Handicapped Children Act, was passed in 1975, just a year before Mrs. Silberstein and Leibish Lefkowitz had their first meeting.[43]

Despite the congruence in the timing, Mrs. Silberstein says she was unaware of these new disability rights and special education laws when she began her own efforts on behalf of special needs children.[44] Her first step after her daughter was born was to assemble a group of parents in Brooklyn who shared her desire for reform within the Haredi world. It was then that she turned to Leibish Lefkowitz, who immediately promised the community's support and the backing of the Rebbe. In addition to financial support, Lefkowitz made a classroom available in the Bais Ruchel school in Brooklyn. There, in 1977 Mrs. Silberstein and her fellow activists opened the first school in the Satmar community for children with special needs.[45]

The emergence of a disability rights consciousness within the Satmar community stands as one of the most significant instances of the absorption of modern American cultural attitudes into Satmar life. At the time, these modern attitudes were as new to mainstream America as they were to the Satmars. And Satmars were as active in bringing about the process of change in their own community as outside actors were in theirs. They did not lag behind the rest of society. Nor were they passive recipients of a more enlightened culture that was thrust upon them. They were active agents who produced their own indigenous movement for reform that was both temporally and philosophically in harmony with the changes taking place in the broader world. It was a perfect example of the process of unwitting assimilation. Neither set of cultural actors directly influenced or took inspiration from the other. Yet the Satmars were clearly, if unconsciously, replicating and responding to changes occurring in the broader culture, in particular to new attitudes that were moving Americans toward a greater acceptance of human differences.

Mrs. Silberstein's advocacy, which began in Brooklyn, reflected this new appreciation for difference. She took that advocacy with her when she and her family moved to Kiryas Joel five years later, in 1982. Her judgment when she first arrived was that "there was nothing for the children in Orange County" except for the BOCES program in Goshen (the county seat), which, she concluded, "was a nice program but it wasn't appropriate for our children."[46] BOCES is the acronym for the Boards of Cooperative Educational Services, a system in New York under which smaller school districts band together to establish shared programs they cannot easily afford to maintain on their own. Monroe-Woodbury was (and remains) part of the Orange-Ulster BOCES, which provides a variety of services, including special education programs, to children from both Orange and Ulster counties. Special education programs were also offered at the Monroe-Woodbury public schools. But none of these programs was deemed "appropriate" by Satmar parents and community leaders for the simple reason that the programs required the children to leave Kiryas Joel.

What Mrs. Silberstein was looking for was what she had helped to create in Williamsburg: a special education program housed within the Satmars' own schools. It did not take her long to renew the advocacy she had initiated in Williamsburg. As she had done there, she sought out and found other parents of children with special needs who shared her desire to develop resources for children and their families. The number of children with disabilities in the community at the time was not large. The overall population of the village was still quite small. And, contrary to widespread belief, there is no evidence that Satmars exhibit unusually high rates of "birth defects" (a stigmatizing term disability rights advocates reject). Nor was there a lack of parental interest in meeting the needs of families of children with disabilities. The same change in sensibility that was occurring in Brooklyn was making itself felt in KJ as well, even before Mrs. Silberstein began organizing there. A meeting she called shortly after her arrival, in 1983, drew a good twenty-five participants.[47] Among them was Wolf Lefkowitz, a stalwart follower of the old Rebbe. Lefkowitz's wife had given birth to a child with Down syndrome earlier that year. A wealthy businessman who owned and managed a successful crystal factory, Lefkowitz (no relation to Leibish Lefkowitz, who also owned a crystal factory) moved to the village in 1980. He was one of the first devotees of the idea of a school for children with special needs in Kiryas Joel. Like Mrs. Silberstein, Wolf Lefkowitz states that from the moment of his child's birth, he knew that helping children with special needs was going to become his life's mission. That mission was clarified for him at the 1983 meeting when a therapist from Monsey who specialized in working with Orthodox children was invited to talk to the group and convinced him of the wisdom of creating a special needs school.[48]

With Lefkowitz's financial backing and the institutional support of R. Moshe and KJ's religious establishment, a school for Satmar children with special needs—really, a school within a school—was opened later that year. Called Shaarei Chemlah (Hebrew for Gates of Compassion), it was given space on the first floor of KJ's own Bais Ruchel girls' school. Though the Shaarei Chemlah children had their own separate classrooms, teachers, and specialized curriculum, they were able to mix with the other children in the school. Fulfilling Mrs. Silberstein's dream of integration, children with disabilities could go to school hand in hand with their siblings and participate with them in various school events and ceremonies.

Like the Bais Ruchel into which it was integrated, Shaarei Chemlah was a private institution, privately administered, privately incorporated, and almost entirely privately funded.[49] Wolf Lefkowitz was the school's major patron and its executive director. The UTA provided the physical facilities and other material resources. Outside funding came from the Kennedy Foundation, a private foundation created by Joseph P. Kennedy in 1946 to promote opportunities for people with intellectual disabilities.[50] The Kennedy Foundation, which long predated the new disability rights laws, was one of the early manifestations of the dawning consciousness in America about special needs. Turning to it for support represented the old model of reliance on private philanthropy, which was then just beginning to be supplemented and supplanted by the new legal regime that made special education a public responsibility.

The resulting coexistence of public and private educational institutions for children with special needs created a quandary for parents of children with disabilities who lived in religious subcommunities—and for the school districts now required to serve them. The right of parents to choose to send their children to religious schools was well established.[51] But so too was the general principle rooted in the Establishment Clause that public funding could not be directed to parochial schools.[52] Unless children with special needs were withdrawn from those schools and sent to public school, it was unclear how, or even if, they could receive publicly funded special ed services to which they were now entitled. But being compelled to send one's children to public over parochial school would violate established parental rights.

The problem was that the distinction between public and private institutions had become muddied. Even before the special education law created this predicament, in 1965 Congress enacted Title I (formally known as the Elementary and Secondary Education Act), which made school districts responsible for providing remedial education to economically disadvantaged children.[53] Up to this time, the line between public and private schools had been relatively clear. Public funding for education went to public schools, while private schools received no public funding (apart from the indirect subsidy of tax exempt status). So long as parents could pay for it, their right to choose a private religious school for their children was secure. But once school districts became responsible for serving all children in their jurisdictions, the line between public and private was blurred. And that raised serious Establishment Clause issues regarding the provision of public services to children in religious schools.

The Establishment Clause, which states, "Congress shall make no law respecting an establishment of religion," is one of two clauses in the Constitution addressing religion. The other, known as the Free Exercise Clause, prohibits Congress from interfering with the free exercise of religion. That guarantee of the free exercise of religion is one of the two constitutional pillars on which the right of parents to choose a religious education for their children, and opt out of public schooling, rests. The second pillar of that parental right is the Due Process Clause of the Fourteenth Amendment, which prohibits the state from "depriv[ing] any person of life, liberty, or property without due process of law." Reconciling the parental right to choose religious education with the

Establishment Clause prohibition on public support for religious education was a problem that long predated the legal problems in Kiryas Joel. Indeed, the tension between the right to free exercise and the prohibition on state support for religion had been evident from the time the Supreme Court first applied the Establishment Clause to state and local governments, which occurred in 1947 in the landmark case *Everson v. Board of Education.*

Everson was a first in several regards. It was the first Supreme Court case to determine that the Establishment Clause, which by its terms prohibits only *Congress* from enacting laws "respecting an establishment of religion," also applies to state and local governments. It was also the first case to make Thomas Jefferson's metaphor of a "wall of separation" between church and state the foundational principle for analyzing Establishment Clause claims.[54] And it was the first to take up the question of whether the government could provide funding, either directly or, as in this case, indirectly, to religious schools.[55] More specifically, it addressed the question of whether state funding for transportation to religious schools was constitutional.

Acknowledging the tension between the Establishment Clause principle of a "wall" between government and religion and the Free Exercise principle that the government cannot burden the exercise of religion, the Court in *Everson* delivered a decidedly mixed message. On the one hand, it insisted that the principle of separation between church and state prohibited government funding of parochial schools. The "wall of separation," it said, must be kept "high and impregnable." That implied, or so it seemed, that there could be no government aid for religious education. On the other hand, the Court stated that religion could not be a basis for disqualifying people from receipt of a public service or benefit. The Court reasoned that a program that funnels public money to parochial schools is constitutional as long as it supports a service that is secular and given to all private schools, not just religious ones. Whether the program in *Everson* actually satisfied this criterion was debatable. The impetus behind the program challenged in *Everson* was clearly to benefit parochial schools. And the lion's share, if not the totality, of the budget went to parents who sent their children to parochial schools. But on its face, the law provided transportation sub-sidies for children going to secular as well as religious schools. Conced-ing that the transportation subsidy program approached the "verge" of breaching the "wall" of church-state separation,[56] the Court concluded that it was nonetheless permissible because the subsidy was provided to assist parents of schoolchildren "without regard to their religious belief."[57]

Following this confounding decision, it was left to states to decide whether or not to provide publicly funded transportation to nonpublic schools. Many states already had programs that subsidized private school bus transportation; others created new ones.[58] New York State, reflecting the growing influence of its Catholic population, was among those that already had such a law in place. It responded to the *Everson* decision by passing a new law reaffirming its commitment to making school districts responsible for providing "sufficient transportation facilities . . . for all of the children residing within the school district to and from the school they legally attend."[59]

It remained an open question after *Everson* what services besides transportation satisfied its criteria for secular benefits. In the 1960s, many states had begun to push the envelope by enacting government programs that provided secular textbooks to private school students or subsidized the salaries of teachers who taught secular subjects in paro-chial schools. These programs were immediately challenged by civil liberties groups, resulting in a confusing series of holdings issued by the Supreme Court between 1968 and the early 1980s. Loans of textbooks to children in private schools were upheld, but loans of other instruc-tional materials (such as laboratory equipment) were struck down. Funds to administer standardized tests in private schools were upheld, but funds to pay for nonstandardized tests were struck down. Funding for diagnostic health services in private schools was upheld, but pay-ments to parochial school teachers to provide remedial teaching, guid-ance, counseling, and other testing services were struck down. And a program providing money to private schools to pay for the transporta-tion costs of field trips also was deemed to be unconstitutional, even though it was another transportation subsidy (for conveying students to and from school) that was the first form of state aid to private schools held to be constitutional. Subsidies for teacher salaries, tuition tax credits, and building maintenance grants likewise were struck down.[60]

Few could find a coherent principle to explain this baffling array of results. Religious conservatives were unhappy with the cases that denied support to religious schools. But liberals also were hard put to justify, let alone celebrate, a doctrine that offered little in the way of guidance to predict where the line between acceptable and unacceptable forms of support would or should be drawn. All placed the blame on the 1971 decision of *Lemon v. Kurtzman,* in which the Court sought to clarify the doctrine that *Everson* had ushered in by formulating a three-pronged test: Did the government program in question lack a secular purpose? Did it have the effect of either promoting or inhibiting religion? And did it foster an excessive entanglement between government and religion? If the answers to any of these questions were yes, the Supreme Court said, then the program should be struck down. Unfortunately, this attempt at clarification seemed only to add to the confusion and unpredictability of the judicial test. Democratic senator Daniel Patrick Moynihan quipped, after noting case law that permitted the government to provide books to parochial schools but not maps, "What about atlases?" The lack of a consistent principle or test was even acknowledged by the Supreme Court justices, who often described the doctrine in this area as an "embarrassment," but struggled to come up with a better approach.

This left it anyone's guess whether providing Title I services to students in private schools would be deemed constitutional. Since the Supreme Court did not directly address the question until 1985, a full twenty years after Title I was enacted, it was left to school districts to decide for themselves which position to take in the face of strenuous advocacy from both parochial school representatives and the civil liberties groups who opposed them.

In that twenty-year period between 1965 and 1985, it was the parochial schools' position that prevailed. Programs were set up in New York State and elsewhere that sent remedial education specialists, employed by local school districts, into parochial and secular private schools.

Under these long-standing programs, the Monroe-Woodbury School District had been providing remedial instruction in English and math to private schoolchildren for years when the Satmars first began to move in. It continued to make Title I services available to private school students, including Satmar children, after KJ was incorporated, just as it continued to make bus transportation available to transport Satmar children to and from their religious schools. There was nothing unique about this arrangement in which public resources were being used to augment the system of private religious education in KJ. It had been state policy to provide these services to children in parochial schools (and secular private schools) for decades. And the Satmars by and large welcomed these services, despite resistance in some quarters to accepting the Title I classes that the district offered.

For the first five years that this arrangement was in place, relations between the Satmar community and the school district were more or less amicable. But that situation began to change in 1983, when a series of incidents made cooperation between the district and the village less tenable. The first thing to cause trouble involved neither remedial nor special education. It was rather the school bus service. Monroe-Woodbury had been dispatching buses to ferry students to and from the private schools in KJ since the late 1970s. By the early 1980s, it was transporting a thousand or so KJ children a day.[61] Initially, the bus service caused no discernible friction. Since boys and girls attended different schools in different locations in KJ, the student population on the buses was effectively, though not officially, sex segregated. Assignments of routes were made at the start of each school year on the basis of a collective bargaining agreement between the bus drivers' union and the school district. Under this agreement, the school district was obliged to honor drivers' requests for routes in order of seniority. Prior to 1983, the seniority rules had yielded only male drivers for the routes that took the boys to the yeshivah.

But at the beginning of the 1983–1984 school year, a woman named Patricia Dugan was assigned to a yeshivah route. For boys to board a bus driven by a woman driver was a clear violation of the Satmars' gender-segregation norms. Ms. Dugan's assignment provoked an immediate protest. When she arrived at the appointed hour, the boys (following their teachers' instructions) refused to board the bus.[62]

Subsequently, in response to the UTA's request for an accommodation, the school district replaced Ms. Dugan with a male bus driver. Seeking to reconcile this action with the bus drivers' collective bargaining agreement, which granted the district discretion to deviate from seniority rules in special circumstances, the district's director of transportation issued a judgment that Dugan lacked "the necessary skill and ability to handle a particular route and to handle the children who will be driving on that route."[63] In short order, the bus drivers' union filed a grievance alleging a violation of the collective bargaining agreement.

Presiding over this controversy—and the Monroe-Woodbury School District—was Daniel Alexander, who had assumed the position of superintendent in 1978. Coming from a previous post at the East Ramapo Central School District in neighboring Rockland County, Alexander was alert to the challenges posed by a large Hasidic constituency for a public school district. In fact, he wrote his PhD dissertation on the subject of "The Political Influence of the Resident Hasidic Community on the East Ramapo Central School District." He began the dissertation while he was still working in Monsey and completed it in 1982, a few years after moving to the job at Monroe-Woodbury. The conclusion he drew then was tempered but prescient: the Hasidic community's influence over the East Ramapo School District was not significant—yet. But he cautioned that the influence of the community could grow and potentially come into conflict with the objectives of the public schools' main constituency, that is, the families who actually sent their children to the public schools.[64]

It would be decades before Alexander's fears for the East Ramapo School District were realized.[65] But in Monroe-Woodbury, it was barely a year after he filed his dissertation that the situation with KJ blew up. The first confrontation, as noted above, was the appearance of the female bus driver on the boys' school route in 1983. Other events were occurring at the same time, both inside and outside KJ, which greatly exacerbated the growing tensions between the village and the Monroe-Woodbury School District: 1983 was the same year that the first new annexation of 370 acres was proposed. It was also the year that the Shaa-rei Chemlah school was founded and the year that Louis Grumet left his post at the state education department and took up a new job as executive director of the New York State School Boards Association, a private nonprofit organization that serves as "the statewide voice for the interests of public boards of education."[66] It would take another seven years and many intervening events for Grumet to be provoked into bringing a lawsuit. But with the Satmars' newfound awareness of the rights of children with special needs and Grumet's new assignment at the School Boards Association, the key elements for that impending legal battle were in place.

1984: A New Flash Point of Conflict

The year 1984 was a turning point both for the confrontations with the Monroe-Woodbury School District and for the internal rifts that had begun to open up in Kiryas Joel following R. Yoelish's death. It was a notable year for the country as well. Deregulation and decentralization were in full swing as Ronald Reagan was elected to a second term as president. The creation of a separate local government by a religious community fit right in with the Reagan-era romance with "localism" that conservatives liked to juxtapose to the totalitarian dystopia in George Orwell's novel *1984*, which lent the year a special frisson. Sup-porters of this conservative vision, like the Harvard philosopher Robert Nozick, whose *Anarchy, State and Utopia* became a kind of libertarian bible in the 1970s and 1980s, portrayed homogeneous subgroups as ful-filling voluntary associations that people were free to join or leave as they chose.[67]

But if Kiryas Joel seemed to exemplify the kind of libertarian mini-utopia that Nozick idealized, it also illustrated how conflict arises in even the most homogeneous groups and how, in the face of such con-flict, such groups are neither exactly voluntary nor even completely homogeneous. Indeed, it was precisely at this moment, at the same time that the situation between KJ and the Monroe-Woodbury School Dis-trict was deteriorating, that the long-simmering internal conflict in KJ bubbled to the surface. A key precipitant was the appointment of Aaron Teitelbaum, Reb Moshe's eldest son, to the newly created position of Village Rov. With both Kiryas Joel and the wider Satmar kingdom expanding, Moshe Teitelbaum found it difficult to attend to the many institutional and religious affairs of the entire community. While he would continue to preside over the worldwide Satmar community as Rebbe and would remain as Chief Rabbi or "Rov" of Williamsburg, he arrived at the conclusion that it made sense to cede direct administrative responsibilities in the second major Satmar center in KJ.

And so, during the intermediate days of Sukkot in October 1984, an assembly of KJ community leaders gathered in Moshe's Sukkah to nominate his eldest son, Aaron Teitelbaum, who was already the head of the main yeshivah in town, as Rov and Mara d'Atras (chief rabbinic authority) of Kiryas Joel. As Samuel Heilman notes, this marked the first time in its history that the Satmar community had set in place a succession plan.[68] The process was noteworthy in that it bore traces of the regal pomp and circumstance of other Hasidic courts.[69] The first Satmar Rebbe, R. Yoelish, had held unquestioned authority and was the object of universal reverence. Not so his successors, for whom ceremonial adornment was an important tool in boosting their contested legitimacy—and very much in line with the practices of other Hasidim.

Thus, *Der Yid* ran a lavish ad on November 9 announcing the "coronation ceremony" to take place the following evening after the Sabbath. The next week's issue of the Satmar paper offered a highly detailed, full-page description of the festive ceremony that was held on Saturday night, November 10, at the main synagogue in KJ, attended by notable rabbis and Satmar yeshivah students alike. This description was accompanied by two full pages of congratulatory notes in *Der Yid* that came from across the Satmar empire, from the local shtetl of KJ to faraway London and Bnei Brak.[70]

These felicitations conveyed the impression that Aaron had broad, if not unanimous, support in the Satmar world. Beneath the surface, however, there was considerable discontent with him, especially within KJ. He was perceived by many to be an imperious and power-hungry newcomer to the community, insufficiently devoted to perpetuating the legacy of R. Yoelish. Moreover, doubts lingered about the intensity of his anti-Zionism, owing to his marriage to his Hebrew-speaking, Israeli-born wife, Sasha. He would remain closely aligned to his father for another fifteen years, during which time he consolidated control in KJ as the dominant religious and, to a great extent, political player in the village. In the course of that time, he also accumulated a growing number of enemies—both in KJ and in Williamsburg—who were opposed to what they perceived as his heavy-handed ways. Those dissidents who had gathered around Alta Faiga saw Aaron as a further step away from the true Satmar way and redoubled their opposition to the regime of his father.

In that same year that Aaron was appointed as Rov, another event occurred that would have major consequences for the education system in Kiryas Joel and for the village at large. The case of *Aguilar v. Felton*, argued before the Supreme Court in December 1984, barely a month after Aaron's coronation, addressed the long-postponed question of whether providing Title I services to children in parochial schools was constitutional. More specifically, it addressed a New York City program that had been established in the 1960s soon after Title I's passage. Under this program, funds received from the federal government were used to purchase materials and pay for the salaries of teachers and specialists who provided remedial education to children. As noted by the Supreme Court, "Of those students eligible to receive funds in 1981–1982, 13.2% were enrolled in private schools" and "of that group, 84% were enrolled in schools affiliated with the Roman Catholic Archdiocese of New York and the Diocese of Brooklyn and 8% were enrolled in Hebrew day schools."[71] The Bais Ruchel school in Williamsburg was one of several Jewish day schools that enjoyed the benefit of Title I services under the New York plan, alongside the Catholic schools that were its primary beneficiary. The teachers and specialists employed by the district who went into Catholic, Jewish, and other private schools were subject to monitoring mechanisms that aimed to ensure that the instruction they provided in parochial schools was secular in nature. This feature distinguished the New York program from the program at issue in a companion case, *Grand Rapids School District v. Ball*, which involved a Michigan program that likewise sent teachers employed by the public school district into parochial schools.[72]

In both cases, the question that had been left lingering for two decades after the passage of Title I—whether such programs violated the Establishment Clause—was squarely addressed. And in both cases, decided on the same summer day in 1985, the Supreme Court declared that sending public employees into parochial schools violated the Establishment Clause. According to Justice Brennan, who wrote the opinions, the inspection necessary to ensure that the service providers do not stray into religious matters "would require a permanent and pervasive state presence in the sectarian schools receiving aid." But without such monitoring, Justice Brennan wrote, "the teachers participating in the programs may become involved in intentionally or inadvertently inculcating particular religious beliefs or tenets." Warning that these programs posed the risk of creating a "symbolic link between government and religion," the Supreme Court held that such programs must be struck down.

Notwithstanding their endorsement by a majority of the justices, the holdings in the two cases generated enormous controversy. Expressing a concern shared by many conservatives, Chief Justice Burger lamented that many children who suffer from dyslexia, require instruction in English as a second language, or need remedial math or reading instruction "now will not receive the special training they need, simply because their parents desire that they attend religiously affiliated schools."[73] Burger was one of four justices who dissented in the two cases. The others included Byron White, Sandra Day O'Connor, and William Rehnquist. Reflecting the Court's deep-seated ambivalence over the issue, which was widely shared, within little more than a decade the dissenters' position would come to prevail in a case known as *Agostini v. Felton*, in which the Supreme Court took the unusual step of reversing its decisions in *Aguilar* and *Ball*.[74] Like the *Aguilar* case that it overruled, *Agostini* involved a program instituted by the New York City school district, which never ceased its efforts to deliver publicly funded services to the parochial schools even after the Supreme Court ruled against it in 1985. That persistence was vindicated in *Agostini* when the

Court decided that it was constitutionally permissible to send Title I providers into parochial schools after all.

Indeed, *Aguilar* and *Ball* marked the high point—or, from the point of view of its critics, the low point—of the Court's adherence to a strict principle of no aid to religious schools. In hindsight, it is clear that these cases were the beginning of the end of a liberal jurisprudence committed to separation between church and state. Following *Aguilar* and *Ball*, the Supreme Court began to retreat from the principle of strict church-state separation announced, if not exactly followed, in *Everson*. *Everson's* commitment to that principle had been fortified by the liberal Warren Court in series of decisions handed down in the 1960s.[75] And the Court continued to adhere to that principle and the corollary no-aid-to-religious-schools doctrine throughout the Burger Court era, notwithstanding the fact that Warren Burger's appointment by Richard Nixon to replace Earl Warren as chief justice in 1969 was supposed to herald a new conservative direction for the Supreme Court. Although the Burger Court (and for that matter the Warren Court as well) sometimes applied these principles to uphold programs providing aid to private schools, it was a grievous disappointment to religious conservatives that it also struck down many school aid programs. It was the Burger Court, after all, that produced the much-maligned *Lemon* decision in 1971 and decided the cases of *Aguilar* and *Ball*. It was only after Chief Justice Burger retired in 1986, one year after *Aguilar* and *Ball* were decided, that the Court became receptive to the ongoing campaign to repudiate those doctrines. Religious conservatives had been waging that campaign since the 1960s, with little success.[76] But after Burger was replaced by William Rehnquist as the new chief justice in 1986, conservatives finally began to score legal victories in the area of religion clause jurisprudence, leading many of them to believe that the time had finally come when the Court would reverse *Lemon* and maybe even *Everson* and the whole idea that the Constitution embodies a principle of separation between church and state.[77]

It is interesting to consider what might have happened had the doctrine established by the Rehnquist Court in *Agostini* in 1997 prevailed in the 1980s. In all likelihood, there would have been no need for a separate school district to address the predicament that special needs children in KJ faced. But in 1985, when *Aguilar* and *Ball* were decided, the doctrine of strict separation between church and state remained the law of the land. With the stroke of a pen, the Burger Court rendered Title I programs in parochial schools unconstitutional. Across the country, school districts that had such programs in place were left to cope with their sudden termination.

In New York City, where the *Aguilar* case had arisen, the school district responded by moving Title I programs for parochial school students out of those schools and into public school buildings. But it also took steps to placate its parochial school constituencies, both Catholic and Hasidic. Fearing that the Hasidim would no longer allow their children to attend remedial education classes, the district came up with a plan to cordon off a separate area for them in the public school in Williamsburg. But the creation of a partitioned-off area for the Hasidim antagonized the minority communities who made up most of the public school's population and led to a federal lawsuit against the district on both Establishment Clause and Equal Protection Clause grounds. Dubbed "the wall" case, that litigation ended in another defeat for the school district of the City of New York and further embittered relations between the Satmars in Williamsburg and their Black and Latino neighbors.[78]

In Monroe, the school district came up with a very different solution to the challenge of serving the Satmar community without running afoul of the Supreme Court decisions. As many parochial school advocates argued at the time, the Court had held only that Title I programs could not be run *inside* religious schools. It took only a little ingenuity for school districts committed to providing special programs to parochial school students to discover a way to circumvent this stricture: by sending Title I service providers to parochial students in mobile instructional units (MIUs), parked outside their school buildings. The use of such mobile units proliferated after *Aguilar* and *Ball*, creating a veritable industry for MIUs. By 1997 when *Agostini v. Felton* lifted the ban on entering the physical premises of parochial schools, one-third of the Title I budget was going to vans, drivers, and garage and maintenance services.[79]

In most school districts that implemented such programs, vans and trailers were the vehicles of choice. In Kiryas Joel, it was an old school bus that was converted by Monroe-Woodbury to house two makeshift classrooms. Children attending the Bais Ruchel school would simply exit the school building and file into the bus parked just steps away. Through the use of this converted bus, Monroe-Woodbury was able to continue the provision of Title I services and minimize the disruptive impact of the Court's 1985 decisions.

Virtually all Satmar children were eligible to receive Title I services, if not for income-related reasons, then because their families did not speak English at home. But most Satmar families chose not to. They were ambivalent about having their children receive remedial instruction from public school teachers. For boys, there were simply not enough hours in the day to complement their rigorous regimen of religious studies with additional classes in secular subjects. More than that, secular studies were viewed with suspicion, as a potential threat to the core values of the community. The fact that Monroe-Woodbury would send instructors into the village did not eliminate the fear that outsiders and their secular culture might infiltrate the community.

When it came to girls, however, attitudes toward secular education were somewhat more relaxed. As a result, both Williamsburg and Monroe-Woodbury had set up remedial programs in their local Bais Ruchel schools prior to the Supreme Court decisions declaring them to be unconstitutional. Despite reservations about bringing a secular educational program into the community, the Title I program in KJ was popular enough that two instructors were holding side-by-side classes of five children at a time inside the village's Bais Ruchel, serving a total of sixty girls throughout the school day.[80]

Indeed, the Bais Ruchel school was a bustling place at the time that the Title I cases were being decided. No fewer than three special programs were operating inside the building in addition to the regular school program at the time the decisions came down. The remedial education program run by the Monroe-Woodbury School District was one. The Shaarei Chemlah school established in 1983 was another. And yet a third program had been established inside the KJ Bais Ruchel during the 1984–1985 school year, just as the Title I cases were being decided. Like Shaarei Chemlah, this was a program for children with special needs. But unlike Shaarei Chemlah, which was a full-time program for children with profound disabilities like Down syndrome, this new program served children with mild disabilities that did not necessitate withdrawal from the regular school but rather required supplementary services. An even more significant difference between Shaarei Chemlah and the new special ed program was that the new one was not privately run. As with the Title I program, it was staffed and administered by the Monroe-Woodbury School District.

There were thus two different programs on the chopping block when the Supreme Court's Title I decisions came down in 1985. Technically, those decisions required only the removal of the Title I program since they did not directly address the constitutionality of special education programs in private schools. But the events of the last two years had made Superintendent Alexander of Monroe-Woodbury extremely wary of trying to continue to placate the Satmars. Instead of looking for a way to continue delivering special ed services to children inside KJ, he simply pulled the plug on the program. Henceforth, in order to receive their legally mandated services, Satmar children with special needs would have to attend the district's public schools.

Alexander's decision can be understood only in light of the events that led to his creating the special ed program in KJ in the first place. Like so much else in KJ's history, that program was not the result of a premeditated plan designed and implemented by the Satmars. Rather, it was a somewhat haphazard solution to a practical problem jointly improvised by KJ's and Monroe's leaders. The problem, simply put, was how to reconcile the competing interests of the two communities: the interest of the Satmars in developing appropriate individualized education programs (IEPs) for their children that would accommodate their cultural differences, and the countervailing interest of the school district in minimizing the burdens associated with making that accommodation.

The improvised nature of the solutions to this problem that Monroe-Woodbury and KJ's leaders jointly devised belies the common image of

the Satmars as devilishly plotting to take over school districts in order
to commandeer public resources to support their private school system.
To be sure, village leaders would come to recognize the economic and
educational benefits associated with the regulatory and financial powers
of a school district. And yet, none of what came to pass with regard to
separate special education programs for the Satmars was planned or
foreseen in advance. Rather, both the future school district in KJ and
the short-lived program in the Bais Ruchel that preceded it were the
result of a serendipitous chain of events that began years before the idea
of them was ever hatched.[81]

The Gathering of a Perfect Storm

It was a chance encounter, back in 1980, that led the district to set up the
short-lived special ed program inside the Bais Ruchel school. It was then
that Mrs. Schayndel Wieder, the wife of Abraham Wieder, had an overnight stay in the hospital, one of the few places where contact between
a KJ housewife and an outsider might occur. There, she had a revelatory
conversation with her hospital roommate, who informed her about the
existence of new organizations dedicated to helping parents of children
with special needs and instructed her in how to advocate for services
from the local school district.[82]

Abe Wieder, KJ's future mayor and close ally of R. Moshe and R.
Aaron, was at that time a member of the village board of trustees, a successful businessman, and a thirty-two-year-old father of a child born
with a hearing impairment. The Wieders had been searching for services
for their daughter from the time she was a young girl. At first they sent
her to the Bais Ruchel, but she struggled to keep up without the benefit
of supplementary services. The Wieders first caught wind of the support
services made available by the new special education laws when a fellow
resident of KJ suggested to them that they send their daughter to
BOCES, where he sent his own hearing-impaired child. The Wieders
took this suggestion and, for a number of months, sent their daughter
to the special education program run by BOCES. Every day she would
board a bus in Kiryas Joel that came to collect her and bring her to the

BOCES facility in Goshen, the county seat about ten miles away. And every day she cried and pleaded with her parents not to go, feeling alienated and uncomfortable as the only observant Jewish child in her class.[83]

Faced with their daughter's distress and the apparent inflexibility of BOCES, Mr. and Mrs. Wieder were at a loss. And then Mrs. Wieder had the visit to the hospital that seemed to her truly *bashert*—meant to be! Her roommate was the mother of not just one but two children with hearing impairments. Even more intriguing to Mrs. Wieder was the fact that each of them had mastered a foreign language in addition to learning English and Sign Language. Mrs. Wieder hung on every word of her roommate's proud recounting of her children's linguistic accomplishments, as language was a particular sore point in the Wieders' dealings with BOCES. As Mrs. Wieder explained to her new acquaintance, BOCES not only required their daughter to be integrated into an English-only speaking environment but also demanded that the entire family speak English at home. The rationale for this demand, which reflected the sameness model of liberalism that still prevailed in many corners of the educational world, was that learning how to participate in more than one spoken language was too confusing for children with hearing impairments.

Mrs. Wieder was therefore all ears when her hospital acquaintance assured her that it was possible to demand instruction in more than one language from the public school special education providers. Acting as an open pipeline to the outside world, her roommate exposed her to the existence of a new approach, a difference model of equality, that rejected language assimilationism in favor of bi- or multilingualism. Equally importantly, she advised Mrs. Wieder on how to advocate for the services to which she felt her child was entitled. Mrs. Wieder shared this newfound knowledge with her husband, and the first thing they did was obtain a private instructor for their daughter recommended to Mrs. Wieder by her acquaintance from the hospital. Over the next three years, Michael Hughes, a well-respected Deaf educator who was hearing impaired himself, came to the Wieders' house to work with their daughter as a private teacher.[84]

It was when that private arrangement came to an end, in 1984, that Mr. Wieder first turned to the Monroe-Woodbury School District. This was also the year that Aaron was installed as the Rov of Kiryas Joel and the school bus controversy was intensifying. With Wieder and other parents from the community pressing the district for special education services that accommodated their linguistic and cultural differences, it did not take long for Superintendent Alexander and his staff to be persuaded of the benefits of delivering services directly to the children in KJ rather than requiring them to come to the public school. Monroe-Woodbury provided special education services inside the Bais Ruchel building, or in some cases at families' homes.[85] This allowed children like the Wieders' and the Silbersteins' daughters to receive what they needed and were legally entitled to with minimal disruption to their participation in the Satmar private schools and their integration into the Satmar community. At the same time, the school district could minimize the friction with the Satmar community and the disruption of its own programs. It was, from both sides' point of view, a mutually beneficial decision—until the Supreme Court handed down *Aguilar* and *Ball*.

While those cases did not directly address special education, their reasoning seemed to many observers to jeopardize programs like the one in KJ. Superintendent Alexander had to decide how and where to deliver special education services to the Satmars after *Aguilar* and *Ball*. He faced not only new legal strictures but also increasingly demanding Satmar parents seeking the best services for their children.[86] Meanwhile, the Satmars' intransigence over women bus drivers was revealing the lengths they would go to insist upon programs tailored to accommodate their religious culture.

It was indeed a perfect storm in which Alexander was forced to take a stand. Feeling he had to do something to prevent Monroe-Woodbury from becoming enmeshed in endless costly accommodations for the Satmars, he declared the special program in the Bais Ruchel to be over just months after it had been established. Under the new policy he announced for the 1985–1986 school year, children in Kiryas Joel would have to attend the public schools in order to receive the special education services that they were entitled to and that the district was legally obligated to provide.

Carrying out this new policy throughout the summer of 1985, Monroe-Woodbury's Committee on the Handicapped conducted individual evaluations of the children who had formerly been receiving special education services inside the Bais Ruchel school. Each was assigned to the public-school program deemed appropriate for his or her individual needs. But the Satmar parents refused to comply with these assignments. Led by Abraham Wieder, they hired private tutors and initiated administrative proceedings, as provided under the special education laws, to challenge the proposed placements.[87]

Before any of these administrative hearings could take place, however, the Monroe-Woodbury School District brought a lawsuit against Wieder and the other parents, seeking a declaratory judgment that it was legally required to provide special education services *only* in "the regular [special education] classes of the public school" and thus that it was not permitted to educate the Satmars "separately from pupils regularly attending the public schools."[88] In support of this position, Monroe-Woodbury relied on the decisions in *Aguilar* and *Ball* as well as a provision of New York State's Education Law that had been enacted in response to the federal Education for Handicapped Children's Act. This provision spoke in seemingly clear terms: "Pupils enrolled in nonpublic schools for whom [special education] services are provided shall receive such services in regular classes of the public school and shall not be provided such services separately from pupils attending the public schools."[89]

Advancing the argument that this made placement in public school mandatory, *Board of Education of the Monroe-Woodbury Central School District v. Wieder et al.* (*Wieder* for short) was the first lawsuit to be brought challenging the separatist practices of the Satmars of Kiryas Joel. A month later, KJ inhabitants found themselves hit with another suit, this one, *Bollenbach v. Board of Education of the Monroe-Woodbury Central School District*, brought by the women bus drivers.[90] This followed by a year the arbitration proceeding that the bus drivers' union initiated on behalf of the women drivers. Although the arbitrator denied a request for back pay for the women drivers on the grounds that "the District had acted in good faith under unusual and difficult circumstances," he found the district to be in violation of the collective bargaining agreement as a result of having fabricated grounds for denying female bus drivers routes in Kiryas Joel. The arbitrator ruled that starting in the spring semester of the 1984–1985 school year, seniority rules had to be adhered to even when that produced women drivers.

It was just two months after the 1984 arbitration judgment that Aaron was installed as Rov of KJ. Under his leadership, the UTA stiffened its resolve to oppose the arbitration ruling and sought the restoration of the accommodation that had briefly been granted by the district. On January 24, 1985, the village, the UTA, and representative parents filed a lawsuit and succeeded in obtaining a temporary restraining order preventing the district from assigning women drivers to the boys' buses.[91] It was thus the Satmars who were the first movers in initiating litigation against outside parties. That in turn prompted the female bus drivers to sue them. On December 26, 1985, the women drivers filed a sex discrimination claim in federal court, naming both the Monroe-Woodbury School District and the village of Kiryas Joel as defendants.[92]

KJ leaders were now contending with two separate lawsuits, one concerning the school bus controversy and the other concerning special education placements. Both arose out of conflicts with the school district, although *Bollenbach* initially positioned KJ and Monroe-Woodbury on the same side, as codefendants and coadversaries of the women bus drivers. That illusory alliance quickly broke down when the district filed a cross-claim against the village, asserting that it was KJ that was responsible for the refusal to assign female drivers to the "male runs." The village and the UTA countered with a cross-complaint of their own against both the district and the drivers.

All this litigation required good legal counsel. Representing the UTA and the village in both suits was George Shebitz, an education law expert. Some years earlier, Shebitz had tangled with—and befriended— Lou Grumet when Grumet was trying to close down facilities in New York City and Shebitz was serving as legal counsel for the chancellor of New York City's public schools. In 2006 Shebitz would die at the relatively young age of fifty-eight, lauded for his labors on behalf of children with special needs and children's rights more generally. Until that time, he served as the de facto in-house counsel for KJ, a role that began in earnest in 1985 with the school bus litigation and the *Wieder* case.

Shebitz was a skilled attorney who developed strong legal arguments for the Satmars in the *Bollenbach* and *Wieder* actions, both of which dragged on for several years and demanded a fair bit of legal ingenuity. In response to the women drivers' claim of sex discrimination in *Bollenbach*, Shebitz argued that the constitutional guarantee of the free exercise of religion required accommodating the Satmars' objections to female bus drivers, which were based on their religious tenets. He also argued that it would not violate the Establishment Clause of the Constitution and the associated principle of separation between religion and state for this accommodation to be made. Ultimately, the women bus drivers would prevail in a 1987 federal court decision. U.S. District Court judge Robert Ward held that the proposed accommodation of removing women drivers violated the Establishment Clause's prohibitions on governmental support for religious groups and also violated the federal employment discrimination statute (Title VII), which prohibits the unequal treatment of women. In short, the court held that the residents of Kiryas Joel did not have a free exercise right to have the district "tailor its busing service to conform to their religious tenets."

Meanwhile, the *Wieder* case was being litigated, addressing the school district's insistence that Satmar children with special needs attend the public schools. The challenge for Shebitz here was how to deal with the state education law, which stated: "Pupils enrolled in nonpublic schools for whom [special education] services are provided shall receive such services in regular classes of the public school and shall not be provided such services separately from pupils regularly attending the public schools."[93] Against this seemingly invincible position, Shebitz's argument was that the New York statute was trumped by the federal special education law, which he interpreted as not just permitting but requiring placements in private settings when that was most "appropriate." He made deft use of the internal tension within the Handicapped Children's

Education Act, which coupled the stated preference for placing children in "the least restrictive" setting with the countervailing principle of accommodation of individual differences. Emphasizing the government's commitment to making individualized judgments about a child's needs, Shebitz argued that while public school might be the most "appropriate" placement in most cases, it could not be said that placement outside of public school was *never* the most appropriate placement.

As for the district's claim that *Aguilar* and *Ball* made it unconstitutional to provide services in the village of Kiryas Joel, Shebitz argued that those cases forbade the delivery of services only *on the site of parochial schools.* That left open the possibility of providing services at a "neutral site," neither inside public school facilities nor inside parochial school buildings, but at some other location. On the basis of these arguments, he sought a court injunction ordering the resumption of services in the Bais Ruchel "annex" (or at another site) and seeking damages to compensate the parents for the expenses incurred for private therapeutic services as well as punitive damages for the emotional injuries allegedly suffered.

It took three years for the case to reach its culmination. In February 1987, a year and a half after it commenced, Shebitz scored an initial victory when Justice Irving Green, who presided over the state trial court that first heard the case, sided with the Satmars. The court ordered the district to provide educational, remedial, and therapeutic services for Satmar children "in a mobile or other appropriate site not physically or educationally identified with but reasonably accessible to the parochial school children" in Kiryas Joel.[94] In other words, it proposed dealing with special education in the same way that remedial education had been dealt with following *Aguilar* and *Ball*: through the use of mobile learning units or stationary sites physically and institutionally separated from the parochial schools.

Soon thereafter, the school district appealed this holding, leading to at least a partial reversal. At the very end of 1987, a state appellate court held that neither party had it exactly right. The court argued against a literal reading of the New York Education Law requiring "pupils enrolled in nonpublic school" to "receive [special education] services in regular classes of the public school." It found that the school district's interpretation of the law was "too rigid and thus fails to take into account those exceptional situations where public-school placement would be inimical to a student's welfare due to the nature or severity of a child's handicap, external factors such as distance and personal safety, or some similarly valid reason."[95]

This would seem to favor the Satmars of KJ. But the court also declared that "we cannot abide the statutory construction advocated for by the defendants [i.e., the Satmars], for it would require that Education Law § 3602-c(9)," the New York law calling for public school placements, "be disregarded and might permit unnecessary placements of children in parochial-school settings for no compelling reason, thereby violating the Establishment Clause."[96] Ruling against Wieder and the KJ plaintiffs, it struck down the injunction issued by the lower court that had called for reinstating the special ed program in a mobile classroom or another site in KJ. Explaining its decision, the appellate court asserted that the "special accommodations sought for these children are prompted" not by the fact that they are "so severely handicapped as to preclude their participation in the regular special education programs offered in the public schools," but rather "by their parents' desires to keep them out of the public schools and insulated from students of dissimilar religious and cultural backgrounds."[97] "Even if we accept the representations made by the defendants at oral argument to the effect that they will not insist upon instruction in the Yiddish language or segregation of the sexes at the court-ordered site," the court concluded, "the creation of a facility for the obvious purpose of accommodating the Hasidic community without regard to secular factors will effectively render it inaccessible to other children." "As such," it held, "it cannot be considered a truly neutral site."[98]

Perhaps appropriately, given the conflicting principles at stake, the appellate decision was a marvel of ambiguity. Declaring that providing special educational services to Satmar children at a neutral site was neither constitutionally prohibited nor constitutionally required, it deferred to the school district to determine whether placement in the public school programs was appropriate, pointing out that parents could "seek administrative review of the propriety of the plaintiff's present placement of each child based upon the child's individual circumstances and educational requirements."[99] In short, the decision gave the school district the authority to decide whether or not to place a child in the public school, while suggesting that it regarded accommodations of the sort sought by the Satmars to be a violation of the separation of church and state.

KJ officials, however, were not to be deterred. Almost immediately, they filed an appeal to the state's highest court. On July 12, 1988, that court handed down its decision with an opinion authored by Judge Judith Kaye, the first woman to sit on the state's highest court and a figure who would go on to play a significant role in the litigation that subsequently engulfed Kiryas Joel. Judge Kaye's opinion in the *Wieder* case also was an object lesson in studied ambiguity. She began by observing that both sides had framed the legal issues as a matter of "musts," with the school district claiming that it must place the Satmar children in the public school and the Satmars answering that it must provide services to them outside the public school. Eschewing both "extremes," she concluded that "neither party's position is compelled by law."[100] The question, she said, was not "what the law compels or requires," but rather "what it permits."[101]

Referencing the "150 Satmarer children" who were now receiving or seeking special education, Judge Kaye laid out a carefully reasoned opinion that demonstrated considerable understanding of the Satmar community. She affirmed the lower courts' conclusion that the state Education Law should be read not literally to require all special needs students to attend public schools, but rather as expressing the basic goal of integrating school students with special needs. More specifically, she understood the goal to be to avoid isolating special needs students who attend public schools from the larger public school community.[102] Rejecting the view that the school district had no choice but to serve the Satmar children on the site of the public schools, she nonetheless affirmed the appellate division's view that the school district has the authority to determine which placement is the least restrictive and meets a child's individual educational needs. At the end of the day, the school district was "neither compelled to make services available to private school handicapped children only in regular public school classes" nor obliged to provide the services at the Satmars' "own schools, or even at a neutral site."[103] Since the Satmars were careful to claim that the accommodation they were requesting was based on nonreligious needs, such as the need to accommodate the use of Yiddish language, Judge Kaye concluded that they could not claim that the accommodation was a constitutionally protected religious right. But neither could the school district claim it was constitutionally prohibited. Instead, she left all possibilities open and subject to the discretion of the school district. It was now up to Monroe-Woodbury to decide whether to continue insisting that the Satmar children receive services inside the public schools or instead institute special education programs at a neutral site.

Any hope that Judge Kaye's rather sympathetic decision might lead the school district to choose the latter option was quickly dashed. Following the high court's judgment, Superintendent Alexander reaffirmed that he had no intention of setting up special ed programs inside Kiryas Joel or at any other site. Under his leadership, Monroe-Woodbury took the view that the entire village of Kiryas Joel was a religious, hence nonneutral, site. KJ's attempt to gain the educational services it wanted through litigation had run into a dead end. It was at this point that KJ officials, having exhausted all their options, turned to their friends in the legislature for help.

What happened next was a study in political sagacity. The truth was that no one knew what to do, except that something had to be done. In keeping with the long Satmar tradition of political engagement, KJ's political leaders had by now established strong connections with local elected officials, and their political clout was growing. The school district, for its part, found itself in a bind. It was not unresponsive to the Satmars' plight and political heft, but it also had to address the concerns of parents and students in Monroe and Woodbury who were increasingly opposed to accommodating the Satmars. Hoping to find a way to broker some kind of compromise, local leaders convened a meeting at the home of Roberta Murphy, the head of the Monroe-Woodbury School Board. The assembled participants included Wieder, representing the village board of trustees, Shebitz, Superintendent Alexander, and Assistant Superintendent Terry Olivo, plus an assortment of local officials from the town of Monroe. In addition, the meeting was attended by a number of state-level elected officials, including U.S. congressman Ben Gilman, state senator Art Gray, and, most notably, the relatively unknown new assemblyman, George Pataki.[104]

As Steven Benardo would later recall, Pataki's presence at the meeting was *bashert*, the same Yiddish term Mrs. Wieder used to describe her fateful meeting at the hospital.[105] Pataki had begun his political career as the mayor of nearby Peekskill from 1981 to 1983. As fortune would have it, Alexander had worked at the public school that Pataki's children attended before assuming his position in East Ramapo. Pataki finished his political career in New York as the popular three-term governor of the state from 1995 to 2006. But back in 1984, Pataki had just been elected to the State Assembly. It was he who came up with the idea of creating a separate school district in Kiryas Joel, apparently on the fly.

The idea of replacing regional school districts with districts composed of a single municipality had been kicking around among New York local government policy makers for years. The motivation behind that plan, as Pataki knew of it, had absolutely nothing to do with the kind of cultural and religious divisions presented by KJ. Rather, it was a way for mayors of small cities, like Peekskill, to increase their power and avoid being subsumed into a larger school district's bureaucracy. New York State had long denied small cities and suburban municipalities the ability to run school districts of their own; it had joined in the enthusiastic consolidation of school districts that swept across America in the early twentieth century, primarily for economic reasons. It was more efficient to have a single district composed of multiple localities than to have a separate district for each one. This rationale was especially persuasive in areas facing population decline, as was the case in rural New York when, in 1917, declining enrollments first prompted the state legislature to abolish small local districts and replace them with "township units."[106] These larger units evolved into the regional school districts that remain the dominant mode of school district organization outside of large cities today.

The move to regional school districts that took place in rural New York State in the 1920s had another underlying motive. At that time, a battle was raging between Catholic immigrants and the anti-Catholic Protestant establishment that then dominated New York political and educational leadership. Indeed, Catholic immigrants had been protesting the unabashed use of public schools as a means of assimilating them into the dominant Protestant culture since the 1840s.[107]

It was in response to this system of enforced Protestantization that the Catholic community in American developed its robust system of parochial schools. But Catholics resisted the cultural hegemony of the public schools in another way as well, foreshadowing the strategy adopted by Satmar Hasidim half a century later. As historian Sarah Barringer Gordon has shown, by forming enclaves in rural and suburban areas, where they constituted a sizable percentage of the population, Catholics were able to escape their position as a minority and influence their local school boards. In some parts of the country, public school districts in majority Catholic areas went so far as to rebrand parochial schools as public schools.[108]

School district consolidation served as a constraint on this process of creating Catholic-dominated school districts. In the early twentieth century, the policy of consolidation was explicitly linked to the ongoing battle on the part of the Protestant Establishment to prevent Catholics from gaining access to funding or influence over the public schools. By the 1980s, the anti-Catholic sentiments of old had passed. But the regionalism that denied homogeneous religious communities the ability to establish their own local school districts remained in place, sustained by both tradition and the economic efficiencies that consolidation was said to bring. The sole force militating against the established consensus was the opposition of mayors of small cities such as Peekskill, who perceived in consolidation a system that undercut the power of smaller municipalities, prompting them to consider legislation that returned control of school districts to the municipal level.

George Pataki's recent experience as mayor of Peekskill had acquainted him with the proposal for creating municipally based school districts—an idea that he now pitched to the leaders gathered on the back deck of Roberta Murphy's house.[109] The Satmars felt an immediate affinity for Pataki, with his Hungarian roots. This did not, however, lead them to embrace immediately the idea he was pitching. As Grumet records in his reconstruction of the meeting that took place that day, Wieder initially "was not keen on the idea of running a secular school district," which would have to conform to the state's "decidedly secular curriculum." On the contrary, Wieder expressed uncertainty that the Satmars could "abide by the voluminous rules of state education law while still remaining true to Jewish law." No one present at the meeting raised any concern about staying true to American law. With no concern about its possible unconstitutionality and no better alternative in sight, by the end of the afternoon both sides to the dispute came around to endorsing the idea of a self-standing school district in KJ. From the standpoint of the Monroe-Woodbury School District, it was a way of washing their hands of the burden of accommodation to the Satmars. From the standpoint of KJ, it was a way to deliver special education to the children who required it without having to leave the village. Recognizing this, KJ's leaders agreed to Pataki's plan, with the approval of the various community leaders and politicians in attendance, apparently with little heed for the possible legal consequences.

Proposing the creation of the district through legislation was only the first step, however. Getting it passed in the state legislature would require the support of a majority of the members of the New York State Assembly and a majority of the State Senate. To accomplish this task, the Satmars' well-oiled political machine in Williamsburg sprang into motion. It took little effort to get Brooklyn's assemblyman Joseph Lentol to cosponsor the bill with Assemblyman Pataki.[110] Together, they used the parliamentary strategy of presenting it to the State Assembly and Senate as part of an "omnibus bill," which bundles together numerous bills on unrelated topics to be voted up or down as a whole, typically with little awareness of the component parts. In this case, no fewer than forty-five "consent bills" were packaged together and submitted to a vote in the final hours of the final day of the 1989 legislative session. It was in the wee hours of the night on the last day of the session that the legislature approved the omnibus bill containing Lentol and Pataki's proposed bill for a school district in KJ. Along with the other items contained in the omnibus bill, Chapter 748, "an act to establish a separate school district in and for the village of Kiryas Joel, Orange county," passed by a nearly unanimous vote of 149 to 1.[111]

Notwithstanding the near unanimity in the New York State Legislature, there were fierce opponents to the bill outside of it. In KJ itself, the dissidents associated with Alta Faiga not only saw the new district as a power play by the KJ establishment associated with R. Aaron but also feared the effects of a village-sponsored public school that would introduce foreign values to Satmar kids. The fact that Satmar religious values would not stand at the heart of regular instruction within the proposed school was, to them, a sacrilege.

But it was Lou Grumet, then the executive director of the New York State School Boards Association or NYSSBA, who would turn the critics' objections into a literal federal case. Based in Albany, Grumet made it his business to monitor legislation that affected school districts. Prior to its passage, Grumet had viewed Lentol's and Pataki's bill with little concern. According to his sources in the legislature, the bill was sure to be shot down because it was plainly unconstitutional. In other words, it was just a sop for KJ officials, a show of support for their plight not expected to yield practical results.[112] Grumet was so confident of this prediction that he did not even entertain the possibility that the bill might pass.

The actual outcome left Grumet stunned. According to his account, it was five o'clock in the morning when he was awakened by a call from one of his aides saying, "Boss, you know that bill? That stupid bill from Monroe-Woodbury? It's about to pass." Five minutes later, the aide called again to report: "It just passed." Grumet was dumbfounded. A dyed-in-the-wool liberal for whom integration, separation of church and state, and public education formed the holy trinity of his secular religion, he was shaken to the core by the prospect of a school district formed to accommodate a religious sect devoted to self-segregation. He was shocked that the bill had passed. Shocked, but not yet dismayed—because he was certain that Mario Cuomo, who was now the governor of the state, would veto the bill once he found out what Chapter 748 contained.[113]

To make certain, Grumet quickly scheduled an appointment with Cuomo with the intention of setting him straight. What happened at that meeting may never be known. Grumet's vivid recollection of the encounter portrays him as a mix of hero and apostate, defying the man for whom he had worked throughout the 1970s when Cuomo was New York's secretary of state. According to Grumet, he had worshipped Cuomo, regarding him as a mentor and crediting him with much of his political education and government career, in particular his previous appointment as assistant commissioner in charge of special education. Grumet simply could not believe that a committed liberal—and a constitutional scholar to boot (as Cuomo was widely regarded)—would knowingly approve a law that created a separate school district for the Satmars.[114] So he was both shocked and dismayed when Cuomo made it clear that he had no intention of vetoing the bill, and indeed actively endorsed it. "What's so egregious about it, Luig?," Grumet recalls Cuomo saying to him—using the Italianate nickname he had bestowed on his onetime Jewish protégé. As Grumet persisted in trying to persuade his former mentor that signing the law would be a blot on his legacy, Cuomo dismissed his concerns with the same jesting tones. "Who's going to sue, Luig?," Grumet recalls the governor saying to him. To which Grumet responded plainly, "I would, governor."[115]

And thus was born the case of *Grumet v. Board of Education of Kiryas Joel Village Union Free School District, Board of Education of Monroe-Woodbury Central School District and the New York State Department of Education*, the lawsuit that would catapult Kiryas Joel from a regional curiosity to an object of nationwide attention. On trial was not just whether a separate school district for KJ was constitutional but whether such separatism was really un-American and how un-American KJ really was. In the eyes of many Americans, KJ's separatist practices were clearly un-American, especially insofar as they were enabled by state law. This was the point of view not only of Grumet but of a wide swath of the American population for whom the liberal principles of integration and separation of church and state had become sacrosanct. But this liberal point of view was being subjected to forceful challenges from the multicultural left and, even more effectively, from the political right. It still remained culturally dominant, as reflected in the media attention the passage of Chapter 748 drew to KJ. Typical of the tone of the coverage was an extensive investigative report on the village and the legal controversy surrounding it broadcast by *60 Minutes*, the widely watched network weekly news show, which ran a story on KJ shortly before the Supreme Court heard the case of *Grumet v. Kiryas Joel* in 1994. "Imagine a town that excludes everyone except members of a certain religion," Ed Bradley, the anchor, solemnly intoned. "Certainly not in America!" he exclaimed in the show's trademark exposé style. "Well, guess again," he continued. "There is such a town and it's just 50 miles north of New York City. It's called Kiryas Joel."[116]

Reflecting the combination of horror and fascination with which Kiryas Joel was coming to be seen, he went on to describe a "town that's unlike any other in America," characterized by "the complete dominance of the Grand Rabbi" whose requirement of "rigorous and all-consuming education" from "dawn to dusk" supplied its "main defense against the outside world." Depicting a town where "anyone who buys or builds a home must give $10,000 to the religious schools," with "no television, no radio, no English newspapers or unapproved books," Bradley conjured up the dubious specter of "a Jewish sect and a voting bloc that makes clear what it wants and, more often than not, gets it come election time." Gravely, he informed the viewing public of the impending Supreme Court decision about the legitimacy of a public school district formed in Kiryas Joel.[117]

Could the state pass a law delegating the public powers of a school district to a community such as Kiryas Joel? According to Grumet and many of the pundits who weighed in on the case, as Ed Bradley of *60 Minutes* had intoned so incredulously: "Not in America!"

But as it turned out, it was not at all clear that a separate school district for a religious community was forbidden by American law. The specific law that Grumet challenged—Chapter 748—reflected the multidirectionality of KJ's unwitting assimilation into American society. Everyone, including Monroe-Woodbury and KJ's leaders, had compromised somewhat, placating some and infuriating others, both inside and outside the village. But the fact of the matter was that while old-school liberals like Grumet and Bradley could declare "Not in America!" and expect a large audience to agree, by the late 1980s a substantial proportion of Americans were willing to accommodate a school district formed to accommodate a religious group devoted to self-segregation. And it was not only conservatives. Many on the left were reconnecting with religion and exhibiting sympathy for subgroups claiming strong rights of cultural and political autonomy. In academia, communitarian thought was in its heyday. And multiculturalism—a new term then—was being introduced into the American lexicon by political theorists such as Will Kymlicka, who published his first book, *Liberalism, Community, and Culture* in 1989 (the year Chapter 748 was passed). Kymlicka argued against communitarian critics of liberalism that liberalism itself was committed to accommodating cultural differences and supporting broad forms of cultural autonomy. These academic trends reflected broader changes in popular liberal sensibilities. Identity politics and the recently dubbed "culture wars" were erupting on both the left and the right. The courting of evangelical Christians by Ronald Reagan continued under the presidency of Republican George H.W. Bush, only to be succeeded by the election in 1992 of Bill Clinton, whom *Newsweek* called the "most pastorized" president in history. His "New Democrat" approach tacked to the center when it came to matters of economic policy, and his administration was "awash in religious rhetoric."[118] This created common ground with conservatives, while evincing support for what left-wing thinkers such as philosopher and social critic Cornel West and feminist philosopher Iris Marion Young dubbed "the new cultural politics of difference."[119]

Under the weight of these new forces, the old model of liberalism, predicated on transcending differences and participating in a common secular culture, was under siege. While it still had many adherents, it was not clear whether it would survive or be bested by a new vision of difference. This was a question that would wend its way to no less an authority than the U.S. Supreme Court, pushed forward by a small village of Hasidic Jews by the name of Kiryas Joel.

CHAPTER 5

Only in America!

Benardo's Building

It takes a long time for a case to arrive at the Supreme Court. The trial court where Louis Grumet filed his lawsuit in early 1990 did not reach a decision about the constitutionality of Chapter 748 until 1992.[1] Two years after that, the U.S. Supreme Court heard an appeal of that state court decision and issued a decision that appeared to strike a decisive blow against the school district. In fact it only prolonged the uncertainty about its constitutionality.[2] Following that, Grumet would spend another six years challenging the creation of the Kiryas Joel School District in state courts.[3] Altogether there would be a full decade of litigation, during which time the legal fate of the district would remain uncertain.[4]

In the meantime, Chapter 748, the law authorizing the establishment of a school district in KJ, remained in force. Unless and until a final pronouncement came down declaring it to be unconstitutional, the Satmars had no need to refrain from doing what the statute authorized, namely, exercising "all the powers and duties of a union free school district under the provisions of the education law."[5] The Satmars had not sought those powers, but they lost no time in exercising them. Immediately following the passage of Chapter 748, KJ village leaders, led by Wieder, convened to figure out how first to build and then to run a school district.

The first order of business was to elect a school board and hire a school superintendent. It would take a person with manifold skills not just to run but to create a brand-new school system. It would require expertise in special education, a still relatively new and complex field. But it would also require building a school from scratch and developing a culturally and linguistically unique program to serve the distinctive needs of Satmar children. Beyond that, the superintendent would be responsible for serving the needs of the entire school-age population of KJ that was eligible for legally mandated state-funded programs. All of the services formerly provided by the Monroe-Woodbury School District—bus transportation, remedial education, diagnostic evaluations to determine the existence of special needs—would be transferred to the fledgling school district. At the same time, the superintendent would have to contend with the ongoing legal challenge and the ever-present threat of the district's dissolution. Clearly, it would take a person with an impressive array of talents—and a lot of gumption.

To the credit of KJ's leaders, such a person was found. Like many other significant developments in KJ, the selection of a superintendent happened more by accident than by design. The assignment initially proposed to the man who assumed the job was simply to draft a blueprint for the new school district that would satisfy the requirements of the New York State Board of Education. Seeking to dispense with this task as quickly as possible so the school would be ready to open in the fall of 1990, the village leaders consulted their legal adviser, George Shebitz. Shebitz in turn placed a call to his good friend, Steve Benardo, who at the time was working as superintendent for special education in the Bronx, one of the largest school districts in the country.[6]

Shebitz and Benardo had become friends eight years earlier when both were involved in *Jose P. v. Ambach*, one of the first class-action suits to be brought under the Education for All Handicapped Children Act.[7] At the time, Grumet was still at the Department of Education, and Ambach, then New York's commissioner of education and the named defendant in the case, was Grumet's boss. Thus, three of the key figures in determining the fate of the KJ School—Shebitz, Grumet, and Benardo—first became acquainted with one another through *Jose P.* They were, as Grumet later recalled, an "unlikely trio,"[8] since they stood on opposite sides of that dispute, with Shebitz serving as counsel to the

Department of Education and Benardo serving as the department's court liaison, while Grumet was supporting the plaintiffs' position that the New York City School District was not in compliance with the special education law.

Bernardo's doctoral training in bilingual special education made him a natural person for Shebitz to turn to when, following the passage of Chapter 748, the need arose to find someone who could develop a plan for the new school district, as was required by state law. Benardo accepted the assignment as a favor to Shebitz, but also out of curiosity. In his work in the Bronx, Benardo oversaw the education of thirty thousand special needs students, located in 186 schools as well as in the juvenile detention facilities that the district superintended.[9] (School districts are responsible for the education of juveniles in detention in their jurisdiction as well as those enrolled in school.) These numbers were the highest of any district in the country.[10] It was the polar opposite of KJ, where only thirteen children with special needs would be attending the new school when it first opened and only a few more were identified as being in need of auxiliary services.[11] Sizing it up, Benardo initially thought it would be no more than a moonlighting job. The joint expectation of both Benardo and the KJ leaders who hired him was that the implementation of the blueprint he designed would be carried out by someone else.

But Benardo's irrepressible curiosity soon got the better of him.[12] The challenge of creating special needs programs for Yiddish-speaking Hasidic children with their unique cultural traits was just too intriguing for an expert in bilingual special education to resist. Conversely, the same skills that made Benardo the obvious person to turn to for formulating the blueprint for the new school district made him equally attractive to KJ's leaders for the permanent position. Thus, a job Benardo thought would be a matter of days, or weeks at the most, evolved into the full-time role of serving as the school district's first superintendent.

Of course Benardo was an outsider to the Satmar community, and his hiring represented a significant intrusion of the outside secular world. But the village leaders perceived that Benardo's outsider status was an asset if they wanted to avoid conflicts with state authorities that would lead to even more intervention. As a public entity, the school district, by law, had to be run as a secular school system. That meant keeping religious teaching and observance out of the school, adhering to secular teacher training, and pursuing secular curricular standards and practices. No one in the Satmar community had the training to adhere to these standards. And, by the same token, none possessed the credentials to serve as superintendent.

Furthermore, an experienced school administrator from outside the community would help to allay the suspicion that many outsiders had that the KJ School District would fail to comply with the separation between church and state. Grumet was by no means the only one watching the implementation of Chapter 748 with concern. The Satmars needed to demonstrate the secular nature of the school district in order to fend off a growing number of critics, including officials inside New York's Department of Education.[13] (As we shall see, the dissidents had the exact opposite fear: that the school district would be thoroughly secular!) Benardo not only had the skills and experience needed to figure out how to satisfy the educational standards prescribed by state law but also had the personality to fill a key task in KJ: that of a cultural translator who was able to explain the requirements of secular standards to the Satmar community and adapt them to their distinctive culture and equally able to explain the Satmars' needs and activities to the outside world.[14]

With Shebitz's strong endorsement, Benardo thus appeared to the village leaders as quite literally a godsend, an impression he cannily confirmed during his job interview, which Wieder kicked off in classic Talmudic style by launching not just one but a whole volley of questions. Starting off with the disarmingly simple "Let me ask you a question," he deftly moved from the practical ("Can you explain what you got to do?") to the topical ("Do you like sports?") to the mystical ("Do you think that God can make both teams win a game?") without a pause. With dry humor, Benardo recounts, "I gave him the answer I knew he wanted," clinching the job with the perfect retort: "God can do anything he wants."[15]

Benardo threw himself into his new work. He acquired the buses used to transport KJ's children to and from the community's private

religious schools and took over the administration of both the bus transportation service and the Title I program. He hired administrators, special ed teachers, and therapists, finding Modern Orthodox educators in
the region who could serve as Yiddish language specialists. For positions such as teacher's aide, janitor, and driver that did not require degrees, he drew from the local Satmar community. The staff that had been
hired to work in the Shaarei Chemlah school constituted a readymade
workforce that he transplanted more or less wholesale into the public
school. The children from Shaarei Chemlah went with them. Last but
not least, Benardo oversaw the construction of a prefab building in
which the new school could be housed on property leased from the
village. Outside this hastily constructed building a flagpole with the
American flag was firmly planted, signifying the secular character of this
emphatically American, yet also clearly Satmar, public school.

All of this activity took place in less than a year, between the end of
the summer of 1989 and the summer of 1990, as Benardo and his new
staff rushed to prepare for the opening of the school in the fall of 1990.
In addition to the thirteen children with special needs from KJ, arrangements had been made to admit children with severe disabilities from
the nearby communities of New Square and Monsey, where other
Haredi groups lived.[16] Plans for providing auxiliary services for children
with less severe impairments (like the Wieders' daughter) were put into
place. Grumet's lawsuit, which was proceeding, lurked in the background. So far, nothing but procedural motions had been heard addressing various technicalities. Shebitz, with whom Benardo was in constant
communication, was on the case, allowing the superintendent to focus
on setting up a state-of-the-art program to meet the needs of Kiryas Joel.

Kiryas Joel's Dissidents

Meanwhile, another controversy in KJ was brewing. Although the
sources of this controversy had nothing to do with the dispute over
special education, the creation of the new public school provided further grist for the mill for the growing number of Satmar dissidents who
were now casting Moshe and Aaron as betrayers of the old Rebbe's holy

way. However, the majority of the community accepted the creation of a secular school district as a necessary price to pay in order to serve children in need and end the conflict with the Monroe-Woodbury School District. Foremost among those who took this position were the longtime advocates for Satmar children with disabilities. For Malka Silberstein, the opening of the public school in KJ was the fulfillment of her dream. At long last, she saw the creation of a learning environment that would promote her daughter's successful integration into Satmar society. In an interview she gave not long after the public school opened, she emphasized "acceptance by the community" as "the name of the game." She lauded the new school for its culturally sensitive programs, which, she said, made "whatever her siblings was doing relevant to what [her daughter] was doing." And she sharply contrasted the new school, where her daughter was "able to participate in all," to the programs offered by Monroe-Woodbury, which Silberstein said exposed her to things that were "offensive to our culture."[17]

For Abe Wieder, the creation of the school district was both a political and a personal triumph. The efforts he and his wife had taken on behalf of their daughter almost a decade earlier had been vindicated. And his leadership in the campaign solidified his emerging role as a powerful political operator. Reflecting his increased influence, Wieder was selected by Moshe and Aaron Teitelbaum to head the slate of candidates that would run for the new school board. Although Wieder would briefly step down from his position on the village board of trustees after being elected to the school board (in order to mollify the dissidents), from this time onward, he was, for all intents and purposes, the outward face and effective secular leader of Kiryas Joel. His warm embrace of Benardo set the tone for the rest of the community's reception.

Benardo himself became a fixture in the community almost instantly.[18] He established a rapport not only with the village leaders but also with the families of the children with disabilities, who welcomed him into their homes. This openness was greatly facilitated by Benardo's genial personality. Along with his professional expertise, Benardo projected a sense of caring and respect for the community. He soon became a kind of ambassador for Kiryas Joel, defending it and explaining its ways to the outside world.

For its part, the community recognized that hiring an outsider to run the school district was not just a legal and political necessity, but the precondition of an unforeseen but welcome opportunity to secure important benefits they otherwise could not obtain. These included the ability to dedicate their property taxes to their own school district, rather than having to support Monroe-Woodbury; the receipt of substantial amounts of federal and state funding for educational services; and, last but certainly not least, the delivery of the special education programs supported by those public funds inside the village—precisely what parent activists and village leaders had been advocating for since 1985, the year the Supreme Court held Title I programs inside parochial schools unconstitutional. The fact that the new public school would have to be staffed and run by outsiders and adhere to a strictly secular curriculum seemed to be an acceptable compromise to the majority of the community.

But not everyone in KJ accepted this logic. In particular, the dissidents strenuously resisted the new school district, opposing it as an unholy intrusion of secular government and culture. They saw the threat that contact with outside educators posed to the Satmars' ability to insulate themselves. And they also saw the school battle as an opportunity to intensify their mounting resistance to Moshe and Aaron. The Rebbetsin and her followers had been trying to protect Reb Yoelish's legacy from Moshe and his followers ever since Moshe took office in 1979. After Moshe appointed Aaron as Rov of Kiryas Joel in 1984, the target of the Faiga faction's opposition expanded to include both Moshe and Aaron. "Faiga's *mentshen*" (Faiga's men), as they came to be known, had been engaged for the previous ten years in a series of complicated financial and legal maneuvers aimed at establishing control over a number of valuable properties in Brooklyn and Orange County. The properties in contention included the Bedford Avenue property in Brooklyn, where the Rebbetsin had lived with her late husband before moving to KJ, as well as the "parsonage," the apartment attached to the back of KJ's grand synagogue, which had been intended for the Rebbe to live in and served as the Rebbetsin's living quarters after his death.[19]

FIGURE 5.1. Main Aroni Synagogue at Back of Which Is Disputed "Rebbetzin's Shul."
Courtesy of Jackson Krule.

By coincidence, the dispute between the Faiga faction and Moshe's camp, which had been simmering for years, boiled over at precisely the same time that the events leading up to the passage of Chapter 748 were heating up. At the end of 1989, as plans for creating the KJ School District were just getting under way, Faiga's mentshen maneuvered to have the title to the Bedford Avenue property transferred to a newly formed shell corporation called 26 Adar Corporation, which was owned and controlled by one of the leaders of her faction, Nachman Brach. While this transaction was in process, but before the transfer was judicially approved, Brach, along with two other of Faiga's mentshen, took out a loan for $1,125,000 secured by the Bedford Avenue property. The bank that provided the loan was led to believe the property still belonged to Faiga and would remain in her hands, for her personal use. In fact, Brach and the others were hatching plans to construct new apartments in the building, which they could sell off at a profit, and establish control over the synagogue that continued to operate inside the late Rebbe's former residence in Williamsburg.[20]

The following year, in March 1990, as the conflict between the Faiga group and Moshe continued to escalate—and as the school district was simultaneously getting off the ground—Brach obtained judicial approval for the transfer.[21] Once he succeeded in establishing legal ownership of the Bedford Avenue property, he installed a metal gate at the entrance in order to keep members of the Moshe faction out.[22] In response, Moshe's supporters brought suit against Brach and his 26 Adar Corporation, challenging the validity of the transfer of the Bedford Avenue property to the corporation that Brach controlled. They argued that the property actually belonged to the Yetev Lev Congregation in Williamsburg and not to Faiga, who, as its former occupant and supposed owner, had purported to authorize its transfer.[23] This litigation would drag on for decades, during the course of which *Der Yid*, the establishment party's paper of record, published an article calling Brach a "robber" and asserting that he had obtained the title to the Bedford Avenue property through "lies and deceit."[24] This would lead to even more litigation when Brach retaliated, accusing *Der Yid* of libel.[25]

While much of this action centered on Brooklyn, the reverberations were keenly felt in KJ, where both Brach and Faiga owned homes, and where another rebellion against the established leadership was being fomented at the same time. This rebellion—the second source of the emerging dissident movement—was spearheaded by families in the village who felt their children were being mistreated in the yeshivah. The controversy over the yeshivah had been brewing since the mid-1980s, when the division between Moshe's opponents (the misnagdim) and Moshe's supporters (the so-called hasidim) began to harden. According to the misnagdim, their children were being teased, bullied, and ostracized by their classmates, often, they suspected, at the behest of the bullies' parents.[26] In addition to the mistreatment their children suffered at the hand of their peers, the misnagdim were convinced that the school administrators were deliberately placing them in classrooms led by teachers aligned with Moshe. Requests to have them transferred to teachers sympathetic to the misnagdim were harshly rebuffed.[27]

While Moshe was the original target of the misnagdim, it was Aaron who became the focal point of the opposition after he was appointed Rov of KJ in 1984. Not only was Aaron perceived to be responsible for the classroom assignments in his role as the UTA's chief administrator, but he also was seen by the dissidents as insufficiently devoted to the old Rebbe's way and generally lacking in the spiritual leadership qualities required of a rebbe. On top of all this, he was regarded as harsh and punitive in the way he responded to his critics, in contrast to his father's gentler style. Instead of finding ways to mollify the misnagdim, Aaron had a high-handed manner that served only to fuel the conflict.[28]

As agitation over the treatment of their children grew, some of the dissidents began to organize. This source of growing opposition to Moshe and Aaron's leadership coincided with, yet was distinct from, the activity of Faiga's mentshen. The latter were chiefly motivated by their view of Moshe as an illegitimate successor to the late Rebbe. The parents' group, by contrast, was chiefly focused on Aaron's perceived transgressions as steward of the UTA. Only a few of them were in Faiga's inner circle. Nonetheless, there was substantial contact between the two groups and overlap in their views about the shortcomings of the leadership.

In fact, by 1987, the threat was perceived to be so great that a special joint meeting of the Kiryas Joel and Williamsburg Yeter Lev congregations was held with the apparent aim of shoring up the KJ establishment. Representing Kiryas Joel at the meeting were Abe Wieder and other lay leaders of the village who sat on the KJ congregation board. Representing the Williamsburg congregation were its board members, including Berl Friedman and Jacob Kahan, who, a decade later, would face off as the leaders of the two rival factions following Aaron and Zalman. In 1987, Friedman and Kahan and the rest of the board of the Brooklyn congregation stood shoulder to shoulder with Wieder and his fellow KJ board members in seeking to suppress the unfolding protest from within.

Taking note of the "internal dissension" in KJ, as well as the financial challenges facing the KJ congregation, the participants at the joint meeting adopted a resolution to transfer title of the KJ cemetery from the KJ congregation to the Williamsburg congregation. In addition, it was decided that the two congregations would share the income from the cemetery, but that the Williamsburg congregation would funnel its share to the support of KJ's yeshivah, at least for the first couple of years of this new arrangement. Finally, the leaders of the two communities decided that governance of the cemetery also would be shared between the two congregations.[29]

If the hope was that this joint effort would quell the unrest, this ambition was quickly dashed. The dissident parents, who had grown increasingly frustrated with the UTA's intransigent response to their requests for transfers to sympathetic teachers, were reaching a breaking point. In the summer of 1988, one disgruntled KJ parent, Avraham Hirsch Weinstock, decided to hire a private teacher, Moshe Mordechai Friedman, for his son Zalman Leib. Soon thereafter, Zalman Leib was joined by five other students whose parents pulled them out of the UTA school. The six boys and their teacher began to meet in various rented rooms in the village through the winter of 1989, at which point hostilities broke out into the open.[30]

Consistent with past behavior, the KJ establishment of Aaron and Moshe did not take kindly to this perceived act of insubordination. They demanded compliance with communal regulations, invoking the legacy and unquestioned authority of R. Joel Teitelbaum. Initially, Moshe's chief aide-de-camp, Moshe (Gabbai) Friedman, was charged with the task of pressuring the parents to shut down their makeshift *cheder* (or *chaider*, rhyming with cider, in the Satmar pronunciation). Dissidents recall Friedman acting like a "bulldozer," as he vainly tried to convince the six defectors to return their sons to their yeshivah.[31]

When it became clear that the parents had no intention of doing so, the ante was raised. The establishment party issued a broadside in the name of the "Administration of the Cong. Yetev Lev," excoriating "a group of people residing in Kiryas Joel [who] have recently rebelled against the ordinance of our late revered Rabbi and Leader." The document went on to state that "it is well known that Rabbi (Joel) Teitelbaum O.B.M. (of blessed memory) dealt especially harsh [*sic*] with nonconformists, and banished them from within the confines of his private institutions." The text then named over forty men who "are totally banished from our Congregation." This meant that they and their families were no longer welcome in Satmar synagogues, educational institutions, and cemeteries. To leave no doubt, a stern warning was sent to those who assisted them "in the act of rebellion." "Let it be known," the missive admonished in Yiddish, "that we will deal with them with asperity."[32]

The rhetorical stakes were raised even higher in a notorious sermon or *drushe* that R. Moshe gave in Williamsburg after Shabbes on Saturday evening, February 25, 1989. The controversial "Ki-sisa drushe" took its name from the weekly Torah portion to be read the following Saturday in synagogue that dealt with the famous biblical episode of the golden calf.[33]

Significantly, the first Satmar Rebbe had commented on this portion in unequivocal terms in his most famous work, the anti-Zionist *Va-yo'el Mosheh* (1959–1960). R. Yoelish analogized the sin of worshipping the golden calf to Zionist "idolators" in modern times. The resulting danger required stern rebuke of those who had succumbed to "disease [that] has spread" among Jews.[34]

Moshe Teitelbaum could not match the commanding presence of his uncle, R. Yoelish. Indeed, the memory of his uncle was likely a burden for him, given the constant comparisons between them in which he always came up short. But he was willing to borrow from his uncle's playbook to deliver a stern rebuke to violators of the true path. Ki-sisa provided the perfect occasion, with the story of the "golden calf," which offered ample opportunity for admonition—and even a measure of identification with a towering ancient namesake. In his sermon, Moshe Teitelbaum moved swiftly from an account of how the biblical Moshe smashed the original tablets of the Ten Commandments when he saw the Israelites dancing around the idol to his own ire over the sins of the parents who had the temerity to pull their children out of the KJ yeshivah.

Moshe enjoined his audience to resist the rebels, stirring up the crowd with a now famous utterance in Satmar lore: "Sheygets aroys" (Gentile, get out!).[35] Labeling the renegade parents with this disparaging Yiddish term—in effect, denying they were Jews—represented a sharp escalation of the conflict between the established leadership and the reviled misnagdim.

Word of Moshe's drushe quickly traveled from Brooklyn to KJ. According to the dissidents, the next day yeshivah students stormed the site where the private lessons for the sons of the six families were being held. Brandishing sticks, they overturned tables and chairs, smashing things and cursing the participants. Parents of the boys who studied there recall being threatened, even receiving death threats for breaking with the community's ironclad discipline.[36]

Aaron Teitelbaum was away in Florida when the violence broke out in KJ. By the time he returned, the negotiations that Moshe Gabbai conducted with the defectors had failed. As the parents saw it, the Ki-sisa sermon—in which Moshe had declared that the children would be placed in separate classrooms if they returned to the yeshivah in order to avoid "infesting" the school—was the last straw.[37] It was now clear to them that pulling their children out of the KJ yeshivah was more than a temporary step; they would have to form a new yeshivah, beyond Aaron's control. This was the beginning of a movement to create a parallel set of institutions in Kiryas Joel that would define itself in opposition to the establishment party from this point forward under the name of Bnai Yoel.

The hardball tactics of the establishment did fortify some of the faithful, but they stirred up sympathy for the opposition as well. Families who had previously stood in the background were now forced to take sides, and more than a few chose to be with the defecting parents. Indeed, as the establishment continued to post the names of the dissidents in public, the ranks of the opponents kept growing in spite of the threat of expulsion. One member of the establishment quipped that perhaps the rabbis should stop publicly posting the dissidents' names since it served only to advertise how rapidly the movement was growing.[38]

These were not the only expulsions that took place within KJ in 1989. Faiga's mentshen were providing support to Bnai Yoel and continuing to challenge Moshe in ways that were guaranteed to lead to their expulsion as well. In addition to their ongoing effort to gain control of the Bedford Avenue synagogue in Williamsburg, Faiga and her mentshen were providing sanctuary to anyone in the community who crossed Aaron and Moshe. Aaron publicly acknowledged this widely known fact when he expelled the Bnai Yoel families, accompanying his formal expulsion decree with a warning that, from now on, they would find only one house of worship open to them. Without naming Faiga, everyone understood he was referring to the congregation known as Bais Yoel (House of Joel) that her mentshen had established in the "parsonage" behind the main synagogue, where Faiga continued to live. Now, with the doors of the main synagogue (and most of the smaller synagogues in KJ) closed to the members of Bnai Yoel, it became their alternative shul. There, they could pray and congregate with other opponents of Moshe and Aaron.[39] The two groups of dissidents, Faiga's mentshen and the families who had withdrawn their children from KJ's schools, thus began to crystallize into a full-fledged dissident movement under the protective eye of the Rebbetsin.

By now, the movement had a name (Bnai Yoel), an objective (the establishment of their own chaider, free from the establishment's control), and momentum. Soon they began to attract financial support. Backers from as far away as London, moved by the children's plight, contributed funds for a new school. Nachman Brach also offered financial support and provided space in one of the buildings he owned in KJ where classes could be held until a permanent building was constructed. Defying pressure from community leaders in Brooklyn and KJ, Faiga continued to open up her home to the members of Bnai Yoel, drawing Moshe and Aron's wrath and confirming the Rebbetsin's role as the dissidents' symbolic leader. What had begun as a temporary act of withdrawing children from a class had turned into a movement to create a new set of moysdes (communal institutions) to serve the growing dissident population.

To combat this movement, the village leaders summoned all the powers at their disposal. But figuring out what powers they had was a learning process in itself. At least initially, KJ's leaders did not deploy the tools of government that village incorporation had conferred on them not, primarily, because they feared external scrutiny but because those powers were new and still, to a significant extent, unknown to them. Instead of exercising their municipal powers, the village leaders' first resort was to utilize the powers they exercised in their private capacity, as synagogue leaders and property owners. Those powers were no less formidable than their public powers. Besides the power to expel members of the opposition, in their private capacity as synagogue officers, KJ leaders possessed the ability to extend their authority over property controlled by the mainstream congregation—or from 1989, by the Vaad hakirya, the "village council" cum development company that acted on the congregation's behalf.[40] In fact, it was in 1989, in response to the political ferment, that Moshe allegedly instituted a ten-thousand-dollar fee on all new buildings in Kiryas Joel, to be earmarked for the council or, in other accounts, to be dedicated to the mainstream faction's system of private schools.

At the same time, the establishment leadership introduced a requirement that contractors and owners pledge not to sell or rent units in KJ to those who did not meet the congregation's approval.[41] Of this requirement, Moshe is said to have declared: "Anyone that rents without this permission has to be dealt with like a real murderer . . . and he should be torn out from the roots."[42] This kind of "covenant" restricting occupancy and ownership to people approved by the congregation recalls the racially restrictive covenants once widespread in American property deeds (and deployed against Jews themselves). Covenants are a way of using private property rights to ensure residential homogeneity, enforce conformity, and discipline people tempted to deviate from the established norms. Their legality is questionable; the use of racially restrictive covenants was deemed unconstitutional by the Supreme Court in 1948, and they could be deemed to violate fair housing statutes as well. But whether these particular covenants would be deemed to be illegal was never squarely confronted, and even their existence was never clearly proved.

In addition to these measures aimed at restricting residential property to people of whom they approved, the establishment now forbade access to the KJ cemetery to dissidents, touching on one of the most elemental and sensitive sources of Jewish ritual observance. Like the expulsions that took place that year, the property restrictions placed on the cemetery and residential properties in the village were all private measures designed to ensure loyalty to the establishment and squelch the opposition. Eventually, the dissidents would challenge these restrictions. In the frenzied year of 1989, however, when the conflict first erupted, the members of Bnai Yoel were simply trying to survive the attacks on them and find a way to ensure their children's religious education.

But in the spring of 1989, a new character came onto the scene, presenting himself as a spokesman for the dissidents with bold ideas for political action. Joseph (or Yosl) Waldman, a longtime resident of KJ, was an idiosyncratic—his critics would say grandstanding—character who occupied an ambiguous place in the village's political landscape. On the one hand, he was a master publicist, enthralled with media and technology, who was chiefly responsible for bringing the dissident movement's existence to public light. On the other hand, he never belonged to any particular dissident group. He considered himself a champion of Bnai Yoel, but he was never a member of it. He did not come from one of the six original families who broke away from the yeshivah in 1989, nor did he send his children to be educated at the Bnai Yoel school, which was founded not long after. Instead, with the exception of a brief period when his children were expelled because of his dissident activities, Waldman insisted on their attending the schools run by the UTA in KJ. He abhorred the treatment of the Bnai Yoel children as "hostages" and held himself out as Bnai Yoel's biggest supporter.[43] But his insistence on sending his children to UTA set him apart from Bnai Yoel's core membership, as did the provocative and publicity-grabbing style of his activism, which alienated many of his fellow dissidents.

Waldman went on to play a central role in founding various umbrella organizations, with names such as the Committee for No School District, the Committee for the Well-Being of Kiryas Joel, and the Kiryas Joel Alliance, that brought together the disparate elements of the growing dissident community. But he always stood apart from the various dissident groups that he helped to promote. While other dissidents went on to form tight-knit subcommunities within which their children were educated and married, Joseph was, as his longtime lawyer Michael Sussman would say after many decades of representing him, "a different cat."[44] Not only was he different from the parents who formed Bnai Yoel; he was different from his own brothers, who were core members of Faiga's mentschen. Indeed, Joseph's older brother, Zalman Waldman, was Faiga's close aide and caretaker, responsible for establishing and superintending the synagogue that ran out of her home.

Joseph Waldman was in many ways an exception to the rules that obtained in Satmar society. He was a fully observant but independent-minded man who resisted constraints and admonitions. He defied the general communal principle of behaving with discretion, quietude, and limited contact toward the gentile world.

That said, it was not until the winter and spring of 1989 that Waldman was prompted to rebel. The triggering event, by his account, was his witnessing of the ongoing harassment of Bnai Yoel kids, who still had no school building of their own. Waldman asserts that on one particularly violent day he watched as they fell victim to attacks by an "army" of yeshivah bokhers whom he perceived to be acting on Aaron's orders.[45] In his view, by encouraging the attacks and expelling families from the congregation and the UTA, Aaron was making clear that he was willing to sacrifice children to preserve his power base.

During this period, Waldman reports, he was "cruising along on the borderline, very, very much on the string," watching from afar—until one Shabbes, when he ventured to make a "kinda supportive message" in favor of the dissidents, in response to which he received a punch in the nose from a supporter of Moshe Teitelbaum. Perhaps because Waldman was still trying to adhere to community norms, Waldman says that he resisted "losing control" and "instead . . . immediately contacted Aaron Teitelbaum" to seek redress.[46] Commencing what would become a trademark tactic of his, Waldman used his cherished electronic equipment to make a secret recording of his conversation with Aaron, which he subsequently posted on a hotline frequented by the more adventurous members of the Hasidic community. In that conversation, Aaron promised, according to Waldman, that he would "take care of" the situation in exchange for Waldman refraining from going to the state authorities. As Waldman recalls his evolution into a dissident warrior, it was Aaron's subsequent failure to keep his end of this bargain that marked the beginning of "my war against him." Shocked to the core, Waldman says, he then told Aaron that "if you're not gonna be responsible, then I have to do what I'm going to have to do."[47] Much like Grumet's response to Cuomo's rhetorical question, "Who's gonna sue, Luig" ("I will, governor"), this was a declaration of war.

A few weeks later, on the night of Lag Ba-Omer, a violent incident occurred that, Waldman avers, "changed my life completely."[48] On that night, Waldman says, he was awakened at one o'clock by "a terrible noise." After calling the state police, he discovered that it emanated from the nearby cemetery. He then jumped into his car and—packing a gun that he had begun to carry for his security business—drove to the cemetery. There, he says, he "saw a scene that is engraved in my mind": a throng of yeshivah students "throwing stones" at the Rebbetsin as she and her entourage came out of their cars.[49]

It was well known to everyone in the community that Faiga was in the habit of making nocturnal visits to the cemetery, especially on ritually significant occasions such as Lag Ba-Omer. Often, she would maintain a silent vigil at her dead husband's graveside for hours at a time. This night, however, was anything but silent. Yeshivah students were throwing stones that were "flying right and left," according to Waldman. Three cars belonging to Faiga's mentshen were "all smashed up" and the windows broken. Only the arrival of state troopers put an end to the shower of stones.[50]

After the police had dispersed the yeshivah students, the Rebbetsin's entourage, led by Waldman's brother Zalman and other aides, returned to her home, with Joseph in tow. Joseph recounts that he watched as they "tried to give her something to drink" and began to place calls to "the *dayunim*," rabbinic judges in Israel. True to form, upon observing the Rebbetsin "shaking" and "ferociously crying," Waldman ran home and returned with his trusty tape recorder so that he could "record her crying" and talking with the rabbis in Israel about the need to shut down KJ's "disrespectful" yeshivah. Eventually, his brother admonished him and took the tape recorder away, but Joseph was undaunted. He ran back home and retrieved another tape recorder. Waldman explains that he thought it likely that village leaders would deny the incident: "that's one thing I learned—that history is in the making." From that night on, he applied his talent for creating videos and tape recordings, which he had previously applied to painting a positive portrait of Satmar life on behalf of the establishment, to documenting the travails of the dissidents and the excesses of the establishment.[51]

More than that, he used his PR skills to stage events that brought the plight of the dissidents to public attention. The first such incident was a battle over KJ's first school board election, which Waldman instantly saw to be an opportunity to expose the corruption and abuse of power he and the other dissidents believed the village leaders were guilty of. The negotiations with Assemblyman Pataki and other state and local politicians that culminated in the passage of Chapter 748 were going on during the very period when the harassment of the dissidents was occurring. With the passage of Chapter 748 on June 21, 1989, shortly after the incident at the cemetery that led Waldman to declare his support for the dissidents, a new front opened up against the establishment.

For example, the prominent businessman and founder of Shaarei Chemlah, Wolf Lefkowitz, never accepted the idea that a public school should replace the private school that he had founded for children with special needs. Unlike many other parents of children in Shaarei Chemlah, who welcomed the arrival of Benardo and the new public school, he strenuously resisted moving the children out of the privately run program that he ran inside the Bais Ruchel girls' school. Like other dissidents, he took the position that all Satmar children should be educated in the physical and cultural confines of the religious schools, including children with special needs.[52]

Lefkowitz, of course, had a personal investment in preserving the school that he founded and ran. But apart from his personal interests, there were a number of reasons why he and others found the creation of the school district objectionable. First, he and other dissidents believed that a public school run in secular fashion was a profanation of the Rebbe's holy way. In the subsequent years, rabbinic figures sympathetic to the dissidents would inveigh against the public school as an abomination. One Bnai Yoel pamphlet from 1994 referred to Steven Benardo as "a transgressor of the foundations of Judaism." The school itself was nothing less than "a calamity for [the idea of] a pure education."[53]

Wolf Lefkowitz and other opponents of the public school district in KJ had other grounds for discontent. The school district, they believed, would significantly expand the powers of the village leaders. Although the district was to be governed by an elected school board that technically would be independent of the village leadership, members of the new school board, like the village mayor and the members of the village board of trustees, would be vetted and approved by Moshe and Aaron. Moshe clearly asserted his power to appoint school board members in this period of upheaval: "It's like this. With the power of the Torah, I am here the Authority in the Rabbinical Leadership. . . . As you know I want to nominate seven people and I want these people to be the people."[54]

And so Moshe and Aaron designated their allies, including Abe Wieder, to fill the seven spots on the school board in what was fully expected to be an uncontested election. In this fashion, the Rebbe and his advisors essentially appointed local political officeholders. In so doing—and in full compliance with the democratic procedures prescribed by state law—the religious leaders of the community exercised control over KJ's secular political institutions. Already, the interlocking political and religious leadership of the village wielded both the powers of municipal government *and* the powers of private governance with which the congregation as a private corporation was endowed. Now, those leaders would effectively control the school board as well.

More specifically, their authority would be augmented by the power to impose property taxes to fund the operations of the school district, the power to receive and distribute funds from the state and federal government for education-related expenses, the power to purchase or lease sites dedicated to schoolhouses and playgrounds and to construct and furnish them, and the power to hire teachers and maintain a transportation force. All of these powers were granted under Chapter 748, in addition to the power to provide remedial and special education services for children in the newly created district.[55] These powers would be directly exercised by the members of the school board, who would be elected after being nominated by the village religious and lay leadership. The consequent augmentation of the village leaders' powers and tightening of the political and religious power structure served to agitate further the growing group of dissidents.

They expressed their political discontent in theological terms. How, they asked, could the arrogation of the powers of a secular school district by village leaders be reconciled with the Rebbe's insistence upon separation from the secular world—the very principle that led Joel Teitelbaum to establish a shtetl at a remove from the city decades earlier? To its Satmar critics, the establishment of the public school system created an impossible choice: either the Satmars would have to lie about the character of the new school system, pretending that it was secular when it was not, or they would have to perpetrate the grave act of removing God and religion from the children's education.[56] Either way, the leaders of the village, with Moshe's blessing, would be violating Jewish law and corrupting Reb Yoelish's holy intent.

These sentiments were widely shared and deeply felt among the dissidents. But it was Joseph Waldman who came up with a plan for turning these feelings into an overt political challenge. His idea was to organize a slate of alternative candidates for school board and thereby demonstrate the political force of the dissidents inside KJ. It was an audacious and paradoxical strategy. If his candidates won, his aim was to get them to use the power of the school board to shut the school down, ideally before it ever opened. If they lost, Waldman reasoned, the election would serve to expose the village leaders' embrace of secular power and the ways they used that power to suppress internal dissent. By appealing to outside authorities such as the county officials charged with supervising school board elections, Waldman hoped to preserve the Rebbe's—and now the dissidents'—vision of withdrawal from the world. It was an ironic quest to stop the secular power grab by enlisting secular support. Only by playing the dirty game of politics could they hope to return the community to its posture of separating itself from such "worldly" affairs.

The only problem with Waldman's plan was that he could find only one person to run on his protest slate: himself. Predictably, after announcing his candidacy, Waldman was formally expelled from the Yeter Lev congregation.[57] Undeterred, he persisted in his plan to turn the school board vote into the village's first contested election. On January 3, 1990, along with the seven candidates who had been selected by Aaron and Moshe, he filed a formal petition declaring his candidacy with the BOCES superintendent in charge of overseeing county school board elections.[58] The next day, Waldman found his tires slashed. He also received a slew of phone calls, warning him that if he did not pull out of the election, he and his family would face repercussions. Waldman made sure to record all of this and pass it on to local reporters. He was an effective, persistent, and often sensationalist source for the local paper, which made it its business to investigate the dissidents' allegations of mistreatment and misuse of power by the establishment, of which there would be many. From this point onward, the *Times Herald-Record* reported regularly on Waldman's claims of harassment and on the dissidents in general.

Even more significant than Waldman's appeal to the press was his appeal to the law. It was after receiving the harassing phone calls that threatened not only him but also his children that Waldman placed a phone call of his own, to Michael Sussman, a local civil rights lawyer who had gained acclaim as the lead lawyer in the Yonkers case, a high-profile housing discrimination suit launched in the 1980s (dramatized in the 2015 television miniseries *Show Me a Hero*).[59] Waldman's question for Sussman revealed his complicated personal and communal agenda: how could he prevent Aaron from throwing his children out of the yeshivah without pulling out of the school board election? Could the secular legal system protect his children, as well as his own electoral prospects?

That phone call changed the course of the dissident movement in KJ, in ways both foreseen and unforeseen. As Waldman well understood, merely making recourse to non-Jewish courts was seriously discouraged in traditionally Orthodox communities even into the late twentieth century. It was deemed far preferable, if not religiously required, to address one's disputes in rabbinical court. Over time, Haredim in KJ and elsewhere had started turning to state courts to resolve disagreements, especially over business. But what Waldman was instigating was far more dramatic than the arbitration of a business dispute. For a Satmar Hasid to turn to secular law to challenge the authority of the community's religious leaders was a shocking breach of precedent and customary norms. Yet bringing a legal complaint against Moshe and Aaron is exactly what Waldman had in mind.

As Sussman recalls of that first phone call, he advised Waldman on the possible courses of action that lay open to him. Addressing Waldman's concern about his children, Sussman explained to him that the law was unclear: On one hand, "there's a strong preference for letting private institutions, particularly religious institutions, decide their own destiny." On the other hand, there was an "equally strong concern about children," which, in light of there being "no other alternative school," could militate in Waldman's favor. The bottom line was that Aaron, as the chief executive of the UTA, was the legally responsible party and could be sued. Waldman then cut to the chase. Sussman recounts: "He said, 'I want to run,' so I said, 'go ahead, run.'"[60]

The lawyer-client relationship established as a result of this phone call would last for many decades. The client group would expand to include not only Waldman but virtually all of the dissidents engaged in battle with the village leadership. In much the same way that George Shebitz served as in-house counsel for the village, Sussman assumed the position of chief legal adviser to the dissidents. Over the ensuing years, he would play an active role in shaping the dissidents' agenda as well as the strategies they would use to pursue their agenda. He would advise them to build their own alternative institutions. He would help them to monitor the elections that took place inside the village. And he would challenge the property restrictions and zoning regulations that the village leaders tried to use to thwart the dissidents from creating their own moysdes. Eventually, he would even lead them to challenge the very constitutionality of the village itself![61] Throughout all of this, he performed the important function of translating the dissidents' complaints about violations of religious law into the language of secular law. Conversely, he introduced the idiom of American law into the language of the dissidents. He thus fulfilled Waldman's paradoxical vision of using secular legal authority to preserve the Rebbe's domain of spiritual sanctity.

At the dawn of 1990, however, Sussman was still new to the area, and the situation of the Satmars in KJ was unfamiliar to him. Sussman's first act for Waldman was modest enough; he assisted Waldman in getting the polling booth moved out of the main synagogue.[62] On January 17, the school board election was held: 1,769 residents cast ballots, the highest turnout for an election since the village had been founded. Although Waldman lost, he could (and did) boast of receiving 673 votes, notwithstanding his assertion that many votes were cast for the establishment candidates by underage students.[63] If it was not quite the stunning defeat of the establishment that Waldman had imagined, it was a revealing demonstration of the extent of the political resistance and a harbinger of the strife yet to come.

This new phase of the conflict inside KJ coincided with the external attack on the new school district that Grumet had set in motion. Just two days after the school board election, Grumet filed his lawsuit against the New York State Department of Education, challenging the constitutionality of Chapter 748. The village's leaders were now facing an external legal challenge and an internal political challenge. The question of whether they were comporting themselves in ways that were consistent with American constitutional principles—and with the late Rebbe's religious principles—could no longer be avoided.

Although they came at the KJ establishment from different angles, Lou Grumet's lawsuit and Yosel Waldman's legal forays proceeded in lockstep. When Waldman was first dreaming up his idea of a protest slate in September 1989, the New York State School Board Association (NYSSBA) was holding its first meeting to discuss how to respond to the recent passage of Chapter 748. The NYSSBA board members all shared Grumet's concerns about the statute, which they feared might create a precedent for other communities to secede from established school districts.[64] Situating that concern in the political context of the day, Grumet later explained that "in the Reagan years, that was a plausible" scenario.[65] (The Reagan administration had ended just one year earlier.) Public education was also facing the challenge of the homeschool movement, which threatened to draw resources away from public school districts composed of students with different backgrounds and levels of wealth. This threat would be greatly exacerbated if communities that wanted to separate themselves from others could command the resources of a public school system. Facing that threat head-on, Grumet's board readily agreed with him that the NYSSBA should do what it could to push back. On January 6, 1990, three days after Waldman and Wieder submitted their respective petitions to run for the school board, the NYSSBA held another meeting at which Grumet's proposal to bring a lawsuit was formally approved. The lawsuit was filed on January 19, two days after the school board election took place.

The complaint initially named the New York State Department of Education, along with the state officials responsible for implementing the law, as the defendants. This choice reflected the theory of the case that Grumet's lawyers had devised. Rather than argue that *the school district* was operating in an unconstitutional fashion, the complaint asserted that it was *the state* that had acted unconstitutionally by granting Kiryas Joel the right to establish its own school district. On this theory, even if the new school district operated in full compliance with the constitutional principle that religion has no place in public education, the statute violated the principle of separation between church and state by bestowing the powers of a public school district on a religious community. The complaint argued that this move was prohibited by the Establishment Clause of the federal Constitution and by a state constitutional amendment, known as the Blaine Amendment, which specifically prohibited the expenditure of public money on schools that are "wholly or in part under the control or direction of any religious denomination."[66] The complaint also rested on the claim that the school district violated the Equal Protection Clause of the Fourteenth Amendment by "carv[ing] out a new school district from an existing district when such an effort will have the effect of creating a segregated school."[67]

Not long after the suit was filed, both the Monroe-Woodbury School District and the Kiryas Joel School District (now formally constituted and run by the newly elected board presided over by Wieder) made motions to intervene. Each argued that it had a direct interest in the outcome of the case and therefore should be added as a codefendant in order to have the opportunity to explain why Chapter 748 should be upheld from its point of view.

While the trial court was taking these motions under advisement, Waldman was turning his attention to a new challenge. Having lost the school board election, but not his political zeal, Waldman announced that he would work to defeat the incumbents on the village board of trustees. Given his recent showing in the school board election, this was no idle threat. Responding to this challenge, Wieder and another member of the village board agreed not to seek reelection. Wieder further agreed that the village leaders would not oppose the creation of the new school that the Bnai Yoel was then in the process of establishing.[68]

This appeared to be a significant concession, but only briefly. On March 18, two days before the village election was scheduled to take place, the congregation decreed that Waldman's children would be expelled from the KJ schools, effective March 27.[69] Four days later, two days after the village election, Wieder sought and was granted the right to intervene personally as a party in the Grumet litigation. The timing of this action reflected the extent to which the Grumet litigation and Waldman's campaign were intertwined, at least from the villagers' point of view. Waldman, for his part, regarded Grumet's lawsuit as an opportunity to achieve what his run for the school board had failed to do: the dissolution of the school district. Meanwhile, Wieder saw fit to intervene in the case in his personal capacity—above and beyond the motion to intervene he had already filed on behalf of the Kiryas Joel School District—in order to widen the theater of battle against the dissidents.

Four days after Wieder made his successful motion to intervene in the Grumet litigation and one day before the appointed date, the congregation carried out its threat to expel Waldman's six minor children. The children were physically removed from KJ's United Talmudic Academy schools and ordered not to return.

Waldman was not unprepared for this development. Far from it. The first thing he did was to make sure that the press and the state police were present to witness the spectacle of his children being removed from the very schools, which he had contrived. "Don't you dare come home," Waldman instructed his children when his son called to report that the principal was throwing them out and sending them home in a car. Instead of accepting the ride, Waldman ordered his children to wait for him outside in the cold, which enabled him to say to anyone who would listen, "They didn't even allow the children, the small children, to wait inside, it was brutal."[70]

The next day, Sussman filed a lawsuit on Waldman's behalf against the KJ UTA. Moving with dispatch, he sought and obtained a temporary restraining order requiring the UTA to readmit Waldman's children, which he personally delivered to Aaron at his home later that day. A full hearing of the case was scheduled for April 11, the first day of Passover.

Aaron's response to this invocation of state authority was defiant. He tossed aside the documents that Sussman had served him, including a handwritten note stating in bold letters, "WARNING. YOUR FAILURE TO APPEAR IN COURT MAY RESULT IN YOUR IMMEDIATE ARREST AND IMPRISONMENT FOR CONTEMPT OF COURT."[71] Aaron let it be known that he would not let the children back into the schools.

Waldman responded to Aaron's display of defiance with an equal display. Knowing full well that his children would be sent away, Waldman packed them off to school the next day anyway. As the children were dutifully reporting to their respective schools, Waldman was serving the order to appear in court on the principal of the Bais Ruchel.[72] Meanwhile, over at the boys' school, the principal was once again ordering Waldman's sons to leave, repeating the scene of the previous day.[73] On cue, Sussman galloped back to court to make the case that Aaron was now acting in contempt of court. Not surprisingly, since Aaron was openly defying the court order to readmit the children pending a full trial of Waldman's case, the judge readily granted Sussman's petition and ordered Aaron to appear in court to explain why the UTA should not be held in contempt.[74]

This was an unprecedented development. Never before had a Satmar religious leader been summoned to a secular court to defend his actions. The order to Aaron to appear in court sliced into the very heart of the Satmar system of religious authority, challenging the supposed autonomy of Jewish law embodied in the figure of the all-powerful Rebbe.

Facing the order of contempt, Moshe and Aaron had little choice but to submit to the order and defend their autonomy from state law in court.

Thus it was that, on March 30, two days after the court's order was issued, Aaron appeared in the courthouse, accompanied by supporters from Brooklyn and Kiryas Joel. It was an amazing spectacle to behold. There, in a room crowded with Satmar Hasidim, Judge Peter Patsalos, the son of Greek immigrants, told Aaron, "The keys to prison are in your pocket; you either allow these children in or you're being imprisoned."[75]

The results of Judge Patsalos's intervention were decidedly mixed. On the one hand, the children were allowed back in school the following day, pending the trial now rescheduled to commence the day after the eight-day Passover holiday. On the other hand, hostility against Waldman within the community intensified. On the same day that Waldman's children were allowed back in school, their family home was surrounded by pro-testers throwing rocks and chanting "Death to Joseph Waldman."[76]

Waldman responded to this act of aggression by again turning to the courts. Michael Sussman, his now notorious lawyer, sought an order of protection, which Judge Patsalos readily granted.[77] The coming of Pass-over provided a further reprieve. With the commencement of school recess, the issue of the children's right to attend the schools was tempo-rarily postponed, and Judge Patsalos took advantage of the lull by trying to get the warring parties to agree to a settlement.[78] But as soon as school resumed at the end of the Passover recess, Waldman's children were again denied entry.[79] This was a particularly brazen act, as it oc-curred on the very day that the hearing of the case of *Waldman v. UTA* was scheduled to take place in Patsalos's courtroom.

Pandemonium was breaking out in Kiryas Joel. Over the course of a tumultuous week, dissidents' cars were torched, houses were pelted with stones, and people were physically beaten. In typical Satmar fash-ion, the violence made its way to Brooklyn, where Moshe's supporters forcibly removed the metal gate that Brach had recently installed to keep them from entering the Rebbe's old abode, prompting the police to be placed on alert.[80] In the midst of this week of violence, Judge Patsalos issued his decision in favor of Waldman and ordered Aaron to readmit the children, at pain of a penalty of $250 for every day they were denied entry.[81]

Three days later, with the children still being denied entry, Sussman was back in court seeking to enforce the fines against Aaron and Moshe for contempt. Three days after that, Louis Grumet filed an amended complaint to his lawsuit, attempting to deny Monroe-Woodbury's and the Kiryas Joel School District's motions to intervene. On May 3, even before the court had had a chance to make its decision, Grumet filed a motion for summary judgment, arguing that it was not necessary to conduct a trial to conclude that the statute was unconstitutional on its face.[82] While the state court considered the pending motions, rioting continued in Kiryas Joel. On May 12, Moshe reprised his infamous "Ki-sisa drushe," issuing another sermon on the heels of the Sabbath that denounced the dissidents. The next day, more than one hundred fifty yeshivah students surrounded Waldman's home.[83]

Over the course of the following week, Moshe and Aaron took a number of steps to get the situation under control. On one hand, they extended an olive branch by negotiating a truce with Waldman in KJ; on the other hand, they detonated a legal explosion by commencing legal action against Nachman Brach in Brooklyn.[84] The terms of the truce allowed Waldman's children to return to the UTA's religious schools in exchange for his making a public apology to Aaron.[85]

The treatment of Brach was less forgiving. The Williamsburg congregation claimed that the transfer of the Bedford Avenue property to Brach's corporation was fraudulent. On May 17, they filed a lawsuit in Kings County (Brooklyn) to "quiet title" and restore the right to possess and use the property to the congregation.[86] This lawsuit, known as *Yeter Lev D'Satmar, Inc. v. 26 Adar N.B. Corp.*, or simply, *26 Adar* (after the name of Brach's corporation), would persist for nearly two decades, outlasting even the Grumet litigation. Eventually, the Adar Corporation would be dissolved and Brach himself would drift away from the center of communal activity and cease to be a significant force in Satmar politics.[87] By the turn of the twenty-first century, he was largely forgotten inside the Satmar community. But the lawsuit against his ghostly corporation would live on.

Back in 1990, Brach's dispute with the leadership was very much alive. The lawsuit filed against him was just the opening salvo in a series of legal battles between him and Satmar leaders that unfolded over the next five or so years. In fact, the lawsuit filed against Brach marked the first time the Satmar leadership brought suit against any of the dissidents. The 26 *Adar* suit served as a warning to the dissidents that appealing to the secular courts to settle the dispute was not a one-way street.

Later in May, the Satmar leaders got the news that the KJ School District's motion to intervene as a codefendant in Grumet's lawsuit had been granted, along with that of Monroe-Woodbury. This was good news for the village but created a serious problem for the plaintiffs. The case had been brought in the name of the NYSSBA (the school board association run by Grumet)—of which Monroe-Woodbury, now formally an adversary, was a member organization. That spelled trouble for the NYSSBA, which now was bringing a lawsuit against a group of defendants that included one of its own members. The complaint had asserted: "The Monroe-Woodbury School District stands, and has always stood, ready and willing to provide appropriate educational services to any and all school age children living within the village of Kiryas Joel on the premises of the Monroe-Woodbury district's public schools."[88] But now Monroe-Woodbury was openly contradicting this, declaring that it supported Chapter 748 and opposed Grumet's claims.[89] In response, Grumet submitted an affidavit arguing that it was not in Monroe-Woodbury's interests to defend Chapter 748. Not mincing words, Monroe-Woodbury's lawyer submitted an affidavit stating, "I am amazed at the condescending and paternalistic tone of the affidavit of Louis Grumet" and further, that "I believe it to be unmitigated chutzpah for plaintiffs, a trade organization and its representatives, to lecture a popularly elected board of education on what constitutes the best interests of the school district which it administers."[90]

The court dealt with this issue by ruling that the NYSSBA did not have standing to bring the lawsuit—but that Grumet, in his personal capacity, did. The same logic applied to Albert Hawk, the titular president of the NYSSBA, who was also a formal party to the litigation, though he never played an active role. Under state and federal law, any tax-paying citizen had standing to bring a lawsuit claiming Establishment Clause violations.[91] Therefore, while neither Hawk nor Grumet could go forward in their capacity as an NYSSBA officer, they both could proceed as private citizens. The case was thus reconfigured so that it was now Grumet and Hawk, not NYSSBA, suing the school districts of Monroe-Woodbury and Kiryas Joel along with New York State's Department of Education.[92]

The Public's Response to *Grumet v. Kiryas Joel*

Public attention to the case grew slowly but steadily. Since the trial court had been asked to rule on a motion for summary judgment, there would be no trial to attract public notice. But the New York State teachers' union had learned of the litigation and filed an amicus brief in support of Grumet's position, guaranteeing that a significant constituency would be paying attention to the outcome.[93] Sure enough, when the trial court issued its decision, in January 1992, it caught the media's eye. In its first story about the case, the *New York Times* reported: "A special public school district in a Hasidic community in Orange County was established in violation of the constitutional separation of church and state, a State Supreme Court judge ruled today."[94] Noting that KJ planned to appeal the decision, the article stated: "If it is upheld, the ruling will effectively close the school, leaving the children to find an education elsewhere" and "throw[ing] into disarray Kiryas Joel's carefully crafted plan to educate its disabled children."[95]

In fact, the village's "carefully crafted plan to educate its disabled children" was undisturbed by the court's ruling. Benardo, the man responsible for crafting the plan, was keeping close tabs on the case and could hardly fail to feel anxiety about its ultimate fate. But his main focus was on fostering the programs, which had been up and running since the fall of 1990. He was relieved to learn they would be allowed to continue pending the case's appeal.[96] The fact that the trial court had ruled the law creating the school district unconstitutional was certainly cause for concern. But the newfound attention to the case gave Benardo and the community leaders reason to hope that the ruling might be overturned on appeal.

That hope was reinforced as the case progressed through the appellate process and various advocacy groups began to rally around it. The more defeats KJ suffered—its petition to reverse the trial court's decision was rejected twice, by New York State's appellate division and then by its highest court, the Court of Appeals—the more support it attracted, in particular from conservative Christian organizations.[97]

Not that the Satmars had sought out their support. But the litigation coincided with a new stage in the history of the Christian right in America, which focused on courts as "the next battleground of conservative Christian activism."[98] Conservative unhappiness with the Court had been brewing for decades. But it was only in 1980 that a "new Christian right" began to emerge with the mission to "take back the Court." Ronald Reagan's election in 1980 made that goal a real possibility.[99] Facing reelection in 1984, he strongly backed the Equal Access Act, passed by Congress in 1984 in response to growing criticism of university policies that denied religious groups access to university venues and funding.[100] He also made a campaign promise to deliver a constitutional amendment protecting the right of states and school boards to reinstitute prayer in public schools.[101] This amendment never came to pass. But thanks to Reagan's focus on judicial appointments, both the Supreme Court and the lower federal courts were increasingly populated by conservatives, who were, to varying degrees, receptive to the positions of the Christian right.

But it was not only conservatives who were moving courts in the direction of greater receptivity to religious groups. In fact, the notion that religious groups deserved equal access to university venues also received broad support from Democrats. The discourse of multiculturalism and equal access for diverse viewpoints was gaining ground among progressives, and conservatives seized upon that to argue that it should apply to religious groups and conservative beliefs too.[102] Liberals could hardly disagree. In 1990, the year the *Grumet* litigation began, the Supreme Court approved the constitutionality of the Equal Access Act and held, further, that it was unconstitutional to deny a Christian club equal access to use of the premises of a high school as an after-school activity.[103] The opinion for the Court was written by Justice Sandra Day O'Connor, a moderate conservative appointed to the Court by Ronald Reagan. But a concurring opinion was written by Justice Thurgood Marshall, one of the two most liberal justices then on the Court. And the decision received the support of all but one of the liberal justices, Justice Stevens, who would stake out an equally singular position in the *Grumet* case four years later.

To recall, 1990 was also the year that saw the formation of the American Center for Law and Justice, the most prominent of the conservative Christian "public interest law firms" that were established in 1990 with the specific aim of reshaping First Amendment doctrine in order to expand religious liberty and weaken the wall of separation between church and state.[104] Founded by the well-known evangelical minister Pat Robertson in 1990 and known by its acronym, the ACLJ (a name clearly intended to echo that of its nemesis, the ACLU), it was part of a concerted campaign to use the tactics of liberal legal advocacy groups in the service of conservative ends. In 1992, Robertson appointed Jay Sekulow, an attorney who had recently won a unanimous ruling in favor of the Jews for Jesus before the Supreme Court and was himself a Messianic Jew, as chief counsel of the ACLJ, a position in which he served from 1992 until 2018.[105] In this position, Sekulow would have a hand in nearly every free exercise and establishment case of note and in notable free speech cases as well, making him one of the most influential agents in transforming the law of the First Amendment.

Between 1990 (the year the *Grumet* case commenced) and 1994 (the year it went to the Supreme Court), Christian-affiliated legal groups such as the ACLJ proliferated, and the number of religious liberty cases they litigated—or participated in as "friends of the court"—grew by leaps and bounds.[106] Some of this burst of energy was stimulated by a surprising source: a decision written by Justice Antonin Scalia, who was widely revered by religious conservatives, and generally regarded as a great supporter of their legal agenda, but who bitterly disappointed them in 1990 by handing down a decision that held that the Free Exercise Clause does not grant religious objectors the right to an exemption from neutral laws of general application. This seeming rejection of the right to religious accommodation, in a case called *Employment Division v. Smith*, pointed up tensions within twentieth-century conservatism that mirrored the tensions that existed within liberalism itself. These tensions manifested themselves in complicated ways. At the same time that liberalism was splitting between a sameness model of equality and a difference model that undergirded the move toward multiculturalism and pluralism, conservatism also was riven between conflicting impulses. Both conservative and liberal thought contained a strand of deep-seated skepticism about the use of state power to regulate behavior and, even worse, thought. Opposition to state-sponsored orthodoxy and indoctrination was a principle of classical liberalism to which both laid claim. On the other hand, both also accepted the necessity of state regulation to maintain social order and protect public safety and basic civil rights, notwithstanding the fact that upholding such regulations inevitably entails some degree of behavioral, and maybe even mental, conformity. The resulting ambivalence regarding the conflicting values of individual freedom and law and order came to a head in the *Smith* decision.[107] Members of the religious right were confused and outraged when Scalia rejected the principle that the Free Exercise Clause confers a broad right to religious exemptions. But in doing so, Scalia was upholding equally conservative principles—of judicial restraint and deference to the authority of the state. Above all, Scalia gave voice in *Smith* to the long-standing conservative principle of law and order and the consequent need for conformity to a single, state-approved, set of rules of conduct. To hold otherwise, he said, "would be to make the professed doctrines of religious belief superior to the law of the land, and, in effect, permit every citizen to become a law unto himself."[108]

The idea that state power and conformity to the law are necessary to keep anarchism at bay was as venerable a principle of conservative political thought as they came. Nonetheless, the conservative political movement, which was growing ever stronger in the early 1990s, rejected Scalia's appeal to law and order swiftly and vociferously—alongside liberal civil rights and civil liberties groups. The coalition of strange political bedfellows that formed in reaction to the *Smith* case was telling. At the same time that it demonstrated the tensions internal to liberalism and conservatism, it also revealed surprising commonalities. These commonalities led to the formation of a political alliance between liberal civil libertarians and religious and political conservatives in the early 1990s that today is almost unimaginable, but was, in the moment, completely consistent with the tacking of liberal Democrats toward the center and the increasing value placed on group identity, including religious group identities, by both the left and the right. Thus it was that the ACLU and other liberal civil liberties advocacy groups joined forces with the ACLJ and other nascent conservative "civil rights firms" to lobby for the passage of a law that was designed in effect to overturn the widely detested *Smith* decision by requiring courts to grant exemptions from laws that impose a substantial burden on the free exercise of religion. Dubbed the Religious Freedom Restoration Act, or RFRA for short, the proposed statute reflected the outrage at the *Smith* decision that was then widely shared. Its passage certainly reflected the growing influence of the religious right and the broader conservative movement of which it was a part. But it also reflected the points of convergence that were emerging between conservatism and progressivism as each embraced identity politics and the value of preserving cultural differences.

The real turning point came in 1993.[109] Ending twelve years of Republican administrations, Bill Clinton, who assiduously courted traditional religious voters as part of his strategy of tacking to the right, was inaugurated president on January 20. One month later, the new Christian right scored its first major legal victory in the case of *Lamb's Chapel v. Center Moriches School District*.[110] Like so many Establishment and Free Exercise Clause disputes, this was a case that focused on schools. More specifically, it was a case in which the Supreme Court ruled unanimously that public schools that open their facilities to secular organizations after hours must make them available to religious groups as well.[111] This was an argument that conservative lawyers had long been pressing, and now, for the first time, it had prevailed. Sensing their momentum, the ACLJ lawyers who won this case, led by Jay Sekulow, were looking around for other cases that could advance their agenda.

Eleven days later, the Supreme Court handed religious conservatives yet another victory in the case of *Zobrest v. Catalina Foothills School District*, which held that the Free Exercise Clause required the school district to provide a Sign-language interpreter to a Deaf child attending a Catholic school and, further, that the Establishment Clause did not prohibit this arrangement.[112] Like *Grumet*, it was a case that involved disability rights as well as the right of religious freedom and presented a sympathetic case for allowing publicly funded services, in religious school settings, for children with disabilities.

Meanwhile, lobbying for the Religious Freedom Restoration Act was in full swing. The bill to approve the new law was formally introduced by then-congressman Charles Schumer of New York on March 11, 1993, fewer than three weeks after *Lamb's Chapel* came down. It passed with near unanimity and was eagerly signed into law by President Clinton in November. In the interim, in the summer of 1993, KJ School District had suffered its final defeat in state court.[113] It did not take long for it to appear on the radar of the new religious rights advocacy organizations, which were casting about for a follow-up to their recent successes in *Lamb's Chapel* and *Zobrest*. *KJ v. Grumet* was, in some ways, an unlikely lawsuit for these advocates to latch onto. But in other ways it was a perfect vehicle for their cause. Logically enough, most of the cases that conservative Christian lawyers took on featured Christian plaintiffs or promoted Christian causes. The organizations they represented made no bones about the fact that their primary agenda was to promote the values of evangelical Christians. But they represented their cause in terms of the general—liberal—principle of "religious freedom," which in theory protected people of every religion. For reasons of both principle and expediency, conservative Christian advocacy groups were happy to support cases brought by members of other religious faiths, so long as the values, legal strategies, and expected outcome were congruent with their own.

This was made possible by the fact that traditional Christians and religious traditionalists of other faith traditions shared certain goals. One such goal was to secure public support—government funding— for private religious education. Another was to return prayer and other

religious practices to the public schools, which was a central plank in
the Christian right's broader platform of returning religion to "the public square." Restoring religion to its previous position as a source of a
public, and not merely private, authority was an objective shared by
traditionalists of many different religious denominations, including Orthodox and especially Haredi Jews. Although most Orthodox and
Haredi Jews had little to no contact with Christians, conservative or
otherwise, they came to understand their affinity with this conservative
Christian cause.[114]

The belief that religion belongs in the public realm was just one point
of affinity between the mainstream Satmar party in KJ and the new
Christian right. Closely related was their shared struggle with the doctrine of separation between religion and state. The Satmars sought to
demonstrate that the creation of the KJ School District was consistent
with the principle of separation that was embodied, according to the
Court in *Everson*, in the First Amendment's Establishment Clause. More
specifically, they sought to show that Chapter 748 satisfied the elements
of the so-called *Lemon* doctrine, named for the 1971 case of *Lemon v.
Kurtzman*, in which the Supreme Court had laid out its three-part test
for determining when the principle of church-state separation is satisfied. All of the lower court decisions rested on the conclusion that
Chapter 748 failed to meet the requirements of *Lemon*'s three-part test.
But by the time the *Grumet* case reached the Supreme Court, some
advocates were arguing not only that it met the *Lemon* test but that the
Lemon test shouldn't be applied at all and that the very notion of a high
and impregnable wall of separation between church and state should be
discarded.

Indeed, *Lemon v. Kurtzman* stood alongside *Roe v. Wade* (the decision in which the Supreme Court recognized the right to abortion) as
one of the chief targets against which the Christian legal movement
took aim. *Lemon* was the most prominent of a spate of "strict separation"
decisions that were handed down following *Everson*, many of which
addressed state programs designed to help subsidize parochial schools.
Lemon specifically held that salary subsidies for teachers who work in
parochial schools are unconstitutional even if the funds are only used

to pay for teachers of secular subjects. At a more general level, it affirmed the strict version of the principle of church-state separation expounded (though not adhered to) in *Everson*. And it sought to operationalize that principle by identifying three separate requirements, each of which state action must meet to escape the judgment that it violated the Establishment Clause. First, according to *Lemon*'s three-part test, a state's action must not have the intent of promoting or inhibiting a religion. Second, it must not have the primary effect of promoting (or inhibiting) religion. Third—and this was the real novelty of *Lemon*, the secular intent and effect requirements having already been articulated by the Supreme Court in prior case law—the law in question must not "excessively entangle" the government with religion.

As much as *Roe v. Wade*, which came down just two years after *Lemon*, and as much as the school prayer decisions issued ten years earlier, the "*Lemon* doctrine" was widely reviled by Christian conservatives, who saw it as the embodiment of everything that was wrong with the liberal approach to religion. They objected to the requirement that the law must have a secular intent. They objected to the requirement that the law could not have the effect of promoting religion, even if that was unintended. And they especially objected to the proposition that the government could not be "excessively entangled" with religion. As they viewed it, this created a catch-22 for religious groups since the second prong of the test required religious institutions to limit their use of government funds to secular functions, while the third prong supported the conclusion that the monitoring mechanisms needed to ensure their compliance with that requirement were too invasive. Indeed, it was precisely this reasoning that had led Justice Brennan to conclude in *Aguilar* that Title I instruction could not take place inside parochial schools. As he saw it, the only way the government could ensure that Title I instructors confined themselves to secular subjects (as required by *Lemon*'s second requirement) was by monitoring what they did in the parochial schools—in violation of *Lemon*'s third prong.

Conservatives were not the only ones who found fault with *Lemon*. There was also lots of liberal handwringing over *Lemon*'s three-part test, which judges and commentators across the political spectrum perceived to be wildly unpredictable in its results. When Senator Moynihan made his famous quip about the inconsistency of decisions that allowed the government to provide secular textbooks to private schools but not maps or other instructional materials ("What about atlases?"), it was the application of the *Lemon* doctrine that he had in mind. But whereas liberals yearned for a better way of applying the principle of separation between religion and state than that provided by the *Lemon* doctrine, one that would uphold the principle while avoiding inconsistent and unfair results, conservatives questioned the principle itself. Some objected to the wall of separation metaphor for being too strict and called for its replacement with a softer line of separation between church and state, one that would allow for some forms of public support for religion and some expressions of religion in the public realm. Others called for a rejection of the principle altogether.

Sensing the wind at their backs, religious conservatives were intensifying their campaign against *Lemon* in the early 1990s. The victory in *Lamb's Chapel* in February 1993 gave them reason to believe that the time was finally ripe to get the Supreme Court to do what they had long only dreamed of doing: overturn it. All they needed was a case before the Supreme Court that involved the Establishment Clause with facts that made a compelling argument for allowing the line between government and religion to be blurred. With its sympathetic subjects (religious children with severe disabilities, not unlike the Deaf Catholic schoolboy in *Zobrest*), *Grumet* seemed like the perfect case.

Thus, it was that the KJ School District's appeal to the Supreme Court became the first opportunity to reconsider *Lemon v. Kurtzman* following *Lamb's Chapel* and *Zobrest*, cases that raised the tantalizing possibility that the Court had had its fill of *Lemon* and strict separation. At the least, it was an opportunity to reconsider whether the *Lemon* doctrine was the right way to think about publicly supported religious education. Even though, technically (and in truth), the Kiryas Joel School District was run as a secular system of education, everyone understood that its creation was an accommodation to the Satmars' way of life that had been necessitated by the Court's past refusal to allow public school districts to provide services to children inside parochial schools. It was the application of the *Lemon* doctrine that had led the Court to conclude in *Aguilar v. Felton* and *Grand Rapids v. Ball* that Title I services could not be provided in parochial schools, and it was the handing down of that pair of cases that had led Monroe superintendent Daniel Alexander to pull the plug on the short-lived special ed program inside KJ's religious school. That in turn was the event that precipitated the passage of Chapter 748. Now, just shy of a decade after those events, *Grumet* seemed like it could provide the occasion for reconsidering both those cases and the *Lemon* doctrine on which they were based.

At least that was the agenda of the new Christian right, which in 1993 began to take an interest in the *Grumet* litigation. Flush with optimism and energized by their recent victories in *Lamb's Chapel* and *Zobrest*, the newly minted Christian legal advocacy firms decided to file amicus briefs in *Grumet*. Taking the lead was the ACLJ, headed by Jay Sekulow. Amicus briefs were filed by numerous other conservative Christian organizations as well, both old (e.g., the Knights of Columbus, the Catholic League for Religious and Civil Rights, and the Archdiocese of New York) and new (e.g., the Rutherford Institute and the Christian Legal Society). Amicus briefs in support of the Kiryas Joel School District also were submitted by the Orthodox Agudath Israel and the National Jewish Commission on Law and Public Affairs (COLPA).[115]

Recognizing the seriousness of the challenge they were facing, all of the major liberal organizations committed to maintaining the separation of church and state submitted briefs in support of Louis Grumet and, more broadly, *Lemon*. The long list of liberal advocacy groups that supported Grumet's position included the ACLU, Americans United for the Separation of Church and State, and, standing in counterpoint to the conservative Jewish advocacy groups that lined up with the conservative Christian advocacy organizations, three venerable Jewish organizations with a long-standing commitment to separation of church and state: the American Jewish Committee, the American Jewish Congress, and the Anti-Defamation League (ADL).

Formed in the early twentieth century, these three groups were united in their desire to fight antisemitism and support equality in America. Two of them, the AJ Committee and the ADL, were among the earliest supporters, one might even say formulators, of the principle of church-state separation adopted by the Supreme Court.[116] The participation of these three Jewish organizations in the *Grumet* case reflected the fact that nested within the broader fight between liberals and conservatives in America was a smaller proxy fight taking place within the American Jewish community between liberal and conservative Jews.

Kiryas Joel School District v. Grumet became a screen onto which this political division was projected. The case had gone from being an obscure lawsuit, followed by only a few interested parties in New York, to a national news story pitting two competing visions of America against each other. On one side stood the vision of America as a country dedicated to integration and inclusivity. On the other side stood the vision of America as a "Christian nation," founded on Christian and biblical values—or, as it was sometimes expressed in more nonsectarian terms, "family values." According to this vision, the state had not only a responsibility to govern in accord with Christian and biblical values but also the right to transmit such values through public support for religious education.

Kiryas Joel's version of a godly place was surely not Christian. But it did challenge the prevailing secularist vision and the more specific proposition that the government should not provide support to religious groups. The controversy generated by KJ's public school was part of a larger debate that cut across religious denominations. That debate reflected an ever-widening division—in fact, a culture war—between traditionalists of different religious persuasions and liberal secularists of different religious and nonreligious bents. The *Grumet* case offered an opportunity not only to stage this debate but—possibly—to reverse the balance of power that up until this point had seemed to favor the liberal position. It thus became one of the many theaters in which the national culture war was being waged.

But it also became a theater for a more local culture war within the American Jewish community. Many, indeed most, of the key players in the litigation were Jews. Beyond the Satmar protagonists themselves, Louis Grumet was Jewish; the lawyers who argued the case for Grumet from the New York State School Association, Jay Worona and Pilar Sokol, were Jewish; George Shebitz, the village's lawyer, was Jewish; Nathan Lewin, the lawyer hired by the village to represent the school district, was Jewish; superintendent Steve Benardo, who testified for the school district, was Jewish; Michael Sussman, who represented Joseph Waldman, was Jewish; Robert Abrams, New York's attorney general, who defended Chapter 748 on behalf of the state, was Jewish; Julie Mereson, the lawyer who argued the case for the state before the Supreme Court, was Jewish; Justice Lawrence Kahn, the trial court judge who issued the first ruling striking down Chapter 748, was Jewish; Judge Howard Levine, who dissented from the Appellate Division's decision to affirm Kahn's ruling, was Jewish. And so, too, was Judge Judith Kaye, the first woman on New York's highest court, who wrote the decision in the *Wieder* case, denying the Satmars the right to force the Monroe-Woodbury School District to provide special ed classes at a neutral site.

Alongside these figures who were directly involved in the *Grumet* litigation, there were others who played key roles in bringing the litigation about and shaping its outcome, a high percentage of whom also were Jews. Daniel Alexander, the former superintendent of the Monroe-Woodbury School District whose refusal to accommodate the Satmars' request for services in Kiryas Joel led to the passage of Chapter 748, was Jewish. Many members of the NYSSBA board, who stood firmly behind Grumet, were Jewish. Curiously enough, even Jay Sekulow, the Brooklyn-born, Long Island–raised lead lawyer for the ACLJ, was a Jew who found Jesus after his family moved to Georgia and then became a Messianic Jew.[117] Together, these men and women represented the full spectrum of political and religious positions occupied by American Jews.

At the far end of that spectrum stood the Satmar Hasidim themselves, defined by their total renunciation of liberal secular values. Closer to this side of the spectrum than his liberal coreligionists, though not nearly as far to the right as the Hasidim, was Nat Lewin, the lawyer whom the Satmars employed to defend the constitutionality of Chapter 748 on behalf of the school district.[118] A top attorney and Orthodox Jew himself, Lewin was well known for his advocacy of Jewish causes, especially Orthodox and ultra-Orthodox ones. Among the many cases he had already argued before the Supreme Court was the "menorah case," in which he represented Chabad, the Lubavitch Hasidic movement, and successfully persuaded the Court to uphold the constitutionality of a public holiday display that included a menorah alongside a Christmas tree.[119] He also argued the "yarmulke case," in which a Jewish officer in the air force sought an exemption from a military regulation forbidding the wearing of head coverings while in uniform.[120] In addition, Lewin had represented the largely Satmar Hasidic community in Williamsburg in a redistricting case, arguing (unsuccessfully) that the use of racial criteria to correct invidious discrimination against nonwhites was unconstitutional.[121]

Lewin's career was a dazzling example of the success of Modern Orthodoxy, with its goal of synthesizing strict observance of Jewish law with full participation in the modern world. Born in Poland, Lewin escaped the Nazis with his family and arrived in New York in 1941. He grew up in the leading Modern Orthodox institutions of New York, excelling at Yeshiva University High School for Boys and Yeshiva College, where he graduated summa cum laude. From there, he went on to become a star student at Harvard Law School, where he befriended an Italian American classmate by the name of Antonin Scalia. When Scalia died, Lewin wrote a eulogy for Scalia titled "The Supreme Court's Jewish Gentile," in which he recalled how the two had bonded as editors on the *Harvard Law Review*. Averring that "we seemed to share identical views on church-state issues," Lewin said the only thing they ever disagreed over when they were students in the early 1960s was how the Court should decide the cases challenging the Sunday Closing Laws that were then being litigated.[122] In contrast to Lewin, Scalia was of the view that requiring everyone, including Saturday Sabbath observers, to adhere to Sunday Closing Laws was perfectly constitutional.

After graduating from Harvard, Lewin clerked for Justice Harlan and served as an assistant to solicitors general Archibald Cox and Thurgood Marshall before working in the Civil Rights Division of the Department of Justice. He then went on to an illustrious career as a Washington lawyer. Throughout it all, he maintained his steadfast commitment to

Orthodoxy and took on pro bono cases supporting traditionally observant Jews. It made perfect sense, then, for Abe Wieder to approach
Lewin at the beginning of the *Grumet* litigation to ask him to represent
Kiryas Joel.[123] When Lewin accepted the invitation, he had no expectation that the case would make its way to the Supreme Court. But he saw
the assignment as falling "squarely within what I had been doing before."[124]
That is, he was "representing a religious Orthodox community in litigation that tested their ability to carry out a function, at public expense,
that they thought was necessary."

If Nat Lewin—hailed as Orthodox Jews' "foremost advocate on legal
and legislative issues"—was the perfect pick to represent the Satmars,
he was also the perfect foil to Louis Grumet, who occupied the opposite
pole of the American Jewish political spectrum with regard to his attitudes toward religion as well as his political attitudes.[125] Married to a
gentile, Grumet had raised two daughters in a completely secular home,
"[telling] them they could make up their own minds" about what to
believe.[126] He himself was raised in West Virginia, in an observant Jewish household, by parents who were both the children of immigrants
from Eastern Europe. But he cast off his family's traditional religious
practices at the same time that his high school was undergoing desegregation. As a teenager, he formed an intense identification with the experience of African Americans, based on his own sense of himself as an outsider. To Jews like Grumet who came of age in the 1950s and 1960s,
secularism and liberalism were very much of a piece. Both pointed in
the direction of integration into a common democratic culture in which
differences of race, creed, and color would fade in importance.

Many American Jews of Grumet's generation and slightly older not
only subscribed to this "liberal consensus" but had played an active role
in creating and promoting it.[127] In the most renowned instance, Jews
were prominently involved in the civil rights movement.[128] Less well
known is the involvement of Jews in crafting the legal doctrines that
articulated the legal secularist theory of religious liberty, according to
which religion belongs in the private realm. Beginning in the late 1940s
and continuing in the early 1960s, Jewish constitutional lawyers assumed
a leading role in articulating the rationales for the "strict separationist"

position, of which *Lemon* was the apotheosis, demanding that a strict separation between religion and state be maintained.[129]

Foremost among these Jewish lawyers was Leo Pfeffer, the longtime head of the American Jewish Congress. Although he was born in Hungary (the home country of Satmar Hasidism as well) and was a resident of Goshen (a mile away from Kiryas Joel), Pfeffer was as far away from the Satmars culturally as a Jew could be. A self-described "secular humanist," who became the AJ Congress's legal adviser in 1945, he was widely acknowledged as the dominant force in church-state litigation throughout the 1950s and 1960s. He retained that position of influence into the 1970s, when *Lemon v. Kurtzman*, which he essentially crafted, was handed down.[130] Pfeffer had been a source of controversy in the internal politics of the American Jewish community for years, owing chiefly to his role in the school prayer cases of the early 1960s and his subsequent role in developing and applying the *Lemon* doctrine. Prior to the school prayer decisions, which held that prayer and devotional Bible reading in public schools violated the Establishment Clause, the American Jewish community had been united in its support for the separationist doctrines that Pfeffer was advancing on behalf of the AJ Congress, along with the ADL and the AJ Committee.[131] His belief that "a secular state would allow private religion to flourish" and that the removal of religion from the public sphere would "promote the integrity of the public school system" was, for a time, the consensus position of the American Jewish communal establishment.[132]

But the school prayer decisions of the early 1960s divided the American Jewish community much as they divided Protestant and Catholic denominations, though not for the same reason. For Jews, the concern was not to maintain the practices of reciting Christian prayers and Bible readings but rather to avoid blame for ending those practices.[133] Even Pfeffer thought it unwise for his organization to participate in *Engel v. Vitale*, the case that ended school prayer in 1962. He sought to dissuade the ACLU from bringing the case. But the ACLU decided to forge ahead. At that point, Pfeffer decided to initiate what he hoped would be a more palatable companion case. His aim was to underscore that removing public support from religious schools was good for religion and therefore should be supported by people of faith as well as secularists. But from that moment on, a rift emerged in the American Jewish community, with the majority siding with Pfeffer's liberal position, but a growing minority rejecting it in favor of a conservative stance.

The school prayer decisions occasioned a clear-cut break. Laura Gifford and Daniel Williams recount in *The Right Side of the Sixties*: "After years of falling in line with the liberal civic agencies on constitutional matters, the chief Orthodox groups dissociated themselves from the litigation and amicus briefs generated by Pfeffer."[134] For the rest of his life, Pfeffer would claim that "the Orthodox consider me the worst enemy they've had since Haman in the Purim story."[135]

In 1964, the Union of Orthodox Jewish Congregations of America, known as the Orthodox Union, formed a new Jewish legal advocacy group called the National Jewish Commission on Law and Public Affairs, better known as COLPA, which was specifically dedicated to combating Pfeffer's brand of church-state jurisprudence. While Pfeffer was busy assisting the ACLU, the Orthodox founders of COLPA were forging a new alliance with Christians who objected to the removal of religion from the public schools. The Jews who created COLPA maintained that the First Amendment guarantees were "meant to protect the wisdom of the devout over the impulses of the licentious" and that the Constitution should be interpreted "to honor God's law."[136] Its chief objective was to counter the forces of secular humanism that its supporters believed were taking over the public schools by persuading the Court that state funding of religious schools was not an establishment of religion. The attorney hired to advance this position was a recent graduate of Harvard Law School: Nat Lewin.[137]

By the time that *Kiryas Joel School District v. Grumet* was being litigated in the 1990s, Nat Lewin and Leo Pfeffer had been squaring off for decades. But while Lewin was still in his prime, Pfeffer was then entering his eighties and no longer actively engaged in litigation. Moreover, the doctrine of strict separationism for which he had tirelessly advocated no longer held sway. The Supreme Court's decision in *Lamb's Chapel*, handed down on June 7, 1993, initiated the process of dismantling what could fairly be called the Pfeffer doctrine. Just three days before that pivotal decision was announced, Leo Pfeffer died at the age of eighty-three of congestive heart failure.[138] Two weeks later, the Supreme Court handed the foes of separationism another victory with the decision in *Zobrest*, the case authorizing the provision of a Sign language interpreter to a Catholic school student.

It was a supreme irony—though perhaps an inevitable development in the dialectics of American Jewish culture—that the process of dismantling Pfeffer's jurisprudence was being led not only by Nat Lewin, but even more aggressively by Jay Sekulow, whose Messianic Judaism fused Jewish belief and Christian evangelicalism. Sekulow's role at the helm of the conservative Christian legal movement symbolized the complex relations between Jewish and Christian religious conservatives. Notwithstanding their profound theological disagreements, chiefly over the status of Jesus, Jewish and Christian conservatives increasingly shared a common religious language and political agenda, beginning with the goal of getting the Court to reject the interpretations of the First Amendment favored by liberal civil rights groups such as the AJ Congress and the ACLU.

In July, a month after the Supreme Court handed down its *Lamb's Chapel* and *Zobrest* decisions, signaling its receptivity to conservative arguments against strict separation, New York's high court moved in the opposite direction. It issued a decision in the *Grumet* case, applying the *Lemon* doctrine to support its conclusion that Chapter 748 was unconstitutional. Leo Pfeffer was no longer around, but Lou Grumet was. A man very much in the model of Pfeffer, he was determined to defend strict separationism on behalf of that large swath of the American population, both Jewish and non-Jewish, that still adhered to the erstwhile "liberal consensus" in favor of a separation of church and state and devoted to the ideal of the public school as the site of integration into a common, democratic, and secular culture.

But if Grumet was the living embodiment of that brand of liberalism, KJ school superintendent Steve Benardo was a sign of its internal contradictions. A New York Jew of Sephardic heritage, Benardo shared Grumet's general outlook. When relating his involvement with KJ, he would always ask: "How did a New York liberal end up being the super of KJ?"[139] The irony embodied in the question clearly tickled Benardo.

But the answer he gave to this question tracked not only the change of attitude that he underwent, but the splintering that liberalism itself was undergoing in the 1980s and 1990s. For much of his career, Benardo subscribed to the belief that the mission of the public schools was to serve diverse communities and integrate them into a common civic culture. But after becoming the "super of KJ" and participating in its legal defense, he came to see the Satmars' claim for accommodation as "the ultimate liberal issue."[140]

It made sense that a proponent of bilingual and special education would see the right to be educated in a separate environment as a liberal claim. As we have seen, disability rights advocates were at the forefront of contesting the hegemony of the "sameness model," according to which the liberal principle of equality requires that every individual be treated the same as every other. In its stead, they argued for a *difference model of equality*, according to which equality requires recognizing differences and accommodating them. This was a position that stood in tension with the regnant idea of "mainstreaming," which called for children with special needs to be put in the same environment as everybody else—a clear application of the sameness model of equality. The difference model of disability rights rests on the recognition that some differences are so profound that children need to be put in a separate environment. Benardo readily transferred the logic of accommodating difference through separation to the cultural and linguistic differences that separate ethnic and religious groups from one another. The disability rights movement was thus an important factor in contributing to the ethos of difference that came to be embraced widely in the 1990s, to the benefit of Kiryas Joel.

Indeed, this new language allowed supporters of KJ to describe religious differences as cultural differences and thereby maintain that they were not asking the state to support a group based on *religious* grounds. This had the effect of fusing together disparate threads into a single argument: a new religious conservatism aimed at overcoming strict separation, the new language of multiculturalism aimed at achieving a "politics of recognition," otherwise known as identity politics, and the new disability rights movement aiming at accommodating special needs.[141]

These were the kinds of claims that Lewin put forth in *Grumet*. In good lawyerly fashion, he argued that (1) the KJ School District was not a religious accommodation, but rather a cultural one, and (2) if it were a religious accommodation, it was constitutionally permissible if not constitutionally required. This two-pronged argument reflected the logic of the difference model, which, by the 1980s and 1990s, was being embraced with equal vigor by liberals and religious conservatives (even if some liberals had qualms). In fact, liberals could be even more expansive in their embrace of the difference model than conservatives given their openness to the project of multiculturalism and its goal of redressing racial and gender bias and exclusion by recognizing difference.

Liberalism itself was fracturing. Some of its proudest adepts—to wit, Lou Grumet—expressed ambivalence about multiculturalism. Others, such as Steve Benardo, supported a group's right to cultural difference. For the latter group, the ideal of integration was no longer possible or even desirable.

A prime example of this change of sensibility was Michael Sussman, the lawyer who represented KJ's dissidents. He represented a generation that came of age in the 1970s. Like Grumet, and like so many Jews born in the decades between the 1930s and the 1970s, Sussman was deeply imprinted by the American struggle for racial equality and inspired by the leaders of the movement for civil rights.[142] But whereas Sussman had an instinctual affinity for the project of integration, he also had an understanding that the time for that ideal may have passed. As the lawyer for the NAACP who led the fight to end housing and school discrimination in Yonkers, he experienced firsthand the disenchantment with the pursuit of integration expressed by most of his African American colleagues and clients.[143] He understood their fatigue and frustration, even as he personally felt duty bound to honor the principle that racial segregation is a violation of the principle of racial equality. He pursued the project of racial integration in the *Yonkers* litigation, but he recognized that it had become passé.

Sussman's sympathetic understanding of the Black community's turn away from desegregation was one manifestation of the changes that white liberals, and Jewish liberals in particular, were undergoing. The work he ended up doing for the dissidents in KJ was another. Sussman saw his work for the dissidents as part and parcel of the larger theory of minority rights and structural discrimination that had animated his work against race discrimination in Yonkers. It was not lost on him that his clients in KJ wanted more, not less, separation from the outside world and less, not more, secularism than even the mainstream Satmar leaders countenanced. His clients were hyper-Satmars, more Satmar by their own estimate than the living Rebbe. But he nonetheless viewed them as a victimized minority being subjected to systemic forms of discrimination. The fact that Sussman saw his support for their cause as an extension of his *liberal* commitments exemplified the contradictory ways that liberalism was being interpreted and applied in Jewish-American circles and in the broader American political scene.

These fractures within liberalism were taking place under the pressure of an even larger struggle between progressive and conservative forces in American political culture. As American politics grew more polarized, there were very few participants in the KJ litigation who did not occupy one pole of the political spectrum or the other. Those who came closest to the middle, or perhaps the center-left, were Grumet's lawyers. Jay Worona and Pilar Sokol were both young Jewish attorneys who had only been working at the NYSSBA for a few years when the litigation started. Born in the late 1950s and early 1960s, theirs was a generation sufficiently removed from the Jewish immigration experience that, for them, integration into the mainstream of America was a given. As a child, Worona attended the Conservative synagogue in Poughkeepsie with his family. After graduating from Albany Law School, he joined a Conservative synagogue there, as did Sokol, who was a member of the same Conservative synagogue attended by Robert Abrams, New York's attorney general.[144] Over the course of the decade that they were fighting on opposite sides of the KJ case, Sokol and Abrams met regularly at their shul.

It was Worona, then in his thirties, who worked on the case from start to finish and served as Grumet's lead lawyer, facing off against the far more experienced Lewin, as the case made its way to the Supreme Court. Worona was Grumet's protégé, or at least Grumet liked to see him that way. He regarded his charge as "a young guy with all this adrenaline," possessing both "a lot of insecurity" and a lot of "raw intelligence."

Worona was certainly a far more modest type than the rest of the cast of characters in the drama (as, apparently, is Sokol, who did not respond to interview requests). In his interviews, Worona frequently used the word "self-deprecating" to describe himself, and equally often condemned "arrogance" as a personality trait, without ever naming whom he had in mind.[145] But if he was less confident, experienced and credentialed than the other lawyers involved in the litigation, he was the one who had the prescience to see that Leo Pfeffer's doctrine of strict separationism, favored by Grumet, was not going to save the day. Worona keenly sensed that the political winds were changing and the days of strict separationism were over. Instead of arguing that the purpose of the Chapter 748 was religious, he proposed that the legal team should attack the constitutionality of Chapter 748 on different grounds, namely, that it was a violation of the Establishment Clause to "single out" a religious community and bestow upon it a benefit that other people and groups did not receive. Grumet fought him tooth and nail, but in the end Worona prevailed, both in his debate with Grumet and in the U.S. Supreme Court itself.

It was a remarkable triumph for such a green lawyer, all the more so given that the more seasoned lawyers who headed the liberal civil rights organizations did their best to elbow Worona aside when it came time to appear before the Supreme Court. In his memoir, Grumet replays the scene over who would argue the case. The discussion took place at the National Education Association's headquarters in Washington, D.C., shortly before the Supreme Court was scheduled to hear the case. Gathered together to conference about the case were all of the lawyers who had filed briefs in support of Grumet's position, both from his own team and from allied groups. As Grumet recalls it, "All the amici are in the room and we're talking about a whole group of very bright, very ambitious, Ivy League lawyers. And Jay is making his presentations and Jay leaves the room to go to the bathroom. At which point they all say to me, you can't let him handle the case. I can handle the case. And of course, everyone was I."

As he recalled it, Grumet "looked up and said, 'he's handled this four times in court so far, and he won in the New York Court of Appeals, which is not chopped liver. And he's lived this case.'" Then Grumet added the kicker: "You guys don't understand. He hasn't been paid for this." Indeed, after the trial court ruled the NYSSBA lacked standing, it was no longer permissible for its legal staff to work on the case. Ever since then, Worona—later joined by Sokol—had been working on the case gratis, "doing this at night basically. And weekends, putting other stuff aside." According to Grumet, the assembled lawyers responded to his explanation of why Worona deserved to argue the case by telling him (in his paraphrase): "'You're going to destroy the First Amendment. You don't understand. The reason this case is coming up has nothing to do with the Hasids and has everything to do with the *Lemon* test. And that's the only reason they're taking this case.'" But Grumet argued forcefully for his protégé, and by the time he returned to the room, it was settled: Worona would argue the case.[146]

One more event occurred before the day of the oral argument, of limited significance at the time, but notable because it involved an individual who later would assume the position of highest judicial authority. As was customary, a "moot court" had been arranged to help Worona practice his courtroom performance. The lawyer brought in to role-play the Supreme Court justices was a young attorney who had clerked for Chief Justice Rehnquist in 1980 and then served as a special assistant to the attorney general in the Reagan administration before joining the Washington firm of Hogan and Hartson, which was hosting the moot. An early product of the conservative legal movement, that young attorney who assisted the Grumet legal team in preparing for oral argument was John Roberts.[147] Eleven years later, he replaced William Rehnquist as chief justice of the Supreme Court.

On March 30, 1994, the long-awaited day arrived. The scene at the Supreme Court was unlike any other the nation had ever seen. And the nation was watching. The courtroom was packed as usual. But the Satmars who filled the benches made for an unusual sight. The Rebbe (Moshe), the KJ Rov (Aaron), KJ's mayor (Leibish Lefkowitz), and Abe Wieder all were present, along with other KJ officeholders and lay leaders. Representing the school district were Superintendent Benardo and Mrs. Silberstein. Waldman had, of course, not been invited to be part of the village entourage. But thanks to the alternative newspaper he had founded to serve as a voice for the dissidents, he managed to wrangle a press pass. Standing outside the courthouse were dozens of dissidents, men in traditional garb, with young boys at their sides, bearing placards with handwritten statements in English such as "Faith and Torah Are Not for Sale," "Jews Resist Secularization," and "Judaism and Secularizm [*sic*] Are Extreme Opposites."[148] Grumet, of course, was in the courtroom and had brought his daughter and wife as guests. Worona had brought his parents and was seated near the podium alongside his co-counsel, Sokol. On the other side of the podium were Nat Lewin, Lawrence Reich, a lawyer who had been hired to represent the Monroe-Woodbury School District, and Julie Mereson, an assistant attorney general, who was representing New York State.

Each side made its arguments and held its own. Justice Sandra Day O'Connor led the questioning by asking why the law took the form of special legislation, which applied to only one community, rather than being a neutral law of general application. Justice Anthony Kennedy asked if it was "fair to say that governmental power was transferred here to a geographic entity based on the religious beliefs and practices of residents," a suggestion Lewin batted away. According to him, the statute did not draw lines on the basis of religion but rather conferred the power to form a school district on residents of the village irrespective of their religion, meaning that, in principle, anybody could buy or rent in the village. A number of the justices challenged these assertions, including Souter and Kennedy, who expressed doubt that the lines around the district had not been drawn on the basis of religion, even if that was not made explicit in the text of the statute. But it was Ruth Bader Ginsburg, then the sole Jewish member of the Court, who dominated the oral argument, speaking even more than the famously garrulous Antonin Scalia, although she had joined the Court only six and a half months earlier.

Like Souter and Kennedy, Ginsburg questioned whether the coinciding of municipal lines with religious affiliation was a mere happenstance.

Expressing her skepticism, she queried both Lewin and Worona about what would happen "if a religious body, say, the board of the synagogue" were given the power to run the school board. In response to Lewin's insistence that KJ's homogeneity was the product of private choice, she asked if it were true that Satmars were free to choose to sell to outsiders, pointing to the allegations that properties in KJ were subject to privately imposed covenants. Justice Scalia, by contrast, displayed considerably more sympathy for the Satmars, as did Chief Justice Rehnquist, who likened the Satmars' situation to that of "a large group of Roman Catholics [who] lived close together in New York State, and they decide they would like a separate school district," a scenario that was presumably perfectly constitutional. Both Rehnquist and Scalia indicated their support for a broad principle of cultural accommodation and invited (or in the case of Worona and Mereson, challenged) the lawyers to distinguish the "purely cultural needs" of a religious group from needs that are religious in nature. And Justice Scalia went a step further, drawing out the broader implications of the issue that made the Satmar village an object of such interest to Christian religious traditionalists. Making the culture war framing plain, he asked Worona to deal with the hypothetical situation of "a community divided by railroad tracks," one side of which is "a very swinging, modern-type crowd, and they like avant-garde education and all that," while "the other side of the tracks, influenced by a reaction to modernity, feminist aversion to obscenity and so forth, want old-fashioned education." Scalia was well on his way toward rehabilitating his reputation as a strong defender of religious liberty and traditionalism, in the wake of the debacle of his 1990 decision. Returning to this scenario, his final words at the oral argument were: "It's like a parent in the hypothetical I gave you who wants her child to have sex education and seeks permission from the school district on the one side of the tracks to send the child to the school district on the other side. What's so wrong about that?"

Scalia and the chief justice had clearly telegraphed how they would rule. The other justices, however, were harder to read. From the questions they had posed, it was anyone's guess how the Court would rule. Over the next three months, suspense continued to build, fostered by the media. Indeed, while Americans paid scant attention to most Supreme Court cases, Kiryas Joel had been turned into a national media spectacle, a phenomenon that began with the *60 Minutes* story broadcast before the Supreme Court argument and now continued as reporters rushed to interview the Satmars and their lawyers on the courthouse steps. Flashing on the frock-coated, bearded Hasidim, the news cameras captured both the village leaders and the village dissidents, which they clearly had trouble distinguishing. Joseph Waldman had little difficulty grabbing the microphone in between dignified speeches delivered by Abe Wieder and Malka Silberstein. Their shared Yiddish accents, rarely heard on national TV, were yet another reminder to the outside world of the otherworldliness of the Satmars. Grumet cut an equally striking figure, sporting one of his trademark canes.[149] As the parade of participants flitted by, it was hard to say who was the more quixotic, Grumet or Waldman, and who was the more likely to succeed in persuading the Court, Worona or Lewin.

What was clear was that through the litigation, the Satmars had become even more of an American cultural phenomenon. Actually, they had been an American phenomenon all along, exemplifying the long history of tolerance for religious subgroups in the United States. But now they had become a phenomenon of national renown, exhibiting to the country the contradictory strands of its political and religious culture. Even as they seemed to the nation to be strange and alien, they were serving as a canvas onto which the ambiguities and ambivalences of American politics and collective identity were splashed. At the very same moment, the Satmars were using the American political and legal systems as tools to defend their separatist institutions and affirm their right to withdraw from the world. It was a perfectly symbiotic relationship.

CHAPTER 6

The Law of the Land
(Is the Law)

On June 27, at the end of the 1994 term, the Supreme Court handed down its decision in *Grumet v. Kiryas Joel*, agreeing with the lower courts that Chapter 748 violated the Establishment Clause.[1] The ruling was a serious setback for KJ and a victory for Grumet, Sokol, and especially Worona, whose theory of the case had prevailed and who had argued it persuasively, notwithstanding the qualms expressed by the more experienced lawyers. But the victory was not a vindication of Grumet's belief that a separate school district for the Satmars was unconstitutional. Nor did it spell the end of the KJ School District. Instead, it laid the ground for the reauthorization of the school district under an emerging doctrine of "neutrality," according to which political separatism was permissible as long as all groups had an equal opportunity to establish their own separate political units, not just Kiryas Joel.

The Supreme Court's growing receptivity to this doctrine reflected the complex political currents that were simultaneously pulling people away from the integrationist paradigm and yet still appealing to the liberal value of equal rights for all. Its rise clearly reflected the increasing influence of the conservative movement. But it also was supported by growing sympathy for group rights and multiculturalism on the left. Even old-school liberals, who emphasized individual over group rights and formal over substantive equality, felt the normative pull of "neutrality."

Indeed, neutrality could be fairly said to be the quintessential liberal value, as liberal political theorists of the time maintained.

Increasingly, though, the doctrine of neutrality was applied by supporters of group rights to make the case that whatever one group got, other groups should get too. Both sides of the political spectrum embraced a doctrine that said, in essence, it is permissible, perhaps even constitutionally necessary, to accommodate cultural differences by granting groups the right to form and maintain their own separate enclaves—so long as this right is granted to all groups on equal terms. It was this same doctrine that underlay the principle of equal access that gave religious groups access to public facilities and services, such as Sign language interpreters for students in parochial schools. Now that doctrine was being used to justify allowing a religious group to establish its own local government.

Supported by this doctrine, the New York State legislature, for reasons having to do primarily with local politics, would pass three more statutes authorizing the KJ School District over the course of six years following the Supreme Court's decision in *Grumet*. Each one sought to satisfy the principle of neutrality enunciated in *Grumet*. Whether they actually did so was a matter of debate. Grumet, for one, was certain they did not, and he carried on his legal campaign against the school district for another five years, up until the time the last of the authorizing statutes was passed. At that point, the torch was passed to the KJ dissidents, who filled the vacuum created by Grumet's departure from the scene by filing a suit themselves, claiming that the KJ School District did not satisfy the requirements of the law. The vicissitudes of this ongoing litigation revealed the extent to which the meaning of the Establishment Clause remained in contention, even as it showed which side was gaining the upper hand.

It was not lost on either side of the debate that protecting the kind of religious separatism that KJ exemplified required a serious modification, if not outright rejection, of the notion that religion must be walled off from the state. Allowing the Satmars to establish their own local government institutions was at odds with the formerly dominant doctrine of strict separation, or at least so it seemed to that doctrine's ardent supporters. After all, the Satmars were demanding more than merely cultural autonomy and the right to preserve their distinctive way of life. They were demanding political autonomy and the right to create their own local government entities that would serve to protect their way of life. Moving beyond the right to practice their *religion* in the private realm to the right to exercise *political* authority in the *public* realm entailed a serious erosion of the wall of separation between church and state.

There was, of course, a counterargument to this proposition. Insofar as the governmental structures established by the Satmars restricted them to the pursuit of secular ends, and otherwise conformed to the requirements of law governing the exercise of political power, the village and the school district could both be said to be wholly secular political institutions that adhered to the principle of separation between religious and secular affairs. Indeed, that was the argument Nat Lewin had made on behalf of the Satmars. Whereas the Satmars' Christian supporters had sought to reverse *Lemon* and, in so doing, get the Supreme Court to repudiate the principle of strict separation between church and state, the Satmars themselves had labored to demonstrate that they were in conformity with the principle.

Inasmuch as this was true, there was a deep irony at work: the Satmars' commitment to withdrawing from worldly affairs (and thereby separating their religious community from secular politics) had led them to establish their own secular political institutions. No one was more alert to this irony than KJ's dissidents. They believed that exercising political power, whether by forming and running a public school district or forming and running a municipality, was fundamentally inconsistent with the Rebbe's vision of a community governed by religious, not secular, law. In this, they were guided by the third-century principle of *dina di-malkhuta dina*, the Jewish legal corollary of "render unto Caesar the things that are Caesar's, and unto God the things that are God's," which holds that Jews should follow the law of the land, with the expectation of being accorded autonomy over religious and communal affairs in exchange for fealty to state law. All Satmars profess to abide by this ancient halakhic principle. As the dissidents interpreted it, which is to say, as they interpreted the position of the Satmar Rebbe, adherence to the principle required that they remove themselves completely from the exercise of secular political power and secular governmental institutions.

Thus, their theological justification for opposing the creation of the school district and the village establishment converged with the argument that the creation of a public school district violated the constitutional principle of separation of religion and state—a secular legal argument the dissidents eagerly adopted as their own. In addition to supporting Grumet's lawsuits on these grounds, they appealed to this principle in a series of lawsuits they themselves initiated, in which they challenged KJ authorities over issues of zoning, housing discrimination, and broader issues of religious autonomy and legal authority. These lawsuits turned on their head the arguments over free exercise that had swirled around KJ from its inception. Whereas Satmar leaders, and supporters of the community, had long portrayed the establishment of Kiryas Joel as an expression of the grand American ideal of religious freedom, KJ's dissidents argued that KJ's political institutions were a threat to religious freedom, rather than its defender. Pushing back against the establishment party's claim that KJ was an island of religious liberty, the dissidents asserted that the village not only blurred the boundary between religious and political power but also deprived them of their own religious freedom.

In making this argument, the dissidents exposed abiding tensions inside KJ. And they also revealed the abiding tension that exists between the Free Exercise and the Establishment Clauses of the First Amendment. American jurists had long recognized the tension between the Establishment Clause principle that government must refrain from providing any kind of support to religion and the competing principle, associated with the Free Exercise Clause, that the government should be evenhanded toward religious and secular beliefs. This principle of evenhandedness—neutrality, by another name—was derived from the Free Exercise Clause on the grounds that if the government did not treat religious activities and groups on equal terms with one another, and with secular activities and groups, that would impose a burden on the free exercise of religion in violation of the clause. When applied to government funding and services, the free exercise principle seemed to mandate equal funding for religious institutions and activities (such as education) and equal access to government services, benefits, and facilities. But giving religious groups government funding and services seemed to involve the very forms of government support for religious institutions and activities that the Establishment Clause was thought to prohibit.

Recognizing this tension, and recognizing that it could never be fully resolved, the law had long been conflicted over which of the two competing principles to elevate: the Free Exercise Clause principle of neutrality and evenhandedness or the competing Establishment Clause principle of separating religion from the state. The latter path entailed interpreting the Establishment Clause broadly, with a consequent narrowing of the Free Exercise Clause. Conversely, the former path involved construing the Free Exercise Clause broadly with a consequent narrowing of the principle of separation between religion and state associated with the Establishment Clause. Proponents of this position fortified their view by arguing that governmental neutrality and evenhandedness were requirements not only of the Free Exercise Clause but of the Establishment Clause too. Thus, they appealed to neutrality both to make the argument that granting religious groups access to government benefits and public forums was required to fulfill the principle of religious liberty and to argue that doing so was not a violation of the principle of separation between church and state.

As we have seen, the religious right was a major promoter of this version of the meaning of the two religion clauses, which they viewed, and welcomed, as a direct repudiation of Leo Pfeffer's call for separation between religion and state. Recognizing that this was the direction in which the Supreme Court was tending, Worona pushed for a legal strategy that was consistent with the principle of neutrality, rather than emphasizing the competing principle of separation between church and state. This contrasted with the style of Establishment Clause argumentation favored by the KJ dissidents, who, in their own legal actions, appealed to the principle of strict separation—with mixed success.

Indeed, of all the lawsuits that swirled around the village in the 1990s, it was only the dissidents' that called upon American courts to consider the stark threat posed to religious freedom (specifically, *their* religious freedom) by a weakening of the wall of separation between religion and state. Some judges evinced sympathy for this view. But it was clear that the tide of history was moving in the other direction—toward the doctrine of "neutrality" that allowed for more blurring of the line between religion and government in American politics and, as the Satmar dissidents saw it, a blurring of religious and political power in Kiryas Joel.

Opinions Will Differ: The Justices Dissect *Grumet*

It took some doing to tease the doctrine of neutrality out of the holding in *Grumet* because the Court was splintered and because within a single judicial opinion, most notably, the plurality opinion, authored by Justice David Souter, multiple, even contradictory, rationales were espoused. While the vote was six to three, there were six opinions, one for the plurality, one for the dissent, and four different concurring opinions, each offering a different view of the Establishment Clause principles that should govern the case. Souter's opinion began by proposing that the problem with Chapter 748 was that it created a "fusion" of political and religious authority.[2] This was a straightforward application of the principle of separation between religion and state. But the opinion failed to explain how the statute constituted a fusion, given Benardo's scrupulous professionalism and the school board's adherence to secular standards. Nor did it explain how to distinguish the situation in KJ from situations where a local government has been established by a religiously homogeneous community without resulting in such a fusion. After all, it was not uncommon for residents of towns and villages to belong to the same faith. Souter himself conceded this point, taking pains to emphasize there was nothing inherently wrong with a religiously homogeneous group exercising political power.[3]

Had he accepted the reasoning from *City of Rajneeshpuram*, the case involving the municipality established by the followers of Bhagwan Shri Rajneesh in Oregon, then his conclusion that Chapter 748 violated the no fusion principle would have made perfect sense. That case, decided ten years earlier in 1984, had dissolved the municipality formed by the Rajneeshees on the grounds that the state's recognition of a government formed within the geographic confines of a parcel of land owned, controlled, and populated by a single religious group violated the Establishment Clause.[4] But *Oregon v. City of Rajneeshpuram* was decided by a lower court, in the federal district of Oregon, not by the Supreme Court. Recognizing that the incorporation of the city of Rajneeshpuram technically vested the powers of local government not in the hands of a religious organization but rather in the hands of the residents of the area (who were legally free to believe whatever they wanted and elect whomever they wanted), the district court took the view that "this distinction may be more formal than substantive."[5] By contrast, the Supreme Court, in this period, was adopting a formalistic approach in the area of Establishment Clause doctrine that preserved the formal distinction between state action and the voters and officeholders who effectively control the state, the very distinction that the *Rajneeshpuram* decision had characterized as an elevation of form over substance that should be rejected.

Liberals and conservatives had been fighting over the definition of state action for decades, with conservatives favoring the formalist view and liberals favoring the realist view according to which the legal distinction between public and private is a formal distinction that is in practice often blurred. Since the mid-twentieth century, when the Supreme Court had applied the realist view to "private" race discrimination in the landmark case of *Shelley v. Kraemer* (which invalidated racially restrictive covenants on the theory that private covenants depend upon state action for their enforcement), conservatives had been engaged in a relentless campaign to restore the distinction between private and state action.[6] By the mid-1990s, the conservative effort to turn back the realist view of state action had made serious inroads but was not yet completely triumphant. Justice Souter's approach to the *Grumet* controversy reflected the ambiguous status of the doctrine during this transitional period as well as his own personal ambivalence, which led him to embrace one theory of the case—the idea that Chapter 784 created an unconstitutional fusion of religious and political authority, which depended on rejecting the formalistic distinction between public and private action—but then to shift to a very different theory of the case: the idea that Chapter 748 violated the principle of neutrality that Worona and Pilar had proposed. Liberal justices and moderates like Souter still clung to the rhetoric of a realist analysis that rejected the elevation of form over substance, but they lacked the votes, and perhaps the philosophical vision, to apply it in a consistent way. Instead, they were increasingly obliged to accept the ever more conservative Court's formalistic view of state action and try to adapt it to their purposes.

The ambiguous nature of Souter's opinion was reflected in its ultimate embrace of Worona's main theory, notwithstanding the fact that this theory made no claims about an inappropriate "fusion" of public and private, secular and religious realms. The central defect that Worona identified in Chapter 748 was not that it effected a "fusion" of secular and religious authority but rather that the legislature had passed a statute that *singled out* Kiryas Joel by name. In other words, New York State was failing to be evenhanded in its treatment of groups. In this manner, Worona—and Justice Souter, who embraced this reasoning—appealed to the ascendant principle of neutrality. This line of reasoning implied that had the school district been formed under "general legislation" that applied equally to everyone—or were it so authorized in the future—then there would be no constitutional defect.

Souter's opinion commanded no more than a plurality. It was joined in part by justices Blackmun, Stevens, Ginsburg, and O'Connor. But not one of the justices concurred with Souter's opinion in its entirety. That made it unclear whether the holding rested on the principle of neutrality or not. The Court's splintering into so many different opinions, each offering a different theory of what the constitutional defect was, reflected the fracturing of the broader American political landscape. And it also reflected the strange reversals that sometimes took place between liberals and conservatives when both endorsed the principle of formal neutrality (which calls for different things to be treated the same), while simultaneously accepting the difference model of equality (which implicitly rejects a formal conception of neutrality in favor of a more substantive view that recognizes the need to accommodate different circumstances, needs, and beliefs).

It was no surprise that the three justices on the right wing of the Court at that time, Chief Justice Rehnquist, Justice Antonin Scalia, and Justice Clarence Thomas, embraced this version of the neutrality principle, which supported the conclusion that groups have a right to cultural accommodation, including the right to form their own political enclaves. The dissenting opinion was written by Justice Scalia, whose reputation among religious conservatives had been badly tarnished by his decision in the 1990 case of *Employment Division v. Smith*, but who now was given the chance to regain his reputation as a strong defender of religious liberty and the right to accommodation, which he seized with his customary relish. What was harder to process was the fact that, of the six justices who supported the decision, many of them, including Justice Souter, who wrote the plurality opinion, also gave voice to the value of accommodating group differences and allowing homogeneous communities to form separate enclaves and political institutions.

These six justices offered a plethora of reasons for concluding that Chapter 748 was unconstitutional, resulting in no fewer than five different opinions in support of striking down the law. Only one, Justice Souter's plurality opinion, characterized the problem as a matter of the "fusion" of religion and state—that is, a violation of the principle of separation between religion and state (although, as we have seen, Souter's opinion also embraced the neutrality theory). Only one other (Justice Stevens's concurrence) saw "state action in aid of segregation" as the constitutional problem. The other concurring opinions shied away from applying either the principle of anti-fusion (that is, separation) or the principle of anti-segregation. Instead, they articulated a confusing combination of reasons for holding the statute to be unconstitutional, which merged the ascendant principle of neutrality with other related but distinct concerns. The end result was a highly ambiguous and somewhat inscrutable decision that expressed the coexistence of a multitude of different principles and ideas.

Thus, Justice Kennedy wrote a concurring opinion arguing that "the real vice of the school district, in my estimation, is that New York created [the school district] by drawing political boundaries on the basis of religion."[7] Characterizing the statute as a case of religious gerrymandering analogous to a racially gerrymandered electoral district, Justice Kennedy asserted that "the Establishment Clause mirrors the Equal Protection Clause. Just as government may not segregate people on account of their race, so too it may not segregate on the basis of religion."[8] Foreshadowing the approach he would take in equal protection cases, where he recognized marriage equality and gay rights, Kennedy's notion of gerrymandering relied on a principle of formal equality that repudiates treating people of different backgrounds and group identities differently, even when doing so (as in the case of creating majority-minority electoral districts) is intended to remedy inequality by politically empowering a minority group.[9] He denounced the use of both racial and religious criteria as a basis for drawing lines around political districts. In this regard, he differed from the liberal justices on the Court, who supported the creation of *racial* majority-minority political districts (for purposes of rectifying power imbalances in electoral districts) but opposed the deliberate creation of a *religious* majority-minority political district that had occurred in Kiryas Joel. And he differed as well from the conservatives who dissented in *Grumet* because they supported the creation of a school district for the Satmars but opposed the deliberate creation of majority Black electoral districts.

This approach might have heartened liberals of Grumet's ilk who saw a common thread between the Establishment Clause principle that public entities should not be defined or dominated by religion and the principle of integration. It might have seemed that, in denouncing Chapter 748 as a "religious gerrymander," Justice Kennedy was upholding the principle of integration. But Justice Kennedy went out of his way to emphasize that "the Establishment Clause does not invalidate a town or State"—or, by logical implication, a school district—"'whose boundaries are derived according to neutral historical and geographic criteria, but whose population happens to comprise coreligionists.'"[10] There was nothing wrong, he wrote, with segregated political units as long as the segregation was de facto (voluntary) rather than de jure (imposed by the state). He went on to conclude his opinion with a ringing statement of the value of community that evoked the communitarian discourse of the eighties and nineties: "People who share a common religious belief or lifestyle may live together without sacrificing the basic rights of self-governance that all Americans enjoy, so long as they do not use those rights to establish their religious faith."[11] In this regard, his opinion was in complete accord with the dissenting opinion written by Justice Scalia.

Indeed, all but one of the opinions endorsed this communitarian vision, which ran contrary to the proposition that group-based segregation and political separatism are in and of themselves impermissible. Only Justice Stevens, joined by justices Ruth Bader Ginsburg and Harry Blackmun, expressed concern about "creating a school district that is specifically intended to shield children from contact with others who have 'different ways.'" Characterizing the legislation that authorized the creation of the school district in KJ as "affirmative state action in aid of segregation," Stevens's opinion unambiguously rejected the principle of "neutrality," according to which political separatism is permissible so long as no group is unfairly singled out and all groups have an equal right to establish their own separate political institutions.[12] In Stevens's view, enlisting the state to enable the separatism of the community was in and of itself an "establishment" of religion.

Stevens's analysis cut to the heart of the debate between old-style liberals and new-style communitarians, of both liberal and conservative persuasions. That conservatives would reject Stevens's anti-separatist position was to be expected. "So much for family values!" was the dissenters' tart retort to his opinion. In his typically sharp tone, Justice Scalia, who wrote the dissenting opinion, blasted the Court for its "astounding" decision. And yet there was very little daylight between Scalia's analytic framework and that adopted by the majority of the justices. Save for Justice Stevens's, all of the opinions, both those that endorsed the outcome and those that dissented, accepted Worona's "singling out" theory. As long as a state did not single out a religious community to receive a privilege not made available to other groups, a law empowering the population of a village to form its own school district would not be found to be invalid. What the dissenting justices and the justices who struck down Chapter 748 on the basis of Worona's argument disagreed about was not whether a State *could* grant the power to form its own school district to all subgroups on equal terms, but whether it *had* or *would* grant that power only to the Satmars. To justices Souter, Kennedy, O'Connor, Blackmun, Ginsburg, and Stevens, Chapter 748 betrayed the intent to single out the Satmars for favor—a conclusion that Justice Scalia said was based on the "flimsiest evidence."[13]

This was a disagreement not over principle but rather over evidence and, further, the timing of the production of evidence. Did New York State have to write the law in a way that *already* granted the authority to form a separate school district to other homogeneous communities? Or was it enough, as Justice Scalia suggested, to give the state the benefit of the doubt and assume that it *would* give other groups the same right to form their own school districts as it had accorded to the Satmars if and when a group with a similar need arose in the future? The principle itself—that the right could be granted to one subgroup if (but only if) it was accorded to *all* such groups—was a position that straddled the differences between liberalism and conservatism—and between the different versions of liberalism represented on the Court.

By the same token, it combined a sameness model of equality (according to which, all groups have the same rights) with a difference model of equality (according to which groups have the right to be separate and different).[14] Such a combination was of course not unheard of. A similar blend of sameness and difference principles had animated the infamous doctrine of separate but equal that functioned to legitimate Jim Crow—the basis of the Supreme Court's decision in *Plessy v. Ferguson* (1896). According to this doctrine, Blacks and whites were treated equally under segregation as each group was equally subject to the edict to separate from the other. Supposedly, that doctrine had been repudiated in *Brown v. Board of Education*, which put forth the proposition that "separate is inherently unequal." But among the many questions that lingered after *Brown* were, first, whether voluntary de facto self-segregation should be treated the same as legally imposed de jure segregation and, second, whether segregation on the basis of religion, culture, or language should be treated the same as segregation by race. These were the questions that were animating debates about communitarianism and religious and racial separatism among political theorists, activists, and the American public in this period.[15] In an indirect, inchoate, but ultimately decisive way, most of the justices of the Supreme Court indicated a readiness in *Kiryas Joel School District v. Grumet* to accept the doctrine of an equal right to separate from other groups and form one's own political institutions, at least when it involved a (white) religious group.

It was Justice Sandra Day O'Connor who spelled out the practical implications of the theory of "singling out" advanced by Worona. "New York," she wrote, "allows virtually any group of residents to incorporate their own village, with broad powers of self-government."[16] In direct contrast to the state's municipal incorporation law, Chapter 748 "benefits one group—the residents of Kiryas Joel."[17] That was the hallmark of "special legislation," as distinct from "general legislation": it singled out one group or an individual for a particular burden or benefit.

But if this was the problem, there was an obvious solution, which did not require dismantling the school district in Kiryas Joel. "There is nothing improper about a legislative intention to accommodate a religious group," Justice O'Connor asserted, "so long as it is implemented through generally applicable legislation."[18] As KJ's lawyers readily perceived, O'Connor had provided a virtual blueprint for new legislation that would allow KJ to set up a school district without running afoul of the Constitution, and the Satmars lost no time in following it.

In Search of the Right Statute

With the state legislature about to break for its summer recess just one week after the Supreme Court delivered its final opinions of the spring 1994 term, the village leaders asked Nathan Lewin to draft a new statute that would meet the Court's objections to Chapter 748—quickly. Reached by fax in Rome, where he was attending a meeting of the International Association of Jewish Lawyers, Lewin obliged and faxed the statute he quickly drafted back to the Satmars.[19]

But Lewin's draft did not prove satisfactory to his clients in KJ or to their political sponsors. As he later recalled, "they ran it past Shelly Silver," referring to the once-powerful State Assembly speaker, "and he and the rest of them said, it's too broad."[20] Of course, the new statute *had* to be broader than the old one; the whole point of the Court's neutrality theory was that Chapter 748 was too specific. Recognizing this necessity, Lewin had produced a statute that articulated criteria that other localities in New York State could satisfy. But precisely because it did so, the Satmars' friends in the legislature deemed it too broad.

The disagreement between Lewin and the Satmars' political sponsors was reflective of a dilemma born of the Court's neutrality theory. The broader the criteria, the greater the number of communities that could satisfy them; the narrower the criteria, the fewer the communities that could satisfy them. If none could satisfy the criteria, it would be worthless. If only the village of Kiryas Joel could satisfy the criteria, then it would run afoul of the holding in *Grumet* and be deemed to violate the Establishment Clause.

But if broad criteria resolved one problem (the "singling out" of a religious group), they created another. As Lewin observed of the Satmar's political patrons, "they were concerned that if it was written in a way that gave other communities the ability to form their own public schools, it could be used for racial segregation."[21] Broad criteria would enable wealthy white communities to form their own separate school districts. To be sure, school districts were already racially segregated—but not by law. The legislators and their liberal supporters were concerned to avoid the appearance of de jure segregation that could be attributed to a statute authorizing racially homogeneous populations to secede and form their own local school districts; the fact that most school districts were already de facto segregated, thanks to deeply entrenched patterns of residential racial segregation facilitated by the exercise of private rights, went unmentioned.

Escaping the horns of this dilemma was a problem that would plague the Satmars for the rest of the decade. Their initial strategy was to respond to the criticism of Lewin's sweeping draft by formulating a far narrower statute that would not empower so many communities to form their own school districts. When Lewin refused to craft such a narrow statute himself, he recalls, "somebody at the New York legislature redrafted it to be so narrow it only applied to Kiryas Joel."[22] The swiftness with which this new piece of legislation was drafted and passed reflected the extent of the Satmars' political influence. Running against the clock, the new statute, titled Chapter 241, was approved by the legislature just a few days after the *Grumet* decision was handed down by the Supreme Court.[23]

Everyone understood the new statute would face an immediate legal challenge. Sure enough, as soon as Governor Cuomo signed Chapter 241 into law on July 6, 1994,[24] Grumet's legal team swung back into action. Twenty days later, Worona and Sokol filed a lawsuit challenging the constitutionality of the new law.[25] Their theory of the case was simple: while the statute did not follow the first in singling out Kiryas Joel by name, it was obvious that the statute was intended to benefit Kiryas Joel, and only Kiryas Joel.

To rebut this claim, the Satmars turned again to Lewin. This time, however, Lewin refused to represent them. As he saw it, the new law was "plainly unconstitutional"[26] under the reasoning of the Supreme Court opinion in *Grumet*. "I can't defend that," he told the village leaders.[27] Acting quickly, the village leaders hired an Albany-based lawyer by the name of George Barber to assist Shebitz in defending the constitutionality of Chapter 241.

The second *Grumet* case, filed under the name of *Louis Grumet v. Mario Cuomo*, reflected the growing enmity between the New York governor and his erstwhile protégé. Ever since their first hostile encounter after the governor signed the first KJ School District law, the two had been at loggerheads. Grumet never got over his deep disappointment in Cuomo, whereas Grumet remained for Cuomo a perpetual thorn in his side. Grumet's second lawsuit, filed in the midst of the 1994 gubernatorial campaign, constituted a threat to Cuomo's bid for a fourth term, particularly among his liberal supporters, who tended to oppose a separate school district for the Satmars. That said, it also represented a political opportunity for Cuomo, since defending the law against Grumet's legal challenge allowed him to display his steadfast commitment to the

Satmars and the broader Orthodox Jewish community. Lest there be any doubt about his intentions to support the new statute, Cuomo made an appearance at a campaign rally held in Kiryas Joel that summer, where he told a cheering crowd that if the second law was declared unconstitutional, he would introduce a third, and if that were declared unconstitutional, he would introduce a fourth, and would never cease in his efforts to support the children of Kiryas Joel and the Satmar community—if he were reelected.[28] Cuomo turned out to be prescient about the fact that no fewer than four statutes would eventually have to be passed, the first three of which would be declared unconstitutional. He was less prescient about the election. He lost the race to the only politician in New York who could claim to be even more devoted to the Satmars, and more beloved by them in return: George Pataki.

While Pataki was taking office, *Grumet II*, as Grumet's second lawsuit came to be known, was proceeding to summary judgment. Presiding over the case was Justice Kahn, the same judge who had adjudicated Chapter 748 to be unconstitutional in *Grumet I*. This time, Kahn evinced much more sympathy with the Satmars for reasons that some found inscrutable and others cynically attributed to his desire to curry favor with New York politicians; a short while later, Kahn was appointed to a federal judgeship.[29] Defying the view that the statute was "plainly unconstitutional," as Nat Lewin himself believed, Kahn pronounced himself satisfied with the neutrality of Chapter 241.[30]

But the state's higher courts were not so sympathetic. A year and a half after Justice Kahn ruled that Chapter 241 was constitutional, his decision was reversed by the Appellate Division.[31] That judgment was affirmed a little less than year a later, on May 6, 1997, by the state's highest court, the New York Court of Appeals. Both the Appellate Division and the Court of Appeals accepted Grumet's argument that only Kiryas Joel could satisfy the law and treated this as evidence of a clear intent to favor the Satmars.

At this point, the Satmars again turned to Lewin in the hopes he would take on the task of petitioning the U.S. Supreme Court to review the New York courts' decision. Lewin, however, emphatically declined, insisting once again that he would not defend Chapter 241 and thereby bringing to an end the appeals process for *Grumet II*.[32] Instead, in evocation of Cuomo's campaign prophesy, the Satmars' political sponsors sprang back into action to produce yet a third statute that would authorize the existence of a school district inside Kiryas Joel. Only this time it was Governor Pataki, not Cuomo, who signed off on the legislation.

The new bill, Chapter 390, was drafted to be less narrow than the second one—though not so broad as to license a mass exodus from the existing regional school districts on the part of municipalities. This was apparently enough of a "broadening" beyond the single village of Kiryas Joel to satisfy Lewin, who agreed to represent the Satmars in the third round of litigation. It was not enough, however, to satisfy the judges who presided over *Grumet v. Pataki*, which became known as *Grumet III*. Joseph C. Teresi, the New York State trial judge who had replaced Judge Kahn, determined the new law to be unconstitutional. So too did New York's appellate court and the state's highest court, both of which agreed with the trial court's analysis that Chapter 390 violated the Establishment Clause because it was not in fact a piece of general legislation.[33]

At this point, eight years into the litigation, with each of the three statutes that had been enacted to authorize the school district having been struck down, it might have seemed that the effort to enact legislation that would pass constitutional muster was doomed. Undeterred, Lewin filed a cert petition asking the Supreme Court for a review of the state's decision in *Grumet III*. He did so because he had good reason to believe that the Supreme Court might take the case and uphold the latest statute's constitutionality. Indeed, over the course of the previous four years, between the Supreme Court's decision in *Grumet I* and 1998, when the final decision in *Grumet III* was handed down, the Court had grown increasingly receptive to the critiques of the doctrine of strict separation between church and state and increasingly supportive of broad principles of religious accommodation that stemmed from both the religious right and the multiculturalist left. By the same token, it had come to embrace the principle of "equal aid" to religious and nonreligious groups,[34] the effect of which was to sweep aside the old Pfeffer doctrine of "no aid" to religious groups that had prevailed in *Lemon*. It still had not reversed *Lemon*. But two years earlier, in *Agostini v. Felton*, it had reversed *Aguilar* and *Ball*, the 1985 decisions that had precipitated the creation of the KJ School District by ending the practice of providing Title I services inside parochial schools.[35] As against *Aguilar* and *Ball*, *Agostini* held that it *was* permissible for public school districts to provide state-mandated and government-funded remedial educational services to private parochial schools. The logical implication was that school districts could provide them with other publicly supported educational services, such as special education, as well.

Agostini specifically credited *Grumet I* with having demonstrated the need for the Court to move away from a strict principle of no aid to religious schools and toward a principle of equal aid, or "neutrality."[36] Under that principle, which the Court now firmly embraced, the state was required to provide publicly funded services and instructors to public and private, religious and secular schools alike.[37] Had this been the position that the Court held when it first confronted the issue, the Kiryas Joel School District would almost certainly not have been created (or even imagined). It is, of course, impossible to know for sure what would have happened if *Aguilar* and *Ball* had come out the other way in 1985. Similarly, it is impossible to know what would have happened had the Supreme Court accepted Lewin's certiorari petition to rehear *Grumet III* in 1998.

Any possibility that it would do so was scuttled when it emerged that the Satmars already had a fourth authorizing statute teed up waiting to be pushed through the legislative process in the event that their effort to get the Supreme Court to reverse the decision in *Grumet III* proved to be unsuccessful. Indeed, as early as January 1998, when *Grumet III* was "was barely under way," it was reported that "the Assembly Speaker, Sheldon Silver is already preparing to try a fourth time, concerned that the last attempt to create a district for the village will also be struck down." Moreover, it seemed likely that George Pataki would sign off on the fourth statute.[38] The preparation of a fourth statute before the third statute had been presented to the Supreme Court reflected the Satmars' concern that not enough other villages qualified under the new law to persuade the courts that the law was sufficiently general. Indeed, it appeared that there was just one community other than KJ that qualified, the village of Stony Point in Rockland County, a wealthy, white enclave in Haverstaw, a racially mixed and overall less affluent town.

At the same time that the Satmars were thinking about the fate of the new legislation and its consequences for their school district, residents of Stony Point were circulating a petition to commence the process of seceding from their regional district.[39] This, of course, was precisely the scenario that liberal opponents of the separate school for the Satmars most feared. As Grumet confessed, "My worst nightmare is that having stopped the state from creating a school district on religious grounds that they will broaden this law to allow anyone to have a segregated school district on any grounds."[40] In the end, the village of Stony Point did not secede from the racially mixed regional school district. But the controversy generated by the petition was a warning sign that there could be resistance to a broader statute.

But the precaution of pushing for a fourth statute before a final adjudication on the third proved to be fatal to the Satmars' chances of getting the Supreme Court to review the New York Court of Appeals decision in *Grumet III*. When Lewin learned of the existence of the draft legislation, he felt honor bound to report it to the Supreme Court. His prediction was that the existence of a draft for a fourth bill would render the controversy over the third statute moot.[41] Sure enough, the Supreme Court declined to hear an appeal of *Grumet III*, leaving the enactment of a fourth statute the Satmars' only recourse.[42]

And so it came to pass that on August 3, 1999, nearly ten years after the passage of the first authorizing statute, a fourth law authorizing the village of Kiryas Joel to run its own school district was enacted by the legislature of New York State.[43] As noted in a NYSSBA press release, "the legislation [was] part of a 231-page budget bill that passed without public debate at the tail end of the 1999 legislative session. Several lawmakers from the region admitted they were unaware the bill contained language applicable to Kiryas Joel."[44] Similar to the second and third bills, it did not single out the village of Kiryas Joel by name. Instead, it formulated neutral criteria pertaining to the size of the population and the tax base that the village of Kiryas Joel (and perhaps a few other municipalities) could satisfy. Signed into law by Governor Pataki, it represented the continuing commitment of New York State—and the unceasing efforts of the Satmars' political friends—to accommodate KJ's special needs and interests.

Chapter 405, as it was titled, was no less vulnerable to constitutional challenge than any of the other three statutes. And it might well have been challenged by the indefatigable Grumet, had he not recently left the NYSSBA and entered into semiretirement. In his absence, neither Worona or Sokol had the will or the wherewithal to bring a fourth lawsuit. Both had been working on the case for free since 1990, serving as Grumet's unpaid personal lawyers after the trial court's early ruling that Grumet could sue only in his personal capacity, not on behalf of the NYSSBA. In the words of local lawyer Benjamin Ostrer, the school boards association was "out of gas."[45] By contrast, the school district had been in continuous operation for almost a decade now, thanks to a series of "stays" from the Court that Lewin had succeeded in obtaining. Lewin counted these stays as his greatest successes in the *Grumet* litigation, and rightly so, since "temporary" stays create facts on the ground that generate their own staying power.[46]

Dissidents v. Establishment:
Persistent Tensions in Kiryas Joel

But there was another party ready to pick up the mantle. Not long after Chapter 405 went into effect, a lawsuit challenging the validity of the Kiryas Joel School District was filed by Menashe Birnbaum, Zalman Waldman, Meyer Deutsch, Isaac Gluck, Naphtali Tannenbaum, and Efram Fischel Gruber against the board of education of Monroe-Woodbury School District, the district superintendent of BOCES, the village of Kiryas Joel, and the Kiryas Joel Union Free School District.[47] Zalman Waldman was the brother of Joseph Waldman and one of the key members of Alta Faiga's "mentshen." Meyer Deutsch, who had punched Joseph Waldman in the nose back in 1989 when he was still a

member of the village establishment, was now himself a leading dissident. The rest of the plaintiffs were also dissident leaders. Indeed, the
dissident movement in Kiryas Joel was alive and well and by this point
accustomed to litigating its grievances in non-Jewish tribunals.

This particular lawsuit, *Birnbaum v. Kiryas Joel School District*, did not
amount to much. Eschewing constitutional arguments, it tried to maintain that Kiryas Joel did not satisfy the new law's population requirements, an argument the court ultimately rejected.[48] Representing the
dissidents was Benjamin Ostrer, Michael Sussman's office mate and co-
counsel on Joseph Waldman's 1990 case against the UTA. In the intervening years, Ostrer had been involved in extensive litigation on behalf
of the dissidents. According to Ostrer, he had been ready to mount a
constitutional challenge to Chapter 405, but his clients were not ready
to pay for such expensive litigation. Wary of being stiffed, he proposed
making a simpler, cheaper, statutory argument.[49] The judge assigned to
the case was Peter Patsalos, who had delivered Joseph Waldman his
victory against Aaron and Moshe in the lawsuit challenging the expulsions of his children from the UTA. Patsalos's KJ decisions neatly book-
ended the first decade of the dissidents' litigious activities, with the first
having been delivered in 1990 and the last in December 1999, when he
issued his ruling in the fourth and final school district case. It was only
a preliminary ruling, denying the dissidents the injunction they requested to prevent the school district from operating until the case was
resolved.

Notwithstanding this ruling, Judge Patsalos wrote that he believed
the dissidents were likely to succeed in their claim at trial.[50] Sensing this
prospect, the village lawyers maneuvered to get him replaced by another
judge by hiring Patsalos's personal lawyer to represent the district. The
appearance of a conflict of interest left Patsalos no choice but to recuse
himself.[51] The case was then transferred to another judge in Orange
County, John K. McGuirk, who, on February 14, 2001, rejected the dissidents' claim that the population of the village was not large enough to
satisfy Chapter 405.[52]

This latest round of fighting between the dissidents and the establishment was but one of several phases in the unfolding political drama

inside Kiryas Joel. The first consisted of the expulsions and harassment that took place during the chaotic year of 1989–1990 when the Bnai Yoel group was forming. In the same period, Brach was maneuvering to take control of Bedford Avenue, Waldman was bringing his legal action against Aaron and the UTA, and Grumet was filing his first lawsuit. The second phase unfolded between 1991 and 1992, as *Grumet I* wound its way through the lower courts. Dubbed by Michael Sussman "the guerrilla warfare" phase, because of the many acts of violence committed by roving bands of yeshivah students in this period, this was a time of intense, often physical strife, during which efforts by the village establishment to restore order were matched by efforts on the part of the dissidents to disrupt it. To be sure, the fighting never reached the point of armed conflict. Neither firearms nor knives ever became part of the arsenal of weapons used by the Satmars. As the *New York Times* noted in 1992, "The State Police see few of the usual crimes in this village of 8,000 Hasidic Satmar Jews. 'No drugs, no D.W.I.,'" a member of the state police force was quoted saying. And yet Kiryas Joel had become "a leading trouble spot in this five-county area," with state troopers receiving "hundreds of calls from people who've been stoned, their house and car and windows broken, their sidewalks stenciled with Hebrew profanities."[53] Incidents of arson, stone throwing, and verbal and physical harassment grew ever more common in the early 1990s, and the state police, whose headquarters stood just outside the entrance to the village, was regularly called in to break up fights.

Throughout all of this, KJ's leaders continually disavowed responsibility, placing all blame for the acts of physical harassment squarely on the shoulders of the young men who committed them.[54] But while the leaders insisted these were just the actions of a few "hotheads," it was clear to everyone that the harassment of the dissidents took place in direct response to their refusal to submit to the leaders' authority. The more the establishment sought to squelch the opposition, the more stubbornly the dissidents resisted, using every tool they could to protect themselves, from calling the police to reaching out to reporters.[55] At Joseph Waldman's direction, all incidents were reported to the local

Times Herald-Record, which churned out stories on a regular basis about the violence and harassment directed against the dissidents. Most provocatively of all, the dissidents kept going to lawyers and bringing their grievances to the state.

This represented a continuation of the strategy inaugurated by Waldman's lawsuit against the UTA. Although Waldman had publicly apologized and agreed to discontinue his suit in exchange for the readmission of his children into the Yetev Lev's schools, his success in getting the court to rule in his favor—and to issue an order of contempt against Moshe and Aaron—emboldened other dissidents to appeal to courts and invoke state law as a basis for protecting their rights. The first person to follow in Waldman's footsteps in this fashion was Joseph (Yosef) Hirsch, a village employee who worked for a time as the village building inspector and then for the village water department before joining the ranks of the dissidents in 1990.[56] As a municipal employee, Hirsch was in possession of information concerning the activities of village officials that he purportedly passed on to the state authorities in charge of monitoring local elections. Subsequently, he participated in the circulation of a petition demanding that voting no longer take place inside the main synagogue. Following revelations that Hirsch had filed a complaint with the local election authority, he was terminated from his position as a municipal employee and publicly denounced as a *moyser* or informer to gentile authorities, a label that carries profoundly negative connotations among traditional Jews. Members of the congregation were instructed to have no further contact with him.[57]

The following year, in 1991, Joseph Hirsch made a bid for a seat on the village board. After losing that election, he publicly considered a run for the school board. Hirsch paid for these acts of hubris by being subjected to physical harassment.[58] In April, he received an unsigned letter denouncing him as a sinner and an informant.[59] In 1992, after tapes surfaced that purportedly recorded him informing to government authorities about voting fraud and the village's misuse of funds, violent demonstrations erupted in KJ. Banners hanging from the main synagogue and the windows of the village hall denounced Hirsch as a moyser. Mobs of young men marched through the streets chanting "death to the traitor," in reference to Hirsch.[60]

Months before the rumors surfaced that he was an informer, the mainstream congregation had already issued a community-wide letter warning parents they would be expelled if they sent their children to the preschool Hirsch now ran for the Bnai Yoel. As usual, the dissidents ignored the threat.[61] Following the demonstrations against Hirsch, the congregation renewed its threats against the rest of the dissidents. Prominent members of Bnai Yoel received a personal letter from the congregation titled "the last warning," which declared (in Yiddish): "We warn you that you are not allowed to send your child to that informer."[62] Notwithstanding the menacing language, the warning had little effect on Bnai Yoel parents. But enmity toward Hirsch in the wider community increased. On September 6, 1992, three Satmar teenagers were arrested on charges of having thrown stones at him while he was driving kindergartners home from the Bnai Yoel preschool.[63]

This period was marked by a transition in lay leadership in KJ. In April 1991, Abe Wieder was appointed deputy mayor, serving under the long-standing Satmar icon Leibish Lefkowitz, who had been mayor since KJ's founding. When Wieder became deputy mayor, Lefkowitz delegated his authority to him, and from this point onward, Wieder served as the village's de facto mayor until assuming the official title in 1997 (which he continues to hold today).[64]

Wieder was the consummate insider politician—so much so that one local journalist dubbed him "Boss Wieder," evoking the transactional approach and assertive control that William "Boss" Tweed exercised over Democratic and city politics in New York in the mid-nineteenth century. Wieder also served as president of the board of the KJ Yetev Lev Congregation, a reminder of the blurred boundary between public (secular) and private (religious) authority in Kiryas Joel.[65] It was on Wieder's watch as president of the congregation that its board sent the letters of warning to the Bnai Yoel parents, demanding they cease associating with Hirsch. Meanwhile, under Wieder's direction as deputy mayor, the village board of trustees was taking other measures against the dissidents. In July 1992, the village board passed a resolution affirming that the next village election (scheduled to take place in June 1993) would be held inside the social hall of the main synagogue.[66] The placement of the polling booths inside the main synagogue was a long-standing grievance of the dissidents, who had been seeking their relocation since 1990.[67] The previous March, a group of over a hundred dissidents had petitioned the town of Monroe to move the voting booths to another location. When the town refused, the petitioners asked the Orange County Board of Elections to order their removal from the synagogue. As evidence of voter intimidation, the dissidents produced letters of warning issued by the Brooklyn and KJ congregations demanding that signatories renounce their opposition to the polling place location or risk expulsion from the congregation.[68]

After an investigation, the election board determined that many of the signatories lived outside of KJ. Concluding that it could not verify the dissidents' allegations of voter harassment, and that there was no alternative polling place large enough to accommodate KJ's voters, the board refused to order the town of Monroe to move the polling booths. In response, the dissidents filed a lawsuit challenging the board of election's conclusions.[69]

That was in early June 1992. Just a few weeks later, the village board of trustees adopted its resolution affirming that the next election would take place in the congregation's social hall. Although it was the town of Monroe, not the village, that had the legal authority to determine the location of the voting booths, the village's affirmation that it would keep the polling booths in the synagogue was a clear slap in the dissidents' face.[70]

The following month, donning his hat as president of the KJ congregation, Wieder delivered a report on the dissidents at a joint meeting of the Brooklyn and KJ congregation boards. Such joint meetings were a rarity, as each of the Yetev Lev Congregations was generally left to run itself. But this special meeting of the General Assembly, as it was labeled in the minutes, was convened for the specific purpose of enlisting the help of the Williamsburg congregation to address the strife inside Kiryas Joel.[71]

Even before this meeting of the general assembly was called, the board of the Williamsburg congregation had been participating in the fight to suppress the dissidents. The Brooklyn-based lawsuit against Nachman Brach was still ongoing (and would, indeed, continue for another seventeen years!). In addition, the Williamsburg congregation, which now held exclusive title to the KJ cemetery, had banned Brach, Hirsch, and other dissidents from the burial grounds. This ban had been instituted just days before the annual commemoration of the Rebbe's yahrtseit on 26 Av (August 25, 1992), in the middle of the escalating fight over Hirsch's preschool.[72] The dissidents responded by instigating not one, but two class-action lawsuits on behalf of the banned dissidents. The first, filed under the name of A. H. Weinstock (the father whose removal of his son from the UTA initiated the creation of Bnai Yoel), represented a vain attempt to obtain a state court injunction that would grant the dissidents access to the cemetery in time for the yahrtseit on August 25.[73] That suit foundered on the legal doctrine that religious disputes are not justiciable.

It was shortly after this abortive lawsuit that a General Assembly was convened with the express purpose of amending the bylaws to merge Kiryas Joel and Williamsburg into a single congregation. There, it was declared that "Kahal Yetev Lev D'Satmar is one large congregation" with "branches in New York, Kiryas Joel, Monsey, Williamsburg, Borough Park and Lakewood" as well as "many other areas." The General Assembly further declared that "the central leadership is in Williamsburg where the Chief Rabbi resides." A second bylaw asserted that this "central governing body" holds exclusive control over all Satmar moysdes, catalogued as "all synagogues, cemeteries, burial societies, butcher stores, matzah bakeries, educational and charitable institutions, free loan societies, children's homes, and Bikur Cholim of Satmar" (society for visiting the sick). Hammering home the point, a third bylaw provided that "no group or individual has any right to establish a synagogue, school, or whichever or any other organization under the name of Kahal Yetev Lev D'Satmar, or Satmar, or Yetev Lev, or Rabbeinu Yoel [our rabbi Joel], or Talmidei Rabbeinu Yoel [students of our rabbi Joel] without permission from the congregation." In case there was any doubt that Bnai Yoel was the target of these admonitions, the third bylaw concluded by stating that "in Kiryas Joel it is not permissible to open a synagogue, or any other school or organization in the entire village and its surroundings without the approval of the central governing body."[74]

According to the minutes of the September 1992 General Assembly meeting, the adoption of these bylaws was followed by an appeal from Berl Friedman, the president of the Williamsburg congregation, to all to participate in city elections. More specifically, he exhorted the attendees to vote in accordance with "the instructions of the leadership," especially of the United Jewish Organizations, because, he candidly explained, "it's extremely important to demonstrate our power so we can benefit from the programs which the city provides to the general public." Turning to the internal crisis at hand, he then appealed to the community to bring disputes to rabbinical courts "and not, God forbid, to the civil court system." He noted that "lately this aspect has been greatly trampled on"—a clear reference to the lawsuits recently initiated by the dissidents, which included a tort action brought by Joseph Hirsch and his wife against Aaron Teitelbaum, Abe Wieder, and other congregation leaders, in addition to the lawsuits seeking access to the cemetery and the removal of voting booths from the KJ synagogue.

Following the exhortation against going to the secular courts delivered by Berl Friedman, Wieder took the floor as president of the KJ congregation to present a report on the village, which was summarized in the minutes as a "sharp protest against the rabble-rousers."[75] Wieder concluded his remarks with an appeal to the central leadership in Brooklyn to help in suppressing the "struggle of enemies" and maintaining "peace in our ranks"—a clear indication that the meeting's true purpose was to form a unified front to respond to the challenge to the leadership taking place inside KJ.

The dissidents reacted to this latest effort to put them in their place in typical fashion: with defiance. The exhortations "to not, God forbid, go to the civil court system" had exactly the opposite effect. Instead of coming to an end, the lawsuits proliferated at a rapid pace. The voting booths and *Hirsch* suits were still pending. A second suit dealing with access to the cemetery had recently ended in the dissidents' defeat, which seemed to affirm the Brooklyn congregation's right to exclude them from the burial grounds. But even though the suits were not successful, they showed the dissidents' growing mastery of the American legal system, including their dawning realization that even a losing legal battle could be a useful means of making trouble for the establishment.

By this point, the dissidents had recognized the need to create a parallel set of moysdes, beginning, of course, with the Bnai Yoel school. Initial funds had been raised to lease a building to house the fledgling school and hire staff to serve its growing student body. But by the summer of 1993, the school was running out of money. As often happened in the Satmar world, crisis begot opportunity, and Bnai Yoel's financial predicament turned into a fundraising bonanza. Infusions of funds from sympathizers around the world allowed its leaders to purchase land to construct a new building in Monroe, just outside of KJ.[76]

Beyond creating their own school system, the dissidents also sought to build their own synagogues, mikvehs, and social halls where meetings could be held and weddings celebrated. In response, the establishment developed new methods to fight the dissidents. Thus commenced a new phase in the conflict between the establishment and the dissidents. Over the course of 1993, the effort to suppress the dissident movement shifted from the streets to the halls of village government. Village officers, led by Wieder, began to flex their municipal muscles, deploying various tools of local government, including the power to assess real estate taxes, the power to regulate land use and construction, and the power to control the provision of public services to private property owners and residents in the village. In addition to these powers that they enjoyed as village officeholders, Wieder and his associates had yet another tool of government available to them: the power to control the allocation of public housing. Although the Kiryas Joel Public Housing Authority was technically a separate entity from the village—it was in fact a federal agency, not a state or local government institution—the same federal law that created local public housing authorities granted localities the ability to appoint the chairman of the authority in their area. In KJ, that position was given to Gedalye Szegedin's uncle, Mayer

Hirsch, the prominent land developer who served as head of the powerful Vaad hakirya. Thus, the same man wielded power over both public and private housing in the village.

It took a while for village officers to become fully aware of these powers and understand how to use them. But once they figured it out, local government measures, such as enforcing building codes and zoning ordinances, came to be common mechanism for preventing the dissidents from gaining power. In turn, the dissidents resorted more and more to legal action to stop these measures.

Ironically, the dissidents' continuing resort to litigation was prompted by the village's adoption of a measure specifically designed to prevent internal disputes from being adjudicated by state courts. This unusual measure was part of a new ordinance dubbed Local Law No. 2. Enacted in May 1993, Local Law No. 2 tightened the requirements already prescribed by Local Law No. 1. Whereas Local Law No. 1 regulated land use and fixed safety standards for buildings in KJ, Local Law No. 2 imposed a new eighteen-month expiration date on building permits. It also, for the first time, established a Building Department charged with the responsibility for administering and enforcing the building code—presided over by none other than Mayer Hirsch.[77]

More controversially, the new ordinance also established a new procedure for enforcing the existing building standards and zoning regulations contained in Local Law No. 1.[78] Instead of submitting disputes to state courts, the usual procedure for adjudicating zoning and building code controversies, Local Law No. 2 stated they should be adjudicated by the village board of trustees, in effect substituting an administrative proceeding, conducted by village officials, for a state judicial proceeding. As Wieder would later explain in a court of law, this provision was motivated by the village leaders' desire to be able to enforce the zoning and building regulations prescribed by Local Law No. 1 themselves, without having to go to secular court.

In point of fact, the village had never sought to enforce its building code and zoning regulations prior to this point in time. Uses of property that ran afoul of suburban zoning laws and safety codes, like the placement of religious and commercial establishments inside residential buildings, were generally tolerated. Indeed, the whole point of incorporating as a separate village had been to create a zoning regime in which such uses would be perfectly acceptable. It would be antithetical to the very rationale of KJ, for example, to shut down the many shtiblekh, or prayer quorums in private homes, that populated the village.[79]

It was, therefore, supremely ironic that the Satmar leaders began to use the same kind of exclusionary zoning tactics against the dissidents that the town of Monroe had used against them. Doing so demonstrated once again the two-sided nature of exclusion: having people who hold to certain beliefs or follow a certain kind of lifestyle *in* the community necessarily depends on keeping people with different beliefs or practices *out*. This need to exclude "undesirables" in order to maintain the sense of belonging in the community is common not only to enclave societies such as KJ or Rajneeshpuram but also to more "typical" suburban municipalities—as can be seen in the exclusionary zoning ordinances and homeowner association regulations that historically served to maintain the racial and socioeconomic homogeneity of American suburbs. KJ officials, who were now in possession of these tools of exclusionary zoning customarily used to keep unwanted outsiders out, now discovered they could use them to restrict the activities of their internal adversaries as well. When they first began to make use of this tool, it might even have seemed possible to drive the dissidents out of the village altogether.

Unlike the typical exclusionary suburb, however, the village of Kiryas Joel had to find an enforcement mechanism other than the courts to achieve its preferred form of homogeneity. This was because of the religious taboo against adjudicating internal disputes in secular tribunals. In order to be able to wield the stick of zoning and building code enforcement, village officials felt they needed to find a way to enforce zoning and building code citations that did not involve resorting to gentile authorities. That was the purpose of the controversial portions of Local Law No. 2, which made the board of trustees in effect the court. It did not make the board the court of last resort, as the ordinance recognized that parties had the right to submit the board's administrative rulings for judicial review. But it did make the board the court of first resort, thereby arrogating to the village an adjudicative function customarily performed by state and local justice courts.[80] This granted village officials a formidable power they could use in their ongoing war against dissidents.

Enacting the new ordinance was just the first step. The next step was to issue citations for alleged violations of the building code. The first intimation of this development came not long after Local Law No. 2 was passed, when a man who had sided with the dissidents, by the name of Morgenstern, was contacted by Wieder and Mayer Hirsch, the latter of whom was now acting in his new roles as head of the village planning board and zoning board of appeals. Wieder and Hirsch told Morgenstern he would be given a citation if he continued to allow members of Bnai Yoel to pray in his home.[81]

Up until this point, not a single enforcement action had been initiated by the village even though violations were rampant, so it might have seemed an empty threat. Indeed, the village did not end up citing Morgenstern. But Wieder's and Hirsch's private chat with him was clearly meant to send a message to the dissidents that this state of affairs was about to change. Indeed, this turned out to be the opening salvo in what would prove to be a very long battle over alleged zoning and building infractions on the part of the dissidents.

In the summer of 1994, the first citation under the new enforcement ordinance was issued. The recipient of this first citation was Avraham Weinstock, who by now was well known to the establishment as an agitator, having been the first of the Bnai Yoel parents to withdraw his son from the mainstream yeshivah. A few years earlier, the Weinstock family had commenced a home renovation project at 3 Van Buren Street, a few minutes' walk from the main synagogue. That project stopped in 1990 with the addition half finished, not as the result of any official interference with the building project but simply because the Weinstock family suspended its completion. Now, in August 1994, in anticipation of the Jewish high holidays when a bigger prayer space would be needed, Weinstock was approached by Zalman and Joseph Waldman and Meyer Deutsch about the possibility of building a synagogue for the dissidents on the Weinstock property.[82]

It already had been an eventful summer. The Supreme Court's decision striking down the original school district statute had been handed down at the end of June and Chapter 241, the second authorizing statute, had been signed into law on July 6. A few weeks later, the village board of trustees submitted a referendum to the KJ voters to reconstitute the public school district and board of education under the new law.[83] A Committee for No School District then formed with the mission of persuading KJ residents to vote against approving the school district, as required by Chapter 241. Led by Joseph Waldman and supported by other dissidents, that campaign never gained traction. On election day, July 25, KJ residents approved the reconstitution of the school district by a vote of 2,798 to 240. As he had before, Waldman claimed he was prevented from running in the school board election by the establishment. Before the month was out, he filed a lawsuit in state court to register his protest. A second lawsuit, alleging voting fraud and voter intimidation in the school board election, was filed by dissidents a month later.[84]

Also in this period, the board of the KJ congregation had passed a resolution banning Yehezkel Roth, the prominent local rabbi known as the Karlsburger Rov, who was a vocal supporter of the dissidents.[85] The state court cemetery case bearing Weinstock's name was decided, dismissing the dissidents' complaint.[86] Meanwhile, Grumet was filing his second lawsuit.[87] All of this activity took place in the two hot months between the end of June and the end of August. Now, with the summer winding down and the high holidays approaching, a plan was hatched to turn the Weinstock property into Bnai Yoel's own grand synagogue.

3 Van Buren Street: The Battle over the Dissidents' Shul

The dissidents had already established smaller prayer spaces scattered around the village. And dissidents continued to frequent Congregation Bais Yoel, as the congregation that met in the Rebbetsin's house was known. For regular daily and Sabbath services, these prayer spaces would suffice. But for the high holidays and other major festivals, a larger space was required in order to accommodate the entire Bnai Yoel community (including the women) in one place. The property at 3 Van Buren Street, which sat a short distance from the village's main synagogue and across the street from the village hall, had already been permitted for an addition. It seemed to be the perfect location for the expanded prayer space the dissidents envisaged. Weinstock agreed and gave the signal to his builder, Moses Indig, to resume construction on the property. No sooner did construction commence, however, than a stop order was issued by Mayer Hirsch.[88]

Undeterred, the dissidents quickly completed a round of construction at 3 Van Buren Street, just in time to inaugurate its use as a synagogue on September 5, the eve of Rosh Ha-Shanah. Throughout the 1994 high holiday season, Hirsch kept issuing citations, and Weinstock and his builder kept ignoring them.[89] The dissidents enjoyed the use of their new synagogue from the evening of Rosh Ha-Shanah through the end of Yom Kippur, as they had intended. The day before the eve of Yom Kippur, Weinstock and his builders received a summons from the building inspector to appear before the newly constituted "hearing board." This hearing board was the creation of the new ordinance, Local Law No. 2. Under its terms, the village board of trustees now possessed the power to hold hearings to determine if building code and zoning violations had taken place—a function ordinarily performed by courts. On September 30, with the holidays now over, the hearing took place, presided over by Wieder and the other village board members. Also present were the village clerk, Gedalye Szegedin, the village attorney, and, representing Mr. Weinstock as his lawyer, Ben Ostrer.[90] The board determined that "the violations here are serious" and imposed a $25,000 fine on Weinstock, while a $10,000 fine was imposed on Moses Indig, his builder.[91]

If the village leaders had hoped that Local Law No. 2 would allow them to impose their will freely (and without going to court), that hope would soon be dashed. Instead of complying with the village's orders, Weinstock and Indig moved ahead with the next phase of the project. First, they established a religious nonprofit corporation called Khal Charidim (Congregation of the Pious), the name they bestowed on the congregation that would occupy the space at 3 Van Buren. Then, on

March 27, the Van Buren Street property was deeded by Weinstock to Khal Charidim.[92] These legal actions were a prelude to the congregation's grand opening. Although the dissidents had refrained from using the Van Buren property since the end of the high holidays in 1994, they planned to hold Passover services there and formally inaugurate the new congregation. Shortly after the legal incorporation of Khal Charidim, in preparation for the Passover holiday, construction on the addition to the building resumed. The village responded by issuing another stop order, and when the dissidents refused to obey, the village issued a flurry of new citations to Weinstock and his builder.[93]

What happened next would permanently alter the dissidents' relationship with the village and, in turn, the village's relationship with American courts. Litigation was by now a constant, even chronic feature of life in KJ. But, other than Waldman's original suit against the UTA, the lawsuits initiated by the dissidents had so far all ended in defeat, leaving little mark on the landscape. That would change when the dissidents, facing citations for building codes violations and intent on using 3 Van Buren Street for Passover, turned to local lawyer Ben Ostrer.

The case that Ostrer filed two days before Passover—*Khal Charidim of Kiryas Joel and A.H. Weinstock v. Village of Kiryas Joel*—began relatively innocuously.[94] Ostrer's first goal was to obtain a preliminary order prohibiting the village from interfering with the dissidents' use of the property during Passover. The judge assigned to the case, Joseph Owen, a native son of the nearby town of Chester, born to Lebanese parents, granted the order allowing 3 Van Buren Street to be used as a synagogue for the duration of Passover. But the dissidents did not simply enjoy the use of the property during Passover. In defiance of the judicial order's time limit, they resumed construction on the building as soon as Passover ended. In June, they held a wedding in the renovated space; the bride was the daughter of Rabbi Morgenstern, the first person to have been threatened with enforcement of the zoning ordinance after Local Law No. 2 was passed.[95]

Celebrating the first wedding in their own synagogue was a moment of triumph for the dissidents. It was also, however, a blatant violation of the legal order that Justice Owen had issued as a temporary injunction ending with Passover. In response to the village's request, Owen now issued more injunctions, this time barring Khal Charidim from engaging in any construction, use, or occupancy of 3 Van Buren pending the outcome of the litigation.

All of this was fairly routine for a building code dispute. Courts commonly issued preliminary orders determining how a disputed building site could be used pending a final decision. What was not so routine was the plaintiffs' challenge to the very constitutionality of the building code itself. As we have seen, Local Law No. 2 went beyond the typical exclusionary zoning ordinance by granting the village power that was usually reserved for courts: to adjudicate zoning disputes and decide for itself if the building authority's claim that the municipal building code was violated was valid. The result was a distinctive kind of law, neither the law of the state administered by courts, nor the law of the Torah that the Satmars professed to live by. It was instead a peculiar kind of secular regulation, intended to be administered by the secular leaders of a religiously homogeneous community for the purpose of avoiding the jurisdiction of secular courts. Technically, the village officials would be conducting an administrative proceeding, exercising the secular powers of government delegated to them by state law. But from their own standpoint, they would be avoiding the exercise of gentile authority over their internal disputes. To the dissidents, this odd hybrid was a perfect example of the exercise of secular power by Satmar leaders that the Rebbe had forbidden.

On their behalf, Ostrer challenged the constitutionality of this peculiar arrangement. But he did not claim that the dissidents' civil liberties were being violated by the village on account of their religious differences. Nor did he claim that the village was violating the principle of separation between religion and state. Instead, the complaint he brought alleged that Khal Charidim's property rights were being violated. More specifically, Ostrer argued that the village was acting unconstitutionally, not by violating the Establishment Clause but rather by violating the Due Process Clause, which protects private property rights. Under this legal theory, the problem with Local Law No. 2 was that it violated the separation of powers, placing the judicial function of resolving disputes in the hands of a legislative body (the village board of trustees). In so doing, the ordinance allowed the village to deprive property owners of their rights without due process of law.

It was an unusual argument, reflecting the unusual circumstances of the case. But it would ultimately prove to be persuasive. On June 27, 1995, Justice Owen ruled that the portions of Local Law No. 2 that permitted village officials to impose onerous fines for building code violations were unconstitutional.[96] He had not yet ruled on the dissidents' more fundamental claim, that the village's arrogation of the right to adjudicate building code and zoning disputes was unconstitutional. And he evinced some sympathy toward the village in ruling that the dissidents were in violation of the building code and that KJ could therefore enjoin the construction of the Khal Charidim synagogue unless and until the necessary permits were obtained. This left the fate of 3 Van Buren Street uncertain. Whether the synagogue could be established inside the Weinstock property now depended on whether the village would grant permits to the leaders of Khal Charidim. Judge Owen encouraged them to submit the necessary applications and "strongly advised" the village "to cooperate in the fullest with any appropriate requests in this regard."[97] But the actual determination of whether to grant the requests was left to the village planning board, which was controlled by Mayer Hirsch.

Between the end of June and the end of August 1995, Khal Charidim submitted no fewer than three applications for a building permit plus a new set of construction plans. The village, for its part, did all within its power to give the dissidents the run-around. On August 24, the village building inspector sent a letter to Zalman Waldman in response to his submitting a building permit application on behalf of Khal Charidim, instructing him that he would have to obtain a special permit, plus site plan approval, and variances before the building could be used as a synagogue.[98]

Months passed before the dissidents submitted the requested application. In the meanwhile, they asked for a re-argumentation of the *Khal Charidim* case. In addition to continuing to maintain that "the [village] Board of Trustees unconstitutionally usurped the function of the courts by holding a hearing," the dissidents challenged the ongoing injunction against their use and occupancy of 3 Van Buren Street.[99] When, just days before Rosh Ha-Shanah, Justice Owen refused to lift the injunction, the dissidents defied his order and held services in the new Khal Charidim synagogue on September 25–26. The village responded to this latest act of defiance by filing contempt proceedings against the dissidents. In early October 1995, Justice Michael Owen found the dissidents to be in contempt of court and issued yet another temporary injunction forbidding them from making use of the building. A full hearing of the plaintiffs' claim to a right to use the building as a synagogue was scheduled for October 12—more than a week after Yom Kippur.[100]

It was at this point that lawyer Michael Sussman reentered the picture to make what the local press called a "last-ditch effort to allow the use of the building during Yom Kippur."[101] Sussman's strategy was to change venues, moving the dispute out of state court and into federal court and, in doing so, to change the topic. Jed Rakoff, the federal judge who ultimately presided over this case, summarized it this way: "The federal complaint—unlike the state court proceeding, which was focused on the property rights of the present and former owners of 3 Van Buren Drive—focuses on alleged unconstitutional infringements of personal freedoms."[102] More specifically, Sussman argued that the village was discriminating against the dissidents by selectively enforcing the zoning code and that its actions constituted a denial of the dissidents' rights to freedom of assembly, the free exercise of religion, and equal protection of the law.

In the same breath, Sussman asserted that the secular and religious leadership of the village overlapped and worked together to oppress the dissidents. His first order of business, however, was to obtain authorization for the dissidents to use the property for Yom Kippur. On October 3, the day after the case was filed, a temporary order permitting use of 3 Van Buren Street for Yom Kippur services was obtained from Judge Barrington Parker, the judge initially assigned the case, just in time for Kol Nidrei that evening.[103]

The same script was followed in advance of Passover, in the spring of 1996. Before that, however, in January 1996, Justice Owen finally issued his ruling addressing the question of the constitutionality of Local Law No. 2. Unlike the federal Khal Charidim suit, which highlighted the religious motivations behind the village's building code enforcement action, the state Khal Charidim case, presided over by Justice Owen, deliberately skirted the religious dimensions of the issue. The dissidents' lawyer in that case, Ostroff, had, as we have seen, challenged the ordinance's constitutionality on separation of power grounds. And Justice Owen himself, from the beginning, sought to keep religion out of the controversy. In a telling footnote to his 1995 decision, he recognized that "unfortunately, underlying this 'cauldron of boiling citations and arguments' is the widely acknowledged and publicized fact that the parties herein are engaged in an ongoing, and at times violent, dispute resulting from their religious differences." But he went on to insist that "the parties and their counsel must understand, however, that the complex determinations before the Court are entirely legal in nature and cannot be governed by the fervent manner with which they seemingly attempt to impose their respective religious beliefs not only upon each other but, through documentary submissions which should be designed solely to represent their *legal* positions, upon this Court." Admonishing that "it is to be expected that counsel and their clients will conduct themselves with the decorum and restraint necessary to facilitate a timely resolution to their *legal* differences," Justice Owen declared that the fact that "the defendant/respondents' actions are motivated primarily not by a concern for village law, but by religious considerations" was irrelevant. His frustration with the parties' "fervent" conduct was clear.[104]

Justice Owen held to the same line in January 1996 when he issued his ruling on the constitutional claim that he had postponed in his earlier decision. The plaintiffs had argued that the board of trustees had unconstitutionally usurped the function of the courts. The village had defended itself against this charge by arguing that it was legally permissible, indeed commonplace, to grant adjudicatory functions to an administrative board and that combining investigative and adjudicative functions in the board of trustees was consistent with this commonplace form of administrative proceedings. Having resisted this conclusion for several years, Justice Owen now determined that the dissidents were correct. It was true that the defendants were right to maintain that there was no general rule against according adjudicatory functions to administrative agencies and local boards. But the general municipal law of New York State—Justice Owen pointed in particular to "general law, 6"—restricted the adjudication of zoning and building code disputes to judicial proceedings. Therefore, Owen concluded that "in enacting Local Law #2, defendant not only usurped the function of the judiciary, but attempted to supersede general law, 6."

The village had lost the state *Khal Charidim* case. But the federal *Khal Charidim* case was still pending. With the hearing in that case not scheduled to take place until after Passover, the leaders of Khal Charidim, including Zalman Waldman, Abraham Weinstock, and Mayer Deutsch, once again appealed to the district court for a temporary restraining order prohibiting the village from preventing them from using the building for services.[105] This time, Judge Parker denied the temporary restraining order, leaving the dissidents unable to use the property that Passover. They remained locked out five months later when the high holidays again rolled around and the federal case still had not gone to trial. An appeal at this time to the state court also fell on deaf ears, when once again Judge Owen denied the dissidents' petition to use Van Buren for Rosh Ha-Shana and Yom Kippur services.[106]

Between these two decisions, the first issued by the federal court in April 1996, the second by the state court in September 1996, two major events took place that further inflamed the conflict. First, in late July 1996, a fire occurred at the maternity center in KJ.[107] Housed in a large building owned by Faiga that sat on top of a hill on the outskirts of the village, the maternity center, to which mothers from far and wide in the Haredi community repaired with their newborn babies to convalesce, was one of the Rebbetsin's pet projects. Its chief administrator was Zalman Waldman, who on that day was expecting to host Rabbi Yehezkel Roth at a fundraiser for the maternity center.[108] Rabbi Roth, we recall, had been banned from giving speeches in the village by the KJ congregation two years earlier. The previous summer, his arrival in the village in defiance of the ban had provoked a mass riot, with some thousand men reported to have been involved.

Characterized by the state police as the most violent incident in the village's eighteen-year history, the riot marked a turning point in relations between the Satmars and the state police. In addition to throwing rocks and eggs at the dissidents, rioters actually pelted police officers.[109] The incident prompted Orange County officials to meet with village leaders after the rioting was over. It also afforded the dissidents with a new opportunity. Not only did they get county officials to meet with them as well; they conveyed their side of the story in the terms that Sussman was using. Local newspaper headlines declared "Religion Tests Civil Rights in Kiryas Joel" and "Dissidents Won't Give In."[110]

That was the summer of 1995. When Yehezkel Roth's return to the village one year later coincided with a fire at the venue he was scheduled to visit, it was hard to suppress suspicions of arson. Earlier that year, Joseph Waldman's car had been subject to an arson attack.[111] Now it was the maternal convalescence center, housing newborn babies and the mothers who had just given birth to them, that was in flames. The dissidents were convinced it was a deliberate act of aggression that marked a resurgence of the violence that had been prevalent in the early phases of the conflict. Many outsiders seemed to agree, although no one was ever convicted and Wieder strenuously denied the allegation, pointing to the fact that his own daughter was in the maternity center at the time.[112]

For Michael Sussman, the fire was a clear demonstration of what Samuel Freedman described in "Jew vs. Jew." Well before it occurred, he had been warned by Joseph Waldman and his other clients to "be careful," a warning he shrugged off, accustomed as he was to being the subject of threats related to the ongoing *Yonkers* litigation. But he recalls the fire in KJ as a sobering moment for his sense, not just of personal safety, but of Jewish identity. Alerted to the news of the fire as it was taking place, he drove to the scene on an early Sunday morning with his father, who had recently moved in with him at his home in the neighboring town of Chester. What stands out most in his memory of the scene is the shocking image of his father, whom he had never before seen cry, "just standing there on the corner, just weeping" at the sight of Jews appearing to be attacking one another.[113]

At this very point in time, Sussman was handed the opportunity to present his understanding of the situation in KJ to one of the finest minds in the federal judicial system. The *Khal Charidim* case had been transferred from Barrington Parker to the newly appointed Jed Rakoff, today best known for presiding over the settlement of the SEC case against Citibank after the 2008 financial collapse and for his regular contributions to the *New York Review of Books*. Like many of the lawyers and judges who played a major role in Kiryas Joel's legal dramas, including Sussman himself, Rakoff was a highly intelligent non-Orthodox Jew with an elite education (Swarthmore and Harvard Law).[114] Appointed to the bench by President Clinton just one year earlier, Rakoff maintained a lifelong devotion to issues of social justice, although his primary field of expertise was securities law and white-collar crime.

On August 5, 1996, just days after the fire at the maternity center, Judge Rakoff rejected the village's motion to dismiss the lawsuit. A hearing was scheduled for October 15, which was subsequently postponed to March 1997.[115] In the interim, a number of other legal developments occurred, further complicating the litigation. First, shortly after Rakoff put a hearing of the *Khal Charidim* case on the calendar, the village planning board finally held its own hearing on Khal Charidim's application for site approval and building permits, but did not issue a decision.[116] Days later, the Appellate Division reversed Judge Kahan's decision upholding the second school district authorizing statute. Calling that statute a "subterfuge" to "camouflage" the legislature's intent to benefit the Satmars with neutral-sounding language, the court struck down Chapter 241 by a vote of four to one.[117] The lone outlier in that case, a longtime fixture in the state judicial system by the name of Edward Spain, disagreed. He asserted that the statute was "not designed to enhance or endorse religion, rather it provides a permissible solution to the religious/cultural dilemma faced by the people of Kiryas Joel . . . in meeting the needs of their handicapped children."[118]

The cloud of legal uncertainty that continued to envelop the school district was at this point old news, a regular part of the KJ landscape to which the community had become accustomed. What constituted a novelty was the impending trial in the *Khal Charidim* case.

To add more fuel to the legal fires raging in the village, in December 1996, Judge Owen issued a decision in yet another case involving the conflict between the KJ establishment and the dissidents. This case, which had escaped public notice up to this point, had been initiated by the Yetev Lev Congregation of Kiryas Joel back in September 1995, just a couple of weeks before the federal *Khal Charidim* case was filed. It marked one of the only times that litigation was initiated by the establishment party against the dissidents, rather than the other way around. Filed under the name of *Congregation Yetev Lev D'Satmar v. Fayga Teitelbaum*, the complaint alleged that the "parsonage"—the apartment at the back of the grand synagogue that had originally been built for the Rebbe and the Rebbetsin where Congregation Bais Yoel now met—had been wrongfully conveyed to Faiga after Reb Yoelish's death. The plaintiff congregation, Yetev Lev, asked the court to nullify the deed and evict Faiga from the premises.[119]

This was not the first time the Moshe-Aaron camp had tried to evict Faiga. According to news reports, Satmar leaders had first sought to commence eviction proceedings against her in the fall of 1990, when the furor against Hirsch acting as an informer first erupted and the public school was opening its doors. That earlier attempt to evict Faiga had been foiled when the rabbi deputized to serve papers against her in Brooklyn was waylaid by a robber and killed.[120] Although that was apparently a random act of violence that had nothing to do with the Satmars' political intrigues, it was evidently enough to dissuade the leaders from filing the case at the time.

Five years later, however, the gloves were off. Under the leadership of Abe Wieder and David Eckstein as president and vice-president of the congregation, the KJ Yetev Lev Congregation sued not only Faiga but also, in another mind-bending twist, several KJ congregation board members, including Leopold Lefkowitz, whom it accused of having made "false and fraudulent statements to the state Supreme Court when the deed was being transferred [to Faiga] in 1981."[121] On this rather curious basis (a strategy known to lawyers as a "collusive lawsuit"), KJ's leaders hoped to oust the dissident congregation, which was now formally incorporated under the name Bais Yoel Ohel Feige (House of Joel Tent of Faiga), and had been meeting in the Rebbetsin's apartment since 1982.[122]

Now, both of the dissident congregations, Bais Yoel Ohel Feige, which had been formed in the early eighties by Faiga's mentshen and met in her apartment at the rear of the main synagogue, and the newer Khal Charidim, formed by the Bnai Yoel group and located down the street in the Weinstock property, were in the crosshairs of the KJ establishment. The Bnai Yoel group and Faiga's mentschen shared a number of key figures such as Zalman Waldman. And both were the subject of contentious litigation presided over by Justice Owen in the Orange County courthouse in the years between 1995 and 1997, at which point the federal *Khal Charidim* case, presided over by Judge Rakoff, took center stage.

Justice Owen's ruling in the *Teitelbaum* case emboldened the dissidents. Not only was Faiga spared eviction, but her title to the building was also upheld. The following July, Faiga transferred the title to the parsonage to the Bais Yoel Ohel Faiga Congregation. The deed was formally recorded in Orange County on July 22, 1997, granting the dissident congregation full rights of ownership over the structure attached to the main synagogue of the establishment congregation.[123]

For a brief moment, it appeared that further conflict might be averted. Four months before the Rebbetsin's apartment was deeded to the Ohel Feiga Congregation, on March 11, 1997, a settlement between the warring camps was reached that seemed to end the Khal Charidim litigation before Judge Rakoff. "Peace at last," the local newspaper trumpeted.[124] Zalman Waldman was quoted as saying: "We are brothers. . . . It's like when two brothers get in a fight and when it is straightened out, everybody is happy."[125] Abe Wieder, for his part, stated: "We have developed a framework of working together. Now our village can move forward as a community whose residents live together in harmony as we build for a bright and prosperous future."[126]

A Short-Lived Truce

One key participant in the dispute who was notably absent from the public celebration of the "peace" announcement was Michael Sussman. What Sussman recalls of the pivotal day of settlement, March 11, 1997, was that "I went home that night and I cried. I swear to God. It's not the first time I cried as a lawyer, but I cried."[127] The fire at the maternity center had not moved him to tears, but the settlement reached by the Satmars had.

To understand the depths of Sussman's disappointment, one has to understand both what led up to it and what followed. Since 1990, when Joseph Waldman first hired him to represent him in his case against the UTA, Sussman had played a unique role in the Satmar community, serving as a kind of in-house counsel for the dissident community, advising them as well as litigating on their behalf. He played a vital role in helping them to create their parallel universe of social and religious institutions, something he took great pride in.[128] He counseled them on their runs for public office. He helped them in their battles over the elections. And, most recently, he had been challenging what he and the dissidents saw as discriminatory denials of tax exemptions.

The tax exemption dispute was another product of the July 1995 village board meeting at which two significant resolutions had been adopted. The first, mentioned earlier, expressed the village's resolve to keep the voting booths inside the main synagogue. The second was a resolution sponsored by Wieder granting the village the authority to determine which properties would be classified as "religious" institutions eligible for tax exemptions. The dissidents believed that the village refused to recognize the buildings that housed their congregations as religious institutions, while granting favorable treatment to the mixed-use properties that the main congregation used for shuls and shtiblekh. Sussman had been threatening to bring an equal protection challenge in federal court claiming that the "extraordinary" difference in taxing between the dissidents and Moshe and Aaron's supporters was a matter of religious discrimination. Faced with this threat, the village tax authority, according to Sussman, "backed off" and settled with his clients.[129]

When Weinstock and the Waldmans first turned to Sussman for help with the Khal Charidim controversy in 1995, Sussman immediately grasped that the case provided him with an opportunity to mount an attack on the village's political system *in its entirety.* Rather than play small ball with this local ordinance, he wanted to demonstrate the systemic nature of the discrimination the dissidents faced with the ultimate aim of bringing the entire system down. It was the same theory of structural discrimination that he had applied to his work on the *Yonkers* case. There he reframed what was originally seen as "'yet another school desegregation case" as more than that—as a school desegregation case *and* a housing discrimination case *and* a police brutality case all at once. His novel legal strategy in that case was to show how different discriminatory practices all worked together to express the majority's hostility toward a minority group. In this manner, he sought to develop a way to prove the systemic nature of race discrimination in terms a court could accept and understand.

Over the course of the preceding five years, as his relationship with the dissident community in KJ deepened, Sussman came to believe that his theory of "unitary discrimination" as he called this theory of the case in *Yonkers*, applied perfectly to their situation as well. From this point of view, the building code dispute over Khal Charidim was just the tip of the iceberg. What was required to defend the rights of the dissidents, as Sussman saw it, went beyond attacking the zoning ordinances, Local Laws No. 1 and 2. His lawsuit on behalf of Khal Charidim became a vehicle for sweeping claims against the village and its officers, alleging that their actions amounted to the denial of the plaintiffs' free exercise of religion, of their right to freely assembly, to due process, and to the equal protection of the law.

Like Grumet, Sussman saw the situation in Kiryas Joel through the lens of race. And, again like Grumet, he saw the problem of race—and its solution—through the lens of integration. The two men were typical in this regard of secular Jews of the postwar generations. To be sure, Sussman, came of age in the seventies, whereas Grumet's formative political experiences took place in the fifties and sixties. As a member of the younger generation who had been involved in progressive politics since college, Sussman was well aware of the limits of the integrationist paradigm. Many of his Black colleagues at the NAACP, where he worked when the *Yonkers* litigation began, had soured on integration, having come to regard it as a failed path. Sussman sympathized with their frustrations. But he continued to believe that equality—and the law, which was constitutionally committed to protect the right to equality—prohibited excluding members of a minority group from access to the same services, benefits, opportunities, and institutions as the majority. Likening the plight of the Satmar dissidents in KJ to that of Black residents in Yonkers, he saw both as minority groups who were being subjected to systemic discrimination.

Still this was a very different kind of lawsuit from the *Grumet* litigation. And it was also different, in scale and in nature, from the other dissident cases thus far. Proving systemic discrimination would require far more evidence than any of the cases Sussman and Ostroff had litigated before. In short, it would require a trial—something the *Grumet* litigation had bypassed. Over the course of the lengthy discovery period that Judge Rakoff allowed for the collection of evidence, Sussman amassed more and more instances of mistreatment of the dissidents, some of which he channeled into a second federal lawsuit filed before the *Khal Charidim* trial had even begun. Whereas the federal *Khal Charidim* case focused on the allegedly selective enforcement of the building code, this new lawsuit made a new claim, reminiscent of the *Yonkers* suit, that the dissidents were being discriminated against by the village's Public Housing Authority. By being denied coveted housing units, Sussman contended, the dissidents were being deprived "of the rights, privileges and immunities secured by the Constitution of the United States, specifically: the rights of the plaintiffs under the First Amendment, as taxpayers, to be free from government funded religious practice, from governmental advancement of religion, and from governmental entanglement with religion."[130]

This was the first time that an Establishment Clause challenge had been formally leveled against the village. Indeed, the complaint in this suit went so far as to characterize the village of Kiryas Joel as a "theocracy." The specific allegations in the suit concerned the long-standing and never fully substantiated claim that the village or, alternatively, the Rebbe required a ten-thousand-dollar contribution to the congregation to build or sell housing units alongside the complaint about the distribution of public housing. But this was just one element of the broader allegation, articulated in the complaint at some length, "that the 'majority' has established a state religion in Kiryas Joel, one impermissibly permeating all forms of secular and political life."[131]

The plaintiffs in this case were, of course, the usual suspects, albeit in new garb: the "Committee for the Wellbeing of Kiryas Joel," a new organization formed by Joseph Waldman and two other dissidents who claimed to have been wrongfully denied public housing.[132] The defendants included the village housing director, Moses Neuman, alongside Wieder and the village itself, with the heads of the federal and state departments of urban housing thrown in for good measure.

Waldman I, as the first federal lawsuit filed in Waldman's name became known, commenced two months before the *Khal Charidim* case went to trial. The trial, which began on March 3, 1997, lasted for five days. The spectacle of a full-scale jury trial airing the dissidents' grievances drew reporters from far and wide. The lawyers gave their opening statements before a packed courthouse. Sussman, who was being assisted by Ostrer, went first. Putting his theory of unitary discrimination into layman's terms, he explained to the jury: "If you hear of jigsaw puzzles, this is a thousand-piece puzzle" that could very well take "two to three weeks" to assemble.[133] "In its most narrow form," he acknowledged, "the evidence in this case is about one building." But, he explained, "what is integral to an understanding of this case is that a small group of men run and have run the village, the synagogue and the United Talmudic Academy as well as another organization that controls land in the village and is integrally involved with the development process for profit in the community, Vaad Hakirya."[134] The upshot, in Sussman's words, was that "the distinction between a school district, a congregation, a village becomes entirely blurred. There is no distinction."[135]

Presenting the case for KJ was Frederick Hafetz, who had joined the village's large team of lawyers.[136] Hafetz was assisted by Susan Necheles, a former Kings County DA, and a young Eric Schneiderman, who would be elected to the state senate in the next year, launching a once-promising political career that ended in 2018 with his ignominious resignation as New York State attorney general due to sexual abuse claims. Hafetz's opening statement was significantly shorter than Sussman's and his point simpler. "This case is not the pilgrims, this case is not the puritans, this case is not about oppression, suppression, persecution of religious minorities." The dissidents, he explained to the jury, were not a religious minority; they were rather a group of "disgruntled individuals" who had political, not religious disagreements with the village leaders. "The differences they manufacture or the differences they state," he argued, "are not in reality differences. They are sham differences for what we submit is a sham lawsuit, not a lawsuit about religious persecution, not a lawsuit about oppression, but a sham manufactured cooked-up lawsuit."[137]

What the case was really about, he asserted, was the decline of the influence the dissidents possessed when the Rebbe was still alive. Worse, the dissidents were disgruntled, he said, because they had lost the ability to profit from "controlling access to the rabbi," which they had granted in exchange for money. Joseph Waldman, Hafetz informed the jury, was just "a person who likes the limelight," "an egomaniac . . . who likes to stir up trouble." Dismissing Michael Sussman's grand theory of systemic discrimination occurring across multiple realms, Hafetz told the jury that the only legally relevant issue was that Khal Charidim did not meet the building code requirements and had "utterly violated the law in every respect, at every turn, at every pass with regard to how one goes about obtaining the permission and constructing and using a place of assembly."[138]

After the opening statements, Sussman put his first witness on the stand. For a day and a half, Sussman coaxed Zalman Waldman to testify to his personal knowledge of many of the events that Sussman had recounted in his opening statement. Sussman was able to establish many of his key points beyond the selective enforcement of the zoning ordinance. Most significantly, Rakoff allowed him to introduce evidence to support his contention about "the blurring of church and state," with a particular focus on the multiple roles that Wieder occupied.[139]

Then Wieder took the stand and, with characteristic savvy, skillfully parried many of the claims against him. There was no basis, he claimed, for blaming the village for the acts of violence and harassment the dissidents endured because those were the actions of private individuals acting of their own volition. Those denied building permits and zoning variances did not qualify for them. The imposition of a building fee by Moshe in 1989, the ten thousand dollars for a building permit supposedly used to support the UTA, never happened. The village was not denying anyone the right to live in KJ, Wieder asserted. The only exclusion going on in Kiryas Joel, he explained, was private exclusion, which private organizations, like the synagogue and the schools, had the right to engage in. What the dissidents portrayed as an effort to kick them out of the village was a matter of access to the services provided by the community's private religious organizations, which those organizations had the right to control.

But while Wieder managed to make a case for distinguishing the public from the private side of the community, he was less successful in maintaining the distinction between religious and secular authority in the public domain. Under Sussman's prodding, Wieder admitted that while, "as a village, under the state constitution and the federal constitution, we are able—a village, a village is able to take someone to court, we, as a religious people, Jewish Satmar people, have an additional prohibition [not] to take any Jew or Satmar into court." In a rare moment of candor, Wieder allowed that this "creates a very difficult problem in handling people who do not comply with the building code, which," he hastened to add, "is a very important safety issue."[140] Sussman then got Wieder to parse the content of what he had just said, step by step. "In your last answer, sir, as I understood your answer, you stated in sum and substance that the village of Kiryas Joel had the authority, but that apart from that authority, there were religious considerations that came into play as to whether you would do that or not. Is that correct?" Sussman queried. To which Wieder responded, "We, as the village board members, have additional restrictions, which we couldn't do that, yes." "And your restrictions that you're referring to are religious in nature, yes?" Sussman further queried. "Yes," Wieder responded. "And your religious restrictions cause you not to go and initiate court action in a secular court?," Sussman clarified. Wieder replied, "That is correct."[141]

Recognizing the trap Sussman had set, Wieder then tried to wriggle out of it. To Sussman's next question—"So when you're sitting on the village board, sir, you're considering religious factors in the discharge of that duty. Is that correct?"—Wieder emphatically answered, "No," adding, somewhat confusingly, that he believed he had "a first amendment right" to act on his religious convictions.[142]

At this point, Sussman switched the topic, but the cat was already out of the bag. All of the carefully constructed defenses of the village's actions that Wieder and his defense team had formulated foundered on his admission that, in his official capacity, he adhered to the religious prohibition against secular adjudications of internal disputes. Although he had sought to justify his reliance on religious considerations as a legitimate exercise of his right to religious liberty, his admission clearly suggested that, as deputy mayor, he placed religious above secular law. The initial complaint had not made an Establishment Clause claim. But as the litigation developed, Sussman edged ever closer to asserting that the village was acting in violation of the Establishment Clause, and that was exactly what Wieder's admission seemed to confirm, at least implicitly.

Wieder, for his part, was appealing to a different vision of the Free Exercise and Establishment Clauses, one that was then being embraced by many religious conservatives in America, and by some on the left as well. It was a given that people of faith, including religious leaders, have the right to hold political office. Less certain was whether public officials have the right to act on considerations of faith. The exchange between Sussman and Wieder reflected the rift that was emerging between competing approaches to the religion clauses of the Constitution, one of which affirmed the right of public officials to act on their faith in discharging their official duties, the other of which refuted it.

At the same time, the colloquy was a fascinating illustration of the extent of legal learning that had taken place in Kiryas Joel by the late 1990s. Wieder's testimony displayed his knowledge about and belief in the First Amendment, another telling instance of the absorption of American cultural norms. At the same time, it threatened to prove that his actions had violated the First Amendment.

Judge Rakoff was clearly alert to this possibility. During a sidebar the following day, he referred to Wieder's admission that he factored religious considerations into his official decisions and asked a pointed question: "Why isn't that a patent violation of church and state?" The defendants' lawyer, Susan Necheles, replied that it is not a patent violation of church and state for a government official to act in accord with his religious beliefs when they conflict with government policy. She recalled the example of renowned Catholic priest Father Robert Drinan, whom she described as "my childhood hero, . . . opposing the Vietnam War when he was a Congressman." Likewise, she observed: "Many people who are D.A.s will not ask for the death penalty . . . on religious grounds," implying that these were examples of the kind of First Amendment rights that Wieder had invoked.

Judge Rakoff, however, wasn't buying the analogy. "I think that is a completely improper analysis," he countered, and offered his own interpretation of Wieder's fateful words. "What he is saying, as I understand it," Rakoff told the lawyers, out of the hearing of the jurors, "is, to draw a slightly more extreme analogy, if a man goes out and commits a robbery, and I'm the local DA, but my religion says you can't prosecute a fellow member of the religion, I, the local DA, will not prosecute that man because of my religious beliefs. That's what he appears to me to be saying." And that, Rakoff concluded, "is a patent violation of church and state."[143]

To Sussman, Rakoff's words were a clear sign that the judge was ready to agree with his argument that the village's actions against the dissidents constituted a violation of the principle of separation between religion and state. Decades later, reflecting on what happened in the trial, Sussman remembers Rakoff as having stated at this point in the proceedings, "I think that I can declare this village unconstitutional on the basis of what I've heard because they're plainly enforcing the law in a way that's entirely dictated by religion."[144] In fact, no such statement appears in the transcript of the hearing, and Sussman's examination of

Wieder actually continued for many hours after the sidebar. But Sussman had good reason to feel optimistic that Rakoff would instruct the jury to interpret the Free Exercise and Equal Protection Clauses, and possibly the Establishment Clause as well, in ways that were supportive of the dissidents. It came as little surprise to him, then, that the village soon indicated it wanted to settle.

What happened next, however, did surprise him, bitterly. In his account, this was "the pivotal moment," not just in the trial, but in the entire history of the KJ dissident movement. As he recalls that moment, he and his clients went into a small room in the new federal courthouse at Pearl Street in Lower Manhattan. There, Sussman says he told his clients, "Guys, this is it. You have them. We did it. You want me to ask the judge to dissolve the village? He's going to dissolve the village. The village cannot function, it's unconstitutional. He understands it. It's simply a religiously controlled entity and it's not permissible."[145] And yet, rather than leap at the opportunity, his clients declined to ask the judge to order the village legally dissolved.

To Dissolve or Not to Dissolve

The dissidents did not reject the opportunity that Sussman presented to them right away. This was, after all, what they had been pursuing for years. As Sussman recalls the events, his clients were initially "in a state of shock." But soon it was he who entered into a state of shock when his clients refused to ask for the village's dissolution. "What can we get, Michael?" he recalls Zalman Waldman asking him when they first entered the conference room. "We can get the end of the village! What more do we want?" Sussman yelled out. The answer was that they wanted less. "Can we get approval for our synagogue? Can we get money?" Sussman recalls them asking. He assured them they could, but cautioned: "This is your chance, gentlemen; we've worked for the last years for this, the record's there, the judge is there, make sure, you're not gonna get, we may not get this chance in our life again."

Whether this was an accurate description of what was actually said on that fateful day or an embroidered memory may never be known.

Nor can we know with certainty why the dissidents turned the opportunity down. Perhaps this was an illustration of the oft-asserted point that participants in internal group conflicts prefer the methods of alternative dispute resolution to the winner-take-all approach of litigation. Perhaps the dissidents, unlike Sussman, did not actually want to detonate the nuclear option of destroying the village, at that time. Perhaps they were scared—of the rupture they might precipitate, of the retaliation they could face, or of the awesome power they would be exercising if they pursued this option, which would stand in opposition to everything they claimed to believe about the exercise of secular power. Or perhaps they simply failed to understand the stakes of the decision they were making and mistakenly believed they would be able to obtain what they wanted through a negotiated settlement, without taking the drastic step of demanding a court-ordered dissolution of the village.

Whatever the true reason was, Sussman would turn out to be right that this was the dissidents' last chance to get the village dissolved. He was also right that agreeing to a settlement was a decision the dissidents would come to regret. That regret would come later, though not much later. For a brief shining moment, as reported in the local paper, there was a shared sense of hope that at long last a peace treaty or, at the very least, a truce between the two sides had been forged.

In keeping with the new—and fleeting—spirit of conflict avoidance, the terms of the truce were hashed out not by lawyers, but by the community's religious leaders. Over the ensuing weekend, intensive settlement negotiations were conducted in Williamsburg, presided over by Usher Anshel Katz, a Brooklyn-based rabbi deemed acceptable to both sides. All of the key players participated in what was billed as a "global" settlement designed to bring an end to all disputes between the dissidents and the KJ establishment. This included the named parties in the *Khal Charidim* litigation (Zalman Waldman, Meyer Deutsch, and Abraham Weinstock, and defendant Abe Wieder), the named parties in the *Waldman I* lawsuit (Joseph Waldman and two other members of the newly formed dissident Committee for the Well-Being of Kiryas Joel), dissident activists Ben Zion Friedman, Chaim Hochhauser, and Yosef Hirsch, and mainstream leader David Eckstein, who, alongside Wieder, presided over the board of the KJ synagogue.[146] The absence of any lawyers at the meeting signified the shared intent of the parties, at least for the moment, to retreat from the public realm of secular law and submit the controversy to rabbinic authority.

The terms of the settlement were announced by Sussman in court the following Monday, interrupting the continuation of Wieder's testimony. They included, in addition to the dismissal of *Waldman I* and the federal *Khal Charidim* case, an agreement on the part of the village of Kiryas Joel not to discriminate against anyone on the basis of their religion; its further agreement that people would serve on only one municipal or public school board at a time; the immediate issuance of a permit by the village to allow the "dissidents" or Congregation Khal Charidim to use the synagogue and a mikvah at 3 Van Buren Drive; the creation of a community resolution board to negotiate solutions to disputes; an agreement on the part of the Khal Charidim members to use this dispute resolution system to solve problems and not to go to the newspapers or secular courts (with the critical proviso that Khal Charidim would expel anyone who violates this provision); and, last and surely not least, the payment of $300,000 to Khal Charidim. As Judge Rakoff sagely observed upon reviewing it, "I think this sounds like a good settlement. But all settlements are only as good as the good will of the people behind them." He concluded on a half-hopeful note: "I look forward to hearing that the settlement has gone very well and that there is nothing for me to resolve."[147]

Needless to say, this was wishful thinking. Almost immediately, the settlement broke down, with each side accusing the other of violating its letter and spirit. The sticking points for the dissidents primarily concerned the failure of the village to issue a certificate of occupancy (CO) for Khal Charidim to operate. The village maintained that the agreement to issue a CO to Khal Charidim was contingent on its satisfying the safety standards prescribed by state law, which it had yet to do. When the parties returned to court to litigate their continued grievances, Judge Rakoff found persuasive the argument that a settlement agreement could not override state safety standards. The parties, he ruled, would have to "mutually agree upon a State Building Inspector" to conduct an inspection and determine whether safety standards were satisfied. Only then would the village be required to permit Khal Charidim to operate its synagogue and mivkah on the premises.[148]

Another grievance motivating the Khal Charidim group to return to court was the failure of the village to allow two dissident representatives to inspect the village books, which, they maintained, continued to be withheld from dissidents. In particular, they claimed that public housing units were being denied to dissidents in discriminatory fashion. They begged the court to go forward with the *Waldman I* litigation despite the settlement's agreement to dismiss it along with the *Khal Charidim* case. Judge Rakoff agreed to this request, persuaded by the argument that the Housing Authority could not be bound by the settlement agreement since it had not been a party to the *Khal Charidim* litigation.[149]

By the same token, the dissidents' lawyers argued that Bnai Yoel was not a party to the *Khal Charidim* litigation and therefore could not be bound by the settlement agreement. It was on this point that the settlement completely broke down. All agreed that the dissidents had pledged to expel anyone from the Khal Charidim Congregation who violated the terms of the settlement. But not all those who identified with Bnai Yoel were members of Khal Charidim. Those who weren't members of Khal Charidim would not be subject to this sanction. "The unresolved vital issue," David Eckstein asserted in a statement submitted to the court, "was how to identify the entire dissident group and to force the dissident group to make the agreement effective as to everyone in the dissident group." Limiting enforcement powers to Khal Charidim was inadequate, he explained, because members of existing groups unaffiliated with Khal Charidim would escape its sanctions. They might even "form new congregations for the sole purpose of avoiding the agreement."[150]

Village leaders pointed to the transcript of the judicial proceedings where the settlement had been announced. There, it was recorded that Sussman, reading aloud the terms, stated that "Khal Charidim certifies that if its members violate that provision, it will take action to expel those individuals from the congregation, which it believes as a private organization it can do, and *it will take further action with regard to atten-dance at the congregation B'Nai Yoel.*" Sussman was then interrupted by Mr. Miranda, one of the village lawyers, who posed the crucial question: "Since one of your plaintiffs is on the board of B'Nai Yoel, Mr. Wein-stock, are you also speaking on behalf of by B'Nai Yoel and binding them?" At that point, Zalman Waldman interjected, "He is not on the board of B'Nai Yoel," while Yosef Hirsch was recorded as saying, "The B'Nai Yoel agreed to all of this." "No problem," Zalman then stated, as Hirsch went on to declare: "And they will have to sign it."[151]

These statements made at the conclusion of the trial might have seemed to confirm the existence of an obligation on the part of Bnai Yoel. But Judge Rakoff brushed Zalman's and Hirsch's statements off. "We can't have these side discussions of semiofficial voices present," he declared, leaving the intent of both the parties and the court with re-spect to this crucial issue mired in ambiguity.[152]

More to the point, when Khal Charidim later returned to court to argue that the village and Wieder should be found in contempt of court because of their refusal to abide by the settlement's terms, Rakoff made a hard-edged ruling. There was no authority, he declared, for binding Bnai Yoel, just as there was no authority for binding the Housing Au-thority, because neither had been a party to the litigation. The irony was that it was a secular court that was making the determination that Bnai Yoel was not, and could not be, bound. As far as the village was con-cerned, the key aim of the settlement was to ensure that any further disputes would be submitted to private arbitration by Rabbi Katz—and that internal disputes would never again be brought to secular courts. According to them, "the Bnai Yoel issue" was itself an issue that should be referred to Rabbi Katz, otherwise the whole purpose of that provi-sion would be defeated.

In the midst of all this back and forth, and with the prospect of a last-ing agreement appearing ever more fleeting, yet another lawsuit was filed by Sussman, with Joseph Waldman as the lead plaintiff. *Waldman II*, as it was referred to in subsequent litigation, was the most frontal challenge to the village yet. In no uncertain terms, the complaint as-serted that the village was a "theocracy" and sought a total dissolution of the village on the grounds that its very existence violated the Establishment Clause. The case was initially assigned to Barrington Parker, who had presided over the *Khal Charidim* lawsuit, before it too was transferred to Judge Rakoff. In an early ruling in *Waldman II*, Judge Parker agreed to grant an injunction requiring the removal of the polling booths from the Yetev Lev Congregation.[153] Once transferred to Rakoff, however, the case was dismissed on the grounds that it was an attempt to relitigate the dispute that had already been settled. Notwithstanding Sussman's best efforts, Rakoff concluded that the plaintiffs had failed to distinguish their new claims from their old ones.[154] On this basis, he rejected the renewed attempt to get an airing of the dissidents' grievances before a secular court.

The appeal of Rakoff's decision dismissing *Waldman II* fared no better. The opinion delivered by the Second Circuit Court of Appeals was written by Judge Guido Calabresi, yet another legal actor in the drama who was of Jewish origin.[155] Judge Calabresi began his opinion by noting: "The behavior Waldman alleges is deeply troubling in that, if true, it describes a town in which public institutions are routinely used as instruments of the dominant religious group and in which members of dissident groups are constantly subjected to threats and discrimination at the hands of their local government."[156] But he agreed with Rakoff that the dissidents had forfeited their right to present the truth (or their version of it) by accepting the settlement of *Khal Charidim*. Only if a fresh dispute arose would there be cause for a court to hear a case brought by the dissidents against the village of Kiryas Joel.

In point of fact, Sussman's earlier prediction was right. The dissidents would never again be granted the opportunity to make the case that the village's retaliatory actions against them constituted a violation of their rights or an establishment of religion. Sussman mounted numerous attempts over the next decade and a half to introduce fresh claims, but Judge Rakoff rejected each one on the grounds of *res judicata* (Latin for the matter already judged).

Why the dissidents were unwilling to seek the dissolution of the village when they had the chance to do so, at the moment of the settlement negotiations, remains unclear. Perhaps their threats to dissolve the village were merely a ploy on the part of the dissidents to get their own shul and moysdes. Perhaps they feared the consequences that would result if they succeeded in getting a court to order the village's dissolution. Perhaps, at the end of the day, they preferred to stay within the confines of their own shtetl, even if ruled by an imperfect but familiar group of Satmar Hasidim.

These questions remain puzzling. The one point that is clear is that the short-lived settlement did not lead the dissidents to cease from political agitation. Indeed, the turn of the century brought a new cycle of frenetic political and legal conflict. In 1998, a year after the settlement debacle, Leibish Lefkowitz died and Abe Wieder was elevated to the position of mayor. A year later, the third statute authorizing the school district, enacted in 1997, was declared by the state's highest court in the case of *Grumet v. Pataki* to be unconstitutional. Meanwhile, the KJ dissidents continued to form new organizations under whose names they brought still more lawsuits.

All of this was but a prelude to an event in 1999 that triggered perhaps the most frenzied round of litigation to take place in the Satmar community: the decision by Moshe Teitelbaum to pass over his eldest son Aaron in favor of his younger son Zalman Leib to take his place as Rov of Williamsburg—and heir apparent to the Satmar throne. Throughout all of this turmoil, the village of Kiryas Joel continued to grow, expand, and thrive, demonstrating the steadfastness and resilience in the face of conflict that marked it from the outset.

PART III

CONFLICT, COMPETITION, AND THE FUTURE OF KIRYAS JOEL

CHAPTER 7

"Two Kings Serving the Same Crown"

THE GREAT SCHISM IN KIRYAS JOEL AND BEYOND

The appointment of Zalman Leib as chief rabbi of Williamsburg added yet another layer of conflict to KJ. His father Moshe, as Samuel Heilman notes in his book on Hasidic succession, was in a state of physical and cognitive decline by the mid-1990s. Heilman further reports that Moshe had been making explicit plans to set in place his eldest son, Aaron, as heir to the entire empire, consistent with the practice of Hasidic dynasties. But the tide of history turned abruptly. For reasons that have never been fully explained, sometime during the spring of 1999, Moshe decided not to appoint Aaron as sole heir in the tradition of dynastic Hasidic succession, but rather to divide the Satmar kingdom into two: Aaron would remain the chief rabbi in KJ; Zalman Leib, who had been serving as the head of the Satmar community in Jerusalem, was called back to serve as rabbi and head of the yeshivah for the main Yetev Lev Congregation in Williamsburg. On June 2, Moshe gathered a small group of leaders and declared: "I hereby reveal my intention publicly in front of the heads of the holy community that I am appointing my son, the great sage, R. Zalman Leib Shlit"a, as rabbi in our community—here in Williamsburg—and his hand is like my hand: to stand at the head of all of the Torah moysdes, be it the yeshivah, the Talmud Torah or the

1989.0644.082

FIGURE 7.1. R. Moshe Teitelbaum, Second Satmar Rebbe.
Courtesy of the National Museum of American History.

Beis Ruchel institutions." Several weeks later, on June 17, the appointment was formalized before a larger group of community leaders at
Moshe's house in Williamsburg.[1]

Der Yid announced that the news was received with "great joy by the
members of the community."[2] But in fact, it came as a shock to many in
the Satmar world who had long assumed that Aaron's appointment as
rabbi of KJ in 1984 presaged his assumption of his father's position as
Satmar Rebbe. The impact of Moshe's decision in 1999 was immediate.
It raised the specter, as Joel Teitelbaum's father warned when he appointed his eldest son town rabbi and told Joel to leave town, of "two
kings serving the same crown." Eschewing this warning, Moshe made a
decision that deepened an emerging rivalry between KJ, where Aaron
and his supporters (the Aronis) were long established, and Williamsburg, where Zalman and his supporters (the Zalis) would base their
new operation. Many KJ dissidents would become Zalis; others, in observance of the time-honored maxim that the enemy of my enemy is my
friend, could be counted as loose allies of the Zali camp. In this way, the
previous fighting between Aaron's followers and opponents inside KJ
became part of a larger schism between the Zalis and Aronis that would
divide the Satmar community worldwide.

Each brother had his own inner circle, whose members had a vested
interest in the success of their candidate in what was shaping up as an
even fiercer battle over leadership in the Satmar community than what
followed the death of R. Yoelish in 1979. With Moshe in decline, han-
dlers of the two contenders understood that what was at stake was not
merely dominance in one or the other of the main capitals, but control
over the worldwide empire. This meant access to the considerable financial holdings of the empire, estimated to be in the hundreds of millions
of dollars.

A key figure in the brewing struggle in the summer of 1999 was Moshe
"Gabbai" Friedman, who was one of the top aides to Moshe Teitelbaum.
The European-born Friedman had survived the Second World War in
hiding in Budapest before making his way to the United States as an
adolescent in 1955. He grew up in Williamsburg in close proximity to

R. Yoelish, to whom he became close. In 1975, Friedman heeded the rebbe's desires and purchased a home in Kiryas Joel.[3]

Following the death of R. Yoelish four years later, Friedman became the chief lieutenant to Moshe Teitelbaum. Among other assignments, he was deeply involved in the leading Satmar Yiddish newspaper, *Der Yid*, of which he is the publisher today. Speculation has it that it was Friedman who persuaded Moshe to divide the empire in 1999 so as to avoid being dismissed by Aaron, who was far more experienced in leading the community than Zalman Leib was. Friedman's own explanation for the divide, as we noted in chapter 1, is something of a legend—and reflects the way in which Satmars have assimilated into the capitalist culture of America. In reflecting on Moshe's decision years after the event, Friedman noted that the Satmar world had grown dramatically at that point in time, reaching a population of a hundred thousand a half century after the Second World War. The Satmar empire contained rich networks of moysdes with combined budgets in the tens of millions of dollars. Not only would it be difficult, Friedman argued, for one person to manage the whole operation, but, he continued, "it's good that there are two hasidic courts." The resulting division would allow the two sides not only to tend their flocks, but to improve them. Rather than a single dynasty under a charismatic rebbe's control, as was long-standing Hasidic practice, Friedman was suggesting an American-style business plan based on free competition between the main camps.[4]

Not all bought into the notion that competition was good for the Satmars. Aaron's camp believed that, as a matter of seniority and erudition, he was the most appropriate successor to his father—and worthy of serving (or ruling) the entire kingdom. His followers greeted Moshe's decision as a declaration of war between followers of the two sons. Over the next year, the two camps solidified into enemy factions, with each seeking to exclude the other from control of key institutions. What resulted was a dizzying series of legal maneuvers, amounting to an increasingly intense and belligerent chess game between the competing sides. Each demonstrated very considerable skill in playing the game against the other, using every trick in the book to gain an advantage.

Recourse to Gentile Courts:
The Labyrinth of Litigation

In Kiryas Joel, Aaron Teitelbaum already had ample experience in dealing with political opponents. In particular, he and his team had a large
stable of lawyers who could help them navigate state and federal courts.
A decade and a half of fierce legal battles with KJ dissidents, Grumet,
and Monroe had endowed the leaders in KJ with a considerable amount
of knowledge of the American legal system. They understood by now
that turning to the courts was a highly effective way to stymie the opposition. In the past, they had mainly been on the receiving end of litigation, playing defense as they were sued, alternately, by the Monroe
School District, the school bus drivers' union, the New York State School
Board Association and Grumet, and the endlessly proliferating dissident organizations. Having been defendants in so many lawsuits, they
realized that initiating litigation was a powerful weapon even if they did
not win. In keeping with this lesson, they already had initiated some
legal actions themselves, including the eviction proceeding against
Faiga and the Rebbetsin's shul and the enforcement actions against Khal
Charidim. They knew their way around the courtroom by the end of
the 1990s. And they understood full well that internal grievances in
the community would end up aired before American state courts.

More specifically, they realized that litigation gave leverage to the
party that lacked effective control over communal resources over the
party in current possession of them. In KJ, they were the party in control, and it was therefore the KJ dissidents who resorted to litigation
most often. Now the positions were reversed. When the Zalis seized
control of the main synagogue in Brooklyn and branded the Aronis as
dissidents, the KJ-based faction knew exactly what to do: follow the
legal playbook of the KJ dissidents.

In addition to using their considerable legal savvy, the leaders in KJ
also understood the power of the press. To promote their perspective,
the Aronis established a new Yiddish newspaper, *Der Blat*, in 1999 to
serve as a counterweight to the existing *Der Yid*. Armed with these two

FIGURE 7.2. Hasid Kissing the Hand of R. Aaron Teitelbaum. Courtesy of Jackson Krule.

sets of resources, the tools of the media and the tools of the American legal system, they went to battle with the Brooklyn-based Zalis and their KJ allies.

Meanwhile, in Williamsburg, the board of the Yetev Lev Congregation was divided. In the wake of the death in 1998 of Leibish Lefkowitz (who had served not only as KJ's mayor, but also as president of the Williamsburg-based Yetev Lev), two men had shared leadership of the congregation: Berl Friedman, son of Lipa Friedman, the former president of the Williamsburg congregation (no relation to Moshe Gabbai Friedman), and Jeno (or Jacob or Yaakov) Kahan (sometimes rendered Kahana), another active member of the synagogue board.[5] This shared governance arrangement, which lasted for less than two years, from 1999 until the end of 2000, would become the source of profound conflict in the wider Satmar community.

Berl Friedman was a staunch supporter of Aaron, and the Aronis were staunch supporters of his. According to them, Friedman was the sole president of the Williamsburg congregation, having been appointed to that position by Moshe after Leibish Lefkowitz died. By contrast, the

Zalis asserted that Kahan was appointed as copresident at the same time. The jockeying for control picked up speed in late 2000 when Kahan and another Williamsburg-based Zali, Shaul Perlstein, circulated a so-called loyalty pledge (also sometimes referred to as "the notorious writ of oath"). The pledge required all congregation members to pledge their allegiance to Zalman Leib in writing.[6] When Friedman and other Aroni members of the board refused to sign, the battle lines between "the Friedman faction" (aka the Aronis) and "the Kahan faction" (aka the Zalis) were drawn.

Within a few days after the loyalty pledge was issued, on January 14, 2001, the Friedman faction gathered and, in the name of the board of the Williamsburg congregation, resolved to hold a new election for president and members of the board. Although this meeting took place in Brooklyn and addressed the fate of the Brooklyn synagogue, prominent members of Kiryas Joel, including Abe Wieder and David Eckstein, were present and indeed prominent representatives of R. Aaron's interests.[7] Not present at the meeting were any members of the Kahan faction, who held their own meeting in the name of the board of the Williamsburg congregation days later at which they announced their own synagogue board election plan.

The dueling synagogue board elections were both scheduled for mid-May. The voting rules established by the Friedman-led Aroni faction allowed all Satmars in the New York area to vote as long as they presented their ballots in person on May 12 or 13. The Zali-Kahan faction permitted mail-in ballots and proxy votes to be cast over the course of May 13–23, but limited the right to vote to members of the Williamsburg congregation, excluding Satmars who resided in KJ, Monsey, or Spring Valley.[8] On May 18, each side announced the results of its election.[9] To no one's surprise, Berl Friedman was declared the winner of the Aroni election, and Jeno Kahan won the election staged by the Zalis. The latter immediately took possession of the Williamsburg board offices, books, and records, which gave him de facto control over the board's business activities.[10] It was at this point that the Aronis found themselves, in Brooklyn, in much the same position in which the dissidents found themselves in the village: ousted from the community's religious institutions and branded as dissidents by the party that was in physical possession and control.

As the Williamsburg congregation descended into chaos, the entire community was engulfed by a sense of ominous change. Not only was Moshe in an infirm state, which heightened the Aronis' suspicion that he was being manipulated to side with the Zalis, but on June 2, the Rebbetsin, Alta Faiga, died, signaling the end of an era. She was the most palpable link to her husband and his generation and, to her many followers, a revered elder, a leader in her own right. Tensions between her and Moshe had generated the first wave of opposition in Kiryas Joel in 1979–1980. Now, more than two decades later, in the year of her death, the opposition assumed new and more acrimonious forms. Four days after she passed, the first contested mayoral election in Kiryas Joel took place, pitting incumbent mayor Abe Wieder against dissident Mendel Schwimmer.[11] Wieder won 57 percent of the vote, but Schwimmer's showing pointed to a large Zali minority in the village.

The political opposition inside KJ spilled over into the wider political world of Orange County when the dissidents' irrepressible attorney, Michael Sussman, decided to run for the position of Orange County executive. He lost, but garnered nearly 40 percent of the county-wide vote and an even higher percentage in KJ, thanks in good measure to the support of the Zalis and other KJ dissidents, whom he vividly recalls crowding into a campaign rally held in the Brooklyn Naval Yard, where they hoisted him up in a chair and paraded him before a crowd of twenty thousand supporters.[12]

That wider political world had changed in a number of ways since the Satmars had first begun interacting with American state and federal officials. Following the Reagan years, during which KJ took shape, eight years of the Clinton administration had ended in what was then, in 2000, the most contested presidential election in American history. Democratic candidate Albert Gore won the popular vote against Republican candidate George W. Bush, but election night returns in Florida favored Bush by such a narrow margin that a recount was required, which would determine who had won the election nationwide. The political battle quickly descended into a bitter legal contest as the Bush campaign challenged the recount process that Gore had initiated. Each side marshaled its own team of lawyers to challenge and defend the validity of the recount under way, but one team (Bush's) was noticeably more aggressive in its legal tactics than the other.[13] In short order, the case went to the Supreme Court, which ruled that the recount process violated the Equal Protection Clause of the Constitution and that no alternative method could be used. In so doing, the Court effectively handed the victory to Bush. It was one of the most controversial judicial decisions in American history.

There was, of course, no causal connection between the American crisis over political succession and the succession crisis in the Satmar world that was occurring at the same time. The Aronis and the Zalis had been on a collision course since at least since 1999, when Zalman was installed as Williamsburg's chief rabbi. The events that led up to the 2000 fight over who was the real president of the Williamsburg congregation—a proxy fight for the bigger question of who was the heir to the Rebbe's throne—would have occurred with or without the spectacle of *Bush v. Gore*. But in hindsight, the temporal parallels are uncanny. Both contests over political succession began in 1999 and came to a head at the end of 2000. The American presidential election and the Satmar presidential election were separated by just a few months. Between November, when the American election took place, and December, when the Supreme Court resolved the controversy in favor of Bush, the Zalis circulated the "notorious writ of oath" demanding a pledge of loyalty to Zalman, and the Friedman-Aroni faction plotted its response. The Aronis and the Zalis announced their dueling presidential elections in mid-January 2001, just a few days before Bush's inauguration, thus precipitating their own election dispute, which, like the American presidential contest, soon devolved into a legal dispute, with each side amassing a team of lawyers, one of which (the Aronis', in the case of the Satmars) was noticeably more aggressive in its legal tactics than the other.

There was one crucial difference between the two election disputes: the contest between the Aronis and the Zalis dragged on for ten years, while *Bush v. Gore* was concluded in a little over two months. And in *Bush v. Gore*, it was the team with the more aggressive lawyers that won, while the opposite was true in the case of the Aronis versus the Zalis. Thanks to the former's aggressive legal tactics, the Satmar election litigation became even more labyrinthine than either the American election litigation or any of the previous or succeeding litigations between the KJ establishment and the KJ dissidents. But while their end dates were a decade apart, their start dates both hovered around 2001, a year that would prove to be as fateful for American politics as it was for the Satmars.

More important than the temporal parallels are the structural and thematic parallels between the two succession crises. As different as the two political systems are—one ostensibly a democracy governed by secular law, the other a community governed by religious law and a supposedly all-powerful rebbe—both relied on elections, and both proved incapable of preventing indeterminate outcomes to elections when the populace was sharply divided. In both contexts, the succession crisis was preceded by increasing political polarization that expressed itself in a bitter split between two sides, which made power-sharing arrangements and compromise an impossibility. The result in both cases was races so close, with voting procedures so unreliable, that it was virtually impossible to tell who the real winner was.

Most important, the absence of a clear outcome in each case led one party to turn to the judiciary to settle the dispute. In this regard, the Satmar succession crisis became a microcosm of the political controversy that was emerging in the United States over the role of the judiciary in dealing with political matters. More specifically, the question that was crystallizing in the winter of 2000–2001 was how courts should deal with disputed election results—if they should intervene at all. In the dispute over the American presidential race, the controversy was provoked by the fact that the judiciary did intervene, in heavy-handed fashion. The Supreme Court's decision brought eight years of Democratic administration to an end, returning the presidency to a Republican administration that sought to continue the conservative economic and foreign policies of Ronald Reagan and George Bush Sr. The spectacle of a court dominated by conservative Republican appointees deciding the election in favor of the Republican candidate on the basis of what was widely perceived to be a flimsy legal argument provoked outrage. Within the legal world, that outrage coalesced around the view that the decision ran afoul of the "political question doctrine"—a longstanding judicial maxim that maintains that courts should not decide political questions because, as the courts put it, political questions are "nonjusticiable."

In this regard, the contemporaneous Satmar controversy made for an interesting juxtaposition. Just as legal critics of *Bush v. Gore* upheld the political question doctrine as a basis for concluding that the courts should not intervene in the electoral process, the courts that were called upon to adjudicate the Satmar election dispute invoked the "religious question doctrine," another American legal doctrine, which maintains that religious questions are nonjusticiable, that is, not to be decided by secular courts. But whereas the political question doctrine fell on deaf ears, the religious question doctrine was eagerly latched onto by judges fatigued by the Satmars' endless disputes. A dizzying number of New York State judges were dragged into the Satmars' succession controversy as a result of the Aronis' aggressive forum shopping, which had them bouncing from the Kings County courts, where Brooklyn is located, to the courts in Orange County, the seat of Kiryas Joel. All told, nine separate lawsuits would be filed seeking a resolution to the question of who the real president of the Williamsburg synagogue was, seven by the Aronis and two by the Zalis, heard in a wide array of courtrooms. With one telling exception, they all concluded in rulings that judges could not adjudicate the dispute without deciding an essentially religious question, in contravention of the constitutional principles of religious freedom and separation between religion and state.

The consequence of these rulings was to permit the Zalis to remain in control of the Williamsburg institutions. To refuse to intervene was, in effect, to allow the party that had seized power to remain in place. This raised the troubling possibility that there is no way for courts to avoid deciding contested elections. Thus, the ultimate question raised by the juxtaposition of *Bush v. Gore* and the Zalis versus the Aronis was not just whether the courts should intervene, but whether it was possible for them not to.

Somewhat paradoxically, the decision not to decide the Satmar election controversy took four years for the New York courts to render, and another three years to be definitively affirmed by the state's highest court, with yet another three years given over to ancillary litigation. By contrast, the decision to decide the outcome of the American presidential election in *Bush v. Gore* was executed and completed within a matter of weeks. Although that seemed like a painfully long time to determine the outcome of an American presidential election, it was nothing compared to the bitter decade-long legal battle that enveloped the Aronis and the Zalis.

The refusal to adjudicate their dispute was not a foregone conclusion. Notwithstanding the religious question doctrine, an equally venerable doctrine holds that judges can and should intervene in disputes over church property and governance if the disputes can be resolved by "neutral principles" of secular law. In the case of the Williamsburg congregation, there was a strong argument to be made that the validity of the dueling synagogue board elections was just the sort of question that could be resolved by neutral legal principles without deciding religious questions. There were other legal strategies available to the Aronis as well. They had many fine lawyers who were perfectly capable of spinning these arguments, and they might well have succeeded in advancing them, were it not for the antics of some members of their legal team.

One of the most unusual members of the team was a man named Ravi Batra, who, unlike many of the other lawyers involved in the Satmars' legal intrigues, lacked a fancy legal pedigree. He maintained an office in the Little India neighborhood of Manhattan and, according to a profile in the *New York Times*, boasted of his skill at helping "lawyers seeking an edge in the unfamiliar world of the Brooklyn courts" by using his personal connections with the judges in the system to gain advantage—a skill that backfired spectacularly in this particular case.[14] He was the first lawyer hired by the Aronis to represent them in their legal challenge to the Zalis' seizure of control in Brooklyn. The basic theory of the case that he was hired to pursue was a good one, one that might well have circumvented the religious question doctrine by asking the court not to decide the validity of the competing elections but rather, to order the Zalis to submit the dispute to the arbitration of a rabbinical court.

This was the dispute-resolution method ostensibly favored by both the Satmars and the American legal system. While frequently honored in the breach, the principle that internal disputes should not be presented to gentile courts continued to be regarded as a vital one by both the Aronis and the Zalis. The problem was that they could not agree upon a neutral rabbinic tribunal. Nevertheless, Satmars on both sides continued to profess their belief in the long-standing Jewish doctrine that disputes among members of the community should not be brought before gentile courts.

That was also the policy strongly favored by the American legal system, not only because of the concerns that underlay the religious question doctrine, but also because of a more general policy in favor of private dispute resolution, which had been aggressively pursued since the early days of the Reagan administration. Private arbitration was a prime example of how Reaganomics, fueled by anti-lawsuit and pro-business libertarian policies, dovetailed with the Satmars' stated preference to be ruled by private, non-state, law.[15]

In keeping with that ostensible preference, the Aronis had first taken their challenge to the validity of Kahan's election to a rabbinical court, in Brooklyn. It was only after the Zalis refused to respond to three summonses that the rabbinical court resorted to by the Aronis authorized them to launch an "Article 75 proceeding," the state's legal mechanism for compelling parties bound by arbitration agreements to submit to an arbitration proceeding. Thus, the initial suit filed by the Friedman faction against the Zalis simply sought a judicial order to submit the dispute to rabbinical arbitration.

That was a strategy that neatly avoided the need for the court to decide any religious questions.[16] And it might have worked, but for the fact that the lawyer selected to pursue this strategy—Ravi Batra—and the person the Aronis selected to bring the petition to compel submission to arbitration, a man by the name of Jacob Brach, engaged in such obstreperous behavior that it drew the ire of the judge, Melvin Barasch, who was assigned to hear the case. Barasch made a series of pretrial rulings that cast the die against them. Jacob Brach (no relation to Nachman Brach, whose cases against the Brooklyn congregation and *Der Yid* were still ongoing) was a curious choice to represent the Aronis. He had only recently finished out a sentence for engaging in business fraud and would forever be referred to by the Zalis in the court proceedings as "convicted felon" Brach.

At the very beginning of the court proceedings, faced with requests from the banks to decide who had authority to write checks on behalf of the synagogue, before the case was even scheduled for trial, Justice Barasch issued interim orders granting the Zalis the right to control the synagogue's day-to-day business affairs, including the exclusive right to sell synagogue seats for the upcoming high holidays. The order further decreed that if anyone else purported to sell seats, they would be held in contempt of court. This order was promptly violated by the Aroni faction on the advice of their lawyer. That created a perfect opening for contempt charges to be brought against Brach by the Zalis' lead attorney, a prominent New York business litigator by the name of Scott Mollen. Mollen, whose toney Park Avenue firm stands at the corner of the aptly named Sholem Aleichem Place in Manhattan, stood as Ravi Batra's opposite in almost every way. A polished, highly respected member of the New York Bar, Mollen later commented he had never seen such questionable legal tricks and ploys in a case as he witnessed being employed by the parade of lawyers who ended up representing the Aronis in their relentless legal battle against the Zalis—and he had represented Leona Helmsley and Donald Trump![17]

The contempt proceedings initiated by Mollen took place at the very beginning of the Aroni versus Zali litigation. But, in ways that could only fully be seen in hindsight, they determined what the ultimate outcome of this litigation ten years later would be. By granting the Zalis de facto control over the synagogue's day-to-day business, the court cemented the facts on the ground and thereby converted the de facto power relations in Brooklyn, where the Zalis, thanks to the court, maintained the upper hand, into a legally unchallengeable reality. This was not so dissimilar to what occurred in *Bush v. Gore*, where the Court's decision to stop the recount left in place a dubious count that gave Bush the lead over Gore by 537 votes. Although the Court adjudicated the latter case, while in the Satmar case the court purported to be making only an interim ruling and ultimately decided not to adjudicate the controversy, in both instances the courts' actions had the effect of leaving the facts on the ground in place, effectively insulating them from legal challenge.

Whether this was evidence that Justice Barasch was biased against them, as the Aronis repeatedly alleged, or simply a practical judgment call on Barasch's part may never be known. Judges routinely issue interim orders granting "temporary" rights of control to those who are in physical possession of the object of controversy. Regardless of Barasch's true motives, this was a decisive judgment, for it perpetuated the Zalis' physical control of the synagogue for the duration of the litigation. That meant that four years later, in 2004, when, following a circuitous course of litigation, Justice Barasch finally issued his decision holding that the court would not intervene to change the status quo, the status quo was precisely what he had decreed it would be back in the summer of 2001. Just as the stay that Nat Lewin succeeded in getting, preventing the KJ School District from being shut down pending the resolution of the *Grumet* litigation, proved to be critical in enabling the school to stay open, the issuance of the interim order granting de facto control over the Brooklyn synagogue to the Zalis proved to be the pivotal moment in the legal battle between the Zalis and Aronis. Similarly, the KJ dissidents' decision to accept the settlement in the *Khal Charidim* case proved to be the decisive moment in the KJ dissidents' battle against the KJ establishment. In each case, a judicial action other than an adjudication of the claims—the kind of procedural ruling that generally escapes public notice precisely because it is not regarded as a decisive judgment—established facts on the ground of the sort that are very difficult to reverse. Indeed, the longer they are allowed (by a court) to stand, the more irreversible they become.

Whether or not the Aronis were correct in their judgment that Barasch was biased against them, they clearly were correct to discern that his interim orders were fatal to their case. That perhaps explains why they decided to violate the orders, on the advice of their lawyer. Brach was the designated fall guy, a role he played to the hilt. Before a hearing on the first charge of contempt of court against Brach was held, Barasch issued a further order barring the Aronis from entering the Williamsburg synagogue for any purposes other than participating in religious services. With the high holidays approaching, Barasch was clearly apprehensive that there would be chaos in the synagogue and in the streets. Following the issuance of this order, on September 7, the Aronis fired Ravi Batra—but continued to engage in the very activities that Batra had encouraged and that Justice Barasch was trying to prevent.

Indeed, both sides were engaging in just the sort of dubious behavior that Barasch was concerned about. Chaos and even violence, as we have seen, were recurrent features of Satmar history. In the latest iteration of intra-Jewish conflict, the two brothers' followers went after each other with ungloved hands. Among the first-rank combatants was a third Teitelbaum brother, Lipa, Moshe's second son, who took the side of Zalman and did not hesitate to use his physical brawn against the Aronis. According to Brach, his own allegedly disruptive acts were entirely a response to Lipa Teitelbaum's physical violence in the synagogue. As he later testified, in broken English, "Whenever the Rebbe [Aaron] came in, Lipa Teitelbaum would stand up on the table and started hitting people." The police were repeatedly called in to restore peace to the Brooklyn synagogue, but, according to Brach, "nobody pressed charges because it's the Rebbe's son."[18]

A month later, matters intensified when Aroni leader David Eckstein came from KJ to the main, Zalman-aligned, shul in Williamsburg, where he was called out as a "moyser"—an informant against the Jewish community—and was allegedly kicked in the head by none other than Lipa Teitelbaum. According to the head of a private security firm employed to provide security guards at the services, "It was wild. There was a lot of shoving, pulling, and pushing, then a lot more punching."[19] Nevertheless, it was the Aronis' representative Brach, and Brach alone, who was accused of being in contempt of Justice Barasch's September 7 order. This time Brach was accused of criminal contempt.

By the time the parties assembled before Barasch for the hearing on the contempt charge, two weeks later, the terrorist attacks on the Twin

Towers had occurred, plunging the city of New York and the entire nation into a state of shock. Yet the Aronis and the Zalis barely paused their fighting to register the events of 9/11. As Americans united in a way that had not been seen since before the Reagan years, the Satmars continued their descent into conflict and chaos. In the courtroom, Brach defended his behavior as a fulfillment of the religious commandment to rebuke wrongdoers. Thus, his new lawyer argued, he had actually complied with Justice Barasch's order to limit his activities in the synagogue to an "exercise of religion." But Barasch, who seemed to enjoy displaying his familiarity with Jewish law, Satmar customs, the impending Sabbath, and the upcoming Jewish holidays, wasn't buying it. He ruled against Brach.

It was at this point, on October 7, 2001, that the Aronis made their first attempt to move their case into a different forum. Believing Justice Barasch was biased against them and would never rule in their favor, their new lawyer made a motion to discontinue the arbitration proceeding—just hours after intervening in an entirely different lawsuit in the hopes of getting the judge presiding over that case to recognize Friedman as the Williamsburg board president.

Confusingly, the case in which the Aronis intervened was the case involving the other Brach, Nachman Brach, whose attempt on behalf of Faiga and her retinue to gain control of the building in Brooklyn where R. Yoelish used to live had spawned numerous ancillary lawsuits, which remained unresolved. Nachman Brach was completely uninvolved in the Aroni-Zali conflict. The 26 Adar Corporation, which he had established for the express purpose of gaining control of the precious Bedford Avenue property, and which was the named defendant in the Williamsburg congregation's lawsuit against Brach, commenced in the 1980s, had recently been dissolved for nonpayment of taxes, which Brach had ceased paying when the court enjoined him from entering the building. But in zombie-like fashion, both the corporation and the litigation had been revived in 2001 at just around the time that the Aroni-Zali conflict commenced. Just recently, the judge in that case, Theodore Jones, had issued a summons to the president of the Williamsburg synagogue.[20] When, owing to the controversy over who the president of the synagogue was, no one responded, Justice Jones issued an order to show cause why the synagogue should not be held in contempt. The Aronis seized on that procedural development as an opportunity to intervene in the 26 *Adar* litigation and press their case that Friedman was the true president of the synagogue. In essence, they repurposed the long-standing *Adar* litigation and used it as a vehicle to try to get a different judge in Kings County to adjudicate their complaint against the Zalis, having become convinced that Justice Barasch would never rule in their favor.

It was an audacious strategy, and for a time it worked. Indeed, it took two years for Justice Jones to uncover fully what was going on and unravel the tangled skein of litigation that issued from the election controversy. In the meantime, the Aronis filed two more lawsuits, one before Justice Jones, seeking to have him void the Zalis' election results, the other, a suit that was filed in the Orange County courthouse. But there were two serious problems with this litigation strategy. Not only were they at best skirting, at worst flouting, the rules against judge shopping; they also were asking judges to decide the question of which election was valid, whereas before they had merely petitioned the judge to order the parties to submit that question to private arbitration by a rabbinical court.

This brought them squarely into the territory of the religious question doctrine, which, as we have seen, functions much like the political question doctrine in that it denies courts the authority to adjudicate certain kinds of disputes. To be sure, there were strong arguments to be made that the dispute could be resolved without addressing religious questions. The core of this argument lay in the claim that the Satmars themselves recognized a distinction between their lay leaders (who ran the board of the synagogue) and their religious leaders, and granted each its own independent sphere of authority. In keeping with this distinction between spheres of secular and spiritual authority, this argument ran, the lay leaders had, in 1948, officially incorporated the Congregation Yetev Lev D'Satmar, Inc. under the New York statute that authorizes and regulates private religious nonprofit corporations—a secular statute that articulates neutral principles of secular law. The

Aronis claimed that the community's founding fathers accepted the application of these neutral principles of secular law to the governance of the congregation and that they had adhered to them by setting up a committee at the time of the synagogue's incorporation to formulate the corporation's bylaws (or "statutes," as they were referred to in Yiddish). All this was done, they said, with the blessing of the Rebbe, who had entrusted the task of running that committee to Berl Friedman's father, Lipa. These bylaws, according to the Aronis' legal argument—and according to the English translation of the Yiddish bylaws that they supplied to the court, which became a further bone of contention in the litigation—recognized the distinction between the Satmars' secular leaders, who ran the synagogue and looked after the community's business and financial affairs, and their religious leaders, whose authority was accordingly limited. Business matters, on this account, as well as issues pertaining to the governance of the congregation, were governed by its bylaws and the state nonprofit corporation statute under which they were adopted. Therefore, the argument concluded, the question of which election was held in accord with the rules could be decided on the basis of neutral secular principles of law.

Competent and reputable lawyers hired by the Aronis repeated this argument in case after case, appeal after appeal, and they made their argument ably. Notwithstanding the existence of strong counterarguments voiced by the other side, the Aronis' position on this matter was at the very least not clearly wrong and arguably correct. If accepted, it would have afforded the courts a basis for asserting jurisdiction over the dispute and rejecting the conclusion that the controversy was religious in nature and hence nonjusticiable. But the presence of other lawyers, such as Ravi Batra, who used questionable tactics may have undermined the ability of the Aroni team to win the courts to their side. Tricks such as filing another case in a different courtroom or, as they did on several occasions, hiring "co-counsel" who conveniently disappeared once they finished discharging their task of allowing the Aronis to claim they had personal ties with the judges or creating the appearance of a conflict of interest that forced the recusal of judges, seem only to have antagonized judges who ended up presiding over their cases and might have otherwise been persuaded by what was, after all, a reasonable legal argument.

The Aronis, it seemed, had not just learned how the American legal system worked, but had overlearned and overestimated the extent to which legal chicanery would be tolerated. Of course, there was a counter-argument to this charge as well. Just as Michael Sussman sought to persuade Judge Rakoff that each new case he brought on behalf of the KJ dissidents related to new incidents and thus raised fresh claims (and was therefore not precluded from being litigated by the doctrine of res judicata), the Aronis defended themselves against charges of forum and judge shopping by contending that each of their lawsuits related to different issues. But they could not avoid the fact that every one of them boiled down to the question of who would be legally recognized as the real president of the Williamsburg congregation. By 2002, Justice Jones had ruled that the two cases before him, and the case filed in Orange County as well, were really just the same dispute as had first been brought before Justice Barasch. Based on this judgment, he ordered all of the election cases to be consolidated and transferred back to Justice Barasch in Brooklyn.

Needless to say, the latter was by this point none too favorably disposed toward the Aronis. That does not mean his ultimate decision was biased against them. Indeed, one could see his final ruling as reflecting a great effort to avoid taking sides. The problem was that he could not decide that the issues were nonjusticiable without rejecting the Aronis' view that the Satmars recognized a distinction between spiritual and secular authority—and accepting the Zalis' contrary view. The Zalis maintained that there was no distinction between spiritual and secular spheres within the Satmar community because everything lay within the spiritual sphere according to their theology. They based this claim on the Hasidic principle of *avodah be-gashmiyut*, according to which God's spirit lies everywhere, in everything, including the material world. By extension, the Rebbe's authority extended to all matters, including governance of the board of the congregation, and it was therefore impossible for courts to make a decision that affected the governance of the board without undermining his spiritual authority.

In rejecting the Aronis' position, Justice Barasch had to side with the Zalis on this matter. Paradoxically, there was no way to avoid deciding the religious question of who the real president of the synagogue board was without deciding the religious question of how the Satmars distributed authority between religious and the lay leadership and whether the Rebbe's authority extended over the governance of synagogue board or not. Justice Barasch confidently asserted that the Satmars believe the Rebbe's spiritual authority is all-encompassing as if this was a finding of fact, not a religious question that was itself subject to dispute in the Satmar world. But this had been a matter of dispute long before the division between Zalis and the Aronis arose. Everyone in the Satmar world agreed on the basic principle of dina di-malkhuta dina, according to which the authority of the state had to be recognized and accepted as a sphere of legal authority separate from the authority of Jewish law. The question over which the Aronis and their various opponents divided was whether a distinction between secular and religious realms of authority was observed within the Satmars' own separate sphere. The Aronis consistently maintained that it was. It was on this basis that they defended themselves against the charge leveled against them by the dissidents that it was a sin for them to run a secular school system. It was likewise on this basis that they had defended themselves against the claim that assuming the powers of secular government to govern a village was in contravention of the Rebbe's dictum that exercising secular power was unacceptable. What once had served as a shield to defend the school district and the village from dissident attacks on their conformity to secular law was now being used by the Aronis as a sword to justify judicial intervention in the Satmars' internal political disputes.

Conversely, the Zalis continued to adhere to the same theological position that the dissidents had asserted in their legal attacks on the KJ establishment, namely, that in order to fulfill the separatist principle of separation *from* the sphere of state power, the Satmars had to abjure the exercise of secular power themselves and conduct their business affairs (like all affairs) in accordance with the will of the Rebbe.

In their earlier legal battles against the KJ dissidents, the KJ establishment had often asserted that there were no religious disagreements between Aaron's supporters and Aaron's opponents, only political ones, the implication being that that the theological objection voiced by the dissidents' lawyers to the lay leaders' actions was not sincere. This was the claim Aaron's side had made in the earlier cemetery disputes, and it was also the position advanced by KJ's leaders in the *Khal Charidim* case and in subsequent cases brought by the dissidents seeking to declare the village a theocracy. According to this line of argument, the KJ establishment couldn't be found guilty of violating the dissidents' civil rights because the dissidents weren't properly deemed to be a religious minority; they were, rather, on this account, just a disgruntled political faction. By extension, the Zalis' view of the Rebbe's sphere of spiritual authority as all-encompassing should be seen not as a deeply rooted theological principle, but rather just a legal strategy. Or so the Aronis claimed.

One cannot entirely rule out the possibility that the theological disagreement expressed in the election cases was cooked up by the Zalis' lawyers because that was the only way to rebut the Aronis' appeal to neutral principles of secular law, which would have authorized the secular courts to intervene in the dispute, potentially in the Aronis' favor. But by the same token, it is just as plausible that the Aronis' theological position regarding the existence of a separation between the spheres of spiritual and secular authority was crafted by their lawyers. Lawyers on both sides played a critical role in translating their clients' beliefs into the language of the law, and in so doing, may well have coaxed out of their clients statements of their beliefs that served to justify their respectively desired outcomes. But even if there is some truth to this, it hardly follows that the Zalis' stated belief in the Rebbe's all-encompassing authority is insincere. Nor does it stand to reason that the Aronis' belief, that the Satmars recognize limits to the Rebbe's authority, is insincere. In point of fact, the lawyers' descriptions of both sides' beliefs had a solid basis in the Satmars' practices. The belief that all matters of Satmar life should be governed by religious law as expounded by the Rebbe had always coexisted with various forms of lay leadership in political and economic life, which endowed the lay leaders with a considerable degree of autonomy. And even if the sharp division between the Aronis' and the Zalis' views about the Rebbe's authority over the Satmars' lay institutions was a product of their respective legal strategies, those views seem to have quickly solidified into sincere beliefs.

In fact, there is good reason to think that both of these beliefs—that the Rebbe's authority is limited and that it is all-encompassing—were there all along. The latter belief, which was one of the most salient features of Hasidism, made it easy for Justice Barasch and other judges to treat their decision to side with the Zalis' view as a factual finding rather than as a decision about how to resolve a religious dispute within the Satmar community. But not all the judges who were called upon to adjudicate the election dispute took this position. Some were more receptive to the Aronis' claims, most notably Justice Stewart Rosenwasser, who presided over a courtroom in Orange County. The Aronis were able to file a suit in Orange County notwithstanding the fact that the dispute was centered in Kings County (the seat of Brooklyn) because they based their claim in this lawsuit on issues pertaining to the Kiryas Joel cemetery. The events surrounding these issues had taken place at the very beginning of the conflict, when the Aronis and Zalis first held their dueling board meetings in Williamsburg. At that time, in January 2001, as each faction announced its election plan, each also resolved to take legal action in the name of the board of the Brooklyn congregation to ensure its control over the KJ cemetery. Indeed, the status of the cemetery in Kiryas Joel was one of the key issues at stake between the two sides. Access to the cemetery was a matter of intense concern not only because Aronis had family members buried there, but also, and most importantly, because this was R. Yoelish's resting place. As we have seen, it was deemed a great mitzvah for Satmars to make an annual pilgrimage to the Rebbe's grave on his yahrtseit, one of the holiest days on the community's calendar.

Access to the cemetery had already been a bone of contention between Aaron's camp and the KJ dissidents. The Aronis clearly apprehended that if the Kahan faction were to gain control over the Williamsburg congregation, the Zalis might do to them what they themselves had done to early opponents of the KJ establishment: ban them and bar them from entering the cemetery. The Aronis were well aware that the Williamsburg congregation had held exclusive rights to the cemetery ever since the joint meeting of the KJ and Williamsburg congregations had been convened in 1987 to respond to the initial unrest. That meeting had concluded with a resolution to transfer the KJ congregation's half ownership of the synagogue back to the Williamsburg congregation. When the conflict between the two factions erupted fourteen years later, the Aroni faction passed a resolution authorizing the leader of their faction, Berl Friedman, to transfer that one-half interest in the cemetery back to KJ in the name of the board of the Williamsburg congregation. That resolution was proposed and adopted at the very same meeting at which the Aronis resolved to hold their synagogue board election.

The conveyance of the half interest in the cemetery from the Williamsburg congregation to the KJ congregation, executed by Friedman as the putative head of the Williamsburg congregation, was formally recorded in Orange County on January 19, 2001. It was a legally savvy move aimed at preventing the Zalis from excluding Aronis from the cemetery.[21] But the Zalis were engaged in preemptive steps of their own. Before the Friedman deed was formally recorded, the Kahan faction managed to file a declaration in Orange County court that, if valid, would prevent the cemetery from being conveyed without their approval.[22] This swift legal action preceded Friedman's recording of the deed of transfer by a matter of hours.

The legal fight for control over the cemetery lay dormant for several years. But in 2005, hoping a judge in Orange County would be more sympathetic to them than one in Brooklyn (in particular, Barasch), the Aroni faction filed a lawsuit seeking a declaration that their transfer of a half interest in the KJ cemetery from the Williamsburg congregation to the Kiryas Joel congregation was valid. Needless to say, the Zalis then counterclaimed that Berl Friedman had no authority to execute the transfer because—according to them—he had by then been formally expelled from the Williamsburg congregation. True to form, this legal dispute dragged on for years, and was but one of several lawsuits brought by members of the Aroni faction seeking to establish their rights to access, if not control, the cemetery, the last of which was filed as recently as 2011.[23] Presiding over this dispute, Justice Rosenwasser repeatedly made rulings in favor of the Aronis, most notably when, after a long and debilitating struggle, Moshe Teitelbaum succumbed to cancer at age ninety-two on April 24, 2006.

The second Rebbe's death inaugurated a new wave of strife. Within hours, Aaron's camp went to court to request that Berl Friedman be deemed the official responsible for funeral arrangements. The initial ruling in their favor in a local Brooklyn court was rejected when the Zalis made a successful appeal to the New York State appellate division. Eventually, a compromise was struck: to accommodate the competing mourners, two funerals were held, one in Williamsburg and one in Kiryas Joel. As *New York Magazine* reported it: "At the funeral on April 25 at the Rodney Street synagogue in Williamsburg, in front of thousands of Satmar men pressed so tightly together a spectator could barely draw a breath, Aaron and Zalman gave a show of unity, sharing a dais as they wailed lamentations and bowed toward their father's wooden casket." But, the report went on, "it soured before the day was over" as "supporters threw punches in the shul in Kiryas Joel, sending two—including Moses Friedman—to the hospital."

Such intrafamilial acrimony was nothing new; just the year before, several of Moshe's grandchildren allied with the Aroni faction had filed a guardianship proceeding seeking to gain control of decision-making in the Satmar community from the Rebbe.[24] In that same period, in a different legal proceeding, the Aronis got a court in Brooklyn to issue a subpoena summoning Moshe to court. Both of these legal actions failed: Moshe never appeared in court, and the guardianship proceeding in a Brooklyn court was dismissed. But their impact was nonetheless felt. Indeed, these steps marked the final rupture between father and eldest son. Moshe believed, and not without reason, that Aaron was seeking to take advantage of him in his infirm state to gain control of the Satmar empire. According to one account, Moshe accosted his son in 2005, branding him a *rushe ben rushe*, an evil person who will be punished in this world—or literally, an evil person who is the son of an evil person, perhaps a sign of his declining mental state.[25] This encounter followed years of litigation, during which each side endeavored to get its claim to be the rightful leader of the Williamsburg congregation—and owner of its many valuable assets—validated by one or another of New York

State's courts. Moshe's physical and mental decline proceeded in parallel with his community's descent into legal conflict and political chaos.

At the funeral in Williamsburg, the Zalis read aloud what they said was Moshe's last will, a claim that was later confirmed by a rabbinical court associated with their side. According to the document, the Satmar Rebbe declared that Zalman "shall occupy my position and succeed me without any shortfall, for effective immediately I have granted him the position."[26] Not surprisingly, the Aronis responded by questioning the will's validity and Moshe's mental competence at the time of its drafting. From that point forward, they steadfastly refused to accept the claim that Zalman was the legitimate heir. And thus, the Satmar kingdom was irrevocably riven into two.

It was not long before this, in early February 2006, that Justice Rosenwasser had issued his final ruling in the cemetery action; he declared that the 2001 Zali declaration purporting to have prevented the transfer of the cemetery without their consent was null and void, and concluded that Friedman had not been expelled from the Williamsburg congregation. This effectively crowned him president. But this was hardly the last word. By the following summer, this decision had been overturned by the Appellate Division of the New York State judicial system. At the same time, the Appellate Division affirmed Justice Barasch's decision, which had been rendered in 2004 and held that the cases touching on the succession controversy could not be resolved without addressing religious questions—and hence were not justiciable.

Strife within the Shtetl

After the death of Moshe in 2006, social relations between the Aronis and Zalis further deteriorated. Regular interaction between the two sides in shul and at the frequent family celebrations (births and weddings) became less common. At the more formal level of rabbinic authority, the Zalis now had to worry about whether they would be formally inscribed in the mainstream congregation's *pinkas*, or registration book, in KJ. If they weren't registered, then their marriages would not be considered legal under Jewish law; and if that were so, then their children would be deemed *mamzerim*, bastards born of an adulterous (in this case, unregistered) relationship.

At the still more formal level of official government action, given the close ties of KJ officials to Aaron, the dissenters continued to maintain that the municipality was discriminating against them and that acts of harassment had the imprimatur of the village and, hence, the state. They had long suspected that the Aroni establishment routinely denied them public housing units and building permits for private residences and home-based religious institutions that were routinely granted to Aaron's followers. Aided, as ever, by Michael Sussman, they continued to press their case in federal court, but to no avail.

One of the hottest sites of controversy in KJ was the small dissident synagogue located at the back of the main Aroni synagogue in what was originally intended as the parsonage and had long been known as Congregation Bais Yoel Ohel Feige or the Rebbetsin's Shul. The history of this small piece of real estate extended back to 1981, when the congregation deeded Reb Yoelish's parsonage to Alta Faiga. A short while later, the Rebbetsin transferred title to the property to the newly formed religious corporation bearing the name Congregation Bais Yoel.[27]

In a rare exception to the general rule that litigation was instigated by the weaker dissident faction, Aaron's team had made repeated efforts to repossess the apartment, including, as we have seen, by filing eviction proceedings against Faiga and challenging the validity of the deed to the property, which she had held since 1981.[28] None of these past efforts succeeded. But in the spring of 2004, the KJ congregation disconnected the sewer line that was attached to the back apartment-shul, launching yet another round of litigation.

The disconnection of the sewer line was received by the dissidents as a declaration of war. Rather than rely on Sussman, whose specialty was civil rights, they turned to Ben Ostrer, the lawyer who had seconded Sussman in the *Waldman* litigation and assisted the dissidents in earlier property disputes and the final challenge to the KJ School District. On June 18, 2005, Ostrer filed suit in state court, calling for state recognition of the dissidents' ownership of Faiga's property and of easements giving them the right to continued provision of utilities.[29] Notably, this was two weeks after Abe Wieder had fended off another election challenge, winning 55 percent of the vote against his latest opponent, one Jacob Banda.[30]

The Bais Yoel case went through many rounds of battle in the New York State courts over the course of the next four years. In 2008, state trial judge Joseph Owen (the same judge who had presided over the state *Khal Charidim* case in the mid-1990s) ruled in favor of the mainstream congregation, declaring the use of the apartment by Bais Yoel to be a nonconforming unlawful house of worship under KJ's zoning laws. He did grant one victory to the plaintiffs, finding that there was a utility easement that prohibited the village from cutting off their water service, but the force of that ruling was limited by his further finding that it could be applied only to residential use.[31] That meant that the village had to turn the utilities back on, but the dissidents were not allowed to use the property as a place of worship.

Owen's ruling did not bring an end to the matter. The apartment continued to be a source of fierce contestation for years. In 2009, the main congregation again shut off the utilities in response to the dissidents' defiance of the order to restrict the property to residential use. At that point, the Rebbetsin's shul, which had been in continuous use as a synagogue since 1981, was shut down.[32] The next year, the legal dispute over the space was reignited, but again Justice Owen ruled in favor of the defendants and, in subsequent proceedings, found the plaintiffs to be in contempt for violating court orders.[33]

Coinciding with the multiyear battle over the Rebbetsin's shul was the ongoing controversy over the cemetery in Kiryas Joel. The two controversies, in fact, were interlocking sites in the struggle between the establishment and dissident factions in KJ from 2004 to 2009. Together they pointed to the continuing importance of private property rights as a tool for establishing communal institutions and as a weapon for defending them or, more aggressively, for attacking one's opponents. In this vein, the KJ congregation continued to exercise control over the cemetery, even though Justice Rosenwasser's ruling in favor of the Aronis had been overturned. Not surprisingly, complaints from the KJ dissidents and Zalis about exclusion from the cemetery persisted. In 2004, the year the sewer line was cut off at the Rebbetsin's shul, another fracas broke out at the cemetery during the commemoration of the Rebbe's yahrtseit. The Aronis alleged that the Zalis were attempting to usurp control over the cemetery and had actually roughed up some of their adherents.[34] The dissidents, in turn, accused the establishment congregation of denying them the right to be buried in the cemetery, where Satmar luminaries—Reb Yoelish, Alta Faiga, and Moshe Teitelbaum— were all interred. In February 2009, the Zali faction sued in state court to prevent the Aronis from "interfering with the contractual and statu- tory rights of the plaintiffs to burial in the Kiryas Joel Cemetery."[35] A half year later, tensions over the cemetery boiled over again, when a forty-one-year-old resident aligned with the Zalis, Esriel Perlstein, died. According to reports, the Aroni faction denied his family access to the cemetery unless a fifty-thousand-dollar fee were paid to the mainstream congregation. Given the legal imperative of a quick burial in Judaism, dissidents went ahead and dug a grave for Mr. Perlstein in an adjacent plot of land, which they immediately consecrated as a cemetery.[36]

Several months later, in October 2009, a Zali-affiliated rabbinical court excoriated the mainstream Aroni faction, accusing it of denying burial rights and stealing community property for its own purposes. At the top of a full-page ad declaring the court's decision that appeared in *Der Yid*, the headline decried the fact that "the cemetery in our community has been taken over by the sect that seeks out gentile courts." Of course, as we have seen, both sides made recourse to gentile courts, with the weaker partner usually as the initiator. In the confusingly named case from that year, *Friedman v. CYL Cemetery*, it was the Zalis, represented by a member of their faction named Wilmos Friedman, who initiated the action against the Aroni faction led by Berl Friedman. Ironically enough, because a beis din had already weighed in, New York Supreme Court justice Victor J. Alfieri ruled in 2010 that a recognized rabbinical court was the appropriate agent to decide the issue. This was in line with past state judicial holdings that internal Satmar-related matters such as the cemetery controversy were religious disputes best addressed by a beis din, and not by a state court.[37]

Strife with Orange County Neighbors

The continual strife within KJ was matched by growing tensions with neighbors just beyond the village's borders. In 2000, barely a year before the Aroni-Zali conflict began, village leaders ignited a new controversy by announcing a plan for Kiryas Joel to build a thirteen-mile pipeline to tap into the underground Catskill Aqueduct. By 2004, opposition had grown considerably, as had the projected budget from an original $22 million to $29 million, most of which was to be drawn from federal sources through the office of U.S. congresswoman Sue Hall. One of the sharpest voices of opposition to the plan came from Charles Bohan, the supervisor of the neighboring town of Blooming Grove. In a letter on June 16 to the Orange County Legislature, Bohan declared with more than a measure of antisemitic stereotyping that "the hardworking commuting taxpayers of my Town will not condone a *parasite community* tearing up local roads . . . in order to facilitate a community who constantly cry persecution as they bury the landscape." Bohan's missive drew stern rebukes from a number of local political officials, but also a host of endorsements from letter writers to the *Times Herald-Record*. One wrote in to say that "Orange County citizens should embrace Bohan's willingness to tackle the issue head-on," while another maintained that "the county needs more leaders, such as Bohan, who will stand against the Kiryas Joel tsunami!"[38] Local residents, supported by the county legislature, which voted twenty to one to oppose the pipeline, were deeply fearful that the pipeline would enable KJ's unrestrained growth and encroachment. By contrast, the official KJ stance was that the pipeline was not optional, but a necessity of life. "It's not that we need the water pipeline to grow," argued one KJ resident. "We need it to exist."[39]

True to form, the village was not of one mind with regard to the issue. In 2001, a new dissident organization called the Kiryas Joel Alliance was formed. It was chiefly associated with the Bnai Yoel, but cast its net widely in search of allies in the fight against Aaron and the KJ leaders. In 2004, it adopted a bold new strategy that breached the customs and boundaries of the shtetl by running paid advertisements in the local newspapers. The KJ Alliance was seeking to connect with the area's increasingly alarmed neighbors by placing itself on the opposite side of the KJ establishment. The opening lines of one KJ Alliance ad captured this sentiment:

> On behalf of the people of Kiryas Joel we reach out to you, our friends and neighbors, in an effort to define ourselves to the general Orange County community in the hope that the words and actions of some, [sic] do not characterize the people of Kiryas Joel as a whole. It is most important to us that you, our neighbors, understand that those words and actions are a cause of great dismay to the people of Kiryas Joel, and is contrary to our very being as a people. The people of Kiryas Joel are deeply aghast at the ludicrous and slanderous accusations being cast upon people who oppose the pipeline project. We strongly maintain that in as much as water is oxygen to our physical bodies, peace is oxygen to our spirits and souls. As a peaceful people we believe only in solutions that can be accomplished in harmony and concurrence with our neighbors.

The ad went on to explain that this position was rooted in Rabbi Joel Teitelbaum's belief in the principle of dina di-malkhuta dina that the dissidents had been invoking since they first set out to challenge the village establishment. In keeping with the spirit of this halakhic counterpart to "render unto Caesar," KJ Alliance stated that it is "a supreme duty of our people . . . to live in accord and peace with the broader community to which exile has brought us."[40] This harmonious sentiment, however, did not carry the day. The Vaad hakirya, the powerful land development agency of the mainstream faction, had been buying property just outside of KJ in Monroe and Woodbury and by July 2004 had accumulated 310 acres. Facing the threat of KJ being denied access to the New York City Aqueduct, the Vaad floated the idea of creating a new, adjacent Satmar village to be called Kiryas Va'Yoel Moshe (the village of Va'Yoel Moshe, after the name of Joel Teitelbaum's famous anti-Zionist book). In response, residents in the neighboring towns of Blooming Grove and Woodbury took a page out of the KJ playbook by proposing the creation of new villages out of their existing towns. This move would afford them greater control over zoning, including the prospect of preventing KJ from building a pipeline on their land.[41] While the second Satmar village was never created, the villages of South Blooming Grove and Woodbury were established two years later, in the summer of 2006.

The constant battling over zoning, water, and municipal boundaries made it difficult to determine who was fighting whom sometimes. In 2010, a group of Satmar developers sued for the dissolution of South Blooming Grove, arguing that the village and its residents had discriminated against them in zoning matters. But this time it wasn't the KJ establishment that stood at the center of the conflict. Rather, it was a dissident faction of Satmars represented by Michael Sussman that sought to dissolve South Blooming Grove.[42]

At the same time, the battle between the mainstream and the dissidents in KJ raged on. While the cemetery dispute continued to simmer in the background, Aaron tightened the screws on the regulation of marriages performed in the village. In late January 2010, members of the Bnai Yoel faction held a wedding ceremony at their school just outside of Kiryas Joel, which young men from the mainstream camp sought to disrupt by denouncing the event over loudspeakers outside of the hall. A few days later, the establishment congregation called on "all kosher Jews to separate and remove themselves from the evil people [who commit] these ugly acts," referring to the rabbi, groom, and father of the bride for daring to conduct a marriage outside of the radius of Aaron's authority.

In February 2010, KJ's chief halakhic expert, Rabbi Getzel Berkowitz, issued a stern warning in the Aronis' Williamsburg-based newspaper Der Blat prohibiting anyone from performing a marriage in the community without his express authorization.[43] Undaunted, the dissidents performed another wedding on February 17, making it clear that their break from the grip of the KJ rabbinic establishment was complete.[44] Later in the summer, dissidents pushed back further against the mainstream. They dumped filled garbage bags on top of fliers that had been distributed throughout the village condemning Bnai Yoel weddings (which included the pictures of grooms and phone numbers of the newlywed couples).[45]

Meanwhile, on a related front, the KJ Alliance filed a lawsuit in 2011 pressing their now familiar claim that the village was a "theocracy" that contravened the Establishment Clause. In addition, they alleged that its actions discriminated against them in violation of the Equal Protection and Free Exercise Clauses and the Religious Land Use and Institutionalized Persons Act (known as RLUIPA), a federal statute that prohibits land-use regulations from imposing burdens on the exercise of religion. Lawyer Michael Sussman produced an inventory of specific actions that he said occurred subsequent to the events addressed in earlier litigation. In his view, these actions constituted fresh claims not precluded by the doctrine of res judicata. Judge Rakoff, to whom the matter was assigned, disagreed. Save for one specific allegation concerning the "community room law," a village ordinance enacted in 2007 that required all building developers to construct "community rooms," Rakoff rejected Sussman's argument that the claims were new. Once again, he dismissed the dissidents' complaint, and in 2012, the Second Circuit Court of Appeals affirmed his judgment, arguing that the agreement reached by mutual consent in 1997—the ill-fated settlement agreement—precluded any further adjudication of the dispute between the dissidents and the KJ leadership.[46] Judge Rakoff's repeated rejections of Sussman's attempts to bring new lawsuits on behalf of the dissidents served to give his settlement order lasting effect. The result was to uphold the existing power structure in Kiryas Joel, preventing the adjudication of the claim that KJ was a theocracy and therefore had to be dissolved. Even though multiple courts, including Rakoff's, recognized that this claim may have been valid, it simply would not be heard.

Strife as a Way of Life

Since 2012, litigation among the disputing Satmar factions inside and outside KJ has largely subsided. So too, the once-dominant measures of social stigma and isolation imposed on dissidents have lessened, as members of different factions have come to terms with, and normalized, the existence of separate camps. Since that time, there have been ebbs and flows to the conflicts between the Satmars and their non-Satmar neighbors. When taking stock of the persistent battles, one can hardly avoid asking: how much strife can a community sustain? Won't endless conflict lead to precipitous decline?

In fact, nothing could be further from the truth. Conflict has been a constant companion of the Teitelbaum family, extending back to nineteenth-century Hungary. Far from being corrosive, the combative impulse has allowed the Teitelbaums to hone the distinctiveness of the Satmar brand, known across the globe for its unyielding defense of the faith. And that brand has been very successful, gaining enough market share to make the Satmars the most populous Hasidic group in the world today.

As Moshe "Gabbai" Friedman observed, competition, in the face of deep conflict, was necessary for the empire after Reb Yoelish's death. The Satmar world had grown to a point that it was no longer governable by a single leader. Forty years after Reb Yoelish's death, the internal rivalries that once produced bitter social tension, seemingly endless litigation, and even physical violence have yielded three flourishing and independent streams of educational and social moysdes associated with the Aronis, Zalis, and Bnai Yoel. Clearly, the effects of a fractured dynasty, and a marked decline in charisma from the founding father, have not been paralyzing. Conflict within, and without, has sharpened, battle-tested, and permitted the growth of the Satmar community—and at an extraordinary clip.

Indeed, in the period between Moshe's decision to divide the empire in 1999 and his death in 2006, Kiryas Joel was the fastest-growing community in the state of New York. It increased in population by 51 percent, growing from 13,273 residents in 2000 to 20,071 in 2006.[47] From that point, the rate of growth has slowed down; the 2010 census counted the population of Kiryas Joel at 20,175. As of 2018, the number of residents has gone up by about 25 percent to 25,292, a slower but still rapid rate of growth.[48]

Two constant constraints on KJ's growth are land and water. But KJ has proved ever resilient in the face of even that seemingly insuperable challenge. As with the public school district, the village administration never relented in its push for access to a water pipeline that would enable KJ's ongoing growth. At long last, construction began on the pipeline to the New York Aqueduct in 2013. Work continues to this day, even as the estimated cost of the project has ballooned to $65 million.[49]

In parallel, the inexorable pull toward more land has continued, with an unexpected twist in the story. Just when it seemed as if KJ's neighbors had finally found a way to thwart the village's further expansion, the establishment faction exhibited once again its political deftness and crafted an alliance with the very external foes against whom it had long battled. The result was a bold new political step that liberated Kiryas Joel from the remaining constraints imposed by the town of Monroe.

From KJ to Palm Tree

From its founding in 2013, United Monroe, the group of activist citizens from the town of Monroe, worked to diminish the influence of the KJ establishment. At times, it joined forces with the dissident Kiryas Joel Alliance. One of the key aims of this partnership was to thwart the efforts of KJ leading citizens, with the support of the village leadership, to annex 507 acres of land from Monroe. The town of Monroe had rejected a petition for the 507-acre annexation in 2015, but it did approve an annexation of 164 acres by KJ from Monroe. United Monroe saw that step as yet another brazen encroachment on the suburban landscape of Orange County. The village of KJ, by contrast, saw annexation as essential to providing adequate housing for its rapidly growing population. For its part, the Kiryas Joel Alliance felt that the tactics of the KJ establishment risked alienating neighbors and the broader host society, and thus constituted a violation of a core premise of Diaspora Jewish life.

In the midst of this confusing environment, the various sides did what they were accustomed to doing; they lawyered up and started to mount legal challenges. The specter of costly and mutually destructive litigation loomed once again, driving the main actors to the negotiating table in the early summer of 2017. During this process, the Kiryas Joel Alliance receded to the background as representatives from United Monroe and the KJ leadership sat down to try to put an end to their

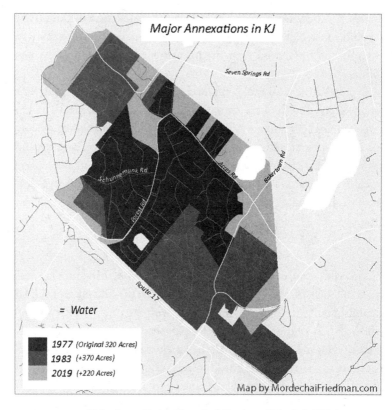

FIGURE 7.3. Major Annexations in Kiryas Joel. Courtesy of Mordechai Friedman.

years of acrimony. Remarkably, the two sides reached agreement on a deal that included the following provisions:

- KJ would not be allowed to annex all of the 507 acres that Satmar residents had purchased in Monroe and sought to incorporate in the village
- KJ *would* be allowed to annex the proposed 164 acres in Monroe
- In order to forestall future annexation conflicts, the two sides agreed that the Satmar enclave should become a self-standing town, the first new town in the state of New York in thirty-five years[50]

In November 2017, a vote was held by the voters of Monroe on the proposed town, which passed overwhelmingly. Several weeks later, on November 20, a settlement to bring an end to existing lawsuits was signed under the supervision of state Supreme Court Justice Paul Marx.[51] It included an additional 56 acres, bringing the total amount of newly annexed land by KJ to 220 acres. It also stipulated that there would be no more annexation of land by KJ from Monroe or Blooming Grove property owners for a ten-year period. The name of the new town would be Palm Tree, English for "Teitelbaum."

On July 1, 2018, Governor Andrew Cuomo signed the bill authorizing the creation of Palm Tree. His signature served as one symbolic bookend to the dramatic rise of Kiryas Joel; the earlier bookend was the signature of his father, Governor Mario Cuomo, who, as New York secretary of state, had authorized the creation of the village of Kiryas Joel forty-one years earlier in 1977. Between the two Cuomo signatures, the Satmar village had grown exponentially—in both demographic and political terms. Reflecting that increase in population and political power, in January 2019 the town of Palm Tree officially took rise.

United Monroe's willingness to arrive at a compromise with its bitter foe, the village leadership, did not signal a complete change of heart regarding the Hasidic village. Rather, it was an act of Realpolitik, based on the expectation that if KJ remained within Monroe, it would only continue to control and demand more of the town. Giving KJ the opportunity to become its own town would obligate it to exit Monroe, since a town in New York, unlike a village, cannot exist within the bounds of another town. That meant that the leadership of Kiryas Joel would no longer be able to make what seemed to United Monroe repeated and excessive demands; nor would KJ's residents be able to decide the fate of elections in Monroe through bloc voting. Agreeing to the town of Palm Tree was, for United Monroe, a long overdue writ of divorce.

For the leadership and many residents of KJ, the creation of a new town offered the prospect of bringing an end to the tensions, threats, and litigation that marred relations with Monroe for decades. The founding of KJ in 1977 had similarly been intended to resolve the acrimonious zoning disputes occasioned by the arrival of the first Satmar settlers three years earlier. But the creation of a Hasidic village within the town of Monroe, while granting the Satmars the right to set their own zoning regulations, did not lead to peace and harmony. Years of accusations and litigation ensued between the two sides. At various points in time, proposals were raised to ameliorate the friction, including the idea raised by former assemblywoman, Nancy Calhoun, in 2003 to allow KJ to become its own city. At the time, Village Administrator Gedalye Szegedin asserted that "there is no sense of urgency to create a city."[52]

But the next year, 2004, relations between KJ and its neighbors were brought to a boil over the village's plans to build the pipeline to the New York City Aqueduct as a way of enabling growth. It was this step that led Supervisor Charles Bohan of neighboring Blooming Grove to call KJ a "parasite community."[53]

In response, Szegedin attempted to explain to local leaders a few months later what residents of KJ felt: "Our constituents, when they go to the gas station, they are being spit at. When they go to the shopping centers, they're looked down on. When I walked into a town hall meeting, someone yelled, 'Bastard.' I don't think that's right. I think this is the United States of America. I think people should be able to practice their religion and practice their lifestyle as long as they're law-abiding citizens, tax-paying citizens."[54] Hostility toward the Satmar population of Orange County has not disappeared overnight. Nor has the fear that it might monopolize valuable resources in the county. Will the creation of Palm Tree herald a new era of peace and harmony? Gedalye Szegedin felt a measure of hope in 2017, when he celebrated the agreement with United Monroe as "an historic new day" that could yield "a recipe for living side by side in peace and mutual respect and understanding."[55] By disengaging from Monroe, he suggested, the Satmars would be able to maintain their distinctive way of life and grow at the rapid clip they desired.

In its continued quest for separation, Kiryas Joel and now Palm Tree stand as Orthodox Jewish versions of the American "city upon a hill," to recall John Winthrop's term from the seventeenth century. Of course, the Satmar community is not "a model of Christian charity," as

Winthrop sermonized in 1630. It did not seek to inspire other communities to emulate it. Nor did it embody Winthrop's evocation of the biblical injunction that one should "love his neighbor as himself." But KJ does exemplify the kind of cities upon the hill that actually *did* take rise in America—religiously and ethnically homogeneous, deeply committed to ritual purity, frequently at odds with surrounding communities, and often riven within.

EPILOGUE

Leaving Kiryas Joel

For many inside Kiryas Joel, the village's existence is the fulfillment of the long-held mission of Rabbi Joel Teitelbaum: to establish a shtetl, a thoroughly separatist, ritually stringent community at a remove from mainstream society that harks back to a mythic past. The Satmars' success in realizing this vision required not only a sense of religious purpose, but very mundane, pragmatic, and often hardball tactics. Drawing on the movement's history of political engagement in Europe, Satmar leaders came to understand well the American system and mastered the art of interest group politics at local and state levels.

This engagement has routinized Kiryas Joel to controversy; disputes with foes both internal and external have shaped it from the beginning and continue to do so, particularly with regard to tensions over land. Indeed, shortly after the agreement to create Palm Tree, which included a moratorium against further annexation, another faction of Satmars proposed the creation of yet another new village, to be called Seven Springs, in Monroe (and thus not under the future control of KJ/Palm Tree, at least initially). The new village they proposed would encompass a terrain of 1.9 square miles, bigger than Palm Tree. Not surprisingly, this new initiative raised the ire of United Monroe, which denounced "a small group of wealthy landowners who wish to skirt local zoning laws."[1] It deepened the fear of surrounding neighbors and communities that Hasidic Jews, with their strange ways, had a limitless appetite for land in the suburban idyll of Orange County, New York.

And yet, it bears repeating that alien as the Satmars may appear to their neighbors, their rise has been perfectly in step with larger trends in American society. KJ's birth in 1977 coincided with the ascendance in American politics of libertarian ideologies that embraced property rights and juxtaposed the supposed virtues of privatization and localism to the sins of big government. Residential segregation, by race and wealth, only accelerated in the years following the formal abolition of legal discrimination, furthered by the reign of the free market that libertarianism glorified.

In parallel, KJ's growth has coincided with the ascent of a newly energized Christian evangelical movement anxious to reclaim the public sphere. Over the past four decades, this movement has had a huge impact on American politics, transforming the complexion of local school boards and state governments, and enabling the victory of Republican presidential and legislative candidates and the seating of a conservative Supreme Court built to last for decades. Both Congress and the Supreme Court under chief justices Rehnquist and Roberts have provided considerable latitude to individuals and groups who seek to opt out of existing laws in the name of religious freedom. At the core of this trend was the philosophical stance clearly stated by Chief Justice Rehnquist in 1985 that the long-standing metaphor of a "wall of separation" between church and state was "wrong as a matter of law and history."[2]

A diverse group of religious and political actors has benefited from the collapse of this wall—most prominently, conservative Christians of a variety of denominations (Protestant, Catholic, Greek and Russian Orthodox), but also members of some non-Christian faith traditions and the many Democrats who supported broadening the right to religious accommodation for their own religious and political reasons. Orthodox Jews, in particular, welcomed and played an important role in bringing about this shift in attitudes about how to reconcile the principle of separation between state and religion with the principle of religious accommodation. Although their agenda has differed in important respects from that of Christian conservatives who sought to abolish the doctrine of church-state separation altogether, it has also overlapped with the Christian right agenda on key issues. Christian conservatives and Orthodox and Haredi Jews who have joined together to fight strict separation are warriors in the identity battles of late twentieth- and early twenty-first-century America.

Often, identity politics is cast as the exclusive or primary preserve of the left.[3] But this is a mistake. Fighting for the right to preserve one's culture is in fact quintessentially American and a form of politics that is often mobilized on behalf of people who define their identity in terms of conservative religious and political beliefs, whether it be the Christian baker who refuses to make a cake for a gay wedding or an Orthodox Jew who practices a controversial form of circumcision. The call to "return religion to the public square" and provide public support for religious institutions (especially schools) is a clear expression of this conservative identity politics. Broadly supported by both conservative Christians and Orthodox Jews, it reflects their shared understanding that the actions and beliefs they seek to protect, as a matter of constitutional right, are not peripheral, but central to their cultural identities. This conservative affirmation of "the right to be different" is not the antithesis but rather the mirror image of the position taken by those on the left, in particular people of color, who make their own claims to their ethnic, religious, or cultural heritage, only to be denounced for their embrace of "destructive" identity politics by conservatives and old-school liberals alike.[4]

America's long history of religious accommodation reveals that identity politics is neither inherently progressive nor un-American. Indeed, both sides of the culture wars that have dominated American politics for half a century espouse the politics of group identity. The battle is not between identitarians and anti-identitarians. Nor is it between those who espouse the value of religious freedom and those who don't. It is, rather, a fight between those who see themselves as protecting *traditional* beliefs, practices, and cultural identity from the corrosive force of secular modernity and those who seek to assert personal cultural or religious identities that are anathema to religious traditionalists.

Kiryas Joel is an especially fascinating manifestation of American identity politics. Notwithstanding its embrace by religious conservatives, it has found support both in the precincts of conservative religious identity politics and within the liberal and multicultural left. For their part, the Satmars have been resolutely nonpartisan for most of their history, seeking and gaining as much support from liberal Democrat governor Mario Cuomo as from Republican George Pataki, while avoiding deep involvement with the conservative movement's ideological and political activities. The Satmars' form of communitarianism has as its chief mission preserving its own cultural and religious identity. Its success in doing so reflects the extent to which America has become dedicated to what Horace Kallen called "cultural pluralism"—the view that group-based cultural difference is not antithetical to, but rather consistent with, classical liberal principles of equality and liberty and the idea of America itself—a version of liberalism that discards the assimilationist melting-pot ideal.[5]

The Satmars' story offers compelling counterevidence to the communitarians' frequent lament that living in a liberal society makes it difficult, if not impossible, to uphold group boundaries and traditional values. Challenging the oft-drawn dichotomies between liberal and communitarian, progressive and conservative, secular and religious forms of identity and society, the Satmars have been able to use the levers of America's bottom-up system of private enterprise to achieve something similar to what has been achieved in Israel through top-down mechanisms, albeit on a much smaller scale: the establishment of a majority-Jewish community where private control over land is coupled with public control over state political institutions. In a twist of historical irony, the Satmars have established their own form of a local counter-Zion.

Kiryas Joel has pursued this path with the blend of combativeness and accommodation that marked Joel Teitelbaum from his days in Hungary and Romania. While fiercely resisting cultural accommodation that might lead to unwelcome intermixing, the community has perfected the art of political accommodation in service of social isolation.

The combination of knowing how to fight *and* how to build alliances, particularly at the local level, has enabled Kiryas Joel to become one of the most successful examples of local sovereignty in American history as well as in the history of modern Jewish communities in the Diaspora.[6]

A Liberal Illiberal Community

The fundamental claim of this book, that the Satmar community of Kiryas Joel is a quintessentially American phenomenon, still grates against common sense. Yet we have seen that the community fits into a larger story of diverse religious groups that have built enclave communities in the United States. Part of the explanation for this trend is the reservoir of sympathy or, at least, tolerance for religion, particularly for strong communal forms of religion, which has been present from the inception of the American Republic.

But that is only part of the explanation. KJ's success also owes a good deal to the classical liberal ideal of private property, which was modernized and absorbed into what legal historian Karen Tani describes as a new American model of governance, which represents a hybrid of a free market regime and an activist state.[7] The Satmars benefited greatly from the fact that in the years between the New Deal and the early 1970s, the American political system took on this new shape, in which power was redistributed among federal, state, and local levels of government in a way that empowered them all, even though it was couched in the rhetoric of decentralization. This new form of federalism was one in which robust forms of local autonomy coexisted with a dramatic expansion of federal and state power. This was no better illustrated than by the federal government's use of block grants, which channeled money to states to implement federal policies; the effect was to empower states and, at the same time, condition their exercise of power on conformity with federal policy. The states in turn channeled money and delegated powers to local levels of government. This is the basic structure of the special education programs that became an increasing part of the budget and programming of public school districts starting in the 1970s, and the Title I programs launched the decade before. The result of the institution of programs such as these has been the creation of a new political frame-work in which power flows throughout the system rather than being concentrated in any one level of government—a political system that is simultaneously centralized yet local, bureaucratic yet entrepreneurial, nationalized yet segregated and communitarian.

Perhaps because they were not perturbed by the coexistence of local forms of political autonomy and the welfare state, the Satmars were able to take full advantage of both. Private agents acting on behalf of the community's religious leaders bought plots of land, developed them, and settled on them, thereby establishing an exclusive community. All of these actions were rooted in the individual right to own private prop-erty. Then, when facing the threat of being zoned out of the community they had settled in, the Satmars transformed their contiguous holdings of *private* property into a legally recognized *public* square through village incorporation. What the followers of the Indian guru Rajneesh had tried to do in Oregon in the 1980s, Skverer Hasidim had done earlier in New Square in 1961, and Mormons of various stripes had done in the nine-teenth century (and again in the twentieth), the Satmars did in the mid-1970s, with astonishing results. Their rapid transformation of private property into a public space—indeed, into a potent form of local political sovereignty—reflected not only the Satmars' prowess in engaging and leveraging but also the American legal and political system's support for communitarianism from the bottom up, a mode of establishing and main-taining insular communities, especially the strong forms of community endowed with collective rights favored by traditionalist religious groups.

Such a pathway to a separatist political enclave would never have been possible in Europe nor, for that matter, in Israel where state estab-lishment of religion and land ownership do not permit such an unfet-tered bottom-up development. And such a pathway is not equally avail-able to all groups in the United States. Like virtually everything in America's market-based system, its availability depends on access to private capital, which itself is a function of government support (or at the very least, the absence of state-imposed impediments to securing loans and other forms of capital) as much as private wealth. The depen-dency of communitarianism from the bottom up on access to capital is paradoxically illustrated in the case of the Satmars who are, per capita, among the poorest communities in America, but who were able to mobilize the economic means and business savvy of a small coterie of wealthy families in their midst. The lesson here seems to be that the more cohesive and illiberal a group's internal organization and culture are, the better able it is to use liberal market-based tools for its own, illiberal, purposes. By steering the resources of its wealthier members toward providing for the needs of the rest, the Satmars were able to maximize their economic clout in much the same way that they have been able to maximize their political clout through bloc voting.

Unwitting Assimilation

Few outside observers would ever imagine Kiryas Joel as a site of assimilation into American society. On the contrary, its language, dress, food, and religious norms all place it at an extreme remove from the cultural mainstream. From its inception, its raison d'être has been to sustain an enclave of purity uncontaminated by the seductions of urban life. Its leaders and residents alike carefully guard the community's boundaries against the importation of foreign values.

And yet, it bears repeating that as committed as Haredi Jews have been to combating assimilation into their host societies, they have never been completely cut off from the social, cultural, and political currents of the day. Even Rabbi Joel Teitelbaum, who dedicated himself to following "the path of the ancient Israel," engaged in innovations, and his flock of adherents has never remained static or entirely immune to larger societal pressures, either in Europe or in the United States.

The assimilation of Satmar Hasidim, if we may call it that, has been unwitting, not in the sense of their being unsophisticated or passive recipients of American culture, but rather, in the sense that it has been an unintended consequence of the very thing that would appear to be the antithesis of assimilation: their cultural and political separatism. On the conscious level, Satmar separatism regards assimilation as a grave danger, even sin. Yet it is undeniable that the community has changed over time, and in accordance with larger patterns in American society.

And the patterns of American society into which the Satmar community fits are themselves increasingly separatist, or supportive of separatism, in nature.

Sociologists a generation ago might have preferred to use the term "acculturation" to describe this process of change; the use of that term is meant to denote far more retention of core cultural values than "assimilation," which implies entry and even disappearance into the societal mainstream.[8] Our own usage here is in the spirit of Gerson Cohen, the eminent Jewish historian who described in 1966 both the ubiquity and "blessing" of assimilation in Jewish history; he was referring to the premise that the constant interaction of Jews with their host societies had strengthened rather than diminished their cultural muscle and yielded a diverse array of robust Jewish cultural traditions.[9]

It is in this sense of the term that one can speak of unwitting assimilation in Kiryas Joel. In fact, there are several layers of assimilation to notice. The form with the deepest roots is the community's political assimilation. Extending back to the origins of the community in Satu Mare—and visually symbolized by Joel Teitelbaum's famous encounter with the Romanian king, Carol II, in 1936—Satmar Hasidim have aligned themselves closely with political authorities in order to advance the interests of their community. In the American context, this tradition of engagement continued through careful cultivation of ties with public officials, but it also expanded to the regular and highly successful exercise of bloc voting in elections. While overtly professing submission to gentile political authority, the Satmars have become thoroughly Americanized in their understanding of the game of interest-group politics. Critics lambast their outsized influence in reshaping the political and physical landscape of Orange County, New York. But much of what they have gained in resources and power comes through their ability to use the ballot box to great effect. There is a dissonance between the seemingly foreign cultural ways of the Satmars and their complete fluency in the language of American politics and democracy. They neither look nor act like traditional, cigar-chomping party bosses, nor do they physically or culturally resemble modern-day politicians. But they have learned the rules of the game and play by them as well as any.

What the Satmars of KJ cannot gain at the ballot box, they can often achieve through litigation, or at least the threat of it. Already from the time of the first zoning disputes with Monroe officials in the mid-1970s, KJ leaders were willing to wield the threat of legal action as a means of achieving their goals. There was nothing of the ethos of subservience to gentile authority in this threat. The Satmars absorbed the legal culture of the United States with relish, in particular, its hyper-litigiousness. Wielding threats of court action was one way they could do so. Another was developing finely tuned powers of discernment when choosing good lawyers (though sometimes they overshot and hired lawyers who were a little too aggressive). Forum shopping, the search for a favorable judge or courtroom in which to seek adjudication, was yet another legal tactic they learned to deploy, sometimes but not always to good effect. Nowhere was this on greater display than in the labyrinth of the Aroni-Zali litigation in which the Satmars drove their penchant for complex legal strategies and forum shopping to mind-boggling extremes.

The Satmars' impressive political and legal acumen was first mobilized to support the twin tasks of creating and defending the creation of the Kiryas Joel Union Free School District. This effort featured a hugely sophisticated use of legal tactics and talent, which was the result of a conscious set of decisions taken by community leaders. Although the political entities they created—the school district and the village itself—were more or less accidental, the project of defending them from legal and political attacks decidedly was not. In the process of defending their institutions, a remarkable amount of legal and political learning occurred, through which the Satmars absorbed both good and bad American political habits and imbibed American constitutional values.

But there was also a more subtle process of assimilation by which KJ tapped into larger currents in American society without any apparent points of contact. This was evident in the push to provide better education for disabled students just at the moment when the American disabilities rights movement was gaining momentum in the 1970s and 1980s. It was also evident in the increasing boldness of KJ leaders precisely as the Christian right, symbolized by the Moral Majority, was becoming a major force to reckon with in American political life. Coinciding with the rise of that movement, they set about to create a powerful institution in the village, the public school, that stretched the limits of religious accommodation and, as a result, encountered stiff opposition within and without KJ from its first day.

The example of the rising consciousness of disability rights reminds us that the Satmars' channeling of American legal culture has had many positive effects from the convergent perspectives of the Satmar and the American mainstream. But there were also some unintended consequences, at least from the point of view of the Satmar establishment. For example, the very legal weapons they used in disputes with the *outside* world came to be brandished by competing factions *within* the Satmar world itself. The long-standing communal preference to resolve legal disputes internally was frequently bypassed, beginning with the disputes between Moshe Teitelbaum and the early dissidents in the 1980s, picking up steam over the course of the public school controversy, and culminating in the rift between the Aroni and Zali camps, which squared off in New York State courts against one another for nearly two decades.

The fact that dissidents were able to marshal the weapons of American law in their battle with the establishment might seem to affirm the existence of the right to exit, which libertarians argue makes illiberal religious enclaves not merely tolerable but deserving of the state's protection. And to some extent, it is true that America's legal regime has afforded members of the community the right to choose to stay or leave.

But leaving Kiryas Joel is not nearly as easy as the notion of the legal right to exit would have us believe. The biggest deterrent to leaving is the fear of alienating one's family members—and perhaps losing custody of one's children, as has often occurred in cases of divorce when one of the former spouses drifts away from the community, while the other remains. These so-called spiritual custody cases, in which New York family law courts routinely enforce so-called Hasidic Upbringing Clauses in divorce and custody agreements, awarding the right to control the religious upbringing of the children to the parent who remains faithful to Haredi ways, raise serious questions about the voluntariness of exit. The role of the courts in enforcing religious edicts in divorce cases, and the response to these judicial practices mounted by organizations such as Footsteps, constitutes one of the most fascinating recent chapters in Satmar history. But that is a story for a future book.

Enough people have left the community to form a critical mass. But that is only because the overall size of the Satmar population is so large; the percentage of defectors, while impossible to pin down, remains small. Far more typical are those who remain members of the community, but who find more inward or subtle ways of defecting or simply modifying and modernizing community norms. One example is the secret "unbelievers" who choose to remain in the community, and in the closet, for a variety of reasons, including the desire to stay connected to their families, fear of the outside world, and an ongoing appreciation for the values and practices of the community, notwithstanding their rejection of its beliefs.

Others remain total and faithful adherents of the religion, yet push the boundaries of its traditional practices in various ways. It is worth mentioning in this context Ruchie Freier, a Hasidic woman from Borough Park who has received a good deal of public attention in recent years. Mrs. Freier defied communal norms by attending college and, even more astonishingly, law school, while remaining a strictly observant mother of six. The source of her greatest fame is that in 2016 she was elected as a judge in Kings County, New York.[10] Such a position for a Hasidic man is unheard of, and in some ways even more remarkable for a Hasidic woman. Judge Freier hardly represents a mass movement; the Hasidic world remains profoundly wedded to a traditional division of gender roles.

That said, it is hard to imagine her election in an earlier, prefeminist era. Even today, very few Satmar woman openly profess support for feminism or, for that matter, declare the desire to undo existing gender norms in the community. It is true that many of the women (and men) who have left the Satmar worlds of KJ and Williamsburg regard themselves as feminists. But that is one of the marks distinguishing those who have left from those who remain, as is the embrace by many of them of LGBTQ identities.[11]

That said, for those who stay in the Satmar or Haredi worlds, there are unarticulated signs of the feminist values that have stuck deep roots elsewhere in America. Most significant is the increasing tendency of women to work outside of the home during long child-rearing careers that can last for thirty years. As noted earlier in chapter 1, it is common for Satmar women to work after high school graduation and before the birth of their first child. But more and more women are entering the workplace and staying there. In 2000, slightly fewer than 20 percent of KJ women were designated as being in the labor force. By 2019, that figure had almost doubled to nearly 39 percent.[12] The first reason is obvious: it is economically useful, if not necessary, for families with anywhere from five to fifteen children. But anecdotal evidence suggests a second reason: employment outside of the home affords women a measure of personal gratification, self-empowerment, and growth.

This trend reflects yet again an unspoken process of assimilation to an American norm that is, on the face of it, at odds with the underlying worldview of Kiryas Joel. How does this happen, given the insular nature of Kiryas Joel? For one thing, women have easier access to sources of knowledge in the outside world by virtue of their higher degree of English-language fluency, relative to men. And yet, until recently, the sources of knowledge available beyond KJ—television, radio, and non-Haredi newspapers—have been quite severely restricted within. What has unsealed the once hermetic border is the internet, with its boundary-busting capacity all the while that it affords a high degree of discretion. In a community such as KJ, one must traverse that border with great caution. Leading Haredi rabbis regularly inveigh against the destructive effects of the internet, among them KJ's chief rabbi, Aaron Teitelbaum, who insisted in 2012 that the internet "claimed many *korbanos* [victims] and destroyed many Jewish homes."[13] Religious schools in the village, it should be recalled, threaten expulsion of children from families that use the internet at home for any reason other than economic livelihood.

It is curious then that one encounters in the course of daily life in KJ people who own and use smartphones, even though that may arouse suspicion in the eyes of the village's Modesty Committee.[14] Users often volunteer that their phones are restricted by "kosher filters" that cut off access to potentially transgressive material, the most dangerous of which is deemed to be pornography. Meanwhile, many other residents of KJ prefer to use, if at all, old-style "dumb phones," which offer no connection to the internet.

Those who are connected to the internet, through either a computer or phone, often live in a state of cognitive dissonance that is increasingly part of life in KJ in the twenty-first century. Notwithstanding the protests of rabbis, the disapproving look of neighbors, and a broad communal taboo, they appear to regard access to the internet—and even the public display of their phones—as a normal part of life. One cannot help but wonder how long this trend can continue without irreversibly throwing open the gates of the shtetl. What happens when the sources of both news and entertainment aren't restricted? What happens when large numbers of Satmars in KJ can access the *New York Times*, Netflix, or Fox News instantly, not to mention unlimited bodies of popular or even scholarly literature that lead away from the prescribed Satmar path? It is no wonder that not only fiery rabbis but sober-minded lay leaders in KJ such as Gedalye Szegedin regard the internet as one of the gravest threats, if not the gravest, that the community faces. They are well aware that the small but growing number of people who leave the community—still a minuscule fraction of the community—are often exposed to and enticed by the outside world through the internet (just as an earlier generation of defectors was enticed away by books).

Against this spate of challenges to its ongoing existence stands a single, incontrovertible data point: Kiryas Joel continues to grow at a fast pace. The village's own projections as part of the planned annexation in 2015 of 507 acres were that its population would reach 42,000 in 2025—and, at that pace, 73,000 in 2035.[15] Even though the new plans for the town of Palm Tree set limits to the expansion of the Satmars, it is highly unlikely that we will see major changes to the practice of having very large families in the community.

What make KJ's growth all the more astonishing are the constant criticism and hostility from the outside and the fractious dissent from within. But then again, if we recall the combative roots of the Teitelbaum family in the nineteenth century, we are reminded that hostility has not been a deterrent, but rather a boon to growth, hardening the will to survive and refining the adaptive mechanisms of the Satmar community. Simply put, constant strife has been a stimulus to the expansion of Kiryas Joel, a self-standing government dedicated to the preservation of the Satmars' distinctive way of life.

But how to square the forces of assimilation with the forces of internal growth? Both are undeniably potent, though not equally visible. They are engaged, in fact, in a race to the finish, a race that will define Kiryas Joel's future—either as the world's first Hasidic city or as a communitarian experiment that succeeded spectacularly before ultimately succumbing to failure.

What Does KJ Teach Us about America?

It is quite possible that KJ will avoid these two extremes, neither maintaining its state of religious homogeneity nor dissolving into atomized, or Americanized, individuals. For the foreseeable future, it will continue to grow at a rapid clip, exerting an outsized influence in Orange County and offering a uniquely supportive environment for those intent on following "the path of ancient Israel." Without the power of clairvoyance, it is difficult to predict precisely what the future holds. But as we leave our subject, we can take stock of what Kiryas Joel tells us about America today.

In the first instance, KJ reminds us that the long tradition of religious communitarianism in America remains alive and well. Hundreds of religious communities have taken rise on American soil whose followers believed that they were separating from society in order to live a life of spiritual virtue. We often regard these groups as freakish, and consign them to the ignominious status of dangerous cults. But they are bell-wethers of this country's extraordinary religious commitments and diversity. They are "cities on the hill" to which others look with a mix of envy, admiration, and repugnance. Their existence supports the view of scholars of secularism, who suggest that we have moved from a secular to a far more religious "postsecular" era—or that we have never been a truly secular country at all.[16] In this regard, Kiryas Joel takes its place in a long chain of American religious communitarian experiments.

To reiterate, this communitarianism is not directly at odds with America's guiding political principles. In fact, it partakes of two American liberal traditions: the country's long tradition of religious pluralism, rooted in the classical liberal principle of religious freedom; and the equally deep-seated tradition of economic liberalism, rooted in the classical liberal rights of private property and private contract on which a market economy rests.

It was that latter principle that enabled the purchase of property on the real estate market and that allowed Satmar Hasidim to build an enclave in suburban Orange County in the early 1970s, after they failed to achieve this goal in other venues in New York and New Jersey. The free market, though constrained by racial, ethnic, and religious bias, permitted the accumulation of sufficient property to create the shtetl that Joel Teitelbaum had dreamt of. In parallel, state law laid out a path for individual property owners to exercise their right of the franchise to transform a neighborhood in Monroe into a public space, indeed, into a bastion of local sovereignty.[17]

Alongside the basic right to vote stood other positive and negative liberties rooted in American liberalism.[18] Members of the village of KJ exercise the freedom of worship, as can members of any other municipality in the United States. And they enjoy the liberty to raise and educate their children largely free from state control, a right of parents known as "spiritual custody" that was recognized by the Supreme Court in a series of decisions in the early decades of the twentieth century.[19] Notwithstanding the absence of explicit enumeration of any such parental right—or any parental rights—in the Constitution, conservatives appear to be at least as committed to their perpetuation as liberals are. Indeed, defending the right to religious education has long been a core plank of the conservative religious platform, and has been an organizing principle for the Satmars. Along with these "classical" liberal rights, which guarantee freedom from state interference, the Satmars also enjoy the protection of a newer liberal regime of antidiscrimination law. This regime, which is the legacy of the civil rights movement, includes statutes that prohibit discrimination on the basis of religion (and race, and other bases of group classification) in the private real estate market, in public housing, in places of employment, and in places of public accommodation. Under these civil rights laws, the Satmars are prohibited from discriminating, as the dissidents have repeatedly argued. But they are also protected from the threat of discrimination on the basis of their religious identity. In fact, it was the specter of legal action to combat alleged religious discrimination that led town officials of Monroe and Satmar leaders to agree to the formation of a village in October 1976.

It is in this founding moment that we see in the KJ story the congruence between religious and economic libertarianism as well as the coexistence of these libertarian regimes with modern forms of state and federal government that selectively subsidize and support some forms of community over others. But along with congruence with American political traditions come the tensions that lie within them, none more palpable than that between the two key religion clauses of the First Amendment. Yes, residents of KJ are entitled to the free exercise of religion. But no, they are not permitted to "establish" their particular brand of Judaism as the official creed of the village. And yet, to a great extent they have been able to do just that, by consigning the work of enforcing religious norms and maintaining religious homogeneity— what critics would describe as the work of religious coercion and exclusion—to the community's private institutions.

All members of the village's leadership are members of the Satmar Hasidic movement, and almost all of them are rabbis as a matter of education, if not vocation. Furthermore, the current leadership is closely aligned with the court of Rabbi Aaron Teitelbaum, with whom it consults on key issues, as did other KJ administrations with the first two Rebbes. It would be inconceivable, given the current state of affairs in KJ, for the political and religious leadership *not* to be tight allies, if not acting as one and the same. Whether this state of affairs constitutes a violation of the Establishment Clause has never been definitively answered, notwithstanding years of litigation raising the question. The courts have been able to duck the question, thanks to a variety of doctrinal and procedural moves, some employed by the judges who were called upon to adjudicate Establishment Clause claims, and some by the parties themselves. Thus, Judge Rakoff has refused to adjudicate the dissidents' continued complaints that the village is an unconstitutional theocracy on the grounds that they voluntarily settled their dispute with the KJ establishment long ago, at the end of the *Khal Charidim* litigation. Likewise, Justice Barasch and the appellate courts that affirmed his ruling maintained that the dispute between the Zalis and Aronis was nonjusticiable. But the one thing all this litigation makes plain is that it is impossible to avoid judicial intervention in Satmar life. The very effort to avoid deciding religious questions (as the religious question doctrine demands) requires courts to determine what is a religious question—and that itself, as we have seen, is a matter of religious dispute.

If one lesson of the Satmars' endless litigation is that religious questions are unavoidable in secular courts of law, the flip-side of that is that it is impossible for the Satmars (or any insular group) to avoid state law. The Satmar fantasy of complete separation from the secular world is just that, a fantasy, much like the American fantasy of personal liberty as an absolute right to freedom from government interference. These fantasies can only be made real if religion is truly divorced from politics. But the story of Kiryas Joel, as exemplified by the many rounds of Aroni-Zali conflict, demonstrates that this is only possible to maintain in the absence of conflict over who the religious authorities are. The legal battles between the competing factions inside the Satmar world reveal the inextricability of religion and politics, and they likewise demonstrate the unavoidability of both political and religious questions in legal disputes. Summoned by one side to decide on internal conflicts, a court might decide to just leave them alone. But as the cases and events surrounding them show, there is no such thing as just leaving a group alone since even a decision not to intervene constitutes a real intervention.

A Final Thought

As we complete this book, we find ourselves in an extraordinary moment in which Haredi Jews have attracted a degree of public visibility they had previously eschewed and escaped. In the spring and summer of 2020, the global COVID-19 pandemic placed Kiryas Joel once again in the news. Media stories abounded of how the Satmars of KJ, along with other Haredi Jews, ignored early warnings to practice "social distancing" and persisted in praying, celebrating, and burying their dead in large numbers.[20] There was the usual whiff of sensationalism that surrounded stories about Haredim, laced with inaccuracies and a sense of their ineradicable foreignness, but it is undeniable that KJ and its residents responded inconsistently and often badly to the threat at hand. The commitment of its residents to preserving their pious way of life—thrice-daily prayers, regular learning, large celebrations and funerals, children's Torah education, and, above all, the communal nature of their existence—was so deeply engrained that it had, for many, overridden the dangers posed by COVID-19, notwithstanding the core Jewish principle of *pikuach nefesh*, which asserts the supreme value of saving human life over other religious obligations. Rather than utilize the community's hierarchical leadership structure to its advantage, KJ's leaders were slow to react and indecisive. They might well have leveraged the cohesion of the various factions in town to create small and self-contained pods for the performance of essential ritual tasks. They did not.

At some level, this failure reflected the decades-long decline in rabbinic authority that began with the death of the founding Rebbe, Joel Teitelbaum, in 1979. But there are also signs of a more recent development that has had a seemingly transformative effect on the Satmar, Haredi, and wider Orthodox worlds in general: the onset of a new ideological stance that closely resembles, and is clearly related to, conservative white Christian political behavior. This ideological outlook includes a sense of grievance shared by fellow disaffected white people, a political identity that combines conservative values with libertarian individualism, and a fierce commitment to religious liberty—newly repurposed to assert the right to defy state authority if state regulations are perceived to be at odds with religious practices and beliefs. In adopting this new ideology, Haredim have left behind their erstwhile identity as a non- or "off-white" minority that knew how to parlay its electoral power into tangible benefits—without regard to party affiliation.[21]

In hindsight, it is easy to connect the dots and view this development as inevitable. We ourselves have documented and emphasized the points of connection between the Christian conservative movement, especially the Christian wing of the conservative legal movement, and the Satmars' legal claims. There have always been certain ideological affinities between traditionalist Jews and traditionalist Christians, in particular, their affirmation of traditional gender roles and sexual rules and their opposition to secularism.

And yet, largely invisibly to outside observers, including ourselves, at some point over the last few years, many Haredim, including KJ residents, appeared to have abandoned the opportunistic pragmatism that has long characterized their community's political behavior and replaced it with the more ideologically grounded conservativism of Trump supporters. It would be hard to imagine a more imperfect vessel of political expression for the Haredi community than Donald Trump in terms of ethics and comportment. But he was an agent of empowerment and an assertive leader whose defiance of liberal norms resonated with many in the community—to the point of his earning an astounding 99 percent of the vote in KJ in 2020.

These two major events of 2020—the COVID-19 pandemic and the presidential election—have revealed the ways in which the Satmars of KJ are different from many Americans, certainly from the overwhelming majority of American Jews. They reveal as well a growing affinity between the Satmar community and white Christian conservatives—a decidedly new phase in the development of Haredi culture in general and Kiryas Joel in particular. It will be interesting to see whether this affinity will continue to solidify in the aftermath of the Trump presidency or whether there will be a return to an earlier Haredi political pragmatism.

In either case, we had already seen signs that the opening chapter in the history of Kiryas Joel had come to an end. The seemingly endless litigation between the KJ dissidents and the KJ establishment, and between the Zalis and the Aronis, has sputtered out for now, yielding to a workable *modus vivendi* on the ground. The long-standing tensions between Kiryas Joel and the town of Monroe have receded with the

establishment of a new town, Palm Tree, which, like KJ, would perpetu-
ate the original Rebbe's name and ways. And plans for the creation of
new towns and villages, one for each Satmar faction, suggested the possibility that the political cohesion that had long produced a singular
voting bloc might soon become a thing of the past, leading perhaps to
an erosion of the Satmars' political strength or, alternatively, to new
forms of partisan politics. Moreover, the emergence of a growing body
of "ex-Haredim," former Satmars prominent among them, making demands for state protection of parental custody and children's educational rights, seemed to portend a new era in Satmar history.

Yet for all that, the Satmars' commitment to preserving their distinctive way of life, and to resisting change, is as strong as ever. There can be
little doubt that Kiryas Joel, New York, remains a distinctive micro-
society on the American landscape, dedicated to maintaining its religious culture and separating itself, to the greatest extent possible, from
the outside world. It is a "shtetl on the hill," challenging, inscrutable, and
ceaselessly dynamic, as this book has shown. It is a community without
parallel in the long history of the Jewish Diaspora, having achieved a
degree of self-governance unthinkable in the "old world." It is also a
community that serves as a revealing mirror of American society, expos-
ing deep roots and fissures in the animating ideals of this country. In
particular, it embodies the coexistence of liberal and illiberal currents
that, far from threatening the Satmar community, have allowed it to
grow at a stunning pace.

This points to the anomaly at the heart of liberalism, indeed, at the
heart of the American constitutional order. The rights to private
property and the free exercise of religion combine to allow illiberal
groups such as the Satmars to create religious establishments. The
policies of the Satmar municipality reinforce and are reinforced by
the nominally private authority structure of Satmar Hasidism. Neither state law nor federal law has undermined Satmar religious dictates
nor the broader illiberal culture of the community. To the contrary,
state and federal legal authorities more often than not affirm the Satmars'
actions or, by refusing to intervene in disputes, effectively shore up the
established power structure. This says as much about the character

of liberalism in America today as it does about an illiberal religious community like KJ.

Some may applaud the growth of such a separatist community as the fulfillment of the spirit of cultural pluralism and of true religious liberty. Others may look aghast at the weakened wall of separation between synagogue and state, as well as KJ's decidedly conservative values on gender, education, and social integration. But none should doubt that Kiryas Joel is an American creation, born and bred in this country, and belonging to a long tradition of strong religious communities that have survived and flourished in the United States. Indeed, it is an American shtetl, which, through a mix of steely resolve, political skill, internal growth, and fortuity, has achieved remarkable success to date—and continues to shed light on the deeply religious and illiberal roots of secular liberal America.

NOTES

Prologue

1. Julie Satow, "A Magnet for Shoppers Is Getting a Makeover," *New York Times*, May 21, 2013.

2. Eric Hobsbawm and Terence Ranger, eds., *The Invention of Tradition* (Cambridge: Cambridge University Press, 1983), 1.

3. Menachem Keren-Kratz, *Ha-kanai: Ha-rabi mi-Satmar, R. Yo'el Teitelbaum* (The Zealot: The Satmar Rebbe, R. Joel Teitelbaum) (Jerusalem: Merkaz Zalman Shazar, 2020). See also Motti Inbari, *Jewish Radical Ultra-Orthodoxy Confronts Modernity, Zionism, and Women's Equality* (New York: Cambridge University Press, 2016), 131–172.

4. See the comparative estimates of Hasidic groups based on family size in Marcin Wodziński, *Historical Atlas of Hasidism* (Princeton: Princeton University Press, 2018), 198–199. Meanwhile, according to *Anshe shelomenu*, the annual address book of the worldwide community from 2018–2019, there are 29,000 Satmar families at present. According to the 2010 census, there are 5.42 people per household in Kiryas Joel. Using that measure, one can estimate a global population of nearly 157,000 souls.

5. Ibram X. Kendi, *How to Be an Antiracist* (New York: One World, 2019), 29.

6. See the report from a protest in Borough Park in "Masks Burn in Streets as Members of Ultra-Orthodox Community Members Protest New COVID Rules," NBC News, October 7, 2020, https://www.nbcnewyork.com/news/local/ultra-orthodox-community-members-gather-to-protest-new-covid-restrictions/2655635/. See also Joshua Shanes, "The Evangelicalization of Orthodoxy," *Tablet Magazine*, October 12, 2020, https://www.tabletmag.com/sections/belief/articles/evangelicalization-orthodox-jews; and David N. Myers, "What the Current Crisis Shows about Haredi Leadership and Politics," *The Forward*, October 12, 2020, https://forward.com/opinion/456262/what-the-current-crisis-shows-about-Haredi-leadership-and-politics/.

7. Just as this book reached the copyediting stage, we received galleys of the book by Nathaniel Deutsch and Michael Casper, *A Fortress in Brooklyn: Race, Real Estate, and the Making of Hasidic Williamsburg* (New Haven, CT: Yale University Press, 2021). *A Fortress* reflects a striking convergence in scholarly interest in Satmar Hasidism, and, in many ways, is a fitting complement to this book. While Deutsch and Casper focus on the large Satmar presence in Williamsburg, this book focuses on the other major Satmar center in Kiryas Joel. Our thanks to Nathaniel Deutsch and Michael Casper for graciously making their volume available to us.

8. The term "Christian nationalism" is drawn from the analysis of Andrew L. Whitehead and Samuel L. Perry, *Taking America Back for God: Christian Nationalism in the United States* (New

York: Oxford University Press, 2020). Thanks to Nathaniel Deutsch, Josh Shanes, Elli Stern, and Shaul Magid for an illuminating conversation about Haredim, race, and religion.

9. On the 2020 presidential election in Kiryas Joel, see the results for the town of Palm Tree, in which Trump won 6,277 of 6,371 votes cast, at https://ny.votereporting.com/ORA/124 /Districts/4464/0/333/. On the Capitol insurrection, see Elad Nehorai, "I Know Why Haredi Jews Joined Neo-Nazis at the Trumpist Riot," *Daily Beast*, January 16, 2021, https://www .thedailybeast.com/i-know-why-Haredi-jews-joined-neo-n.

10. Sidney Ratner, "Horace M. Kallen and Cultural Pluralism," *Modern Judaism* 4, no. 2 (May 1984): 185–200. See also Epilogue, n. 5.

11. Marc Dollinger, *Black Power, Jewish Politics* (Waltham, MA: Brandeis University Press, 2018), 105ff.

12. Ruth Graham and Sharon LaFraniere, "Inside the People of Praise, the Tight-Knit Faith Community of Amy Coney Barrett," *New York Times*, October 8, 2020, https://www.nytimes .com/2020/10/08/us/people-of-praise-amy-coney-barrett.html.

13. William Alexander Linn, *The Story of the Mormons from the Date of Their Origin to the Year 1901* (New York: Russell & Russell, 1963), 459.

14. William Martin, "The Church of What's Happening," *Texas Monthly*, January 1981.

15. If one widens the lens to include communities that are not officially incorporated but nonetheless style themselves as cities or towns, another example is Islamberg, a hamlet established in the 1980s by a community of Black Muslim families in the foothills of the Catskills, not far from Kiryas Joel. See Rick Rojas, "They Created a Muslim Enclave in Upstate N.Y.: Then the Conspiracy Theorists Came," *New York Times*, January 28, 2019, https://www.nytimes.com /2019/01/28/nyregion/islamberg-ny-attack-plot.html.

16. See Nomi Maya Stolzenberg, "Challenging the Sovereign Shtetl: Communitarianism from the Bottom Up," *Jewish Studies Quarterly* 23 (2016): 247–266; Stolzenberg, "The Culture of Property," *Daedalus* 129 (2000): 169–192.

17. Carol Weisbrod, *The Boundaries of Utopia* (New York: Pantheon Books, 1980).

18. See Robert Bellah, Richard Madsen, William M. Sullivan, Ann Swindler, and Steven M. Tipton, *Habits of the Heart: Individualism and Commitment in American Life* (Berkeley: University of California Press, 1985), viii. See also the key works by Alasdair MacIntyre, *After Virtue: A Study in Moral Theory* (Notre Dame, IN: University of Notre Dame Press, 1981); Michael J. Sandel, *Liberalism and the Limits of Justice* (Cambridge: Cambridge University Press, 1982).

19. Foster Stockwell, ed., *The Encyclopedia of American Communes* (Jefferson, NC: McFarland, 1998) is a valuable compendium that lists 516 communes established during the years 1663–1963.

20. Liav Orgad, "Illiberal Liberalism," in *The Cultural Defense of Nations: A Liberal Theory of National Rights* (Oxford: Oxford University Press, 2015), 53–106.

21. *Wallace v. Jaffree*, 472 U.S. 38 (1985).

22. Sarah Barringer Gordon, *The Mormon Question: Polygamy and Constitutional Conflict in 19th-Century America* (Chapel Hill: University of North Carolina Press, 2003).

23. *State of Oregon v. City of Rajneeshpuram*, 598 F. Supp. 1208 (D. Or. 1984).

24. See, for example, Adam Rovner, *In the Shadow of Zion: Promised Lands Before Israel* (New York: New York University Press, 2014), as well as Michael Chabon, *The Yiddish Policemen's Union* (New York: HarperCollins, 2007).

25. Philip Roth, "Eli, the Fanatic," in *Goodbye Columbus and Five Short Stories* (Boston: Houghton Mifflin, 1959), 255. On an actual controversy on which the story may be based, see Julian Levinson, "Roth in the Archives: 'Eli, the Fanatic' and the Nitra Yeshiva Controversy of 1948," *American Jewish History* 101 (2017): 57–79, https://muse.jhu.edu/article/645162.

26. Alfred Kazin, *A Walker in the City* (New York: Harcourt, Brace, 1951).

27. Samuel G. Freedman, *Jew vs. Jew: The Struggle for the Soul of American Jewry* (New York: Simon & Schuster, 2000).

Chapter 1: Life in the Shtetl

1. Group interview in Kiryas Joel, May 7–8, 2016.

2. Y. Schreiber, "Kiryas Yoel'—a holem vos iz gevorn a metsies," *Der Yid*, September 1, 1978; the article is included in the book-length history of Kiryas Joel by the late Satmar scholar Shlomo Yankel Gelbman, *Retson tsadik* (Monroe, NY: n.p., 1998), 153. See now the two-volume Yiddish history compiled by Shmuel Shlomo Teller, *Kiryas melekh rav*, vol. 1 (1948–1974) and vol. 2 (1974–1977) (Brooklyn: Hamatik, 2018–2019).

3. See the study of Kiryas Joel's proposed annexation of 507 acres in the town of Monroe undertaken by CGR Inc., "Kiryas Joel's Proposed Annexation of Unincorporated Land in the Town of Monroe," August 21, 2015. See also "Census Shows Growth: KJ Is Fastest-Growing in N.Y.," *Times Herald-Record*, June 28, 2007. A chart of Kiryas Joel's dramatic rise in population can be seen at "Kiryas Joel: Population," http://population.city/united-states/kiryas-joel/. See also the projections in the survey conducted by Tim Miller Associates as part of Kiryas Joel's proposed annexation of 507 acres from the town of Monroe from April 29, 2015, http://kjseqra.com/507Acres/DGEIS%20Vol%201%20Text%20Sections/KJ%203.2%20Demography%20and%20Fiscal.pdf.

4. Interview with Gedalye Szegedin, May 7, 2016. For an assessment of the full measure of Moses, see the authoritative biography of Robert A. Caro, *The Power Broker: Robert Moses and the Fall of New York* (New York: Knopf, 1974). Even critics of Szegedin admit that he is a talented man who does a good job in many aspects of his job. Group interview, May 7–8, 2016.

5. See "Growing Pains of a Hasidic Village as it Gets Younger, and Bigger, with Age," *New York Times*, December 11, 2008.

6. Reports of pressure, intimidation, and violence came from interviews with F, September 14, 2011; group interview, May 7–8; and Z, May 11, 2016.

7. Interview with D, May 9, 2016.

8. Gedalye Szegedin, "Thoughtful Planning Can Strengthen MW and KJ Schools," *Times Herald-Record*, March 6, 2016, http://www.recordonline.com/article/20160306/OPINION/160309769.

9. The average number of persons per household in Kiryas Joel, 5.6, is more than double the average of 2.7 in the tri-state area. See the figures in the Census Reporter, https://censusreporter.org/profiles/16000US3639853-kiryas-joel-ny/.

10. The tense relationship between KJ and its neighbors become a central focus of a full-length documentary film, *City of Joel*, released in 2018. *City of Joel* was produced and written by Jesse Sweet, along with Federico Rosenvit and Hannah Olson. See the long post from July 30,

2016, on the Facebook page of United Monroe written by its leader Emily Convers. According to the post, the KJPE includes supervisor Harley Doles, town of Monroe board member Gerard McQuade, KJ spokesperson Ari Felberman, KJ village administrator Gedalye Szegedin, and KJ public school superintendent Joel Petlin. https://www.facebook.com/UnitedMonroeNY/posts/533069280215419. The term "KJPE" appears in websites of opponents of the establishment party in Kiryas Joel, including from some within the community. See, for example, the site kiryasjoelvillage.com, run by a Satmar Hasid from the village whose goal is to "expose the corrupted and fraudulent actions of the religiously controlled Kiryas Joel Village."

11. See the 2019 voter registration figures available at https://www.orangecountygov.com/ArchiveCenter/ViewFile/Item/995.

12. Chris McKenna, "Kiryas Joel Blocs Played Small Role in Election," HudsonValley.com/blogs, November 9, 2016, http://blogs.hudsonvalley.com/fray/2016/11/09/kiryas-joel-blocs-played-small-role-in-election/. For an analysis of Haredi voting trends in 2016, see Nathaniel Deutsch, "'Borough Park Was a Red State': Trump and the Haredi Vote," *Jewish Social Studies* 22, no. 3 (Spring/Summer 2017): 158–173.

13. See Jeremy Sharon, "'We Are Not Americans,' Says Satmar Grand Rabbi," *Jerusalem Post*, December 7, 2020, https://www.jpost.com/diaspora/we-are-not-americans-says-satmar-grand-rabbi-651419. On the sense of being in exile, interview with YT and interview with BR, MJ, SF, and HG on November 15, 2016.

14. For example, according to census data from 2017, Kiryas Joel has 3,840 housing units per square mile, as opposed to 559 in the town of Monroe. See "Kiryas Joel, New York Housing Data," http://www.towncharts.com/New-York/Housing/Kiryas-Joel-village-NY-Housing-data.html.

15. See the data in the Census Reporter, https://censusreporter.org/profiles/16000US363 9853-kiryas-joel-ny/. On the atypical layout of this unusual suburban space, see Eric McAfee, "Demography and Destiny: America's Youngest Community," *New Geography*, March 21, 2015, http://www.newgeography.com/content/004873-demography-destiny-americas-youngest-county.

16. In commenting on the report that Kiryas Joel did not have a master plan, the only municipality in Orange County without one, village administrator Gedalye Szegedin maintained in 2003 that KJ was "a model of 'smart growth'" and "one of the best-planned communities." See "Kiryas Joel: Leaders Consider Growth Options," *Times Herald-Record*, April 27, 2003.

17. The 2018 figures represent a significant *improvement* from past years; see "Kiryas Joel Village, New York, U.S. Census, Bureau," https://www.census.gov/quickfacts/kiryasjoelvillage newyork. By contrast, in reporting on Kiryas Joel in 2011, *New York Times* writer Sam Roberts reported that 70 percent of the community lived below the poverty line. He opened his story by stating: "The poorest place in the United States is not a dusty Texas border town, a hollow in Appalachia, a remote Indian reservation or a blighted urban neighborhood. It has no slums or homeless people. No one who lives there is shabbily dressed or has to go hungry. Crime is virtually nonexistent." Roberts, "A Village with the Numbers, Not the Image, of the Poorest Place," *New York Times*, April 20, 2011, http://www.nytimes.com/2011/04/21/nyregion/kiryas-joel-a-village-with-the-numbers-not-the-image-of-the-poorest-place.html?_r=0.

18. Interviews with two women who left the community, S and J, on February 14, 2013.

19. Shulem Deen, *All Who Go Do Not Return* (Minneapolis: Graywolf Press, 2015).

20. The term "derekh Yisra'el sava" abounds in writing about the Satmar Rebbe's commitment to the preservation of traditional Jewish ritual norms, including in the biographies by A. Fuchs, S. Deutsch, and Sh. Y. Gelbman. The term has its origins in Midrash Rabba Bereshit 74, where the patriarch Jacob, also known as Israel, is called "Yisra'el sava" (Israel the Elder). The term "derekh Yisra'el sava," which connotes adherence to traditional Jewish practice, appears to be of modern vintage, though its precise origins are unknown. On the use of the term more generally, see Samuel C. Heilman, *Defenders of the Faith: Inside Ultra-Orthodox Judaism* (New York: Schocken Books, 1992), 13.

21. The Hatam Sofer (born Moses Schreiber in 1762 and died in 1839) was a German-born rabbi who moved to Pressburg in Hungary, later Bratislava in Slovakia, where he established a large yeshivah and gained renown as a conservative traditionalist.

22. "A Woman Scorned in KJ," *Times Herald-Record*, September 7, 2007, http://www.recordonline.com/article/20070907/News/709070320.

23. Dovid Meisels, *The Rebbe: The Extraordinary Life & Worldview of Rabbeinu Yoel Teitelbaum* (n.p.: Israel Bookstore, 2010), 354–361, 356.

24. On the Rebbe's shifting views, see Meisels, *Rebbe*, 346–352.

25. See the account of the former Satmar woman Deborah Feldman, who left the community in part because of her unpleasant experiences in the *mikveh*. Feldman wrote a widely sold book about her experiences. See Feldman, *Unorthodox: The Scandalous Rejection of My Hasidic Roots* (New York: Simon & Schuster, 2012), 140–157.

26. Interviews with S and J.

27. Feldman reports that the obsession with thinness leads to anorexia in the Satmar community in Williamsburg. See Feldman, *Unorthodox*, 73.

28. The figures are taken from the semiofficial Yiddish monthly in Kiryas Joel in a full-page announcement titled "Der 'dires krizis' in Kiryas Yoel—un di lezung fun Annexation" (The Housing Crisis in Kiryas Joel—and the Solution of Annexation), April 16, 2016, 31.

29. Leading the push for annexation were Kiryas Joel mayor Leopold Lefkowitz and two veteran Satmar officials close to Rabbi Joel Teitelbaum: Moshe Friedman and Shlomo M. Rosner. A Monroe-based group named the Committee for Orderly Growth led the opposition. See "Aneksirung fun frishn bodn tsu Kiryas Yoel bevilgt gevorn," *Der Yid*, May 13, 1983. See also two articles by *Times Herald-Record* reporter Ruth Boice on the annexation: "Plan Would Double Size of Kiryas Joel," *Times Herald-Record*, January 5, 1983, and "Monroe, Kiryas Joel OK Annexation," *Times Herald-Record*, May 10, 1983.

30. On the attempt to build a pipeline, see Peter Applebome, "Sometimes, a Pipeline Is a Lightning Rod," *New York Times*, June 20, 2004. On the plan to build a new community, see Chris McKenna, "KJ Residents Plan to Build Village," *Times Herald-Record*, July 11, 2004.

31. At a loud and cantankerous meeting on September 8, 2015, in which a thousand residents were present, the smaller proposal was approved. See Chris McKenna, "Monroe Board Approves 164-Acre Annexation by Kiryas Joel, Rejects 507-Acre Proposal," *Times Herald-Record*, September 8, 2015, http://www.recordonline.com/article/20150908/NEWS/150909424. In May 2016, the Monroe board approved a ninety-day moratorium on building in the town, thereby forestalling the KJ annexation plans. See Yvonne Marcotte, "Moratorium a Multifaceted Challenge for Monroe," *Epoch Times*, May 11, 2016, http://www.theepochtimes.com/n3/2062828-moratorium-a-multifaceted-challenge-for-monroe/.

32. In a conversation with Gedalye Szegedin on May 7, 2016, he articulated the view that by maintaining territorial contiguity and not establishing new Satmar satellites, Satmar Hasidim could be assured that they were exercising control only over themselves, not over their neighbors. See also the op-ed by Gedalye Szegedin, "Thoughtful Planning Can Strengthen MW and KJ Schools," *Times Herald-Record*, March 6, 2016.

33. See the detailed account on the tensions between Orthodox Jewish and other residents of Ramapo around the East Ramapo school board by Benjamin Wallace-Wells, "Them and Them," *New York Magazine*, April 21, 2013, http://nymag.com/news/features/east-ramapo-hasidim-2013-4/. For other perspectives, see Batya Unger Sargon, "The Blame Game," *Tablet*, September 8, 2014; Ben Calhoun, "A Not-So-Simple Majority," *This American Life*, September 12, 2014, https://www.thisamericanlife.org/534/a-not-so-simple-majority; David J. Butler, Randall M. Levine, and Stephanie Schuster, "Inside the East Ramapo Central School District Case," *Tablet*, May 5, 2017.

34. See the census figures from 2015 to 2019, U.S. Census Bureau, "Kiryas Joel Village, New York," https://www.census.gov/quickfacts/kiryasjoelvillagenewyork.

35. The above quotes are taken from the *melaveh malkah* conversation in a private home in Kiryas Joel on May 7–8, 2016.

36. Group interview, May 7–8, 2016. Regarding Satmar attitudes toward marijuana, it is interesting to note that Leo Friedman, son of one of the most prominent lay leaders in the Satmar community, Moses Friedman, joined with a Gerer Hasid to submit an application to manufacture medical marijuana in New York. Moses Friedman is known as Moshe Gabbai for his role as a chief aide to Rabbi Joel Teitelbaum and his successor, Rabbi Moshe Teitelbaum. See Hella Winston, "Kosher Cannabis? Ger and Satmar Duo Apply for Medical Marijuana Manufacturing Permit, Though Quietly," June 21, 2015, http://www.thejewishweek.com/news/new-york/kosher-cannabis.

37. Interview with three women on May 9, 2016, and group interview with men on May 7–8, 2016.

38. See interview with YK, December 1, 2009.

39. See Census Reporter, https://censusreporter.org/profiles/16000US3639853-kiryas-joel-ny/.

40. Interviews with S and J.

41. Interview with Footsteps staff, November 3, 2015. Footsteps was established in 2003 to address the needs of the rising number of people who left the Haredi world by providing them with "a range of services, including social and emotional support, educational and career guidance, workshops and social activities, and access to resources." For a description of the organization's mission, see its website: http://footstepsorg.org.

42. On this ban in the Satmar world, see Frimet Goldberger, "Ban Me from Driving—Please!," *The Forward*, May 1, 2014.

43. Rosalind Rosenberg, *Beyond Separate Spheres: Intellectual Roots of Modern Feminism* (New Haven, CT: Yale University Press, 1982).

44. See the U.S. Census Bureau QuickFacts data for Kiryas Joel (regarding language spoken at home for the period between 2014–2018), https://www.census.gov/quickfacts/fact/table/kiryasjoelvillagenewyork#. See also the discussion in Ayala Fader, *Hidden Heretics: Jewish Doubt in the Digital Age* (Princeton: Princeton University Press, 2020), 229–231.

45. Israel Rubin, *Satmar: An Island in the City* (Chicago: Quadrangle Books, 1972), 126.

46. The average cost of a home in Kiryas Joel, according to U.S. Census Bureau figures from 2018, is $406,100, compared to a price of $260,300 in Orange County at large. See U.S. Census Bureau, "Kiryas Joel Village, New York," https://www.census.gov/quickfacts/fact/table/kiryasjoelvillagenewyork/PST045218.

47. Interview with three women, May 9, 2016. See Fader's superb ethnographic study of New York Haredi "double lifers," who conceal their abandonment of ritual observance at home but connect to other rebels online. The book contains poignant stories of women mentally opting out of a rules-bound system in which they do not believe or which they find oppressive. Fader, *Hidden Heretics*, esp. 103–112.

48. For a description of a typical Hanukah menu, with recipes, see the food column of Joan Nathan, "From Hungary to Hanukah, From Long Ago," *New York Times*, December 13, 2006.

49. In the early years of the community, when Joel Teitelbaum first moved to the village, a number of his followers joined him in walking forty minutes each way from his home on the outskirts of town to the sole synagogue in KJ. See Sh. Y. Gelbman, *Moshi'an shel Yisra'el* (Kiryas Joel: Sh. Y. Gelbman, 1984), and interviews.

50. This claim was made powerfully by the German-Jewish philosopher Hermann Cohen. See his essay "The Significance of Judaism for Religious Progress," translated and introduced by Alan Mittleman in *Modern Judaism* 24 (February 2004): 36–58.

51. Interview with BR, November 14, 2016.

52. The classic text making this claim is Joel Teitelbaum, *Va-yo'el Mosheh* (1959; 2nd ed., Brooklyn: Deutsch, 1970).

53. Interview with Z, November 14, 2016.

54. For example, Neturei Karta members burned an Israeli flag in Kiryas Joel on May 6, 2016, on Lag Ba-Omer. See "Israeli Flag Burned in the Anti-Zionist Village of Kiryas Joel," https://www.youtube.com/watch?v=c5G7xSfFdrQ.

55. Gelbman, *Retson tsadik*, 336–337, and Meisels, *Rebbe*, 563–567.

56. The *Post* article, "They Came by Bus, by Taxi, by Plane," August 21, 1979, was included in the multilanguage volume commemorating Joel Teitelbaum's death and funeral, *Sheki`at ha-hamah* (Brooklyn: Gross Brothers, 1980), 6 (English section).

57. See the video of R. Aaron lighting the Lag Ba-Omer bonfire in 2013, "Satmar Grand Rebbe Aron Teitelbaum Lighting Bon Fire Kiryas Joel, NY Lag Bomer 2013," https://www.youtube.com/watch?v=iH1gRRrIPQo.

58. The designation "Satmar kingdom" (*malkhus Satmar*) hints at the imperial ambition of the first Satmar rebbe to create, or rather re-create after the Holocaust, a global Satmar community. For use of the term, see Elchonon Josef Hertzman, *Malkhus Satmar: Satmarer kenigraikh in Amerike* (Brooklyn: E. J. Hertzman, 1981).

59. An important consequence of this placement is that the United Talmudic Academy system is served by the Kiryas Joel public school, whereas the other two Satmar systems are served by the neighboring Monroe-Woodbury public school district.

60. On the decision to create a girls' school, see Meisels, *Rebbe*, 462–466, as well as the recollections of the long-standing principal for English studies, Hertz Frankel, in *The Satmar Rebbe and His English Principal: Reflections on the Struggle to Build Yiddishkeit in America* (Brooklyn: Menucha, 2015), 31.

61. Quoted in Meisels, *Rebbe*, 148.

62. A summary of the twenty-point set of guidelines for parents is included in Gelbman, *Retson tsadik*, 265–268.

63. This paragraph draws from Israel Rubin's discussion of a typical Satmar boy's education in Williamsburg in *Satmar: As Island in the City*, 144–149.

64. For example, a textbook published in multiple editions in Kiryas Joel covers the entire course of Jewish history in 150 pages, using maps, tables, and the Hebrew (rather than the Gregorian) calendar system. See Yehuda Friedman, `Al ha-rishoynim ve-`al ha-ahroynim: seder ha-dores farn yugnt*, 5th ed. (Kiryas Joel: Lilmod u-lelamed, 2005).

65. The schedule was described to one of the authors by the father of a yeshivah ketana student in Kiryas Joel in an email exchange of June 6, 2016.

66. *Meyer v. Nebraska*, 262 U.S. 390, 402 (1923). See also *Pierce v. Society of Sisters*, 268 U.S. 510 (1925); *Wisconsin v. Yoder*, 406 U.S. 205, 213 (1972).

67. On Yaffed, see Young Advocates for Fair Education, "Spreading Awareness. Creating Change," https://yaffed.org/. On Naftuli Moster's background and aims, see Jennifer Miller, "Yiddish Isn't Enough: A Yeshiva Graduate Fights for Secular Studies in Hasidic Education," *New York Times*, November 21, 2014, http://www.nytimes.com/2014/11/23/nyregion/a-yeshiva-graduate-fights-for-secular-studies-in-hasidic-education.html.

68. Later that year a group of former Rockland County yeshivah students and their parents filed a class-action lawsuit against the state of New York, alleging that its lack of supervision of Haredi schools amounted to "willful blindness" with respect to the inadequate secular education given to boys. See Amy Sara Clark, "Bid for Better Secular Ed in Yeshivas Headed toward Court," *Jewish Week*, March 10, 2015, http://www.thejewishweek.com/news/new-york/bid-better-secular-ed-yeshivas-heading-toward-court, and Clark, "Suit Claims 'Willful Blindness' over Secular Ed," *Jewish Week*, November 24, 2015, http://www.thejewishweek.com/news/new-york/suit-claims-willful-blindness-over-yeshiva-secular-ed.

69. The lawsuit stemmed from the introduction into the 2018 New York State budget of the "Felder Amendment," named after state senator Simcha Felder, who represents a district in Brooklyn with a large Haredi population and who sought to have an exemption from the requirement that yeshivahs provide "substantial equivalent instruction" in secular subjects. See the Yaffed announcement of its lawsuit from July 23, 2018, at https://www.yaffed.org/lawsuit1.

70. "State Education Chief Unveils Retooled 'Substantial Equivalency' Rules for Private Schools," *Lohud*, May 31, 2019, https://www.lohud.com/story/news/local/rockland/2019/05/31/new-york-puts-forth-new-private-school-education-guidelines/1300079001/.

71. Frankel, *Satmar Rebbe*, 64.

72. Drawn from the Jewish studies curriculum outlines for years 9–12 at the Bais Ruchel high school in Kiryas Joel. See also the account of Satmar educational norms for girls in Meisels, *Rebbe*, 462–485.

73. Email exchange with S, September 2, 2016.

74. Ibid.

75. Some of the college degrees counted in the 7.5 percent come from credit-granting yeshivahs rather than secular colleges or universities, thus making the actual figure of college graduates, in the conventional sense of the term, lower. Compare the results of the 2013 Pew study,

http://www.pewforum.org/2013/10/01/jewish-american-beliefs-attitudes-culture-survey/, to the U.S. Census Bureau data, https://www.census.gov/quickfacts/kiryasjoelvillagenewyork.

76. Ginia Bellafante, "In Brooklyn, Stifling Higher Learning among Hasidic Women," *New York Times*, September 2, 2016.

77. Interviews with Malka Silberstein and Rabbi Eliezer Kohn in Kiryas Joel, February 2, 2012.

78. For a discussion of Pataki's proposal, as part of a detailed description of the legal history of the Kiryas Joel School District, see Louis Grumet with John Caher, *The Curious Case of Kiryas Joel: The Rise of a Village Theocracy and the Battle to Defend the Separation of Church and State* (Chicago: Chicago Review Press, 2016), 40–41. Grumet and Caher point out that Pataki's idea was initially rejected by KJ's mayor, Abraham Wieder, who had a special needs child himself. Wieder, they contend, "was not keen on the idea of running a secular school district." Ibid., 41.

79. Ibid., 248.

80. See *Kunteres milhemet hovah* (Brooklyn: n.p., 1995).

81. Interview with Steven Benardo, August 26, 2003.

82. These figures come from a mix of sources. For public school budget figures from 2014–2015, see the comprehensive tables based on New York State Education Department figures at Syracuse.com, http://www.syracuse.com/news/index.ssf/2014/05/nys_school_budgets _2014-15_look_up_compare_any_district.html?appSession=41639770325438038115527144 9738885125397808530625814117534333280659091791212759442782323189842629547 75184462742050761685945809731&PageID=2&PrevPageID=2&cpipage=1&CPIsortType =desc&CPIorderby=Total_Proposed_Tax_Levy_201415&cbCurrentPageSize=. Additional data come from Pauline Liu, "Our Per-Pupil Costs Climb amid Nationwide Drop," *Times Herald-Record*, September 8, 2013, http://www.recordonline.com/article/20130908/NEWS /309080325, as well as an email exchange with Superintendent Petlin from September 21, 2016.

83. The figure of $70,000–80,000 per pupil in Kiryas Joel came from the email exchange with Petlin from September 21, 2016. Meanwhile, the figure for New York from 2017–2018 can be found at https://data.nysed.gov/fiscal.php?year=2018&instid=800000049018. Meanwhile, the annual Syracuse.com database of New York State school budgets places KJ's annual expenditures per student at $165,000, nearly five times that of the next school district, https://www .syracuse.com/schools/2020/06/ny-school-budgets-2020-how-much-does-each-district -spend-per-student-lookup.html?appSession=9CU7T39W2TU6P55B94F0UF8JARSE1BFH 99JG8D20DQT0UC3O4JE9WT0PK762J193R1N393D3U73AGT72130JY62QZ9298X 228I635TVOH79SV2396NA8WWCAM2594CCB.

84. See, for example, Matt Schaertl, "How Not to Run a School District," originally posted in the *Webster Post*, February 13, 2011, and reposted on *Yeshiva World News* at http://www .theyeshivaworld.com/news/headlines-breaking-stories/83965/kiryas-joel-how-not-to-run-a -school-district.html.

85. As of 2019, there is village website to allow for the payment of tax, water, and sanitation bills: https://kiryasjoel.org/.

86. According to New York State law, "Minutes of open meetings must be made available within two weeks of the meeting; minutes of executive sessions must be made available within one week of the executive session." See the Committee on Open Government of the NY Department of State, http://www.dos.ny.gov/coog/openmeetinglawfaq.html#speak.

87. Joel Petlin estimates that $4.6 million of the school district budget goes to transportation costs. See Pauline Liu, "Our Per-Pupil Costs Climb amid Nationwide Drop," *Times Herald-Record*, September 8, 2013, https://www.recordonline.com/article/20130908/NEWS/309080325.

88. See the data for 2017–2018 from the New York State Department of Education at https://data.nysed.gov/enrollment.php?year=2018&instid=800000040287.

89. For the claim that the insularity of Satmar is the cause of a higher rate of birth defects, see the comments section to the article by Allan Nadler, "The Riddle of the Satmar," *Jewish Ideas Daily*, May 23, 2013, http://www.jewishideasdaily.com/6538/features/the-riddle-of-the-satmar-2/. See also Pauline Liu, "Kiryas Joel Has Come Long Way in Service [*sic*] Special Needs Students," *Times Herald-Record*, July 4, 2014, http://www.recordonline.com/article/20140704/News/407040336. Interview with Joel Petlin and Jehuda Halpern, May 11, 2016.

90. Sam Roberts, "A Village with the Numbers, Not the Image, of the Poorest Place," *New York Times*, April 20, 2011, http://www.nytimes.com/2011/04/21/nyregion/kiryas-joel-a-village-with-the-numbers-not-the-image-of-the-poorest-place.html.

91. See the figure from U.S. Census Bureau QuickFacts at https://www.census.gov/quickfacts/fact/table/US/PST045219. By comparison, in the poorest large city in the United States in 2015, Detroit, 48 percent of the population had incomes under $25,000. Cf. Bruce Kennedy, "America's 11 Poorest Cities," *CBS MoneyWatch*, February 18, 2015, http://www.cbsnews.com/media/americas-11-poorest-cities/. For the 2019 number, see U.S. Census Bureau, "Kiryas Joel Village, New York," https://www.census.gov/quickfacts/kiryasjoelvillagenewyork.

92. Interview with BR, November 2, 2016.

93. On the trend in Lakewood, see Mark Oppenheimer, "The Beggars of Lakewood," *New York Times*, October 16, 2014, http://www.nytimes.com/2014/10/19/magazine/the-beggars-of-lakewood.html?_r=0/.

94. On food stamps, see "KJ Highest US Poverty Rate, Census Says," *Times Herald-Record*, January 30, 2009, http://www.recordonline.com/article/20090130/NEWS/901300361. On Medicaid, see Chris McKenna, "New Data: 93% in KJ on Medicaid," *Times Herald-Record*, June 5, 2014, http://www.recordonline.com/article/20140605/News/406050314.

95. McKenna, "New Data."

96. Interview with Emily Convers, February 8, 2016. Convers was defended by the Kiryas Joel Alliance in an advertisement in the *Times Herald-Record*, June 16, 2015.

97. In response to an article by Emily Convers denying that antisemitism was at play in United Monroe's work, one of the commentators to her letter wrote: "A parasite needs a host to survive." See Convers, "The Situation in Monroe Is Not 'Hopeless' or 'Unwinnable,'" *Photo News*, January 17, 2014. See also the blog post "Kiryas Joel—Parasite Village Filled with Jews" on the white supremacist website White Biocentrism from April 29, 2014.

98. See "12 Family Members Accused of $20 Million Mortgage Fraud," *CBS New York*, November 13, 2014, http://newyork.cbslocal.com/2014/11/13/12-family-members-accused-of-20-million-mortgage-fraud/. In the case from 2015, the two KJ men were part of a larger group of thirty yielded in the sweep. See Heather Yakin, "Welfare Fraud Sweep Nabs 30 Orange County Residents, 2 Corporations in Kiryas Joel," *Times Herald-Record*, July 1, 2015, http://www.recordonline.com/article/20150701/NEWS/150709958.

99. Regarding the claim of arson, investigators determined that the fire was set in eighteen places on April 21, 1990. The villager had already received $100,000 from a $360,000 grant from

the U.S. Department of Housing and Urban Development. After the fire, the village sued its insurer for $1 million. In dismissing the claim, U.S. district judge John F. Keenan wrote that the insurers "presented evidence tending to show that plaintiff (i.e., the village) may have had a motive to commit arson, as well as evidence suggesting the possibility of arson." See the investigative story by Edward F. Moltzen and Christopher Mele, "Burned Money Arson Covers HUD Dollar Trail," *Times Herald-Record*, June 6, 1993. Five years later, Mele and Paula McMahon wrote a detailed follow-up investigative piece in which the application for HUD funding was labeled a "farce." See Mele and McMahon, "Evidence Shows KJ Fraud," *Times Herald-Record*, April 21, 1998.

100. See the sidebar "Probes of KJ Prove Difficult" in Mele and McMahon, "Evidence Shows KJ Fraud."

101. Were it not for the support of those politicians, KJ would not have received $10.5 million in state and federal aid needed to create a fifty-six-bed postpartum convalescence home for mothers that opened in 2008. Chris McKenna, "Kiryas Joel Gets $10.5 Million in Grants for Women's Center," *Times Herald-Record*, July 20, 2008, http://www.recordonline.com/article /20080720/NEWS/807200312.

102. Data on the amount of government support and percentage of employed in Kiryas Joel (and nationally) can be found at the U.S. Census Bureau QuickFacts page, https://www.census .gov/quickfacts/table/PST045215/3639853,00. Cf. the census data from 2000, in which 19 percent of women and only 34 percent of the total population participated in the labor force, at http://censtats.census.gov/data/NY/1603639853.pdf. The census figures include total number and percentage employed and total number and percentage of women employed. The figures on male employment—64 percent in KJ and 68 percent nationally—are calculations devised by Leah Boustan in an email exchange from October 8, 2016. We thank Professor Boustan for her assistance in this matter.

103. See the data from the American Community Survey (2010–2014) at "Data USA: Kiryas Joel," https://datausa.io/profile/geo/kiryas-joel-ny/#housing.

104. The old website www.kjpoultry.com no longer functions, but the figure of 250 employees can be gleaned through a Google search reference to the website.

105. The twenty-page federal complaint against the plant, *United States v. KJPPP*, is at https:// www.justice.gov/sites/default/files/usao-sdny/legacy/2015/03/25/United%20States%20v .%20KJPPP,%2014%20Civ.%208458%20(VB)%20-%20Complaint.pdf. See also Chris McKenna, "Kiryas Joel Slaughterhouse Fined $330,000," *Times Herald-Record*, October 24, 2014, http:// www.recordonline.com/article/20141024/NEWS/141029704.

106. Interview with Gedalye Szegedin, May 8, 2016.

107. Five percent of KJ residents commute between 60 and 90 minutes and 11.7 percent commute longer than 90 minutes. See "Data USA: Kiryas Joel," https://datausa.io/profile/geo /kiryas-joel-ny/#housing.

108. Interview with DN, October 28, 2009.

109. On the 2001 election, see Chris McKenna, "Voter Fraud Found in Kiryas Joel Mayoral Election," *Times Herald-Record*, July 17, 2001, http://www.recordonline.com/article/20010717 /NEWS/307179999. The 1997 investigation by two journalists revealed that eighty-four names were found to have been used in two different places in the same election. See Christopher Mele and Paula McMahon, "Voter Fraud, Take 2," *Times Herald-Record*, October 19, 1997.

110. Interviews with Szegedin, December 7, 2009, and April 29, 2010.

111. Steven J. Dubner, "Leibish Lefkowitz: The Rabbi's Riches," *New York Times,* January 3, 1999.

112. On the origins of the KJ fire department and its erstwhile problems, see Chris McKenna, "KJ Firemen Face Unique Problems," *Times Herald-Record,* January 9, 2002, http://www.recordonline.com/article/20020109/NEWS/301099994.

113. In fact, Szegedin, while the highest paid employee of KJ, is one of eight employees to earn over $100,000. See "Eight Kiryas Joel Officials Earn over $100,000," *Suburban.com,* February 19, 2016, http://www.suburbanites.com/news/eight-kiryas-joel-officials-earn-over-100k/.

114. "Synagogue Faction Allegedly Wrecks School," *Newsday,* October 27, 2005.

115. Interview with Moshe Gabbai Friedman, October 20, 2013.

116. Nomi Maya Stolzenberg and David N. Myers, "Community, Constitution, and Culture: The Case of the Jewish *Kehilah,*" *University of Michigan Journal of Law Reform* 25 (1991–1992): 633, 639.

117. See David N. Myers, "The Rise of a Sovereign Shtetl: Communitarianism from the Bottom Up in Kiryas Joel, N.Y.," *Jewish Studies Quarterly* 23 (2016): 222–246.

Chapter 2: Satmar in Europe

1. According to followers, the Rebbe never imagined the creation of a legally recognized entity but rather wanted a place of refuge from the city with the possibility of providing sufficient housing to his rapidly growing flock. Interview with Shlomo Yankel Gelbman, February 2, 2010. See Sh. Y. Gelbman, *Retson tsadik: hityasdut `ir Kiryas Yo'el* (Kiryas Joel, NY: Executive Printers, 1998), 7. Gelbman is the author of a nine-volume biography of Joel Teitelbaum, *Moshi'an shel Yisra'el,* among other publications.

2. See SHOAH Resource Center, "Satu Mare," http://www1.yadvashem.org/odot_pdf/Microsoft%20Word%20-%207459.pdf. The Romanian census figures of 1930 place the population of the city at 49,917. See *Indicatorul statistic al satelor și unităților administrative din România: Cuprinzând rezultatele recensământului general al populației din 29 Decembrie 1930* (Bucharest, 1932), xxviii.

3. For an overview of the cultural spheres of Hungarian Jewry, see Jacob Katz, *A House Divided: Orthodoxy and Schism in Nineteenth-Century Central European Jewry,* trans. Zipporah Brody (Hanover, NH: University Press of New England, 2002), esp. chaps. 5 and 6.

4. See Avraham Fuchs, *Ha-Admor mi-Satmar* (Jerusalem: Abraham Fuchs, 1980), 79. Fuchs uses an expression from Isaiah (29:6) referring to the force of God being visited upon Ariel (Jerusalem) "with thunder, and with earthquake, and great noise, with *whirlwind and tempest,* and the flame of a devouring fire." I have translated "whirlwind and tempest" as "stormy ferocity."

5. See, for example, Hertzman, *Malkhus Satmar.* In evocation of this motif, there is even a Facebook page titled "Malchus Satmar" that attracts correspondents interested in Satmar Hasidism. See http://www.facebook.com/group.php?gid=2204746126.

6. On the origins of the Hasidic court, see David Biale, David Assaf, Benjamin Brown, Uriel Gellman, Samuel Heilman, Moshe Rosman, Gadi Sagiv, and Marcin Wodziński, *Hasidism: A New History* (Princeton: Princeton University Press, 2018), 225–230.

7. On the role of the *tsadik* as "ladder," see Arthur Green, "The *Zaddik* as *Axis Mundi* in Later Judaism," *Journal of the American Academy of Religion* 14, no. 3 (1977): 338. The literature on the role and image of the *tsadik* is considerable. Moshe Idel discusses it, as well as the image of the

tsadik as vessel, instrument, and palace, in his *Hasidism: Between Ecstasy and Magic* (Albany: State University of New York Press, 1995), 191–207, 365n1.

8. Gelbman, *Moshi'an shel Yisra'el*, 4:145.

9. David Sorotzkin offers a genealogy of radical Hasidic thinkers engaged in battle against the modern world that includes Tsvi Elimelekh of Dinov, Elimelekh of Lizhensk, Naphtali of Ropschitz, and Yoel Teitelbaum in "Binyan erets shel mata ve-hurban erets shel ma'alah: Ha-Rabi mi-Satmar veha-ukhlusiyah ha-ortodoskit ha-radikalit," in *Erets Yisra'el ba-hagut ha-Yehudit ba-me'ah ha-`esrim*, ed. Aviezer Ravitzky (Jerusalem: Yad Ben-Zvi, 2004), 133–167.

10. The first edition of the book, published in 1959, revolved around Teitelbaum's reading of the Three Oaths. Subsequent editions included two additional sections dealing with settlement in the land of Israel and the question of language (modern Hebrew vs. the "Holy Tongue"). See Teitelbaum, *Va-yo'el Mosheh*. See also Sorotzkin, "Binyan erets shel mata," 161.

11. The oaths are: "One, that Israel not ascend the wall; two, that the Holy One, blessed be He, adjured Israel not to rebel against the nations of the world; and three, that the Holy One, blessed be He, adjured the idolaters not to oppress Israel overly much." Babylonian Talmud (Ketubot 111a). For a lucid explication of the oaths and how various modern Jews interpret them in radically divergent ways, see Aviezer Ravitzky, *Messianism, Zionism, and Jewish Religious Radicalism*, trans. Michael Swirsky and Jonathan Chipman (Chicago: University of Chicago, 1996), 63–66, and the appendix devoted to the oaths, 211–234.

12. Teitelbaum, *Va-yo'el Mosheh*, 9ff.

13. In the marketplace of Jewish nationalist ideas, Autonomists such as Simon Dubnow and the Bund favored a regime of national cultural autonomy in Eastern Europe rather than territorial concentration or political sovereignty in Palestine. See Simon Rabinovitch, *Jewish Rites, National Rites: Nationalism and Autonomy in Late Imperial and Revolutionary Russia* (Stanford, CA: Stanford University Press, 2014), as well as Rabinovitch, ed., *Jews and Diaspora Nationalism: Writings on Jewish Peoplehood in Europe and the United States* (Waltham, MA: Brandeis University Press, 2012). On Birobidzhan, see Robert Weinberg, *Stalin's Forgotten Zion: Birobidzhan and the Making of a Soviet Jewish Homeland: An Illustrated History, 1928–1996* (Berkeley: University of California Press, 1998).

14. In similar fashion, the authors of *Hasidism: A New History* refer to the "dialectical engagement to its secular opponent that defines Hasidism as a modern movement." Biale et al., *Hasidism*, 11.

15. See the census figures in Ladislau Gyémánt, *The Jews of Transylvania: A Historical Destiny* (Cluj-Napoca: Institutul Cultural Român, 2004), 186. See the competing set of numbers in Tamás Csíki, "Satu Mare," in *YIVO Encyclopedia of Jews in Eastern Europe*, http://www.yivoencyclopedia.org/article.aspx/Satu_Mare. Csíki notes that "by 1869 the Jewish Population had grown to 1,357; by 1890 to 3,427; and by 1910 to 7,194 (representing 7.4 percent, 16.5 percent, and 20.6 percent of the total population, respectively). By 1941, there were 12,960 Jews in Satu Mare—24.9 percent of the total number of residents.".

16. Raphael Mahler, *Hasidism and the Jewish Enlightenment: Their Confrontation in Galicia and Poland in the First Half of the Nineteenth Century* (Chapel Hill: University of North Carolina Press, 1984), 100–102.

17. Still, the number of Hasidic residents of Sátoraljaújhely who followed Rabbi Moshe Teitelbaum was small—a mere eighty families—compared to one thousand non-Hasidic

families. See Michael K. Silber, "The Limits of Rapprochement: The Anatomy of an Anti-Hasidic Controversy," *Studia Judaica* 3 (1994): 134.

18. On the Kossuth legend, see Michael K. Silber, "Kossuth Blessed by a Rabbi: The Metamorphosis of a Legend," in *Making History Jewish: The Dialectics of Jewish History in Eastern Europe and the Middle East: Studies in Honor of Professor Israel Bartal*, ed. Pawel Maciejko and Scott Ury (Leiden: Brill, 2020), 70–110, as well as Fuchs, *Ha-Admor mi-Satmar*, 23.

19. See the discussion in Katz, *House Divided*, 48.

20. See Michael Silber's discussion of this slogan in his entry on the Hatam Sofer in the *YIVO Encyclopedia of Jews in Eastern Europe*, https://yivoencyclopedia.org/article.aspx/Sofer_Mosheh.

21. See Moshe Teitelbaum's commentary on the weekly portion of Balak in *Yismah Mosheh* (Berlin: Hotsa'at Pardes, 1927–1928), 252.

22. Joel Teitelbaum looked to his forebear, Moshe, along with the Hatam Sofer and the later Hungarian rabbi Chaim Halberstam (1793–1876), as the guiding lights of traditionalist Judaism in its war of survival against a hostile modern world. See Gelbman, *Moshi'an shel Yisra'el*, 2:58ff.

23. The resolutions are included in Alexander Guttmann, *The Struggle over Reform in Rabbinic Literature during the Last Century and a Half* (Jerusalem: World Union for Progressive Judaism, 1977), 264–265. See also Michael K. Silber, "The Emergence of Ultra-Orthodoxy: The Invention of a Tradition," in *The Uses of Tradition: Jewish Continuity since Emancipation*, ed. Jack Wertheimer (New York: Jewish Theological Seminary of America, 1992), 39, 50–59; and Katz, *House Divided*, 77–85.

24. See the Sighet memorial volume *The Heart Remembers: Jewish Sziget*, ed. Yitzhak Alfasi, Eli Netzer, and Anna Szalai (Matan: Association of Former Szigetian in Israel, 2003), 19.

25. See Silber, "Limits of Rapprochement," 134, as well as Gelbman, *Moshi'an shel Yisra'el*, 2:395.

26. Gelbman, *Moshi'an shel Yisra'el*, 3:225.

27. Ibid., 2:468.

28. David N. Myers, "'Commanded War': Three Chapters in the 'Military' History of Satmar Hasidism," *Journal of the American Academy of Religion* 81, no. 2 (June 2013): 311–356.

29. Katz, *House Divided*, 149–153.

30. This quote and many details informing the following biographical sketch of Joel Teitelbaum come from Gelbman, *Moshi'an shel Yisra'el*, 1:57ff.

31. Ibid., 1:97–98.

32. Although prohibited from fasting as a youngster, Joel Teitelbaum asked for his father's blessing on his wedding day to have the strength to be able to fast so that he could serve God. He also tended to fast after recalling a dream as a means of purifying himself. Gelbman, *Moshi'an shel Yisra'el*, 1:381.

33. Gelbman, *Moshi'an shel Yisra'el*, 1:84–88.

34. See the hagiographic account of a close associate of Joel Teitelbaum, Alexander Sender Deutsch, *Sefer Botsinah Kadishah* (Brooklyn: Tiferes, 1998), 1:51. See also Fuchs, *Ha-Admor mi-Satmar*, 65.

35. Gelbman, *Moshi'an shel Yisra'el*, 1:82.

36. See Allan Nadler, "The Riddle of the Satmar," *Jewish Ideas Daily*, February 17, 2011, http://www.jewishideasdaily.com/content/module/2011/2/17/main-feature/1/the-riddle-of-the

-satmar/r&jtahome. For a discussion of Teitelbaum's fastidious attention to cleanliness, see two recent works in English: Y. Y. Weisshaus, *The Rebbe: A Glimpse into the Daily Life of the Satmar Rebbe Rabbeinu Yoel Teitelbaum* (Lakewood, NJ: Mechon Lev Avos, 2008), passim, and Meisels, *Rebbe*, 23–25.

37. Gelbman brings this recollection in *Moshi'an shel Yisra'el*, 1:386–387.

38. Ibid., 4:114.

39. Fuchs, *Ha-Admor mi-Satmar*, 70.

40. The town, which is today part of Ukraine, was known in Hungarian as Irshava and in Yiddish as Orshava.

41. Gelbman, *Moshi'an shel Yisra'el*, 4:180, 192.

42. See Joel Teitelbaum, *Divre Yo'el*, Even ha-ezer, Siman 121 (in Gelbman, *Moshi'an shel Yisra'el*, 4:223).

43. Gelbman, *Moshi'an shel Yisra'el*, 4:203, 211.

44. Ibid., 4:303.

45. Ibid., 4:306–308.

46. Interview with two Satmar Hasidim (W and A), October 1, 2010.

47. A telling indication of this concern was the Hebrew word play invoked by several of Teitelbaum's colleagues, especially the Munkaczer Rebbe: Balfour was referred to as "Ba`al Pe`or," the Midianate idol whose worship prompted Phineas to murder a man and woman who followed it (Numbers 25:7–8). See Gelbman, *Moshi'an shel Yisra'el*, 4:399, as well as Allan Nadler, "The War on Modernity of R. Hayyim Elazar Shapira of Munkacz," *Modern Judaism* 14 (1994): 246.

48. The rabbinic declaration is reproduced in Gelbman, *Moshi'an shel Yisra'el*, 4:413.

49. See Nadler, "War on Modernity," 240.

50. An account of the Csap meeting, including the declaration, can be found in Moshe Goldstein, *Sefer tikun `olam: yakhil kitve kodesh mi-maranan ve-rabanan neged shit`at ha-mithadshim* (Mukacevo: Guttmann, 1935–1936), 31–40. See also the concise summary in Ravitzky, *Messianism, Zionism, and Jewish Religious Radicalism*, 42–46, in which the author argues for the "decisive influence" of the Munkaczer Rebbe on Joel Teitelbaum.

51. H. Shamir, "Ha-`ir Satu Mare ve-Yehudeha," *Zakhor et Satmar*, 52 (Hebrew section).

52. Ibid.

53. Gelbman, *Moshi'an shel Yisra'el*, 4:327–332. See also Menachem Keren-Kratz, "R. Yo'el Teitelbaum: The Satmar Rebbe (1887–1979)" (in Hebrew; PhD diss., Tel Aviv University, 2013), 68.

54. See JewishGen, http://data.jewishgen.org/wconnect/wc.dll?jg~jgsys~shtetm~-1040239.

55. See Gelbman's discussion of Joel Teitelbaum's arrival and first steps in Carei in *Moshi'an shel Yisra'el*, 5:1–47, esp. 23.

56. Teitelbaum wrote a lengthy rabbinic responsum in which he maintained that unless and until the Status Quo group submitted to the authority of the main Hungarian Orthodox organization (established after the failed Jewish congress of 1868), it could not be called "Orthodox." Ibid., 5:48–54.

57. Gelbman, *Moshi'an shel Yisra'el*, 5:7–8.

58. In the midst of this fight, Teitelbaum's proponents published a book in 1929 called *Milhemet mitsvah he-hadash* (A New Commanded War). This title calls to mind the book from forty

years earlier, *Milhemet mitsvah* (Commanded War), in which Joel Teitelbaum's grandfather, the Yetev Lev, figured prominently. In the latter case, the enemies included not only the "band of modernizers" (*kat ha-mithadeshim*) but traditionally Orthodox "Ashkenazim" who remained vehemently opposed to a Hasidic rebbe as chief rabbi of their city. See *Milhemet mitsvah he-hadash* (Satu Mare: Tip. Hirsch, 1928–1929), 2. The volume provides a chronologically ordered compendium of documents related to the controversy. See also Keren-Kratz, *Ha-kanai*, 104–106.

59. This account, which appeared in the Hungarian Jewish paper *Hoemesz* on March 9, 1934, is reprinted in Gelbman, *Moshi'an shel Yisra'el*, 6:116–117.

60. The account from *Hoemesz* of March 1, 1934, is found in Fuchs, *Ha-Admor mi-Satmar*, 86–87.

61. The regulations are recorded in Gelbman, *Moshi'an shel Yisra'el*, 6:195–196.

62. *Zakhor et Satmar*, 40 (Hebrew), 46 (Hungarian). We thank Daniel Viragh for his assistance in translating the Hungarian text.

63. See the data on Satu Mare's Jewish population in 1930 assembled by Gyémánt in *Jews of Transylvania*, 254.

64. See Shamir, "Ha-`ir Satu Mare," *Zakhor et Satmar*, 53.

65. See the report of the meeting of King Carol II and Rabbi Teitelbaum from November 15, 1936, in *Hoemesz*, reported in Fuchs, *Ha-Admor mi-Satmar*, 96. See also Deutsch, *Sefer Botsinah Kadishah*, 1:79–80. It should be noted that a year later Carol appointed the far-right antisemite Octavian Goga as prime minister of Romania, for which he earned the wrath of Jews.

66. Keren-Kratz, "R. Yo'el Teitelbaum," 152.

67. See Randolph Braham, *The Politics of Genocide: The Holocaust in Hungary*, 2 vols. (New York: Columbia University Press, 1981), as well as the account of Kamenets-Podolsk from the United States Holocaust Memorial Museum, http://www.ushmm.org/wlc/en/article.php?ModuleId=10005442.

68. Reflecting the former impulse, Teitelbaum once related, when asked in what Jews should invest their money in this perilous environment, that "they should invest everything only in [the performance of] commandments and good deeds." Gelbman, *Moshi'an shel Yisra'el*, 9:20.

69. Teitelbaum's exposition of the relationship between the violation of the oaths and the Holocaust is found in *Va-yo'el Mosheh*. For a critical reading, notable for its attempt to understand Teitelbaum on his own terms, see Norman Lamm, "The Ideology of the Neturei Karta: According to the Satmarer Version," *Tradition* 13 (1971), 38–53, esp. 48–49.

70. Lamm follows on Rabbi Menachem Kasher in identifying major problems in Teitelbaum's reading of the famous Three Oaths, most significantly his imputation of an unmistakably legal-halakhic status to them (in contravention of Maimonides). See Lamm, 45–48.

71. Fuchs, *Ha-Admor mi-Satmar*, 104–105. On Teitelbaum's trips to Budapest, see Gelbman, *Moshi'an shel Yisra'el*, 9:21ff. For a deeply informed account of Teitelbaum's activity in the 1940s, see Menachem Keren-Kratz, "The Satmar Rebbe and the Destruction of Hungarian Jewry, Part I," *Tablet Magazine*, July 15, 2014, https://www.tabletmag.com/sections/arts-letters/articles/satmar-rebbe-1. The second part of Keren-Kratz's study is an indictment against Teitelbaum for his incompetence and irresponsibility before, during, and after the Holocaust. See Keren-Kratz, "The Satmar Rebbe and the Destruction of Hungarian Jewry, Part II," *Tablet Magazine*, July 16, 2014, https://www.tabletmag.com/sections/arts-letters/articles/satmar-rebbe-2.

72. See the account in Deutsch, *Sefer Botsinah Kadishah*, 1:114–119.

73. Ibid., 122–123.

74. For example, the version of Kasztner as demon can be found in Ben Hecht, *Perfidy* (New York: Julian Messner, 1961); a far more laudatory account comes from a fortunate member of the "Kasztner transport," Ladislaus Löb, in *Dealing with Satan: Rezső Kasztner's Daring Rescue Mission* (London: Jonathan Cape, 2008); see also the more scholarly account of historian Yechiam Weitz in *Ha-ish she-nirtsah pa`amayim* (The Man Who Was Murdered Twice) (Jerusalem: Keter, 1995). Meanwhile, a gripping film of Kasztner and the controversy around his legacy in Israel, *Killing Kasztner*, appeared in 2008.

75. Deutsch, *Sefer Botsinah Kadishah*, 1:127.

76. Gelbman, *Moshi'an shel Yisra'el*, 8:155–158.

77. See Meisels, *Rebbe*, 115.

78. See the account of Ference Kenedi recorded in Fuchs, *Ha-Admor mi-Satmar*, 119.

79. Michael Dov Weissmandl (1903–1957) was a Hungarian-born rabbi and scholar who returned from England to East-Central Europe in 1939 and engaged in active efforts at informing the Western world about the Nazi genocidal campaign and bribing German forces to secure the release of Slovakian Jews. Weissmandel was en route to Auschwitz before jumping off the train and hiding in a bunker, from which he was rescued by Kasztner in 1944.

80. The author of a memoir, Rose Farkas, recalls: "There were many other Orthodox Jews who stayed [in Europe], persuaded by Rav Yoylish that it was the right thing to do." See Farkas with Ibi Winterman, *Ruchele: Sixty Years from Szatmar to Los Angeles* (Santa Barbara, CA: Fithian Press, 1998), 246. See also the account of a onetime follower of Rabbi Teitelbaum, Itzik, in an interview for the online Israeli news service Ynet, http://www.ynet.co.il/articles/0,7340,L-3538199,00.html.

81. Teitelbaum, *Va-yo'el Mosheh*, 5–6, 11.

82. The preferred, indeed only, language that a Torah-observant Jew should speak and teach was Yiddish; both modern Hebrew and secular languages bore within them great risks. Teitelbaum insisted on a sharp distinction between two languages: an impure Hebrew (`Ivrit) and a pure Holy Tongue (*loshn koydesh*). This position came in the latter of two essays added to the original 1959 version of *Va-yo'el Moshhe*, one devoted to settlement of the Land of Israel (*Ma'amar yishuv Erets Yisra'el*) and one to the Holy Tongue (*Ma'amar leshon ha-Kodesh*). For a helpful explanation of this view, see Oded Schechter's essay (under the pseudonym O. from Volozhin) "Haside Satmar," in *50 le-48: Momentim bikortiyim be-toldot medinat Yisra'el*, ed. Adi Ophir (Tel Aviv: Van Leer Institute and Hakibbutz Hameuchad, 1999), 523–533, as well as "'Leshonam ha-tame' she-kar'uhu `Ivrit: ben leshon ha-Kodesh veha-Aramit: Le-gene'ologyah shal ha-`Ivrit," *Mi-ta`am* 2 (2005): 123–138.

Chapter 3: Satmar in America

1. The Yiddish-speaking autonomous region established in the Soviet Union in 1928, Birodizhan, would be one obvious exception to the rule.

2. Eric L. Goldstein offers a detailed analysis of the often rocky path of midcentury American Jews to gain full acceptance in white America in *The Price of Whiteness: Jews, Race, and American Identity* (Princeton: Princeton University Press, 2006).

3. See the important early sociological study by Rubin, *Satmar*.

4. Richard Rothstein, *The Color of Law: A Forgotten History of How Our Government Segregated America* (New York: Liveright, 2017). See also Ruth Knack, Stuart Meck, and Israel Stollman, "The Real Story Behind the Standard Planning and Zoning Acts of the 1920s," *Land Use Law*, February 1996; Stuart Meck, "Model Planning and Zoning Enabling Legislation: A Short History," in *Modernizing State Planning Statutes*, vol. 1 (Chicago: American Planning Association, Planning Advisory Service, Report Number 462/463, 1996).

5. Douglas S. Massey and Nancy A. Denton, *American Apartheid: Segregation and the Making of the Underclass* (Cambridge, MA: Harvard University Press, 1993), 74.

6. The manifest of the *Vulcania*, which departed from Port Haifa, contains the names of Joel and Alta Faiga Teitelbaum. See www.ancestry.com.

7. Gelbman, *Moshi'an shel Yisra'el*, 9:334ff.

8. Ibid.

9. Menachem Keren-Kratz chronicles Rabbi Teitelbaum's economic difficulties, as well as within the ʿEdah Haredit, in Keren-Kratz, "R. Yoʾel Teitelbaum," 231–234.

10. Ibid., 249.

11. Meisels, *Rebbe*, 141–144.

12. George Kranzler, *Williamsburg: A Jewish Community in Transition* (New York: P. Feldheim, 1961), 17. For an interesting recent autobiographical view of the transition, see Philip Fishman, *A Sukkah Is Burning: Remembering Williamsburg's Hasidic Transformation* (Minneapolis: Mill City Press, 2012).

13. Kranzler, *Williamsburg*, 37–41, 219.

14. Quoted in Meisels, *Rebbe*, 149.

15. Deutsch, *Sefer Botsinah Kadishah*, 2:61.

16. Emphasis added. New York State Court of Appeals judge Eugene Pigott, in a 2007 dissenting opinion, pondered whether this bylaw meant "all of the Grand Rabbi's decisions bind every member, or only that they bind every member 'in all spiritual matters.'" See his dissent of November 20, 2007, in *Congregation Yetev Lev d'Satmar et al. v. Jacob Kahana et al.*

17. Deutsch, *Sefer Botsinah Kadishah*, 2:43.

18. See Gelbman, *Retson tsadik*, 6; Deutsch, *Sefer Botsinah Kadishah*, 2:53; and Meisels, *Rebbe*, 420ff.

19. Deutsch, *Sefer Botsinah Kadishah*, 2:58–60; Meisels, *Rebbe*, 465ff.; Chaim Moshe Stauber, *The Satmar Rebbe: The Life and Times of Rav Yoel Teitelbaum zt"l* (Jerusalem: P. Feldheim, 2011), 164.

20. Deutsch, *Sefer Botsinah Kadishah*, 2:67–70.

21. George Kranzler discusses the densely Jewish parts of Williamsburg—the "Jewish Triangle"—in detail in *Hasidic Williamsburg: A Contemporary American Hasidic Community* (Northvale, NJ: Jason Aronson, 1995), 9–16.

22. Deutsch, *Botsina Kadisha*, 2:258–259.

23. "'Der Yid' in hent fun nayer administratsye," *Der Yid*, February 17, 1956.

24. Meisels, *Rebbe*, 177. See, for example, the article from February 1957 that branded Rudolf Kasztner not as a hero who saved the Rebbe but as a murderous collaborator with the Nazis. *Der Yid*, February 15, 1957.

25. Fishman, *A Sukkah Is Burning*, 37–44.

26. Caro, *Power Broker*, 847.

27. "Hassidic Jews Win on Forming Rockland Village," *New York Times*, July 14, 1961. For more on the origins of New Square, see Jerome Mintz, *Hasidic People: A Place in the New World* (Cambridge, MA: Harvard University Press, 1992), 199–200.

28. New Square is smaller, less visible, and less controversial than Kiryas Joel, though it has not been free of conflict. In 2012 it made headlines when a religious dissident was badly burned in an arson attack. The community also became a source of controversy when President Clinton, in one of his final acts in office, pardoned two of its residents who had been convicted of fraud, after the community voted en masse to support Hillary Clinton in her run for a U.S. Senate seat.

29. Although family size is big in New Square (5.47 people per home), the village has not grown as dramatically as Kiryas Joel, in large part because of the Skverer community's practice of encouraging women who marry men from outside of the community to go live near their husband's families rather than in New Square. For details on New Square's demographics, see the 2018 census update at https://www.census.gov/quickfacts/newsquarevillagenewyork.

30. "Growing Pains for a Rural Hasidic Enclave," *New York Times*, January 13, 1997.

31. Knack, Meck, and Stollman, "Real Story Behind the Standard Planning and Zoning Acts of the 1920s"; Meck, "Model Planning and Zoning Enabling Legislation." See also Rothstein, *Color of Law*, 51.

32. Rothstein, *Color of Law*, 56.

33. See Kenneth Jackson, *Crabgrass Frontier: The Suburbanization of the United States* (New York: Oxford University Press, 1985), 4.

34. Isabel Fattal, "A Heavy Blow to One of America's Most Controversial School Boards," *Atlantic*, November 17, 2017, https://www.theatlantic.com/education/archive/2017/11/another-blow-to-one-of-americas-most-controversial-school-board/546227/. For the perspective of former school board president Morris Kohn, see episode 534 of *This American Life* from September 12, 2014, "A Not-So-Simple Majority," devoted to the East Ramapo district, https://www.thisamericanlife.org/534/a-not-so-simple-majority.

35. See Gershon Bacon's description of the traditionalist Orthodox political organization in Poland, Agudat Yisrael, in *The Politics of Tradition: Agudat Yisrael in Poland, 1916–1939* (Jerusalem: Magnes Press, 1996), 227.

36. Gelbman, *Retson tsadik*, viii, 25.

37. Ibid., 28–29.

38. Ibid., 28–29, 31. On Friedman, see Mintz, *Hasidic People*, 31–32.

39. "Jewish Sect to Build a Community in New Jersey," *New York Times*, June 7, 1962.

40. "Jews Ask Jersey Court's Aid in Fight on Tract," *New York Times*, September 25, 1962.

41. Freedman offers a rich description of the struggle in Beachwood, 80 percent of whose residents were Jewish, in his *Jew vs. Jew*, 286. The Orthodox residents were intent on moving out of the home-based synagogues in which they had been praying in Beachwood, whose presence violated existing zoning regulations. They purchased land with the intent of creating the kinds of institutions that would enable and enrich their way of life. The Beachwood Planning and Zoning Commission, all of whose members were Jewish, was called upon to debate the shift in status of the newly purchased land from residential to institutional. Unanimously, the commission voted down the proposal, prompting bitter recriminations by one group of Jews against another, including charges of antisemitism.

42. "Orthodox Jews Battle Neighbors in a Zoning War," *New York Times*, June 3, 1991.

43. *United States v. Village of Airmont*, 839 F. Supp. 1054, 1062–63 (S.D.N.Y. 1993). For further discussion of the original case and its appeal, see Nomi Maya Stolzenberg, "The Puzzling Persistence of Community: The Cases of Airmont and Kiryas Joel," in *From Ghetto to Emancipation: Historical and Contemporary Reconsiderations of the Jewish Community*, ed. David N. Myers and William V. Rowe (Scranton, PA: University of Scranton Press, 1997), 75–108. See also "Federal Court Finds Bias in Village's Zoning Rules," *New York Times*, September 23, 1995.

44. See http://www2.census.gov/prod2/decennial/documents/1970a_ny1–01.pdf.

45. "Bargain and Sale Deed with Covenant, John A. DeVos to Monwood Realty Corp.," recorded in Orange County Clerk's Office, May 2, 1967.

46. See, for example, the early and passing reference to the Monwood Realty Corp. in an article in the *Times Herald-Record* of neighboring Middletown that discussed a number of different development projects, "Monroe Apartment Project Subject to Public Hearing," *Times Herald-Record*, May 11, 1967. Monwood's request to have the Rosewood Village property recognized as a subdivision suitable for building was discussed at meetings of the Monroe town board on June 1, 1970, July 12, 1971, and April 13, 1972. The separate town planning board granted final approval to the Monwood subdivision on July 11, 1972.

47. Interview with H. H. Leimzider, March 22, 2012.

48. The Satmars attempted to purchase land at Congers Lake in Orange County, but a public referendum was held in November 1969 in which residents of the area voted not to permit development on the land purchased by the Satmars. Meisels, *Rebbe*, 541.

49. Biographical details are contained in the *New York Times* obituary, "Leibish Lefkowitz, a Satmar Leader, Dies at 78," http://www.nytimes.com/1998/08/09/nyregion/leibish-lefkowitz-a-satmar-leader-dies-at-78.html. See also Meisels, *Rebbe*, 543.

50. Interview with DF, December 8, 2009.

51. Interview with H. H. Leimzider, March 22, 2012.

52. Ibid.

53. Minutes of town of Monroe board, July 12, 1971. At that meeting, attorney Herbert Fabricant argued against the assembly hall.

54. Minutes of town of Monroe planning board, June 12, 1973, July 10, 1973, August 14, 1973.

55. "Brooklyn Hasidim Believed Planning Large Colony at Upstate Resort Site," *New York Times*, September 16, 1974. See also Gelbman, *Retson tsadik*, 104.

56. Minutes of town of Monroe board, April 1, 1974. See also "Development Accused of Fraudulent Advertising," *Times Herald-Record*, April 2, 1974.

57. Minutes of town of Monroe board, May 6, 1974. See "Monroe Drops Developments Stop Order," *Times Herald-Record*, May 11, 1974.

58. See Town of Monroe Local Law No. 2 (June 7, 1965). James Sweeney, who served as Monroe town attorney from 1968 to 1988, emphasized the desire to preserve the rural character of the town. Interview with James Sweeney, September 14, 2011. On the fifty-fifty breakdown between rural and urban residence in Orange County, see U.S. Census Bureau, "1970 Census of Population, 1:34 (New York), Table 9: Population and Land Area of Counties," 34–21.

59. Notice of Public Hearing, town board of the town of Monroe, May 16, 1974.

60. See Knack, Meck, and Stollman, "Real Story Behind the Standard Planning and Zoning Acts of the 1920s"; Meck, "Model Planning and Zoning." See also Rothstein, *Color of Law*, 51–56.

61. See the special section with accompanying surveys conducted by the *New York Times* in January 1974, "New Yorkers Speak Out on New York." On the city's dire economic state, see Jeff Nussbaum, "The Night New York Saved Itself from Bankruptcy," *New Yorker*, October 16, 2015.

62. Stuart Meck and Rebecca Retzlaff, "The Emergence of Growth Management Planning in the United States: The Case of Golden v. Planning Board of Town of Ramapo and Its Aftermath," *Journal of Planning History* 7, no. 2 (May 2008): 113.

63. *Moore v. City of East Cleveland*, 431 U.S. 484 (1977).

64. *Village of Belle Terre v. Boraas*, 416 U.S. 1 (1974).

65. See *U.S. Department of Agriculture v. Moreno*, 413 U.S. 528 (1973), https://supreme.justia.com/cases/federal/us/413/528/. Four years later, the Supreme Court ruled in *Moore v. East Cleveland* that a local zoning ordinance could not dictate who made a family by preventing a grandmother from living with her grandchild. See *Moore v. City of East Cleveland*, 431 U.S. 484 (1977), https://supreme.justia.com/cases/federal/us/431/494/.

66. Terry Rice, "Exclusionary Zoning: Mt. Laurel in New York?," *Pace Law Review* 6 (1986): 135, 182.

67. Gelbman, *Retson tsadik*, 114.

68. "Iber hundert Satmarer familyes tsien zikh aroys fun Vilyamsburg," *Algemeiner Journal*, May 24, 1974.

69. Gelbman, *Retson tsadik*, 131.

70. Ibid., 108. Interview with H. H. Leimzider. On Zupnik, see the volume in honor of his seventieth birthday, *Yisra'el oseh hayil* (Jerusalem: Mosdot ha-Yahadut ha-Haredit, 1975).

71. Gelbman, *Retson tsadik*, 104, 117. See also "Brooklyn Hasidim Believed Planning Large Colony."

72. "1st Hasidic Families Move into Monfield," *Times Herald-Record*, August 28, 1974.

73. "How Many People? Monroe Officials Jittery," *Times Herald-Record*, July 17, 1974.

74. "Hasidic Settlers Face Uphill Fight," *Times Herald-Record*, July 18, 1974.

75. "Hasidim Attempting to Buy Out Monroe Neighbors," *Times Herald-Record*, July 21, 1974.

76. Interview with DT, September 15, 2011. In its report on the new community, the *New York Times* also noted that "the only adverse public reaction came from non-Hasidic Jews in the town," "Brooklyn Hasidim Believed Planning Large Colony."

77. Letters to the editor, *Times Herald-Record*, July 27, 1974.

78. See "Monroe Sect Leader Fled Nazi Persecution," *Times Herald-Record*, August 4, 1974; and "Satmar Spiritual Leader Comes to Monroe," *Times Herald-Record*, September 1, 1974.

79. "Monroe Planners Stall Housing Plans by Hasidim," *Times Herald-Record*, August 14, 1974.

80. The Satmars' tendency to reveal little and, at times, dissemble was rooted not only in the recent past but in a deeper distrust of the gentile world—a function of their historical experience in Europe, as well as of Rabbi Teitelbaum's quasi-theological pronouncement that "dwelling among the [gentile] nations leads to woes and destruction." See `Al ha-ge'ulah ve-`al ha-temurah (Brooklyn: Sender Deutsch, 1967), 10, 205. Israel Rubin notes the ancient theological distinction found in Satmar thought between the biblical Jacob, the progenitor of the Israelites, and his brother Esau, the prototypical gentile. Rubin, *Satmar*, 52.

81. David Swanson, "Hasids in Monroe: A Clash of Cultures or Point of Law?," *Times Herald-Record*, October 10, 1976.

82. Gelbman, *Retson tsadik*, 120–121.

83. Ibid., 117.

84. "Kiryas Yoel: A Velt's Vunder," *Der Yid*, July 30, 1974. According to Gelbman, Rabbi Teitelbaum gave the settlement its name, which he drew from a Satmar neighborhood in Bnai Brak in Israel. *Retson tsadik*, 122.

85. The term "duped" is how Satmar author Dovid Meisels describes Monroe officials. Meisels also called Monfield Realty and the other players in the drama "puppets of the Satmar community." Meisels, *Rebbe*, 546.

86. See "Hasidic Sect Wins Monroe Go Ahead on 40 Homes," *Times Herald-Record*, October 9, 1974; and "Hasidim Plan Synagogue, Ritual Bath," *Times Herald-Record*, October 12, 1974. See also "Brooklyn Hasidim Believed Planning Large Colony."

87. Interview with H. H. Leimzider, March 22, 2012.

88. Israel Rubin, "Satmar's Arrival in Monroe No Cause for Alarm," *Times Herald-Record*, December 22, 1974; and "Satmarer Can Live in Peace with Neighbors," *Times Herald-Record*, December 23, 1974.

89. The *Times Herald-Record* interviewed a number of Monroe residents, Satmar and non-Satmar, in a long article under the headline "Hasidim 'Good Neighbors' in Monroe," *Times Herald-Record*, July 20, 1975.

90. Gelbman, *Retson tsadik*, 140.

91. "Hasidim 'Good Neighbors' in Monroe."

92. "Impact Could Be Immediate," *Times Herald-Record*, October 7, 1975, and "122 Register in Monroe District," *Times Herald-Record*, October 21, 1975.

93. Minutes of town of Monroe board, July 12, 1971.

94. *Yoga Society of New York v. Town of Monroe*, Appellate Division of the Supreme Court of the State of New York, Second Department (March 7, 1977). Details of the case come from an interview with lawyer Bernard (Bernie) Davis from March 9, 2012.

95. "Attorney Blames Inspector for Hasid Woes," *Times Herald-Record*, July 14, 1976. Notwithstanding this assertion, Barone was a constant visitor to Satmar buildings, inspecting and issuing violation notices when he discovered them.

96. Interview with James Sweeney, September 14, 2011.

97. "Angry Monroe Residents Urge Enforcement against Hasids," *Times Herald-Record*, July 13, 1976.

98. Interview with Alan Lipman, September 14, 2011.

99. "Zoning Law Beats Dietary Law," *Times Herald-Record*, June 4, 1976.

100. "Zoning Violations Halt Satmar Construction," *Times Herald-Record*, June 24, 1976; and "Monroe Hasidim Charged with Zoning Violations," *Times Herald-Record*, July 8, 1976.

101. "Hasidim Deny Housing Charges," *Times Herald-Record*, July 10, 1976.

102. Gelbman, *Retson tsadik*, 175–176.

103. At the town of Monroe board meeting on September 13, 1976, speakers from the floor included a number of Jewish residents, including a longtime critic of the Satmars, Lillian Roberts. Minutes of town of Monroe board meeting, September 13, 1976.

104. Leibish Lefkowitz, "Letter to the Editor from the Satmar Hasidic Community in Monroe," *Monroe Gazette*, July 29, 1976.

105. The latter two suggestions were made by the *Times Herald-Record* journalist Jane Stuart in "Hasidim [*sic*] Development Could Avert Flap with Town," *Times Herald-Record*, August 2,

1976. On the same day, Lefkowitz raised the idea of a planned unit development in "End to Zoning Dispute Sought," *Times Herald-Record*, August 2, 1976.

106. Interview with Shlomo Y. Gelbman, February 2, 2010.

107. Gelbman, *Retson tsadik*, 175.

108. Lefkowitz's letter is included in Gelbman, *Retson tsadik*, 164.

109. Gelbman's accounts on the hiring of Rubinstein and the local lawyer are found in ibid., 162–163, 176–177.

110. Interview with Bernie Davis, March 9, 2012. See also "Hasids Charge Selective Zone Enforcement," *Times Herald-Record*, September 2, 1976.

111. In New York State, the Supreme Court is the lowest of three levels of jurisdiction. It is a trial court whose cases are heard on appeal at the appellate division and then at the highest realm, the New York Court of Appeals.

112. Minutes of town of Monroe board meeting, September 13, 1976. See also "Residents Rap Monroe Actions on Monfield," *Times Herald-Record*, September 14, 1976.

113. "Hasids Take Steps to Form Separate Village," *Times Herald-Record*, September 15, 1976.

114. *Local Government Handbook*, 6th ed. (Albany: New York State Department of State, 2009), 68, http://www.dos.ny.gov/lg/publications/Local_Government_Handbook.pdf.

115. Minutes of town of Monroe board meeting, September 29, 1976. See also "Supervisor Will Battle Satmar Separation Try," *Times Herald-Record*, September 28, 1976.

116. Interview with Alan Lipman, September 14, 2011.

117. With a trace of exaggeration about the ability to choose a judge, Gelbman writes that the Satmars "went to New York [City] to find a judge who would agree to handle the case. . . . We went from judge to judge, but no one wanted to take the case." Gelbman, *Retson tsadik*, 178.

118. "Hasids' Attorney: Civil Rights Violated," *Times Herald-Record*, October 22, 1976.

119. Interview with Alan Lipman, September 14, 2011.

120. Gelbman, *Retson tsadik*, 184–186.

121. "Monroe Supervisor Approves Petition for Hasidic Village," *Times Herald-Record*, December 12, 1976; and "New Village—Right Move, Wrong Reason," *Times Herald-Record*, December 14, 1976.

122. "Satmar Hasidim Set to Create Own Village," *Times Herald-Record*, February 7, 1977; and "Satmar Unfazed by Merger Proposal," *Times Herald-Record*, February 10, 1977.

123. There was a total of 174 registered voters out of some 600 residents. See "Hasids Vote to Form Village," *Times Herald-Record*, February 16, 1977.

Chapter 4: Not in America?

1. For a thorough account of the Brownsville controversy, see Jerald E. Podair, *The Strike That Changed New York: Blacks, Whites, and the Ocean Hill-Brownsville Crisis* (New Haven, CT: Yale University Press, 2002), 125 (Baldwin quote). On the longer-term process of Jews identifying and being identified as white, see Goldstein, *Price of Whiteness*, passim.

2. Max Weber's classic discussion, "The Nature of Charisma and Its Routinization," is found in his book *The Theory of Social and Economic Organization*, translated by A. R. Anderson and Talcott Parsons (New York: Oxford University Press, 1947).

3. On R. Nahman, see Biale et al., *Hasidism*, 113–115; on the Lubavitcher Rebbe, see Samuel Heilman and Menachem Friedman, *The Rebbe: The Life and Afterlife of Menachem Mendel Schneerson* (Princeton: Princeton University Press, 2010). See also Mintz, *Hasidic People*, 126.

4. A number of scholars have clarified the process by which a successor was found. Mintz, *Hasidic People*, 126–138; and Samuel C. Heilman, *Who Will Lead Us? The Story of Five Hasidic Dynasties in America* (Oakland: University of California Press, 2017), 152–209.

5. On the Sigheter Rov in Brooklyn, see Mintz, *Hasidic People*, 127. On the tension between the Rebbetsin and Moshe, see Heilman, *Who Will Lead Us?*, 178–179.

6. See Mintz, *Hasidic People*, 89, 125.

7. "Ha-rov ha-godol ha-tsadik mi-Sighet ShLiT"A oyfgenumen als AB"D d'Kahal Yetev Lev d'Satmar," *Der Yid*, September 14, 1979, 1. See also Heilman, *Who Will Lead Us?*, 186.

8. "Ha-rov ha-godol ha-tsadik mi-Sighet," 1. See also Mintz, *Hasidic People*, 129. On the origins of the Hasidic notion of the rebbe or *tsadik*, see Biale et al., *Hasidism*, 165–170.

9. Mintz, *Hasidic People*, 129.

10. See the front-page story "Toyzenter khsidim un hunderter rabonim bay hakhtarah fun Kh"K Maran ShLiT"A," *Der Yid*, August 15, 1980, 1. The front page of this edition of *Der Yid* is mistakenly dated August 8; the rest of the pages carry the correct date of August 15.

11. Heilman, *Who Will Lead Us?*, 187–188.

12. Z, interview by author, May 10, 2016.

13. "Faiga Teitelbaum, 89, a Power among Satmar Hasidim," *New York Times*, June 13, 2001.

14. On Faiga's relations with Roysele and Moshe, see Mintz, *Hasidic People*, 87–90. See also Keren-Kratz's discussion of Faiga and Roysele, "R. Yo'el Teitelbaum," 151–152.

15. Mintz, *Hasidic People*, 90.

16. On Brach's activity in Williamsburg, see the extensive discussion in Deutsch and Casper, *Fortress in Brooklyn*, 151ff.

17. Mintz, *Hasidic People*, 315, 320–321. Mintz describes Brach as a successful importer and exporter of electronic components.

18. See http://population.us/ny/kiryas-joel/.

19. See Albert Samaha, "All the Young Jews: In the Village of Kiryas Joel, New York, the Median Age Is 13," *Village Voice*, November 12, 2014, as well as Gerald Benjamin, "The Chassidic Presence and Local Government in the Hudson Valley," *Albany Law Review* 80, no. 4 (2017), http://www.albanylawreview.org/Articles/vol80_4/1383%20Benjamin%20PRODUCTION.pdf.

20. Ruth Boice, "Monroe, Kiryas Joel OK Annexation," *Times Herald-Record*, May 10, 1983.

21. *State of Oregon v. City of Rajneeshpuram*, 598 F. Supp. 1217 (D. Or. 1984).

22. Interview with Malka Silberstein (MS), November 2013.

23. Ibid.

24. Ibid.

25. Ibid.

26. See Rubin, *Satmar*, 161–184.

27. See Joseph P. Shapiro, *No Pity: People with Disabilities Forging a New Civil Rights Movement* (New York: Times Books, 1994); Doris Zames Fleischer and Frieda Zames, *The Disability Rights Movement: From Charity to Confrontation*, 2nd ed. (Philadelphia: Temple University

Press, 2011); Samuel R. Bagenstos, *Law and the Contradictions of the Disability Rights Movement* (New Haven, CT: Yale University Press, 2009).

28. *Brown v. Board of Ed.*, 347 U.S. 483 (1954).

29. Civil Rights Act of 1964, Pub. L. 88–352, 78 Stat. 241 (1964).

30. Individuals with Disabilities Education Act, 20 U.S.C. § 1400 et seq. Five years earlier, in 1970, an amendment was made to the 1965 Elementary and Secondary Education Act, titled the Education of the Handicapped Act, a forerunner to the landmark legislation of 1975. See Advocacy Institute, "Legislative History of Special Education" (n.d.), https://www.advocacyinstitute .org/academy/Dec10IDEA35/Special_Ed_Legislative_History.pdf. The 1965 Education of the Handicapped Act created grants for discretionary programs. The 1975 act was the first to clearly enunciate that special education was a right.

31. See Ruth Colker, "The Disability Integration Presumption: Thirty Years Later," *University of Pennsylvania Law Review* 154, no. 4 (April 2006): 789–862; Samuel Bagenstos, "Abolish the Integration Presumption? Not Yet," *University of Pennsylvania Law Review* 156, no. 1 (October 2007): 157–164.

32. See Harlan Lane, *The Mask of Benevolence: Disabling the Deaf Community* (New York: Vintage, 1992), 129–164; Andrew Solomon, "Defiantly Deaf," *New York Times Magazine*, August 28, 1994.

33. The most prominent proponent of the integrationist approach was Alexander Graham Bell. That approach was attacked by Deaf activists and advocates for Deaf separatism in the 1970s leading to heated battles. See Paul Arnold, "The Education of the Deaf Child: For Integration or Autonomy?," *American Annals of the Deaf* 129 (1984): 29–37; Jessica Murgel, "Oralism, Philosophy and Models Of," in *The Sage Deaf Studies Encyclopedia*, ed. Genie Gertz and Patrick Boudreault (Thousand Oaks, CA: Sage, 2016), 724.

34. Interview with Louis Grumet, March 12, 2012. Also see Grumet with Caher, *Curious Case of Kiryas Joel.*

35. Grumet interview; Grumet, email to author, May 10, 2019.

36. The religious roots of the worldwide Camphill movement and its affinities with Catholic Worker communities are discussed in Dan McKanan, *Touching the World: Christian Communities Transforming Society*, 3rd ed. (Collegeville, MN: Liturgical Press, 2007).

37. Interview with Bernard Wolf, December 7, 2012.

38. Grumet interview.

39. On Kenneth Clark, see Damon Freeman, "Kenneth B. Clark and the Problem of Power," *Patterns of Prejudice* 42, nos. 4–5 (October 2008): 413–447, https://doi.org/10.1080 /00313220802377362; Damon Freeman, "Reconsidering Kenneth B. Clark and the Idea of Black Psychological Damage, 1931–1945," *Du Bois Review: Social Science Research on Race* 8, no. 1 (Spring 2011): 271–283, https://doi.org/10.1017/S1742058X11000099. On Mamie Clark, see Leila McNeill, "How a Psychologist's Work on Race Identity Helped to Overturn School Segregation in 1950s America," *Smithsonian*, October 26, 2017, https://www.smithsonianmag.com /science-nature/psychologist-work-racial-identity-helped-overturn-school-segregation -180966934/.

40. Grumet interview.

41. Ibid.

42. Wolf interview.

43. Silberstein interview.

44. Ibid.

45. Ibid.

46. Ibid.

47. Interview with Wolf Lefkowitz, August 31, 2014.

48. Ibid.

49. Ibid.; Petlin interview. According to Benardo, Lipa Gross was a major donor. Benardo, interview by author, September 5, 2014.

50. Silberstein interview.

51. See *Pierce v. Society of Sisters*, 268 U.S. 510 (1925).

52. See *Everson v. Board of Educ.*, 330 U.S. 1 (1947); *Lemon v. Kurtzman*, 403 U.S. 602 (1971).

53. Elementary and Secondary Education Act of 1965, H.R. 2362, 89th Cong., 1st Sess., Public Law 89–10.

54. The U.S. Supreme Court first invoked Jefferson's metaphorical wall of separation between church and state once before, in the case of *Reynolds v. United States*, 98 U.S. 145 (1879), which upheld the constitutionality of an anti-polygamy law against a Free Exercise Clause challenge brought by Mormons in 1879. But the doctrine of separation between religion and state then lay dormant until the Court reinvigorated it in *Everson*, making it a foundation of modern Establishment Clause jurisprudence.

55. *Everson v. Board of Educ.*, 330 U.S. 1 (1947).

56. *Everson*, 330 U.S. at 16.

57. See Sarah Barringer Gordon, "'Free' Religion and 'Captive' Schools: Protestants, Catholics, and Education, 1945–1965," *DePaul Law Review* 56, no. 4 (Summer 2007): 1177–1220.

58. According to Gordon, thirteen states, including New York, had programs providing free transportation to private schools in place by 1938. See ibid., 1183.

59. N.Y. Educ. Law § 3635(1) (McKinney 1981 and Supp. 1986).

60. *Board of Educ. v. Allen*, 392 U.S. 236 (1968) (upholding textbook loan program); *Lemon v. Kurtzman*, 403 U.S. 602 (1971) (striking down teacher salary subsidies); *Tilton v. Richardson*, 403 U.S. 672 (1971) (upholding construction grants for institutions of higher education); *Levitt v. Comm. for Pub. Educ. & Religious Liberty*, 413 U.S. 472 (1973) (funding for administration of nonstandardized tests struck down); *Commissioner for Pub. Educ. v. Nyquist*, 413 U.S. 756 (1973) (striking down building and maintenance grants and tuition subsidies); *Meek v. Pittenger*, 421 U.S. 349 (1975) (upholding the provisions to private schools of "auxiliary services," such as counseling, testing, psychological services, and hearing and speech therapy, and upholding loans of instructional materials such as maps and periodicals, but striking down loans of instructional equipment such as film projectors and laboratory equipment); *Mueller v. Allen*, 463 U.S. 388 (1983) (upholding state income tax law allowing taxpayers to deduct costs of tuition, textbooks, and transportation to school).

61. According to the 1980 census, there were 840 children between five and seventeen in Kiryas Joel, with 543 younger than five. U.S. Census Bureau, "New York," in *1980 Census of Population 1980*, vol. 1, chap. B, pt. 34 (Washington, DC: Government Publishing Office, 1982), https://www2.census.gov/prod2/decennial/documents/1980/1980censusofpopu80134unse_bw.pdf. By 1983, the number of children in the older group had undoubtedly surpassed 1,000.

62. *Bollenbach v. Board of Educ.*, 659 F. Supp. 1450 (S.D.N.Y. 1987), 1453.

63. Ibid., 1453.

64. Daniel Alexander, *The Political Influence of the Resident Hasidic Community on the East Ramapo Central School District.* (New York: New York University Press, 1982).

65. The conflict between Haredi Jews and the rest of the East Ramapo School District population that erupted in 2014 has been amply covered in the press. See, e.g., Batya Unger-Sargon, "The Blame Game," *Tablet*, September 8, 2014, https://www.tabletmag.com/jewish-news-and-politics/183757/east-ramapo-schools; Ben Calhoun, "A Not-So-Simple Majority," in *This American Life*, September 12, 2014, podcast, 60:53, produced by Ben Calhoun, https://www.thisamericanlife.org/534/a-not-so-simple-majority; David J. Butler, Randall M. Levine, and Stephanie Schuster, "Inside the East Ramapo Central School District Case," *Tablet*, May 5, 2017, https://www.tabletmag.com/scroll/232394/inside-the-east-ramapo-central-school-district-case; Isabel Fattal, "A Heavy Blow to One of America's Most Controversial School Boards," *Atlantic*, November 17, 2017, https://www.theatlantic.com/education/archive/2017/11/another-blow-to-one-of-americas-most-controversial-school-board/546227/.

66. See https://www.nyssba.org/about-nyssba/nyssba-overview/.

67. Robert Nozick, *Anarchy, State and Utopia* (New York: Basic Books, 1974). Foreshadowing his popularity in the Reagan era, Nozick was publicly heralded as the "philosopher of the new right" in the *New York Times Sunday Magazine* in 1978. Jonathan Lieberson, "Harvard's Nozick: Philosopher of the New Right," *New York Times Sunday Magazine*, December 17, 1978.

68. On the process of Aaron's ascendance to Rov of KJ, see Heilman, *Who Will Lead Us?*, 180–184.

69. For a discussion of the "regal way" of Hasidism, especially associated with R. Israel of Ruzhin, see Biale et al., *Hasidism*, 304–309.

70. See the coverage of the selection and coronation of Aaron Teitelbaum as Rov of KJ in the leading Satmar weekly: "Satmarer shtetl 'Kiryas Yoel' nemt oyf mara d'asra, R' Arn Teitelboym," *Der Yid*, October 26, 1984, 1, 5; "Fayerlikhe 'mesibas hakhtarah' fun nayem rov in Kiryas Yoel farganenem motse Shabes," *Der Yid*, November 16, 1984, 2, 27; see also in that issue the two pages of ads congratulating Aaron, 16–17.

71. *Aguilar v. Felton*, 473 U.S. 402 (1985).

72. *Sch. Dist. v. Ball*, 473 U.S. 373 (1985); *Aguilar v. Felton.*

73. *Aguilar v. Felton*, 419.

74. *Agostini v. Felton*, 521 U.S. 203 (1997).

75. See *Engel v. Vitale*, 370 U.S. 421 (1962) (ruling prayer in public school unconstitutional); *Sch. Dist. of Abington Twp. v. Schempp*, 374 U.S. 203 (1963) (finding devotional Bible reading in public school unconstitutional); *Epperson v. Arkansas*, 393 U.S. 97 (1968) (striking down state law that prohibited the teaching of evolution in public school). See also *McCollum v. Board of Educ.*, 333 U.S. 203 (1948) (finding unconstitutional a "released time" program that allowed children to receive religious instruction in public school).

76. Rob Boston, "Everson at 60," Americans United, January 2007, https://www.au.org/church-state/january-2007-church-state/featured/everson-at-60.

77. In *Wallace v. Jaffree*, 472 U.S. 38 (1985), Chief Justice Rehnquist wrote in dissent: "There is simply no historical foundation for the proposition that the Framers intended to build the 'wall of separation' that was constitutionalized in *Everson.*"

78. *Parents' Assoc. of P.S. 16 v. Quinones*, 803 F.2d 1235 (2d Cir. 1986).

79. Benardo interview.

80. Abraham Wieder, interview by author, May 2, 2014.

81. The litigation of *Aguilar v. Felton* actually commenced in 1978, the year after the village of Kiryas Joel was incorporated.

82. Mr. and Mrs. Wieder, interview by author, November 16, 2014.

83. Ibid.

84. Ibid.

85. Petlin, email message to author, November 14, 2013.

86. According to Terry Olivo, "Whenever they didn't get 100 percent of what they want, they would go to an impartial hearing," which "ties up an enormous amount of resources." Olivo, interview by author, September 10, 2014.

87. *Board of Educ. v. Wieder*, 132 A.D.2d 409, 412 (N.Y. App. Div. 1987).

88. Ibid.

89. *Wieder*, 132 A.D.2d at 412, citing Education Law § 3602-c(9).

90. *Bollenbach v. Board of Educ.*, 659 F. Supp. 1450 (S.D.N.Y. 1987).

91. Ibid., 1454.

92. Ibid., 1454.

93. N.Y. Educ. Law § 3602-c(9).

94. *Board of Educ. v. Wieder*, 512 N.Y.S. 2d 305, 308 (Sup. Ct. 1987).

95. *Board of Educ. v. Wieder*, 522 N.Y.S.2d 878, 880 (App. Div. 1987).

96. Ibid., 881.

97. Ibid.

98. Ibid., 882.

99. Ibid.

100. *Board of Educ. v. Wieder*, 527 N.E.2d 767 (N.Y. 1988).

101. Ibid., 769.

102. Ibid., 772.

103. Ibid., 774.

104. Grumet with Caher, *Curious Case of Kiryas Joel*, 39.

105. Benardo, interview by author, July 9, 2014.

106. James D. Folts, *History of the University of the State of New York and the New York Education Department 1784–1996* (Albany: New York State Education Department, 1996), https://files .eric.ed.gov/fulltext/ED413839.pdf.

107. See Ian C. Bartrum, "The Political Origins of Secular Public Education: The New York School Controversy 1840–1842," *NYU Journal of Law and Liberty* 3, no. 2 (2008): 267–348.

108. Historian Sarah Barringer Gordon notes in her important study of this neglected topic, "In more remote areas" where Catholics predominated "there had never been a distinction between Catholic and public education." See Gordon, "'Free' Religion and 'Captive' Schools," 1202.

109. The description of this meeting is drawn from Grumet. See Grumet's account in Grumet with Caher, *Curious Case of Kiryas Joel*, 40–41; and Grumet, interview by author, January 28, 2013.

110. A detailed account of the legislative process can be found in Grumet with Caher, *Curious Case of Kiryas Joel*, 45–55.

111. 1989 N.Y. Laws, chap. 748.

112. Grumet interview.

113. Ibid.

114. Ibid.

115. Ibid.

116. *60 Minutes* episode, November 6, 1994.

117. Ibid.

118. Marci Hamilton, "Religion and the Law in the Clinton Era: An Anti-Madisonian Legacy," *Law & Contemporary Problems* 63 (2000): 359.

119. Cornel West, "The New Cultural Politics of Difference," *October* 53 (1990): 93–109; Iris Marion Young, *Justice and the Politics of Difference* (Princeton: Princeton University Press, 1990).

Chapter 5: Only in America!

1. *Grumet v. New York State Educ. Dep't.* (*Grumet I*), 579 N.Y.S.2d 1004 (Sup. Ct. 1992).

2. *Board of Educ. v. Grumet*, 512 U.S. 687 (1994).

3. See *Grumet v. Cuomo* (*Grumet II*), 681 N.E.2d 340 (N.Y. 1997); and *Grumet v. Pataki*, 720 N.E.2d 66 (N.Y. 1999), *cert. denied, Pataki v. Grumet* (*Grumet III*), 528 U.S. 946 (1999).

4. In addition to the three lawsuits filed by Grumet, the school district's authorization would also be challenged a fourth time in *Birnbaum v. Board of Educ.*, No. 7306–99, 2001 WL 36241683 (N.Y. Sup. Ct., February 14, 2001).

5. "Union free" is a technical term referring to local school districts that are free of the restriction on operating a high school that applies to "common" school districts. It has nothing to do with the presence or absence of labor unions.

6. Steven Benardo, interview by author, July 9, 2014.

7. *P. v. Ambach*, 669 F.2d 865 (2d Cir. 1982). On the importance of the *Ambach* case for the disability rights movement, see Fleischer and Zames, *Disability Rights Movement*, 186.

8. Grumet with Caher, *Curious Case of Kiryas Joel*, 127.

9. Benardo interview, July 9, 2014.

10. Ibid.

11. Grumet with Caher, *Curious Case of Kiryas George*, 68n30. Geraldine Baum, "Crossing the Line: A School for Disabled Children Has Some Worried about Separation of Church and State," *Los Angeles Times*, December 19, 1993.

12. See Mintz, *Hasidic People*, 319.

13. According to Benardo, "The State Education department did everything they could to do me in," noting in particular that "they sent an evaluation team into the school district six weeks into the creation of it" and that "BOCES showed up on the very first day." Steven Benardo, interview by author, September 2014.

14. See Elizabeth Kolbert, "Village Wants Hasidic Public School District," *New York Times*, July 21, 1989, https://www.nytimes.com/1989/07/21/nyregion/village-wants-hasidic-public -school-district.html; Elizabeth Kolbert, "Suits Contests Hasidic District," *New York Times*,

January 21, 1990, https://www.nytimes.com/1990/01/21/nyregion/suit-contests-hasidic
-district.html; Associated Press, "Cuomo Signs Bill to Create Hasidic Town School District,"
New York Times, July 26, 1990, https://www.nytimes.com/1989/07/26/nyregion/cuomo-signs
-bill-to-create-hasidic-town-school-district.html.

15. Benardo interview, July 9, 2014.

16. *Grumet v. Cuomo*, 617 N.Y.S.2d 620, 694 (N.Y. Sup. Ct. 1994) ("several of the neighboring
districts send their handicapped Hasidic children into Kiryas Joel", so that two thirds of the
full-time students in the village's public school come from outside").

17. Malka Silberstein, interviewed by C-SPAN in "Kiryas Joel Village," C-SPAN, March 30,
1994, https://www.c-span.org/video/?55762-1/kiryas-joel-village.

18. See Mintz, *Hasidic People*, 320.

19. See Complaint at 1, *In re Bais Yoel Ohel Feige v. Congregation Yetev Lev D'Satmar of Kiryas
Joel*, No. 2004–4075, 2004 WL 5531517 (N.Y. Sup. Ct. June 21, 2004) (referencing Faiga's ownership of the parsonage).

20. See *Congregation Yetev Lev D'Satmar v. 26 Adar N.B. Corp.*, 641 N.Y.S.2d 680 (App. Div.
1996). See also Appellant's Brief at 12, *Congregation Bais Rabbenu v. 26 Adar N.B. Corp.*,
723 N.Y.S.2d 711 (App. Div. 2001).

21. *Congregation Yetev Lev D'Satmar v. 26 Adar N.B. Corp.*, 641 N.Y.S.2d at 682. See also *Bedford Avenue Deed, Beth Feige, Inc. to 26 Adar N.B. Corp.*, December 6, 1989.

22. *Congregation Yetev Lev D'Satmar v. 26 Adar N.B. Corp.*, 641 N.Y.S.2d at 682.

23. Ibid. See also Mintz, *Hasidic People*, 321.

24. See *Brach v. Congregation Yetev Lev D'mar, Inc.*, 696 N.Y.S.2d 496 (App. Div. 1999).

25. Ibid.

26. Z, interview by author, May 10, 2016.

27. Ibid.

28. In the dissidents' official history chronicling the rise of the Bnai Yoel faction, the appointment of Aaron Teitelbaum as Rov of KJ is cast as "against the will of the public, against the will
of most residents of KJ and of most of the elders and disciples of our holy Rabbi of blessed
memory, who have held that it [the appointment] is a betrayal of our holy Rabbi of blessed
memory." *Ben ʾarbaʾim le-vina* (Yiddish), ed. Yoel Laufer and Avraham Wolf Markovitz (Monroe, NY: Der Oitzer, 2013–2014), 70.

29. Minutes of September 22, 1987, meeting.

30. For accounts of this development, see *Ben ʾarbaʾim le-vina*, 72; Mintz, *Hasidic People*,
313; and William Berezansky, "The Untold Rebellion," *Times Herald-Record Sunday Magazine*,
March 25, 1990, 5.

31. Z interview.

32. "Letter sent by the Administration of Cong. Yetev Lev, Adar I 5749/February 1989," private collection.

33. In modern Hebrew, that Torah portion is known as "Ki Tisa," or in the pronunciation
favored by Eastern European Jews, "Ki-sisa."

34. See Joel Teitelbaum's introduction to *Va-yo'el Mosheh* (Jerusalem: Jerusalem Publishing,
1961), http://www.mysatmar.com/docs/shite_hakdoshe/vayoel_moshe.pdf. I thank Shaul
Magid for calling my attention to this passage and for his fine translation of the introduction.

35. Z interview; Waldman interview, August 2, 2010.

36. Z interview; Waldman interview.

37. Waldman interview.

38. Z interview; Waldman interview.

39. Waldman interview; Z interview.

40. On the formation of Vaad hakirya, see Albert Samaha, "All the Young Jews," *Village Voice*, November 12, 2014.

41. *In re Khal Charidim Kiryas Joel, et al. v. Village of Kiryas Joel, et al.*, complaint, copy of announcement in *Der Yid*.

42. Jeffrey Rosen, "Village People," *New Republic*, April 10, 1994, https://newrepublic.com /article/73752/village-people. Rosen reports on a public notice in *Der Yid* from 1989 that stated: "It is forbidden for any contractor or owner of a house, in our village, to sell or rent an apartment in Kiryas Joel to a new resident without receiving permission in advance, in writing." (See also new restrictions imposed in 1993.)

43. Waldman interview.

44. Michael Sussman, interview by author, July 7, 2017.

45. Waldman interview.

46. Ibid.

47. Ibid.

48. Ibid.

49. Ibid.; cf. Heilman, *Who Will Lead Us?*; and Mintz, *Hasidic People.*

50. Waldman interview.

51. Ibid.

52. Lefkowitz interview.

53. Among the rabbinic figures consulted were the Montevideo Rov, the Kashover Rov, and the Karlsburger Rov (R. Yehezkel Roth). The Bnai Yoel pamphlet from 1994 was called *Kunteres ʿal tigʿu be-meshihi*; a year later, a group of Brooklyn-based Hasidic, but non-Satmar, rabbis issued *Kunteres milhemes hoive* (A Pamphlet on Obligatory War). On the controversy, see Myers, "'Commanded War.'"

54. Rosen, "Village People," 11–12.

55. See, for example, *Grumet v. Board of Educ.*, 81 N.Y.2d 518, 522 n.1 (1993).

56. Sussman interview.

57. See *Waldman v. United Talmudical Acad.*, 558 N.Y.S.2d 781, 781 (Sup. Ct. 1990) ("Joseph Waldman, who owns a home in the village, was expelled from membership in the Congregation Yetev Lev D'Satmar on October 8, 1989").

58. William Berezansky, "Eight Enter Kiryas Joel School Race," *Times Herald-Record*, January 4, 1990.

59. *United States v. City of Yonkers*, 880 F. Supp. 212 (S.D.N.Y. 1995); *Show Me a Hero*, written by David Simon and William F. Zorzi, directed by Paul Haggis (HBO, August 16, 2015), adapted from Lisa Belkin, *Show Me a Hero: A Tale of Murder, Suicide, Race, and Redemption* (New York: Little, Brown, 1999).

60. Sussman interview.

61. Ibid.

62. See William Berezansky, "Trustee Says Candidate Is Not Harassed," *Times Herald-Record*, January 6, 1990; William Berezansky, "Kiryas Joel Candidate Denounces Dirty Campaign Tactics," *Times Herald-Record*, January 15, 1990.

63. See William Berezansky, "Maverick Loses Kiryas Joel Bid," *Times Herald-Record*, January 28, 1990.

64. Grumet's Complaint at 5, *Grumet v. Board of Educ.*, No. 1054–90 (N.Y. Sup. Ct., Albany County, January 22, 1992).

65. Grumet interview.

66. N.Y. Const. art. XI, § 3.

67. Grumet's Complaint at 28, *Grumet v. Board of Educ.*, No. 1054–90 (N.Y. Sup. Ct., Albany County, January 22, 1992).

68. William Berezansky, "Kiryas Joel Board Will Change: Two Trustees Fail to File for Re-election," *Times Herald-Record*, February 21, 1990.

69. Petition at Exhibit H, *Waldman v. United Talmudical Acad.*, 558 N.Y.S.2d 781 (Sup. Ct. 1990).

70. Waldman interview.

71. Record on Appeal at 602–603, *Grumet v. Board of Educ.*, 618 N.E.2d 94 (N.Y. 1993).

72. Ibid., 600.

73. Ibid.

74. William Berezansky, "Judge Calls Rabbi to Court over Pupil Expulsions," *Times Herald-Record*, March 29, 1990.

75. Sussman interview.

76. Record on Appeal at 608, *Grumet v. Board of Educ.*, 618 N.E.2d 94 (N.Y. 1993) (Supplemental affidavit in *Waldman v. United Talmudical Acad.*, 558 N.Y.S.2d 781 [Sup. Ct. 1990]).

77. Record on Appeal at 624, *Grumet v. Board of Educ.*, 618 N.E.2d 94 (N.Y. 1993) (Exhibit H, *Waldman v. United Talmudical Acad.*, 558 N.Y.S.2d 781 [Sup. Ct. 1990]).

78. Ibid.

79. Ibid.

80. Bob Liff, "Satmar Unrest Puts B'Klyn Cops on Alert," *Newsday*, April 21, 1990.

81. *Waldman v. United Talmudical Acad.*, 558 N.Y.S.2d 781 (Sup. Ct. 1990).

82. *Grumet v. New York State Educ. Dept.*, 579 N.Y.S.2d 1004, 1008 (N.Y. Sup. Ct. 1992).

83. William Berezansky, "Kiryas Rioters Stone Dissident's Home," *Times Record-Herald*, May 14, 1990.

84. *Congregation Yetev Lev v. 26 Adar N.B. Corp.*, 641 N.Y.S.2d 680 (App. Div. 1996).

85. William Berezanksy, "Kiryas Joel Factions Make Peace," *Times Herald-Record*, May 18, 1990. This incident was not the last time by any stretch of the imagination that Waldman would find himself at odds with the village's leadership. In 1993, KJ's religious authorities, led by chief halakhic decisor Getzel Berkowitz, accused him of the serious transgression of informing and profaning the name of God. They then issued "a severe prohibition on reading any of his deceitful writings, for he is full of defects." See the rabbinic edict published in *Der Yid*, January 21, 1994.

86. See *Congregation Yetev Lev v. 26 Adar N.B. Corp.*, 641 N.Y.S.2d 680 (App. Div. 1996).

87. Cara Buckley, "After Evacuation, Artists Begin an Effort to Save Their Haven," *New York Times*, February 10, 2008, https://www.nytimes.com/2008/02/10/nyregion/10building.html.

88. Grumet's Complaint at 9, *Grumet v. Board of Educ.*, 618 N.E.2d 94 (N.Y. 1993).

89. Motion to Intervene (Monroe-Woodbury), *Grumet v. Board of Educ.*, 618 N.E.2d 94 (N.Y. 1993).

90. Reply Affidavit of Lawrence W. Reich at 2, *Grumet v. Board of Educ.*, 618 N.E.2d 94 (N.Y. 1993).

91. Establishment Clause taxpayer standing doctrine was established in *Flast v. Cohen*, 392 U.S. 83 (1968).

92. Record on Appeal at 396, *Grumet v. Board of Educ.*, 618 N.E.2d 94 (N.Y. 1993) (Stipulation and Order Releasing Original Defendants at 2).

93. Record on Appeal at 253, *Grumet v. Board of Educ.*, 618 N.E.2d 94 (N.Y. 1993) (Answering Affidavit [Grumet] at 4).

94. Sarah Lyall, "Hasidic Public School District Is Unconstitutional, Judge Rules," *New York Times*, January 23, 1992.

95. Ibid.

96. Lewin interview.

97. *Grumet v. Board of Educ.*, 592 N.Y.S.2d 123 (App. Div. 1992); and *Grumet v. Board of Educ.*, 618 N.E.2d 94 (N.Y. 1993).

98. Steven P. Brown, *Trumping Religion: The New Christian Right, the Free Speech Clause, and the Courts* (Tuscaloosa: University of Alabama Press, 2002), 5.

99. Ibid., 24.

100. Robert C. Boisvert, Jr., "Of Equal Access and Trojan Horses," *Law & Inequality* 3 (1985): 373, 378.

101. "State of the Union Address," C-SPAN, January 25, 1984, https://www.c-span.org/video/?123864–1%2F1984-state-union-address.

102. Michael W. McConnell, "Multiculturalism, Majoritarianism, and Educational Choice: What Does Our Constitutional Tradition Have to Say?," *University of Chicago Legal Forum* 1991 (1991): 123.

103. *Board of Ed. v. Mergens*, 496 U.S. 226 (1990).

104. "Robertson Leads His Religious Forces into the Legal Arena: Civil Rights: Televangelist's American Center for Law and Justice Provides Free Counsel in Battling 'Anti-God, Anti-Family' Groups: The ACLU Is a Major Target," *Los Angeles Times*, October 10, 1992.

105. Rosalie Beck and David W. Hendon, "Notes on Church-State Affairs," *Journal of Church and State* 34, no. 4 (1992): 931.

106. Brown, *Trumping Religion*, 100.

107. *Employment Div. v. Smith*, 494 U.S. 872 (1990).

108. Ibid., 879 (quoting *Reynolds v. United States*, 98 U.S. 145 [1879]).

109. While *Widmar v. Vincent* came before 1993, the decision in *Lamb's Chapel* represented the court's increasingly accommodationist stance toward religion. In *Lamb's Chapel*, Justice Scalia wrote: "The Constitution affirmatively mandates accommodation, not merely tolerance, of all religions. . . . Anything less would require the 'callous indifference' we have said was never intended" (*Lamb's Chapel v. Center Moriches Union Free School District*, 508 U.S. 384 [1993]).

110. Brief for Petitioner Board of Education of the Monroe-Woodbury Central School District, *Board of Educ. v. Grumet*, 512 U.S. 687 (1994).

111. *Lamb's Chapel v. Center Moriches Union Free School District*, 508 U.S. 384 (1993).

112. *Zobrest v. Catalina Foothills Sch. Dist.*, 509 U.S. 1 (1993). The lawyer representing the child and his parents in *Zobrest*, William Ball, was a notable advocate for conservative religious causes whose work predated and, in important ways, set the path for the conservative religious advocacy groups associated with the "new Christian right." A Roman Catholic who served as vice chairman of the National Committee for Amish Religious Freedom, he is the lawyer who successfully represented the Old Amish Order in the 1972 landmark case of *Wisconsin v. Yoder*, 406 U.S. 205 (1972) and argued on behalf of Bob Jones University in the case of *Bob Jones Univ. v. United States*, 461 U.S. 574 (1983). See "William Ball Is Dead at 82: Defended Religious Rights," *New York Times*, January 18, 1999.

113. *Grumet v. Board of Educ. of Kiryas Joel Vill. Sch. Dist.*, 81 N.Y.2d 518, 618 N.E.2d 94 (1993), *aff'd*, 512 U.S. 687 (1994).

114. On the manifestation of this position in Orthodox Jewish support for conservative Christian advocacy in the *Lamb's Chapel* and *Zobrest* cases, see Deborah Kalb, "High Court Hears 2 Religion Cases Followed Closely by Jewish Groups," *Jewish Telegraphic Agency*, February 25, 1993, http://pdfs.jta.org/1993/1993-02-25_037.pdf.

115. *Board of Educ. v. Grumet*, 512 U. S. 687, 689–90 (1994).

116. Formed in the early twentieth century, the three groups were united in their desire to fight antisemitism and support equality in America. Two of them, the American Jewish Committee and the Anti-Defamation League, were early and strong supporters of the principle of church-state separation. See Jonathan D. Sarna, *American Jews and Church-State Relations: The Search for "Equal Footing"* (New York: American Jewish Committee, 1989), 1–43, https://www .brandeis.edu/hornstein/sarna/christianjewishrelations/Archive/AmericanJewsandChurchS tateRelationsEqualFooting.pdf; Sarah Barringer Gordon, *The Spirit of the Law: Religious Voices and the Constitution in Modern America* (Cambridge, MA: Harvard University Press, 2010); Noah Feldman, *Divided by God: America's Church-State Problem—and What We Should Do about It* (New York: Farrar, Straus and Giroux, 2007).

117. Jay Sekulow, "How a Jewish Lawyer from Brooklyn Came to Believe in Jesus," *Jews for Jesus*, January 1, 2005, https://jewsforjesus.org/our-stories/jay-sekulow-how-a-jewish-lawyer -from-brooklyn-came-to-believe-in-jesus/. See also David Kukoff, "The Life and Career of Jay Alan Sekulow," *Law Crossing*, https://www.lawcrossing.com/article/327/Jay-Alan-Sekulow/ (describing "the life and career that have taken him from the postwar Jewish shtetl of Long Island to the post-civil rights battleground of the South").

118. Initially, Shebitz presided over the case, but he decided to outsource the litigation to the leading lawyer in the field of constitutional law and church-state issues, Lewin. Worona interview.

119. *City of Allegheny v. ACLU*, 429 U.S. 573 (1989).

120. *Goldman v. Weinberger*, 475 U.S. 503 (1986). Although the Supreme Court denied Lewin's client the right to wear a yarmulke, the case led Congress to enact a law allowing "a member of the armed forces [to] wear an item of religious apparel while wearing the uniform of the member's armed force." 10 U.S.C. § 774(b) (2010).

121. *United Jewish Orgs., Inc. v. Carey*, 430 U.S. 144 (1977).

122. *McGowan v. Maryland*, 366 U.S. 420 (1961); *Braunfeld v. Brown*, 366 U.S. 599 (1961).

123. Lewin interview.

124. Ibid.

125. "Lewin, Nathan," in *Encyclopedia Judaica*, 2nd ed., ed. Cecil Roth (New York: Macmillan, 2006).

126. Grumet interview.

127. Louis Hartz, *The Liberal Tradition in America* (Orlando, FL: Harcourt Brace, & World, 1955), 3–5; Lionel Trilling, *The Liberal Imagination* (New York: Viking, 1950), 12–15.

128. Maurianne Adams and John H. Bracey, *Strangers & Neighbors: Relations between Blacks & Jews in the United States* (Amherst: University of Massachusetts Press, 1999). But see now Dollinger, *Black Power, Jewish Politics*.

129. Gordon, *Spirit of the Law*; Gregg Ivers, *To Build a Wall: American Jews and the Separation of Church and State* (Charlottesville: University of Virginia Press, 1995).

130. See Lee Epstein, *Contemplating Courts* (Washington, DC: Congressional Quarterly, 1995), n. 18 (Leo Pfeffer is "as close to the historical architect and guide of the legal separationist position as can be imagined"). On the concept of legal secularism, see Feldman, *Divided by God*, 8.

131. Jonathan D. Sarna, "Church-State Dilemmas of American Jews," in *Jews and the American Public Square: Debating Religion and Republic*, ed. Alan Mittelman, Robert Light, and Jonathan D. Sarna (Lanham, MD: Rowan & Littlefield, 2002), 57.

132. Ivers, *To Build a Wall*, 122.

133. Ibid., 113–114.

134. Laura Jane Gifford and Daniel K. Williams, *The Right Side of the Sixties: Reexamining Conservatism's Decade of Transformation* (New York: Palgrave Macmillan, 2012), 113.

135. Leo Pfeffer, "Speech Before the 8th National Convention of the Freedom from Religion Foundation, Minneapolis, Minnesota" (September 29, 1985), reprinted in *Freethought Today*, January/February 1986.

136. Gifford and Williams, *Right Side of the Sixties*, 121–140.

137. Ibid.

138. Eric Pace, "Leo Pfeffer, 83, Lawyer on Staff of the American Jewish Congress," *New York Times*, June 7, 1983, https://www.nytimes.com/1993/06/07/obituaries/leo-pfeffer-83-lawyer-on-staff-of-the-american-jewish-congress.html.

139. Benardo interview, July 9, 2014.

140. Ibid.

141. See Charles Taylor, "The Politics of Recognition," in *Multiculturalism: Examining the Politics of Recognition*, ed. Amy Gutmann (Princeton: Princeton University Press, 1994), 25–73.

142. Sussman interview. See also Victor Porcelli, "A Lifelong Democrat and Famed Civil Rights Attorney, Michael Sussman, Runs for Attorney General as a Green," *Gotham Gazette*, October 9, 2018, https://www.gothamgazette.com/state/7976-a-lifelong-democrat-and-famed-civil-rights-attorney-michael-sussman-runs-for-attorney-general-as-a-green.

143. Sussman interview.

144. Worona interview.

145. Ibid.

146. Grumet interview; Grumet with Caher, *Curious Case of Kiryas Joel*, 89.

147. Grumet with Caher, *Curious Case of Kiryas Joel*, 198.

148. "Kiryas Joel Village," C-SPAN, March 30, 1994, https://www.c-span.org/video/?55762-1/kiryas-joel-village.

149. Recalling the scene many years later, Terry Olivo, then assistant superintendent of Monroe-Woodbury, said, "I can still see him on the steps of the Supreme Court with a black cape and a cane with a silver handle, waving his cane." The cape appears to be apocryphal—the television footage shows him dressed in sober gray suit and red tie—and cane. Terry Olivo, interview by author, September 10, 2014.

Chapter 6: The Law of the Land (Is the Law)

1. *Board of Educ. v. Grumet* (*Grumet I*), 512 U.S. 687 (1994).

2. *Grumet I* at 696 (citing *Larkin v. Grendel's Den*, 459 U.S. 116 [1982]).

3. *Grumet I* at 708 ("We do not disable a religiously homogeneous group from exercising political power").

4. *Oregon v. Rajneeshpuram*, 598 F. Supp. 1208 (D. Or. 1984). See Stolzenberg, "Culture of Property," 169.

5. *Rajneeshpuram* at 1208.

6. *Shelley v. Kraemer*, 343 U.S. 1 (1948). Another case in which the Supreme Court adopted the liberal view of state action was *Reitman v. Mulkey*, 387 U.S. 369 (1967). See generally, "Developments in the Law: State Action, and the Public/Private Distinction," *Harvard Law Review* 123, no. 5 (2010): 1248–1314, http://www.jstor.org/stable/40648486.

7. *Grumet I* at 722.

8. *Grumet I* at 728.

9. See *Obergefell v. Hodges*, 576 U.S. 644 (2015); *Romer v. Evans*, 517 U.S. 620 (1996).

10. *Grumet I* at 730.

11. Ibid.

12. *Grumet I* at 711–712. The first opinion in a religion case to give voice to this view was Justice Douglas's dissent in *Wisconsin v. Yoder*, 406 U.S. 205 (1972), the Amish case in which the Supreme Court recognized the right of a religious community to opt out of compulsory education laws if they threatened its "way of life." Douglas's dissent, lamenting that the Court's decision deprived Amish children of "exposure to the new and amazing world of diversity that exists today," is a clear forerunner to Justice Stevens's concurrence in the *Grumet* case. See Reva Siegel, "From Colorblindness to Antibalkanization: An Emerging Ground of Decision in Race Equality Cases," *Yale Law Journal* 120, no. 6 (2011): 1278–1366.

13. *Grumet I* 512 U.S. at 749.

14. See, e.g., Karma Chavez, Yasmin Nair, and Ryan Conrad, "Equality, Sameness, Difference: Revisiting the Equal Rights Amendment," *Women's Studies Quarterly* 43, nos. 3–4 (2015): 272–276; Martha Minow, *Making All the Difference: Inclusion, Exclusion, and American Law* (Ithaca; NY: Cornell University Press, 1990).

15. For examples of scholarship, see Sandel, *Liberalism and the Limits of Justice*; MacIntyre, *After Virtue*; Michael Walzer, *Spheres of Justice: A Defense of Pluralism and Equality* (New York: Basic Books, 1983); Seyla Benhabib, *Situating the Self: Gender, Community, and Postmodernism in Contemporary Ethics* (New York: Routledge, 1992). For examples of activism, see Dana R. Shugar, *Separatism and Women's Community* (Lincoln: University of Nebraska Press, 1995); and

Bette S. Tallen, "Lesbian Separatism: A Historical and Comparative Perspective," in *For Lesbians Only: A Separatist Anthology*, ed. Sarah Lucia Hoagland (London: Onlywomen Press, 1988), 132–145. For public discussion, see, e.g., Amitai Etzioni, "The New Rugged Communitarians," *Washington Post*, January 20, 1991; and Fareed Zakaria, "The ABCs of Communitarianism: A Devil's Dictionary," *Slate Magazine*, July 26, 1996.

16. This presumably explained why the fate of the *village* of Kiryas Joel, whose constitutionality went unchallenged in the *Grumet* litigation, was different from the fate of the Kiryas Joel *school district*. *Grumet I*, 512 U.S. at 712.

17. *Grumet I* at 716.

18. Ibid.

19. Nathan Lewin, interview by author, March 20, 2011.

20. Ibid.

21. Ibid.

22. Ibid. See also Grumet with Caher, *Curious Case of Kiryas Joel*, 236 ("Lewin himself did not defend it").

23. Lewin interview.

24. N.Y. Session Laws chap. 241 (1994).

25. *Grumet v. Cuomo (Grumet II)*, 625 N.Y.S.2d 1000 (Sup. Ct. 1995), *rev'd*, 647 N.Y.S.2d 565 (N.Y. App. Div. 1996), *aff'd*, 681 N.E.2d 340 (N.Y. 1997).

26. Lewin interview.

27. Ibid.

28. Grumet with Caher, *Curious Case of Kiryas Joel*, 237.

29. Lewin interview.

30. *Grumet v. Cuomo*, 615 N.Y.S.2d 1000 (Sup. Ct. 1995).

31. *Grumet v. Cuomo*, 647 N.Y.S.2d 565 (App. Div. 1996).

32. Lewin interview.

33. *Grumet v. Pataki (Grumet III)*, 720 N.E.2d 66 (N.Y. 1999); *Grumet v. Pataki*, 675 N.Y.S.2d 662 (App. Div. 1998).

34. See *Zobrest v. Catalina Foothills Sch. Dist.*, 509 U.S. 1 (1993); *Witters v. Wash. Dep't of Servs. for Blind*, 474 U.S. 481 (1986); *Mueller v. Allen*, 463 U.S. 388 (1983).

35. *Agostini v. Felton*, 521 U.S. 203 (1997).

36. *Agostini* at 214 ("Specifically, petitioners pointed to the statements of five Justices in *Board of Educ.* v. *Grumet*, 512 U.S. 687 (1994), calling for the overruling of *Aguilar*").

37. *Agostini* at 234–235.

38. Richard Perez-Pena, "Special School District's Backers Gird for 3rd Suit and More," *New York Times*, January 23, 1998.

39. Ibid.

40. Ibid.

41. Lewin interview.

42. *Pataki v. Grumet*, 528 U.S. 946 (1999). The litigation around Kiryas Joel has attracted the attention of legal scholars including Abner S. Greene, "Kiryas Joel and Two Mistakes about Equality," *Columbia Law Review* 96:1 (1996), 1–86; Christopher L. Eisgruber, "The

Constitutional Value of Assimilation," *Columbia Law Review* 96:1 (1996), 87–103; Ira C. Lupu, "Uncovering the Village of Kiryas Joel," *Columbia Law Review* 96:1 (1996), 104–20; Jonathan Boyarin, "Circumscribing Constitutional Identities in Kiryas Joel," *The Yale Law Journal*, 106:5 (1997), 1537–1570; and Richard Thompson Ford, "Geography and Sovereignty: Jurisdictional Formation and Racial Segregation," *Stanford Law Review* 49:6 (1997), 1365–445.

43. N.Y. Laws chap. 405, § 83 (1999).

44. See the press release of the New York State School Boards Association from August 23, 1999, http://faculty.history.umd.edu/BCooperman/NewCity/Kiryas%20Joel%20site/Website /New%20York%20State%20School%20Boards%20Association%20Lawmakers%20Approve %20Kiryas%20Joel%20Bill.htm.

45. Ben Ostrer, interview by author, December 18, 2018.

46. Lewin interview.

47. *Birnbaum v. Board of Educ.*, No. 7306–99, 1999 WL 35015446 (N.Y. Sup. Ct. Dec. 20, 1999).

48. Ibid.

49. Ostrer interview.

50. Motion decision, *Birnbaum v. Board of Educ.*, No. 7306–99, 1999 WL 35015446 (N.Y. Sup. Ct. Dec. 20, 1999).

51. Ostrer interview. See Recusal Order, *Birnbaum v. Board of Educ.*, No. 7306–99, 1999 WL 35015446 (N.Y. Sup. Ct. Feb. 18, 2000).

52. *Birnbaum v. Board of Educ.*, No. 7306–99, 2001 WL 36241683 (N.Y. Sup. Ct. Feb. 14, 2001).

53. Michael Winerip, "On Sunday: Pious Village Is No Stranger to the Police," *New York Times*, September 20, 1992.

54. Transcript of Trial at 785, *Khal Charidim Kiryas Joel v. Village of Kiryas Joel, (Federal Khal Charidim Suit)* 95 CIV. 8378 JSR, 1998 WL 601077 (S.D.N.Y. Sept. 9, 1998) (Wieder testimony, referring to Exhibit 217, a village press release condemning the acts of "a few young students"). See also Albert Samaha, "All the Young Jews," *Village Voice*, November 12, 2014 ("Aaron Teitelbaum told the *Wall Street Journal* the violence was caused by 'a few youths who sometimes get out of control'"), https://www.villagevoice.com/2014/11/12/all-the-young-jews-in-the-village -of-kiryas-joel-new-york-the-median-age-is-13/.

55. Minutes of the 1992 General Assembly Meeting Amending By-Laws to Provide for One Congregation, Including Kiryas Joel, Monsey, Williamsburg, Borough Park, & Lakewood (hereinafter Minutes of the 1992 General Assembly), contained in Exhibit J of the Petitioners' Reply Exhibit Book in the Void Election Proceeding and in Exhibit J of the Wertheimer Affirmation in the Void Election Proceeding.

56. Affirmation of Yosef Hirsch in Opposition to Defendants' Motion for Summary Judgment (hereinafter "Yosef Hirsch Affirmation"), *Federal Khal Charidim Suit*.

57. See Winerip, "On Sunday"; Transcript of Trial at 224–225, 227, 229, *Federal Khal Charidim Suit* (S.D.N.Y. Sept. 9, 1998) (testimony of Z. Waldman) (Z. Waldman testifying that Exhibits 5 and 6 were said to be "approximately '92 or the end of '91").

58. See "Civil Rights Lawyer Cries Foul Play in Kiryas Joel," *Times Herald-Record*, April 9, 1991.

59. Ibid.

60. Transcript of Trial at 236, *Federal Khal Charidim Suit* (S.D.N.Y. Sept. 9, 1998) (testimony of Z. Waldman); Transcript of Trial at 672, 718, 744, *Federal Khal Charidim Suit* (testimony of A. Wieder).

61. Transcript of Trial at 230, *Federal Khal Charidim Suit* (S.D.N.Y. Sept. 9, 1998) (Testimony of Z. Waldman) (Exhibit 5, 6, or 7).

62. Transcript of Trial at 233, 235, *Federal Khal Charidim Suit* (testimony of Z. Waldman) (Exhibit 10). See also Yosef Hirsch Affirmation; Exhibit 1 (letter in Yiddish from Congregation Yetev Lev D'Satmar-Kiryas Joe to Hirsch's daughter instructing her that she could not operate her own daycare center unless she agreed not to admit any children from Bnai Yoel and not to operate out of her father's home).

63. Winerip, "On Sunday."

64. Transcript of Trial at 573, 579, *Federal Khal Charidim Suit* (Wieder Testimony). See also Samaha, "All the Young Jews."

65. Transcript of Trial at 583, *Federal Khal Charidim Suit* (Wieder testimony).

66. Transcript of Trial at 778–780, *Federal Khal Charidim Suit* (Wieder testimony) (minutes of the board of trustees of the Village of Kiryas Joel, July 2, 1992, Exhibit 97, referenced in Wieder direct) (hereinafter minutes of July 2, 1992, village board meeting).

67. William Berezansky, "Trustee Says Candidate Is Not Harassed," *Times Herald-Record*, January 6, 1990.

68. Exhibit 1 accompanying Affirmation of Joseph Waldman in Opposition to Defendants' Motion for Summary Judgment, November 1, 1996, *Khal Charidim Kiryas Joel v. Village of Kiryas Joel*, 95 CIV. 8378 JSR, 1998 WL 601077 (S.D.N.Y. Sept. 9, 1998).

69. Appellant Brief, *Friedman v. Orange Cty. Bd. of Elections*, 642 N.Y.S.2d 528 (App. Div. 1996).

70. Minutes of July 2, 1992, village board meeting; Wieder direct testimony, Transcript of Trial at 779–780, *Federal Khal Charidim Suit* (Wieder direct testimony).

71. Minutes of the 1992 General Assembly.

72. *Brach v. Congregation Yetev Lev D'Satmar, Inc.* (*Brach Cemetery Suit*), 57 F.3d 1064 (2d Cir. 1995), *cert. denied*, 516 U.S. 1173 (1996); Petition for writ of certiorari at 3a, *Brach v. Congregation Yetev Lev D'Satmar, Inc.*, 516 U.S. 1173 (1996) (Appendix C, Memorandum and Order by District Judge Sifton).

73. *Weinstock v. Congregation Yetev Lev D'Satmar, Orange County*, Index No. 5788–92 (N.Y. Sup. Ct. Orange Cty., Aug. 24, 1992), discussed in *Brach Cemetery Suit*, 3.

74. Minutes of the 1992 General Assembly.

75. Minutes of the 1992 General Assembly.

76. Z, interview by author, May 10, 2016.

77. Village of Kiryas Joel, N.Y., Local Law No. 2.

78. Village of Kiryas Joel, N.Y., Local Law No. 2., §7(C)(4). See Transcript of Trial at 31, 187, 794, *Federal Khal Charidim Suit* (Hafetz opening statement, p. 31; Z. Waldman testimony, p. 187; Wieder testimony, p. 794).

79. In local legalese, they were known as "rabbinical home occupations" or RHOs. Transcript of Trial at 843–847, *Federal Khal Charidim Suit*. See also Rule 3(g) Statement, 56, 57.

80. The ordinance did not make the board of trustees the court of last resort.

81. Transcript of Trial at 498, *Federal Khal Charidim Suit* (Z. Waldman testimony).

82. *Federal Khal Charidim Suit.*

83. See *In re* Chaim Hochhauser, 34 Ed Dept Rep, Decision No. 13415, 1995 WL 17958460 (May 12, 1995).

84. See *In re* Chaim Hochhauser.

85. Transcript of Trial at 254, *Federal Khal Charidim Suit* (Z. Waldman testimony).

86. *Weinstock v. Congregation Yetev Lev*, Index No. 5798 (N.Y. Sup. Ct., Aug. 24, 1992).

87. *Grumet II.*

88. Transcript of Trial at 1, *Federal Khal Charidim Suit* (opening statements).

89. Transcript of Trial at 20–40, *Federal Khal Charidim Suit* (Hafetz opening statement); Transcript of Trial at 426, *Federal Khal Charidim Suit* (Z. Waldman testimony).

90. Transcript of Trial at 435, *Federal Khal Charidim Suit.*

91. Transcript of Trial at 31, *Federal Khal Charidim Suit* (Mr. Hafetz opening).

92. See *In re Khal Charidim v. Village of Kiryas Joel, ("State Khal Charidim Suit")* 1995 WL 17060400 (N.Y. Sup. Ct. June 27, 1995).

93. Ibid.

94. *State Khal Charidim Suit.*

95. Transcript of Trial at 73, 141, *Federal Khal Charidim Suit* (Z. Waldman testimony).

96. *State Khal Charidim Suit.*

97. Ibid.

98. Transcript of Trial at 43, 153, 162, 163, 170, *Federal Khal Charidim Suit* (Z. Waldman testimony).

99. *Joel v. Joel*, No. 2147/95, 1995 WL 17960400 (N.Y. Sup. Ct. June 27, 1995).

100. *Joel v. Joel*, No. 2147/95, 1995 WL 17960402 (N.Y. Sup. Ct. July 14, 1995) (contempt order).

101. Paula McMahon and David Kibbe, "Court Bars Door," *Times Herald-Record*, October 3, 1995.

102. *Federal Khal Charidim Suit.*

103. David Kibbe, "Dissident Temple Opened," *Times Herald-Record*, October 4, 1995.

104. *State Khal Charidim Suit.*

105. Memorandum and order discussed in *Federal Khal Charidim Suit.*

106. Transcript of Trial at 462, *Federal Khal Charidim Suit* (Z. Waldman testimony).

107. Robert Hanley, "In the Ashes of Arson at Kiryas Joel, Tensions of Bitter Factionalism," *New York Times*, July 29, 1996.

108. Transcript of Trial at 511, *Federal Khal Charidim Suit* (Z. Waldman testimony).

109. Mike Levine, "How Bitter the Tyranny in KJ," *Times Herald-Record*, January 15, 2007, https://www.recordonline.com/article/20070115/News/70115783; Evelyn Nieves, "Our Towns: A Village Faces Another Kind of Storm," *New York Times*, January 14, 1996; Paula McMahon and Christopher Mele, "KJ Leader Apologizes to State Police for Riot," *Times Herald-Record*, August 3, 1995.

110. Paula McMahon, "Religion Tests Civil Rights in Kiryas Joel," *Times Herald-Record*, August 3, 1995; Paula McMahon, "Dissidents Won't Give In," *Times Herald-Record*, August 11, 1995.

111. Evelyn Nieves, "Our Towns: A Village Faces Another Kind of Storm," *New York Times*, January 14, 1996.

112. Robert Hanley, "In the Ashes of Arson, Tensions of Bitter Factionalism, *New York Times*, July 2, 1996.

113. Sussman interview.

114. Jed S. Rakoff, "Will the Death Penalty Ever Die?," *New York Review of Books*, June 8, 2017, https://www.nybooks.com/articles/2017/06/08/will-the-death-penalty-ever-die/.

115. *Federal Khal Charidim Suit,* 935 F. Supp. 450 (S.D.N.Y. 1996).

116. Transcript of Trial at 174–175, *Federal Khal Charidim Suit* (Z. Waldman testimony).

117. *Grumet II.*

118. *Grumet v. Cuomo,* 647 N.Y.S.2d 565, 570 (App. Div. 1996) (Spain, J., dissenting).

119. *Congregation Yetev Lev D'Satmar v. Teitelbaum,* 666 N.Y.S.2d 867 (App. Div. 1997). See Josh Margolin, "Kiryas Joel Feud Intensifies: Congregation Seeks to Evict Rabbi's Widow," *Times Herald-Record*, September 11, 1995.

120. Ibid.

121. Transcript of Trial at 639, *Federal Khal Charidim Suit* (Wieder direct testimony).

122. See Brief for Plaintiffs-Appellants-Respondents, *Bais Yoel Ohel Feige v. Congregation Yetev Lev D'Satmar of Kiryas Joel*, No. 2008–1657, 2008 WL 8622850 (N.Y. App. Div. Oct. 2, 2008).

123. See *Bais Yoel Ohel Feige v. Congregation Yetev Lev D'Satmar of Kiryas Joel*, No. 2004–4075, 2004 WL 5531517 (N.Y. Sup. Ct. June 21, 2004).

124. Paula McMahon, "Peace at Last: Dissidents Win Right to Worship, Both Sides Say It Means the End to Tension in Kiryas Joel," *Times Herald-Record*, March 11, 1997; Joseph Berger, "Dissidents Gain with Kiryas Joel Pact," *New York Times*, March 12, 1997.

125. Paula McMahon, "Peace at Last: Dissidents Win the Right to Worship, Both Sides Say It Means the End to Tension in Kiryas Joel," *Times Herald-Record*, March 11, 1997.

126. Ibid.

127. Sussman interview.

128. Ibid.

129. Ibid.

130. *Waldman v. Village of Kiryas Joel (Waldman I)*, 97-Civ-00074 (S.D.N.Y. Apr. 15, 1997).

131. Quoted in *Waldman v. Village of Kiryas Joel (Waldman II)*, 39 F. Supp. 2d 370, 375 (S.D.N.Y. 1999).

132. See *Waldman II*, 39 F. Supp. 2d at 374.

133. Transcript of Trial at 4, *Federal Khal Charidim Suit.*

134. Ibid, at 12.

135. Ibid, at 13.

136. Sussman interview.

137. Transcript of Trial at 22, *Federal Khal Charidim Suit.*

138. Ibid, at 27.

139. Ibid, at 239.

140. Ibid.

141. Ibid, at 571–72.

142. Ibid, at 572.

143. Ibid, at 681.

144. Sussman interview.

145. Ibid.

146. Affirmation of David Eckstein at 3, *Federal Khal Charidim Suit.*

147. Transcript of Trial at 862, *Federal Khal Charidim Suit.*

148. July 15, 1997 Order, Joel v. Village of Kiryas Joel, 95 CIV. 8378 (JSR), 1997 WL 543091, at *1 (S.D.N.Y. Sept. 4, 1997).

149. *Waldman II.*

150. Affirmation of David Eckstein at 2, *Federal Khal Charidim Suit.*

151. Transcript of Trial at 853, *Federal Khal Charidim Suit.*

152. Ibid.

153. *Waldman II* (citing *Waldman v. Village of Kiryas Joel*, 97 Civ. 7506 [S.D.N.Y. Oct. 27, 1997]).

154. *Waldman v. Village of Kiryas Joel*, 207 F.3d 105 (2d Cir. 2000).

155. A former dean of Yale Law School, Calabresi was the scion of the famed Italian Jewish Finzi-Contini family that was the subject of *The Garden of the Finzi-Continis*, a book remade into a film about the experience of Italian Jews before and during the Holocaust. His family found refuge in New Haven, where his father was a member of Yale medical school faculty. Calabresi was raised Catholic after his mother converted to Catholicism and defined himself as "ethnically Yale." See the discussion with Judge Calbresi at the Centro Primo Levi New York, "We Were Outsiders: Conversation with Guido Calabresi," https://primolevicenter.org/we-were -outsiders-conversation-with-guido-calabresi/.

156. "We Were Outsiders."

Chapter 7: "Two Kings Serving the Same Crown"

1. For a copy of Moshe's letter of appointment, see *Der Yid*, June 4, 1999, 1, 4. The letter was reprinted on the tenth anniversary of the appointment in an article extolling "the historic date" a decade earlier and the growth of the Zali community and moysdes. See "Ha-ʿasiri yihyeh kodesh la-Shem," *Der Yid*, June 12, 2009, 58–61. For a thorough recounting of the succession battles in Satmar, see Heilman, *Who Will Lead Us?*, 194ff.

2. *Der Yid*, June 18, 1999, quoted in Heilman, *Who Will Lead Us?*, 196.

3. Interview with Moshe Gabbai Friedman, October 20, 2013.

4. "Controversial Legendary Satmar Gabbai in First-Ever Interview. Two Chassidic Courts? Of Course, It's Good," excerpted from an interview in *Sha'ah Tovah* in the online Haredi publication *Voz Iz Neias?*, October 1, 2019, https://www.vosizneias.com/39238/2009/10/01 /williamsburg-ny-controversial-legendary-satmar-gabbai-in-first-ever-interview-two -chassidic-courts-of-course-its-good/; interview with Moshe Gabbai Friedman, October 20, 2013.

5. Verified Article 75 petition, RA-34, Adar action, p. 6. On September 12, 1998, Berl Friedman succeeded Leopold Lefkowitz as the president of Satmar. ¶11 Affirmation of Petitioner Oberlander et al., *Yetev Lev D'Satmar v. 26 Adar N.B.*, Corp. Void Election proceeding, petitioners' reply memorandum. January 4, 2002, A-964.

6. See undated letter issued by Friedman faction, Exhibit D, A-235. ¶12 Affirmation of Petitioner Oberlander et al., *Yetev Lev D'Satmar v. 26 Adar N.B.*, Corp. RA-83, Ex. 3 to verified Article 75 petition-document of obligation, RA-83-RA-87.

7. Minutes of the January 14 meeting.

8. See ¶20, 2001 Affirmation of Oberlander et al. *Yetev Lev D'Satmar v. 26 Adar N.B.*, Corp. (ET). See also 2001 affirmation of Oberlander et al. in the *Yetev Lev D'Satmar v. 26 Adar N.B.*, Corp. case (¶¶20–21) (ET). Article 75 Petition, RA-44, par. 28.

9. February 13, 2004 hearing, A-1–18.

10. Ibid. at ¶23.

11. David Chen, "A Hasidic Village Gets a Lesson in Bare-Knuckled Politicking," *New York Times*, June 9, 2001.

12. John-Henry Doucette, "Diana Easily Defeats Sussman in County Exec Race," *Times Herald-Record*, November 7, 2001; Sussman interview. Among his most vivid memories from that time is being hoisted onto the shoulders of several Satmar men at a campaign rally at the Brooklyn Naval Yard, where he was paraded in front of twenty thousand people, including a large throng of KJ dissident supporters.

13. Jeffery Toobin, "What Comes Next," *New Yorker*, September 28, 2020, 34.

14. Kevin Flynn and Andy Newman, "Friend of the Court: One Lawyer's Inside Track: Cozying Up to Judges and Reaping Opportunity," *New York Times*, November 11, 2003.

15. Myriam Gilles, "The Day Doctrine Died: Private Arbitration and the End of Law," *University of Illinois Law Review* 2016 (2016): 371.

16. Article 75 Proceeding.

17. Mollen interview.

18. Transcript of the Proceedings Held Before the Honorable Melvin S. Barasch, November 30, 2001, RA-336-RA-477, p. 53.

19. Susan Edelman, "Rabbi-Rousing Row: Holy Hell as Synagogue Feud Comes to Fisticuffs," *New York Post*, March 10, 2002.

20. Justice Jones, a Black lawyer born in Brooklyn and raised in Queens, was appointed to the State Supreme Court in Brooklyn in 1989, the year 26 Adar was incorporated, and elevated to the Court of Appeals in 2007. He died at the age of sixty-eight in 2012, three years after the *Adar* litigation came to a conclusion. Dennis Hevesi, "Theodore T. Jones, Jr., Judge on New York's Top Court, Dies at 68," *New York Times*, November 9, 2012.

21. *Congregation Yetev Lev D'Satmar of Kiryas Joel v. Congregation Yetev Lev D'Satmar*, 9 N.Y.3d 297 (2007); Scher action complaint, Summons and Verified Complaint, Dated July 11 2005, Exhibit A, A-56. This seems to have actually happened on January 14. See Scher action, A-90-A-96.

22. Scher Action, Ex. C to Complaint. ScanPro3368. A-68. Arbitration proceeding, Verified Article 75 Petition, RA-42, par. 21. RA-88, Declaration by Congregation Yetev Lev D'Satmar, Inc., Dated January 18. Exhibit 4. Declaration, Dated January 18, 2001. Actually dated January 19.

23. *Wilmos Friedman, Herman Kahan, Zigmond Brach, et al. v. CYL Cemetery, Inc., Congregation Yetev Lev D'Satmar, Inc. et al.* aka *Friedman v. CYL Cemetery*, Index No. 33481/08; 80 A.D.3d 556 (2011).

24. Chris McKenna, "Who Will Be the Rebbe's Keeper?," *Times Herald-Record*, September 22, 2005.

25. Michael Powell, "Hands On, Gloves Off," *New York Magazine*, April 28, 2006; see also Heilman, *Who Will Lead Us?*, 202. On the *rushe ben rushe* quote, see Berakhot 7A.

26. Andy Newman, "Dispute over Rabbi's Successor Heats Up," *New York Times*, April 25, 2006; "Hasid Rabbi Dies—Power Struggle Looms for Rabbis," *New York Post*, April 25, 2006; "Hasid Holy Wars; Rivals Brawl at Satmar Funeral," *New York Post*, April 26, 2006.

27. See *In the Matter of Bais Yoel Ohel Feige v. Yeter Lev D'Satmar of Kiryas Joel*, 2004 WL 5531517 (N.Y. Sup.) (Trial Pleading) (June 21, 2004).

28. See ibid.

29. 2004 WL 5531517 (N.Y. Sup.) (trial pleading)

30. Chris McKenna, "Wieder Re-elected in KJ," *Times Herald-Record*, June 2, 2005, http:// www.recordonline.com/article/20050602/news/306029992.

31. Proceedings summarized in Bais Yoel Ohel Feige, 65 A.D.3d 1176, 885 N.Y.S.2d (Appellate Division, 2009).

32. *Kiryas Joel Alliance v. Village of Kiryas Joel*, June 13, 2011 complaint, par. 183, p. 26.

33. *Bais Yoel Ohel Feige v. Congregation Yetev Lev D'Satmar of Kiryas Joel*, 78 A.D.3d 626 (Appellate Division, 2010).

34. Scher action complaint, A-41.

35. *Friedman et al. v. Congregation Yetev Lev d'Satmar*, February 17, 2009, referenced in *Friedman v. CYL Cemetery, Inc.*, 80 A.D.3d 556, 914 N.Y.S.2d 305 (2011).

36. Chris McKenna, "Cemetery Burials Latest Flashpoint between Kiryas Joel's Feuding factions," *Times Herald-Record*, August 21, 2009.

37. "Beis ha-hayim de-kehilosenu vos di kas ha-holkhim be-arka'os habn zikh mishtalet geveyn," *Der Yid*, October 2, 2009, B53. See also "New York Judge Orders Satmar Dispute over Cemetery Must Go to Beis Din," *Voz iz Neias?*, July 22, 2010.

38. For a text of Bohan's letter to the County Legislature, see "KJ in the News Again," *Times Herald-Record*, June 23, 2004, emphasis added. Among those writing in support of Bohan were Phil Pillet (July 8, 2004) and Simone Celio Jr. (July 10, 2004), "Letters to the Editor," *Times Herald-Record*.

39. On the county legislature vote, see Brendan Scott, "KJ Plan Runs Out of Steam," *Times Herald-Record*, July 2, 2004; and Chris McKenna, "Border Battle of Kiryas Joel Getting Hot," *Times Herald-Record*, July 4, 2004.

40. "An Open Letter to the People of Orange County from Your Neighbors in Kiryas Joel" (2004).

41. Chris McKenna, "Myriad of Deals Done to Carve Out New Village," *Times Herald-Record*, July 11, 2004.

42. John Sullivan, "New Shift in Hasidic-Village Construction Battle," *Times Herald-Record*, October 16, 2010.

43. On the initial wedding and protest, see "Dissident Clashes at Kiryas Joel Bring Out Police for Four Days," *Mid Hudson News*, January 31, 2010. The call to separate from the three "transgressors" came in a broadside calling for an "Urgent Protest" issued in the name of the Congregation on January 31, 2010 (16 Shvat). The admonitions came in a brief halakhic ruling by R. Getzel Berkowitz in *Der Blat*, February 5, 2010, 19, and in a longer, multipage ruling by him, "Pesak halokhe ve-daas Toyre," *Der Blat*, February 12, 2010, 12–13.

44. Chris McKenna, "Dissidents Planned Wedding Draws Ire of KJ Mainstream," *Times Herald-Record*, March 2, 2010.

45. "Chris McKenna, "Garbage Dumping in Kiryas Joel Stems from Dispute over Unauthorized Weddings," *Times Herald-Record*, August 23, 2010.

46. Kiryas Joel Alliance; Congregation Bais Yoel Ohel Feige; Zalman Waldman; Meyer Deutsch; Bernard Tyrnauer; Congregation TA of KJ, Inc.; Samuel Eisenberg; Isaac Srugo; Joseph Waldman; Moses Tennenbaum; David Wolner; and Joel Waldman v. Village of Kiryas Joel; Jacob Reisman, Village Trustee; Jacob Freund, Village Trustee; Samuel Landau, Village Trustee; Abraham Weider, mayor of the Village of Kiryas Joel; Moses Witriol, director, Village of Kiryas Joel Department of Public Safety; Congregation Yetev Lev D'Satmar of Kiryas Joel; David Eckstein; Town of Monroe; and Cesar A. Perales, sued in his official capacity as acting New York Secretary of State. *Kiryas Joel Alliance v. Village of Kiryas Joel*, 12–217-CV (2d Cir. 2012). The long list of plaintiffs and defendants represents a veritable who's who of the notable parties and entities on each side of the everlasting feud.

47. Sewell Chan and Jo Craven McGinty, "Explosive Growth Since 2000 in State's Hasidic Enclaves," *New York Times*, June 29, 2007.

48. See the census figures at https://www.census.gov/quickfacts/kiryasjoelvillage newyork.

49. Chris McKenna, "Latest Estimate Finds Kiryas Joel Pipeline Could Cost $65 Million," *Times Herald-Record*, November 25, 2018, May 27, 2019.

50. Chris McKenna, "Kiryas Joel, United Monroe Agree on New Town," *Times Herald-Record* June 16, 2017, http://www.recordonline.com/news/20170616/kiryas-joel-united-monroe-agree-on-new-town.

51. *Stipulation of Settlement and Discontinuance of Proceeding No. 2.*

52. Calhoun's proposals was discussed by Oliver Mackson in "Contemplating the City of Kiryas Joel," *Times Herald-Record*, November 14, 2003. The idea was not pursued at the time by KJ officials. See Chris McKenna, "Kiryas Joel Not Pushing City Idea," *Times Herald-Record*, November 28, 2003.

53. See Chris McKenna, "Heat's on Bohan over Remarks," *Times Herald-Record*, June 23, 2004. See also McKenna's special report on the struggle by Satmar Hasidim to purchase property outside of KJ in Woodbury in "Worlds Apart," *Times Herald-Record*, December 5, 2004. A catalog of other antisemitic slurs against KJ prompted by the pipeline is chronicled in the affirmation of Gedalye Szegedin in the case of *Orange County v. Village of Kiryas Joel*, index 2004–7547, 40–41.

54. For a transcript of Szegedin's and others' remarks at the town hall meeting, see Chris McKenna, "KJ: Two Sides to the Story," *Times Herald-Record*, August 15, 2004.

55. McKenna, "Kiryas Joel, United Monroe Agree on New Town."

Epilogue

1. Chris McKenna, "Hasidic Property Owners Seek to Form a New Village," *Times Herald-Record*, July 2, 2018, http://www.recordonline.com/news/20180802/hasidic-property-owners-seek-to-form-new-village.

2. The critique of the wall metaphor came in Rehnquist's dissent to *Wallace v. Jaffree*, 472 U.S. 38, 107 (1985). Supreme Court justice Kavanaugh waxed eloquently about Rehnquist's jurisprudence in this and other areas in the 2017 Walter Berns Lecture at the American Enterprise Institute, "From the Bench: The Constitutional Statesmanship of Chief Justice William Rehnquist," http://www.aei.org/publication/from-the-bench-the-constitutional-statesmanship -of-chief-justice-william-rehnquist/.

3. See, for example, Mark Lilla, *The Once and Future Liberal: After Identity Politics* (New York: HarperCollins, 2017).

4. Michael McConnell, "On Religion, the Supreme Court Protects the Right to Be Different," *New York Times*, July 9, 2020, https://www.nytimes.com/2020/07/09/opinion/supreme -court-religion.html.

5. See Kallen's use of "cultural pluralism" in the collection *Culture and Democracy in the United States* (New York: Boni and Liveright, 1924). On Kallen and this tradition, see Daniel Greene, *The Jewish Roots of Cultural Pluralism: The Menorah Association and American Diversity* (Bloomington: Indiana University Press, 2011).

6. The state of Israel is another story, representing the realization of state-based sovereignty that Zionist political leaders had imagined. There, the state, along with the quasi-state land acquisition body Jewish National Fund, has historically owned over 90 percent of the land, preventing intentional communities from being created from the bottom up through the acquisition of private property and concentrating land in the hands of the Jewish majority. See Nomi Maya Stolzenberg, "Facts on the Ground," in *Property and Community*, ed. Eduardo Penalver and Gregory Alexander (New York: Oxford University Press, 2010), 107–139.

7. Karen Tani, *States of Dependency: Welfare, Rights, and American Governance, 1935–1972* (New York: Cambridge University Press, 2016).

8. For a good summary of these terms, see Herbert J. Gans, "Toward a Reconciliation of 'Assimilation' and 'Pluralism': The Interplay of Acculturation and Ethnic Retention," *International Migration Review* 31, no. 4 (Winter 1997): 877–878.

9. Cohen, "The Blessing of Assimilation in Jewish History" (commencement address, Hebrew Teachers College, Boston, June 1966).

10. See Sharon Otterman, "Judge Ruchie, The Hasidic Superwomen as Night Court," *New York Times*, November 17, 2017, https://www.nytimes.com/2017/11/17/nyregion/judge-ruchie -the-hasidic-superwoman-of-night-court.html.

11. See Orit Avishai, "Anticipating the LGBTQ Moment in Haredi Communities," *The Haredi Moment: An Online Jewish Quarterly Review Forum (Part 3)*, https://katz.sas.upenn.edu /resources/blog/haredi-moment-online-forum-part-3.

12. The percentage of women in the labor force in 2000 was 19.3 percent, a very slight decline from the 1990 rate of 20 percent. See U.S. Census Bureau, "American Fact Finder: Profile of Selected Economic Characteristics" (2000). Meanwhile, the rate jumped from 32.2 percent in 2015 to 38.9 percent in the 2020 census. For the latter figures, see the U.S. Census Bureau figures for people in Kiryas Joel over sixteen at https://www.census.gov/quickfacts/kiryasjoelvillage newyork.

13. See "Satmar Rebbe Rav Aaron Teitelbaum Gives Passionate Detailed Speech about Dangers of Technology and Internet" (2012), http://thepartialview.blogspot.com/2012/02/satmar -rebbe-rav-aAaron-teitelbaum-gives.html.

14. See the 2015 news item "Satmar Hasidic Village of Kiryas Joel, NY Issues New Smart-phone Modesty Rules," September 20, 2018, http://failedmessiah.typepad.com/failed_messiahcom/2015/08/satmar-hasidic-village-of-kiryas-joel-ny-issues-new-smartphone-modesty-rules-234.html.

15. For the 2025 number, see the "Demographics and Fiscal" section of the report by Tim Miller Associates for the Village from April 29, 2015, http://www.kj-seqra.com/507Acres/DGEIS%20Vol%201%20Text%20Sections/KJ%203.2%20Demography%20and%20Fiscal.pdf. The 2035 projection is found in Chris McKenna, "Kiryas Joel Expected to Double by 2015," *Times Herald-Record*, May 12, 2015, http://www.recordonline.com/article/20150512/NEWS/150519776.

16. For an insightful and measured view of this transition, see Jürgen Habermas, "Notes on a Post-Secular Society," *signandsight*, June 18, 2008, http://www.signandsight.com/features/1714.html.

17. Myers, "Rise of a Sovereign Shtetl," 222–246.

18. See the iconic references to these terms in the 1958 essay by Isaiah Berlin, "Two Concepts of Liberty," in *Four Essays on Liberty* (Oxford: Oxford University Press, 1969), 118–172.

19. *Meyer v. Nebraska*, 262 U.S. 390 (1923); *Pierce v. Society of Sisters*, 268 U.S. 510 (1925).

20. Kevin Roose and Matthew Rosenberg, "Touting Virus Cure, 'Simple Country Doctor' Becomes a Rightwing Star," *New York Times*, April 2, 2020; David N. Myers, "Coronavirus Is No Excuse to Demonize Haredim," *Foreword*, March 23, 2020, https://forward.com/opinion/442172/coronavirus-is-no-excuse-to-demonize-Haredim/.

21. The term "off-white" is borrowed from Laura E. Gomez, "Off-White in an Age of White Supremacy: Mexican Elite and the Rights of Indians and Blacks in Nineteenth-Century New Mexico," *Chicano-Latino Law Review* 25 (2005): 9.

GLOSSARY OF HEBREW AND YIDDISH TERMS

Av Beis Din (Hebrew and Yiddish): Lit., "father of house of law"; head of a rabbinical court.

bashert (Yiddish): Destiny or fated to be, as when finding one's life partner.

beis din (Hebrew and Yiddish): Lit., "house of judgment"; rabbinical court to which many traditionally observant Jews bring personal matters (marriage and divorce) and civil disputes.

Bnai Yoel (Hebrew and Yiddish): Lit., "Sons of Joel," the name of the dissident group in Kiryas Joel that regards itself as adhering to the true path of R. Joel Teitelbaum.

bokhers (Yiddish): The Yiddish version of the Hebrew word *bahurim* for boys, referring to yeshivah students.

chaider, or cheder (Hebrew and Yiddish): Lit., "room," referring to a traditional Jewish primary school where students study the Hebrew Bible and basic Jewish law and practice.

chavrusa (Aramaic and Yiddish): Lit., "companionship," referring to a small study circle or pair, or to the person with whom one studies traditional rabbinic texts.

dayanim or dayunim (Hebrew and Yiddish): Judges of a rabbinical court.

Der Yid (Yiddish): "The Jew," the flagship Satmar Yiddish newspaper now associated with the Zali camp in Williamsburg.

derekh Yisra'el sava (Hebrew and Aramaic): "The path of the ancient Israel," connoting a path of adherence to the traditional Judaism of one's forebears for Satmar Jews.

din Torah (Hebrew and Yiddish): Lit., "Torah Judgment," referring to a matter that could be formally brought before a "beis din" for resolution.

dina di-malkhuta dina (Aramaic): Lit., "the law of the land is the law" referring to the ancient doctrine of subordination to gentile rule adhered to by observant Jews.

drushe (Hebrew and Yiddish): "Sermon," referring to a weekly Torah-based lesson given by the rabbi.

gabbai (Hebrew and Yiddish): A person who serves either as a beadle in a synagogue, assisting with prayer services, or as a chief assistant to the Rebbe.

golus (Hebrew and Yiddish): Lit., "exile."

halakhah (Hebrew and Yiddish): Lit., "the way to walk"; Jewish law.

Haredi (Hebrew and Yiddish): Lit., "one who trembles," referring to a traditionally observant Jew who proudly follows the path of ancestors and rejects modern secular culture and modifications in religion.

Hasidim (Hebrew and Yiddish): "Lit," "pious ones," referring to a large group of Haredi Jews whose origins extend back to the late eighteenth-century and early nineteenth-century Eastern European pietist movement.

Kaf Alef Kislev: The twenty-first day of the Hebrew month of Kislev, marking the date of liberation of R. Joel Teitelbaum from Bergen-Belsen, December 7, 1944.

kahal (alternatively, k'hal or k'hul) (Hebrew and Yiddish): Community.

Kiryas Joel (Yoel): Lit., village of Joel.

kollel (Hebrew and Yiddish): Lit., "collecting/collection"; institution for advanced Talmudic
studies intended for married men, who may receive a stipend for their studies.

Lag Ba-Omer: The thirty-third day of the Omer period between Passover and Shavuot, marking
the death of the ancient sage R. Shimon bar Yochai, considered a great source of inspiration
to later mystics; the day is often commemorated, as in Kiryas Joel, with a big bonfire.

malkhus Satmar (Hebrew and Yiddish): "The Kingdom of Satmar," the title of a number of
books about the Satmar world.

mamzerim (Hebrew and Yiddish): Lit., "bastards," referring to children born of an incestuous
relationship or of an adulterous married woman, according to Jewish law.

matsah (also matso, Hebrew and Yiddish): Unleavened flatbread eaten by Jews during
Passover.

mehitsah: Lit., "partition," referring to a physical barrier separating men and women into separate spaces, principally in a synagogue.

mentshen (as in Faiga's mentshen) (Yiddish and German): Lit., "men."

mikveh (Hebrew): Jewish ritual bath for use by women after menstruation and men in preparation for daily prayers or the Sabbath.

minyan(im) (Hebrew and Yiddish): Lit., "count (n)," referring to the requirement of ten men
for a prayer quorum in Orthodox Judaism (or ten people in Conservative and Reform
Judaism).

misnagdim (Hebrew and Yiddish): Lit., "opponents," referring to the late eighteenth- and
nineteenth-century opponents of Hasidim. In Kiryas Joel, the term was used by the opponents of the mainstream establishment faction.

mitzva/mitzvos (Hebrew and Yiddish): Lit., "commandment," referring to the ritual laws and
regulations that traditional observant Jews scrupulously observe. Can also mean a good deed.

moysdes (Hebrew and Yiddish): Lit., "institutions," referring to the educational, religious, and
social welfare institutions of the Satmar community.

moyser (Hebrew and Yiddish): Lit., "one who turns over," referring to a Jew who informs on
another Jew to gentile authorities.

niddah (Hebrew and Yiddish): Lit., "moved," referring to a woman in a state of separation during menstruation.

peyes (Hebrew and Yiddish): Lit., "sidelocks" or "earlocks," referring to the hair in front of the
ears that Haredi men refrain from cutting in adherence to biblical law.

Rebbe: Yiddish variant of Hebrew "rav" or "rabi," used to refer to a venerated rabbinic leader or
teacher. The term applies to the leader of a Hasidic court such as Satmar.

Rebbetsin (Yiddish): Wife of a Rebbe.

Rov/Rav (Hebrew and Yiddish): Rabbinic leader of a community. In the case of the Satmar
community, the Rov was in charge of the entire network of moysdes, or institutions.

Shabbes/Shabbat (Hebrew and Yiddish): The Jewish Sabbath. "Motse Shabbes" (lit., the leaving of the Sabbath) refers to Saturday evening after the Sabbath.

shadkhan (m); shadkhente (f) (Hebrew and Yiddish): A marriage matchmaker.

sheitel (Yiddish): A wig worn by Orthodox women to conform to the long-standing custom of women covering their hair as an act of modesty.

shi'ur (or shir) (Hebrew and Yiddish): A lesson or class, usually on a rabbinic text, in yeshivah.

shpitzel (Yiddish): A head covering used by Haredi (and Satmar) women that contains a partial wig in the front and a covering over the rest of the head.

shtadlan (Hebrew): Jewish figure who represents or intercedes on behalf of the Jewish community with non-Jewish authorities.

shtetl (Yiddish): Lit., "small town," referring to towns or cities with large Jewish populations, or in the case of Kiryas Joel, an all-Jewish town.

shul/shil (Yiddish): Lit., "school," but used ubiquitously as synagogue.

shtibl (Yiddish): Lit., "little room," referring to a meeting place for prayer, oftentimes in a private home (particularly the basement).

streimel (Yiddish): Decorative fur hat worn by married Haredi men on special occasions, including the Sabbath.

tichel (Yiddish): Lit., "little piece of cloth," referring to the head scarf used by Orthodox women to cover their hair.

tsadik (Hebrew and Yiddish): Lit., "righteous one," referring in the context of Hasidic history to the position of Rebbe, or spiritual leader, who is possessed of extraordinary powers.

tsnius (Hebrew and Yiddish): Modesty.

tzitzis (Hebrew and Yiddish): Prayer fringes that Orthodox men wear as a matter of religious obligation that are part of the tallit (tallis) worn by Jews in morning prayer services.

upsherin (Yiddish): Lit., "shearing off," referring to the ceremonial first haircut for a three-year-old Orthodox boy.

Vaad ha-chinech (Hebrew and Yiddish): Education committee.

Vaad hakirya (Hebrew and Yiddish): Village council that serves as the main land development agency in Kiryas Joel.

Vaad hatsnius (Hebrew and Yiddish): Modesty committee.

yahrtseit (Yiddish): Lit., "time of year," referring to the day that marks the anniversary of the death of a Jew.

yeshivah (Hebrew and Yiddish): Lit., "sitting," referring to the main institution of learning where Orthodox Jewish boys study traditional rabbinic sources as the main part of their educational diet.

STEVEN BENARDO: The first superintendent of the Kiryas Joel Free Union School District as well as a designated spokesperson for the community to the outside world. Benardo was a non-Orthodox Jew who formerly served as head of special education in the Bronx for the New York public school system.

NACHMAN BRACH: Satmar businessman who provided early financial support to the development of Kiryas Joel, but then joined the opposition upon the appointment of Rabbi Moshe Teitelbaum as second Satmar Rebbe. He was involved in a host of business transactions on the side of the dissidents in both Kiryas Joel and Williamsburg.

MARIO CUOMO (1932–2015): The three-term governor of New York who previously served as New York secretary of state and in 1977 formally authorized the creation of the village of Kiryas Joel. He later approved the creation of a public school district in Kiryas Joel that would become a source of bitter legal dispute.

PATRICIA DUGAN: Female school bus driver employed by Monroe-Woodbury School District whose assignment to drive male students to UTA in 1983 and filing of grievance against Monroe-Woodbury School District when they reassigned her precipitated the first conflict between KJ and M-W school districts.

DAVID ECKSTEIN: Prominent Satmar businessman who has served as one of the closest allies to Rabbi Aaron Teitelbaum in Kiryas Joel. Previously had been aligned with R. Moshe Teitelbaum in battles with internal KJ dissidents.

OSCAR FISHER: The brother-in-law of Leibish Lefkowitz who played a key role in purchasing land in the town of Monroe in the early 1970s on which the first Satmar settlement was built. A Hungarian-born Jew, Fisher was neither Satmar nor Orthodox, and thus did not face obstacles to purchasing land in Upstate New York.

MOSHE (GABBAI) FRIEDMAN: One of the closest advisors to R. Moshe Teitelbaum, who, in 1999, supported the leadership of R. Zalman Leib Teitelbaum and became one of his chief advisors. During the time of R. Moshe's leadership, he became the publisher of *Der Yid.*

MOSHE (MONROE) FRIEDMAN: An advisor to R. Joel Teitelbaum who, in 1976, was one of the key Satmar interlocutors responsible for negotiating with Monroe officials and intermediaries Kiryas Joel's creation as a village.

MOSHE MORDECHAI FRIEDMAN: The first teacher hired by parents in the summer of 1988 who would later become the Bnai Yoel.

LOUIS GRUMET: Leading figure in the legal fight against the public school district in Kiryas Joel. Grumet, who was trained as a lawyer, served as executive director of the New York State School Boards Association, in the course of which he initiated the legal action against the KJ public school (an act that was immortalized in the case, *Board of Education of Kiryas Joel v. Grumet*). He previously served as a special assistant to then–New York secretary of state Mario Cuomo.

MAYER HIRSCH: Highly influential and successful Satmar real estate developer who has been one of the close allies of R. Aaron Teitelbaum. He has exerted a great deal of influence in Kiryas Joel through his role on the Vaad hakirya, the village's powerful land development authority.

JUDITH KAYE: Prominent Jewish jurist who was the first woman to serve as chief judge of the New York Court of Appeals and wrote the decision in the case that denied the Satmars the right to force the Monroe-Woodbury School District to provide special ed classes at a neutral site.

LEOPOLD "LEIBISH" LEFKOWITZ (1920–1998): Founding mayor of Kiryas Joel and one of the most important associates of R. Joel Teitelbaum. Born in Hungary in 1920, he came to the United States in 1946. He served as president of the Satmar congregation in Williamsburg and then as one of the chief financial backers of the settlement project in Kiryas Joel.

WOLF LEFKOWITZ: Satmar businessman and resident of Kiryas Joel who was a prime mover behind the Shaare Chemlah (Gates of Compassion) school for students with special needs.

HERMAN HAIM LEIMZIDER: Known as Herman the Hammer, he was a close Satmar associate of R. Joel Teitelbaum and played a key role in overseeing the construction of the twenty-five single-family homes and eighty garden apartments in Monroe that would become the first Satmar enclave. He himself was an early resident of Kiryas Joel.

NATHAN LEWIN: Prominent Orthodox Jewish lawyer who represented Kiryas Joel in its defense of the KJ public school, including most prominently in the U.S. Supreme Court in 1994.

GEORGE PATAKI: The three-term governor of New York who also served as a New York State assemblyman and senator (1984–1990, 1992–1994), during which time he worked closely with the Kiryas Joel leadership to advance the idea of a public school in the village to educate special needs children. On his father's side, Pataki is of Hungarian origin, which led Satmar Hasidim to feel a sort of cultural bond with him.

JOEL PETLIN: The second superintendent of the Kiryas Joel Free Union School District. He first worked as a legal advisor to the first superintendent, Steven Benardo, before taking over the top position. Petlin is a Modern Orthodox lawyer who lives in neighboring Monsey but is not part of the Satmar community.

JAY SEKULOW: Prominent conservative lawyer and evangelical Christian (of Jewish origin) who served as the director of the American Center for Law and Justice and submitted an amicus brief on behalf of the KJ public school in the Supreme Court hearing of *KJ v. Grumet*. He served as President Donald Trump's personal lawyer and as part of the defense team in the first Trump impeachment trial.

MICHAEL SUSSMAN: Prominent New York–area Jewish civil rights lawyer whose greatest renown was his successful battle against housing segregation in an epic twenty-seven-year lawsuit in Yonkers, New York. From the earliest signs of dissent, Sussman has been the preferred lawyer of the KJ dissidents, whom he sees as victims of unfair discrimination by the establishment party in the village.

MALKA SILBERSTEIN: Legendary principal of the Bais Ruchel girls' school in Kiryas Joel associated with the mainstream faction. Silberstein moved from Williamsburg to Kiryas Joel where she was the parent of a child with special needs and one of the earliest advocates for bringing children with learning challenges "out of the closet."

GEDALYE SZEGEDIN: The powerful village administrator of Kiryas Joel and town clerk of Palm Tree and a close ally of R. Aaron Teitelbaum. Born in New York, Szegedin acquired his considerable skills as an administrator without specialized training or higher education. He is effective as an ally, feared as an opponent, and known among state politicians in Albany as a forceful player.

AARON TEITELBAUM (B. 1947): The eldest son of R. Moshe Teitelbaum, Aaron was appointed village rabbi in Kiryas Joel in 1984. In 1999, his father surprised him by dividing the Satmar empire, leaving Aaron in control in Kiryas Joel, but not Williamsburg. Since that time, he has been the leader of the dominant religious and political establishment in Kiryas Joel. Rejecting his father's act of division, he regards himself as the Satmar Rebbe, which places him in conflict with his brother, Zalman Leib. His followers are known as Aronis.

FAIGA TEITELBAUM (1912–2001): Born Faiga Shapiro in Poland, she married R. Joel Teitelbaum after the death of his first wife, Chava. She was half the age of R. Joel at marriage, though the couple were never able to have children. She came to be known as "Alta Faiga" (Old Faiga) and was widely revered as an elegant and compassionate maternal figure who also fiercely protected her husband's health and reputation. After his death, she became a formidable counterweight in her own right to Joel's successor, Moshe Teitelbaum, gathering around her circles of dissidents, many of whom became part of the Bnai Yoel group.

JOEL TEITELBAUM (1887–1979): Born in Sighet, Hungary, the charismatic founding Satmar Rebbe known as Reb Yoelish established the Satmar community in Satu Mare, Romania, in 1934. After surviving the Second World War in a Nazi concentration camp as part of the "Kasztner Transport," in 1946 he made his way to the United States, where he reestablished the Satmar community in Brooklyn. Through the force of his personality, the community took rise in New York and throughout the world. In 1974, the first Satmar settlers made their way to Monroe, New York, where they established Kiryas Joel, the Village of Joel.

MOSHE TEITELBAUM (1914–2006): Born in Hungary, he survived Auschwitz, where he lost his first wife and three children. He immigrated to the United States with his second wife in 1947 and settled in Brooklyn, where he served as the Sigheter Rov. Upon the death of his uncle Joel, Moshe Teitelbaum, who was known as the "Beirach Moshe," was appointed to succeed him. From the beginning of his tenure, he faced opposition from Faiga Teitelbaum as well as other loyal followers of Joel Teitelbaum. His initial alliance with his son Aaron broke down in 1999, when he decided to divide the Satmar empire into two capitals, Williamsburg and Kiryas Joel, overseen by his sons Zalman Leib and Aaron, respectively.

ZALMAN LEIB TEITELBAUM (B. 1951): The third son of Moshe Teitelbaum, he was called back to New York in 1999 from his post as rabbi of the Satmar community in Jerusalem. In that year, his father shocked the Satmar world by splitting the empire into two rather than handing the mantle of leadership solely to his older brother, Aaron. At that point, Zalman Leib became the chief rabbi of the largest Satmar community in Williamsburg and has come to be regarded by his followers, known as Zalis, as the genuine Satmar Rebbe.

JOSEPH WALDMAN: One of the earliest and most outspoken dissidents to the reign of Moshe Teitelbaum (and then Aaron Teitelbaum), Waldman went further than others in filing a suit in federal court calling for the dissolution of the village of Kiryas Joel on the grounds that it is a violation of the separation of church and state.

AVRAHAM HIRSCH WEINSTOCK: A leader among the group of Satmar parents disgruntled over the quality of education in Kiryas Joel; in the summer of 1988, he hired a private tutor to teach a group of students outside of the main UTA school system, which deepened enmity between the establishment and the dissidents.

ABRAHAM WIEDER: Satmar businessman and longtime associate of Rabbis Moshe and Aaron Teitelbaum, who served on the KJ school board and, from 1991 to 1997, as deputy mayor to Leibish Lefkowitz. In 1997, he assumed the position of mayor of Kiryas Joel, which he remains today. In January, he also became supervisor of the newly created town of Palm Tree.

SCHAYNDEL WIEDER: Resident of Kiryas Joel and wife of Mayor Abraham Wieder. After meeting a fellow mother of a special needs child in a hospital room, she became a forceful advocate who insisted on better educational services for her daughter and other special needs children in Kiryas Joel than those previously provided by Monroe-Woodbury School District and the state-sponsored BOCES program.

JAY WORONA: Close associate and mentee of Louis Grumet, who worked at the New York State School Boards Association from 1984 and became its general counsel in 1990. Despite his lack of experience in Supreme Court litigation, he successfully argued the *Kiryas Joel v. Grumet* case in 1994.

INDEX

Page numbers in *italics* refer to figures.

Hasidim: death of leader not accepted by some groups of, 170; of Hungarian Unterland, 84; misnagdim and, 30; Moshe's supporters known as, 230; nineteenth-century Viennese attitude toward, 88; tensions between Brooklyn Black community and, 135, 167. *See also* Satmar Hasidic community

Hasidism: oppositional assimilation in, 86; rise of, 85

Hatam Sofer (Moshe Sofer), 36, 89, 90, 94

Hay Iyar, 52–53

head coverings: for men, 37, 102–3; for women, 38

health center, 33

Hebrew: boys' instruction in, 58; Joel Teitelbaum's dual attitude toward, 113, 413n82; modern version forbidden to be spoken, 149; spoken by Aaron Teitelbaum's wife, 199

Heilman, Samuel, 198, 337

"heretics," Satmar on deviant Jews as, 99

Hildesheimer, Esriel, 93

Hirsch, Joseph (Yosef), 299–300, 302, 303, 318, 329, 332

Hirsch, Mayer, 28, 71, 304–5, 307, 309, 312

Hobsbawm, Eric, 1–2

Hochhauser, Chaim, 329

Hoffman, Joseph, 94

holidays of Jewish calendar, 52

Holocaust, 3–4, 83, 108–9, 110, 112–13

Hoover, Herbert, 140

Horthy, Miklós, 108

housing discrimination: lawsuit against New York for, 135. *See also* zoning laws

Hughes, Michael, 206

Hungarian Jews: consequences of World War I and, 100–101; emigrating by the thousands to Williamsburg, 119–20; intense nineteenth-century conflict among, 90–92, 93–94; Joel Teitelbaum's reputation and, 103; Joel Teitelbaum's willingness to accommodate and, 114; return of Satu Mare to Hungary and,

108; World War II presaging danger to, 108

Hungarian Unterland, 83–84; rise of Joel Teitelbaum in, 96–98; Yismah Moshe in, 89–90, 94. *See also* Satu Mare

IDEA (Individuals with Disabilities Education Act), 184, 185. *See also* Education for All Handicapped Children Act

identity politics, 221, 256, 269, 378–79

illiberal liberalism, 16, 19

Ilosva (Orshava, later Iršava), 97–98, 101, 102

Indig, Moses, 309

individualism: Kiryas Joel placing collective above, 16–17, 36; liberal, 14; libertarian, 393

individualized education programs (IEPs), 184, 204

innovation: forbidden as a matter of Torah, 36, 89, 93, 94, 101; Joel Teitelbaum's opposition to, 98, 101

integrationism: of disability rights movement, 183–84; liberalism and, 165, 219, 270; of Malka Silberstein's vision for special needs, 183, 190; Sussman and Grumet seeing situation in terms of, 321–22

internet use, 42, 387–88; admonitions against, 42, 52, 387, 388; income derived from, 69, 75; UTA ruling against women seeking college education and, 62; women critical of restrictions on, 63

Israel: professional money raisers from, 71; state establishment of religion and land ownership in, 381, 442n6. *See also* anti-Zionism of Joel Teitelbaum

Jefferson, Thomas, 192, 422n54

Jehovah's Witnesses convention center, 137, 152

Jewish holidays, 52

Jewish law (*halakhah*): entwined with American law by KJ authorities, 81; establishment and dissidents committed to, 30; Joel Teitelbaum's vision of society dominated by, 86, 93; secular political power and, 279–80; supposed autonomy of, 248–49

A NOTE ON THE TYPE

This book has been composed in Arno, an Old-style serif typeface in the
classic Venetian tradition, designed by Robert Slimbach at Adobe.